ROSALIE LIGHTNING

FOR INFORMATION, ADDRESS ST. MARTIN'S PRESS, 175 FIFTH AVENUE, NEW YORK, N.Y. 10010.

WWW.STMARTINS.COM

THE LIBRARY OF CONGRESS CATALOGING-IN-PUBLICATION DATA IS AVAILABLE UPON REQUEST

ISBN 978-1-250-04994-0 (HARDCOVER)
ISBN 978-1-4668-5100-9 (E-BOOK)

OUR BOOKS MAY BE PURCHASED IN BULK FOR PROMOTIONAL, EDUCATIONAL, OR BUSINESS USE. PLEASE CONTACT YOUR LOCAL BOOKSELLER OR THE MACMILLAN CORPORATE AND PREMIUM SALES DEPARTMENT AT (800) 221-7945, EXTENSION 5442, OR BY E-MAIL AT MACMILLANSPECIALMARKETS@ MACMILLAN.COM.

FIRST EDITION: JANUARY 2016

10 9 8 7 6 5 4 3 2 1

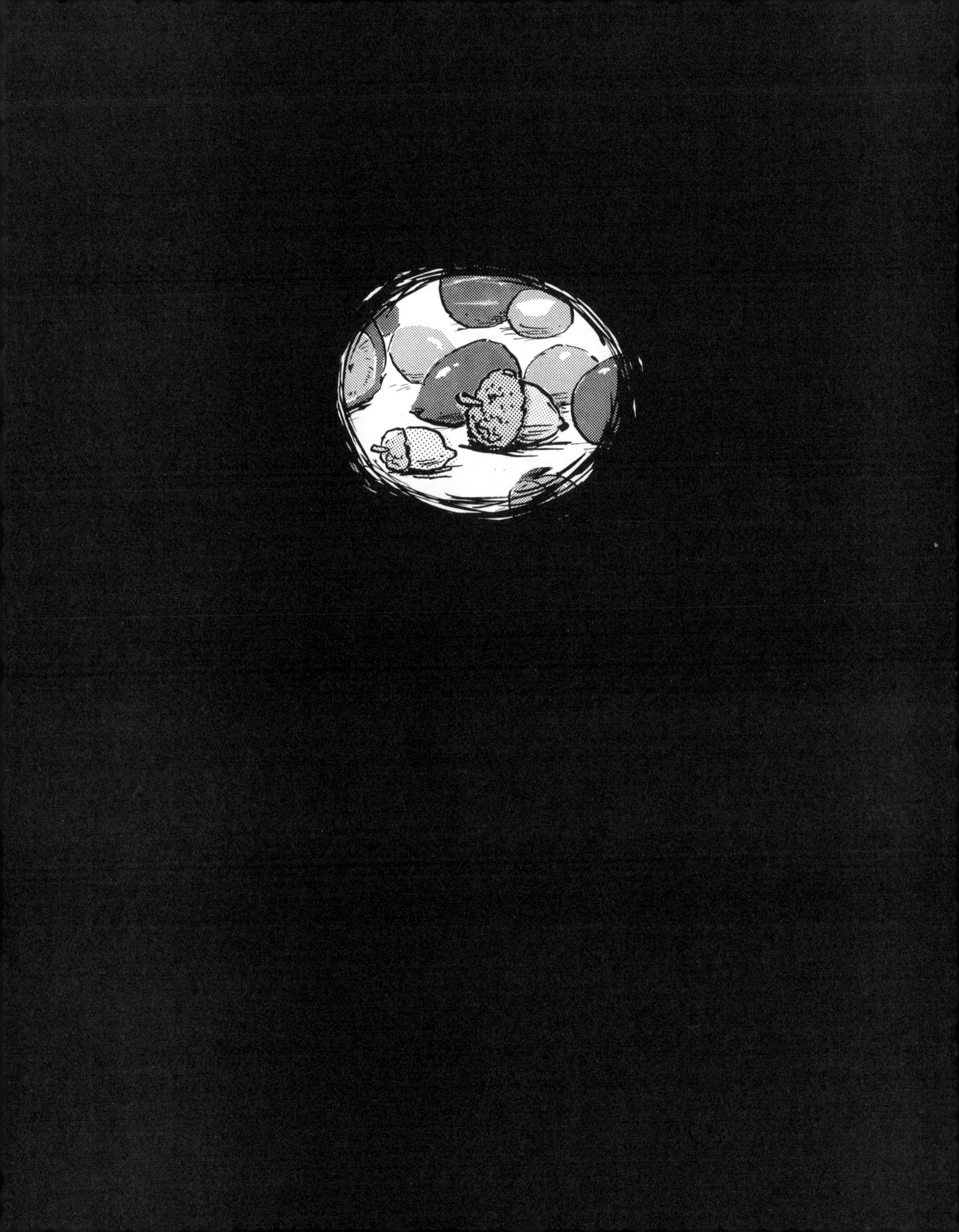

ROSALIE LIGHTNING

BY TOM HART
AND ROSALIE LIGHTNING
AND LEELA CORMAN
AND THE RESIDENTS OF NEW YORK CITY,
GAINESVILLE, FLORIDA, NEW MEXICO,
AND HAWAII, AS WELL AS
VARIOUS SINGER–SONGWRITERS,
FILM DIRECTORS, ACTORS, ANIMATORS,
COMIC ARTISTS, DONORS, LOVERS
AND FRIENDS.

ST. MARTIN'S PRESS
NEW YORK

THE AUTHOR ACKNOWLEDGES WITH GRATITUDE THE WORK OF HAYAO MIYAZAKI AND STUDIO GHIBLI, ROLAND BARTHES, JACK DAVIS, JOHNNY CRAIG, STAN AND JAN BERENSTAIN, METAPHROG, BUSTER KEATON, CHESTER BROWN, ROGER MOORE, IDRIS ELBA, IAN FLEMING, THICH NHAT HANH, DANIELLE HART, CAROLINE PAQUITA, various manga artists, LAURIE ANDERSON, OUM KALTHOUM, AHMED SHAFIK AND MOHAMMED ABDEL WAHAB, MICHAEL, AKIRA KUROSAWA, JOHN LENNON AND PAUL McCARTNEY, BILLY DeBECK, WERNER HERZOG, LES BLANK, OSAMU TEZUKA, TITIAN, MARK EITZEL, JOSH BAYER, PHILIP K. DICK, FRANK KING, LEELA CORMAN, PATRICK DOUGHERTY, HAROLD GRAY, JOHN BERGER, GUSTAVE VERBEEK, GEORGE HERRIMAN, ITALO CALVINO, BRIAN ENO, AND TIM BUCKLEY.

FOR
TOM WOODRUFF,
WHO TAUGHT ME
TO LOOK AT
IMAGES.

AND FOR MOLLY ROSE.

THIS BOOK IS ABOUT
YOUR SISTER, BUT ABOUT
GOD AND LOVE AND
YOU, TOO.

Then, where despair had been, the voice
Of Nina Simone. Parentheses open
On a new gender crossed with stars
Ari removes the bobby pins. Night falls
There is no such thing as non sequitur
When you're in love.

-Ben Lerner
MEAN FREE PATH

I

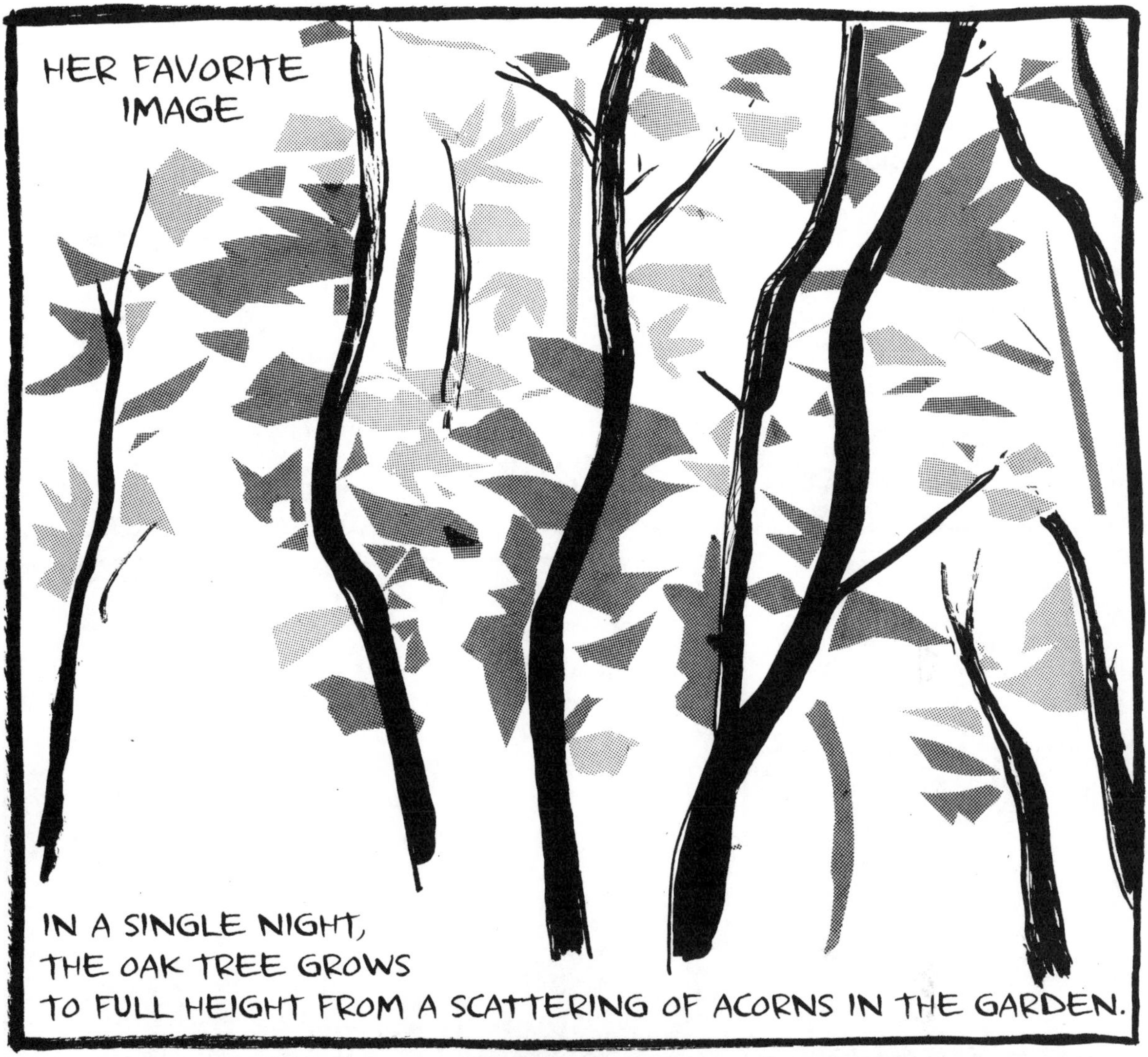
HER FAVORITE IMAGE
IN A SINGLE NIGHT, THE OAK TREE GROWS TO FULL HEIGHT FROM A SCATTERING OF ACORNS IN THE GARDEN.

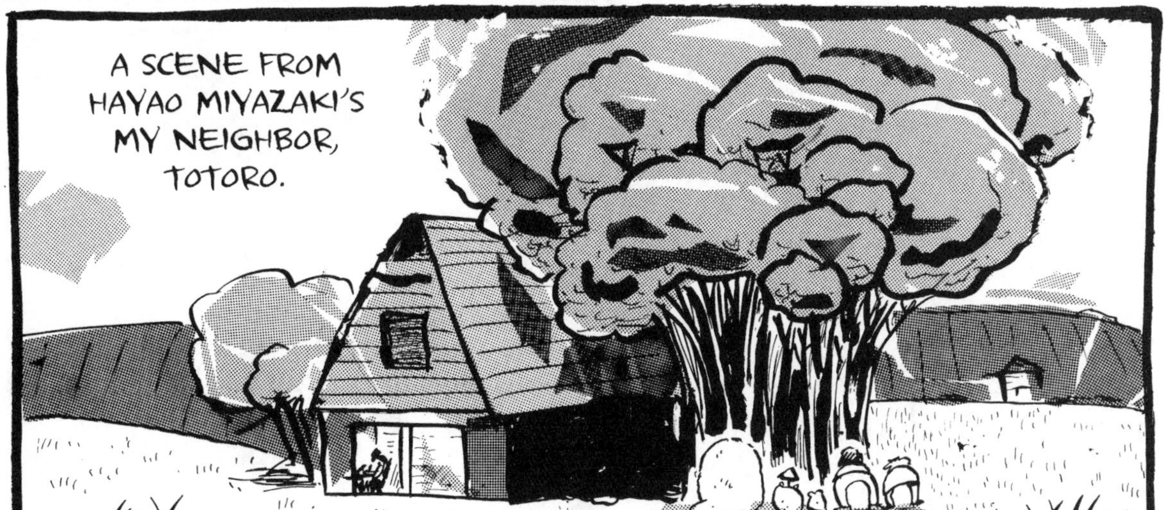
A SCENE FROM HAYAO MIYAZAKI'S MY NEIGHBOR, TOTORO.

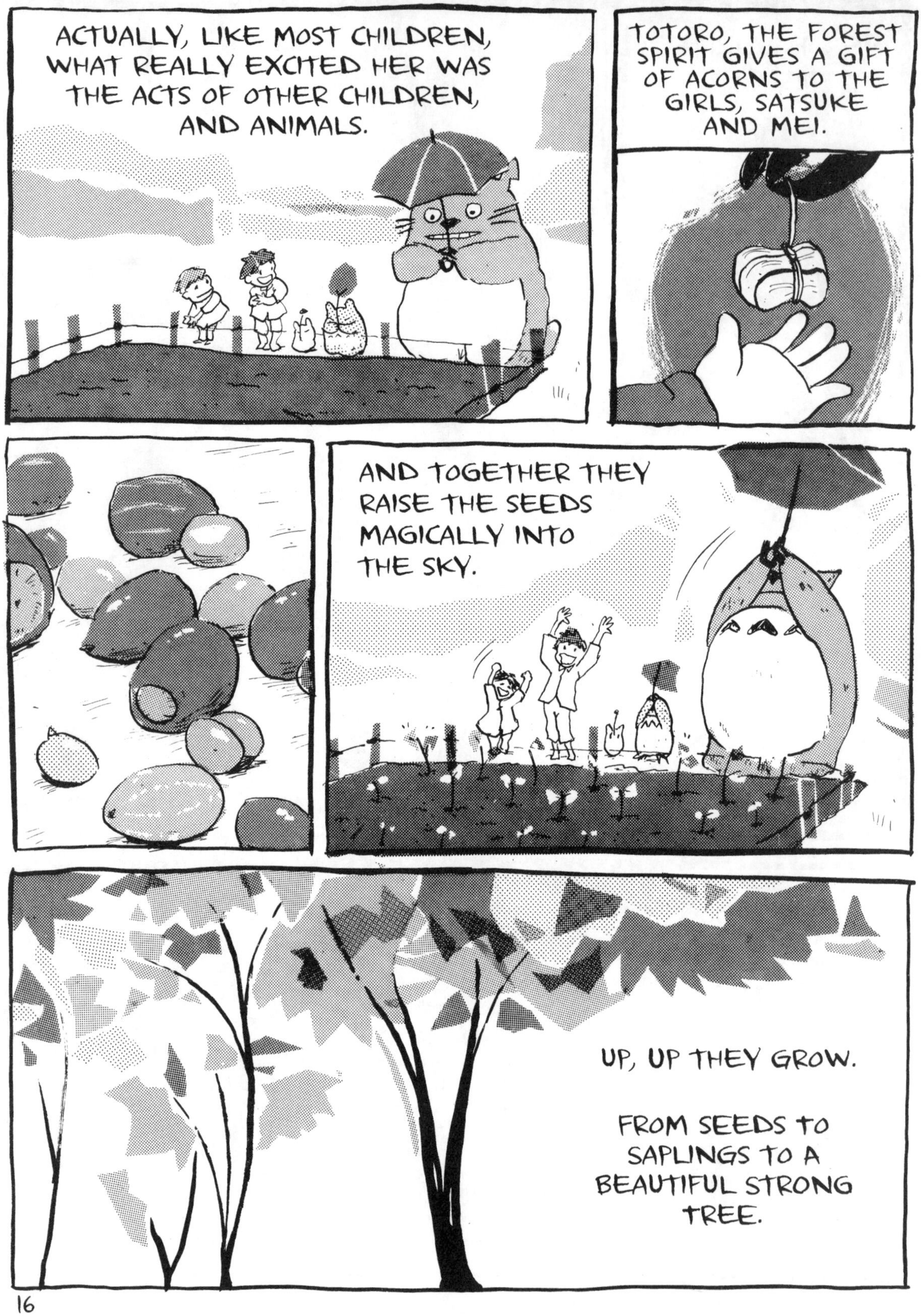
ACTUALLY, LIKE MOST CHILDREN, WHAT REALLY EXCITED HER WAS THE ACTS OF OTHER CHILDREN, AND ANIMALS.
TOTORO, THE FOREST SPIRIT GIVES A GIFT OF ACORNS TO THE GIRLS, SATSUKE AND MEI.
AND TOGETHER THEY RAISE THE SEEDS MAGICALLY INTO THE SKY.
UP, UP THEY GROW.
FROM SEEDS TO SAPLINGS TO A BEAUTIFUL STRONG TREE.

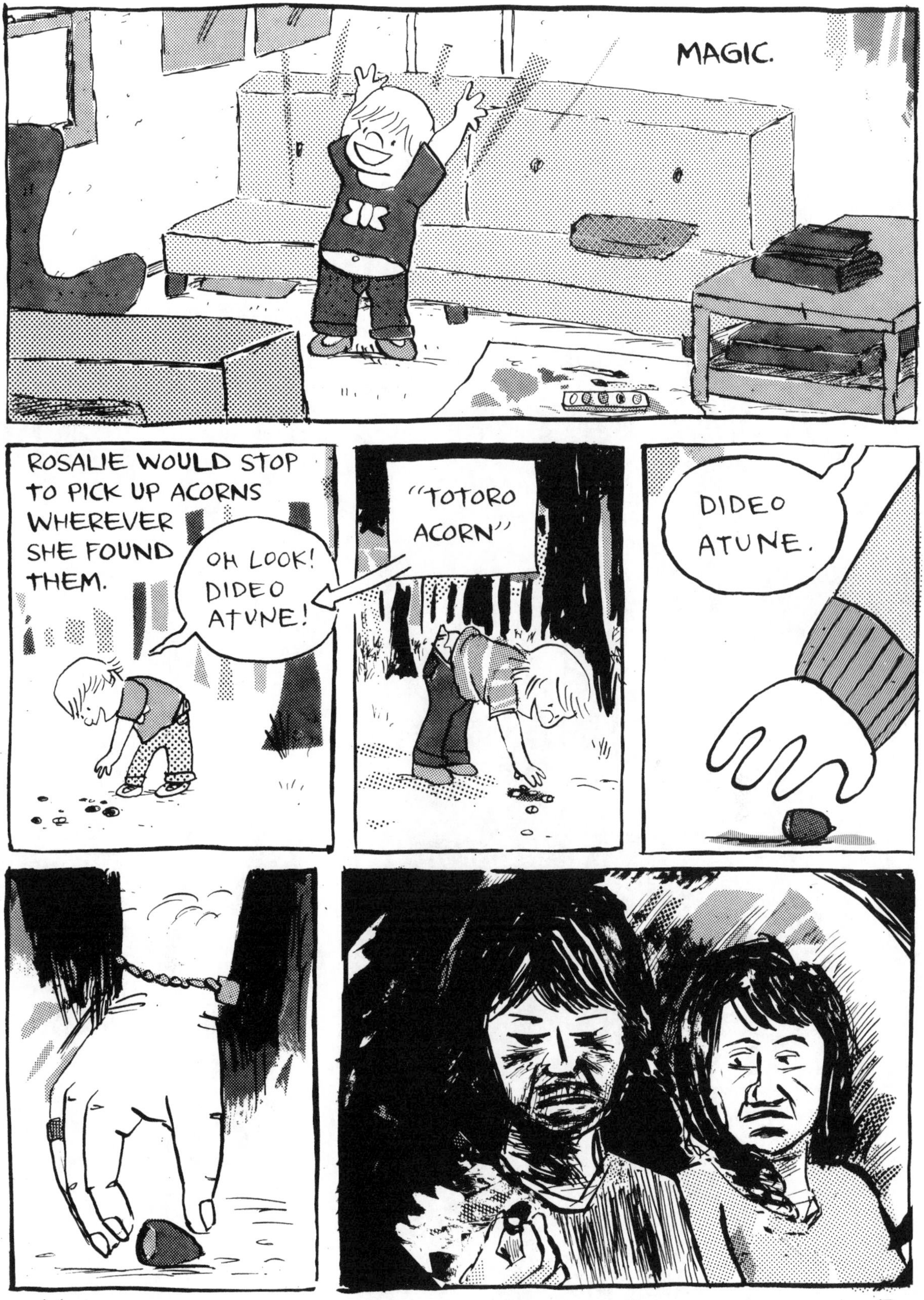
MAGIC.
ROSALIE WOULD STOP TO PICK UP ACORNS WHEREVER SHE FOUND THEM.
OH LOOK! DIDEO ATUNE!
"TOTORO ACORN"
DIDEO ATUNE.

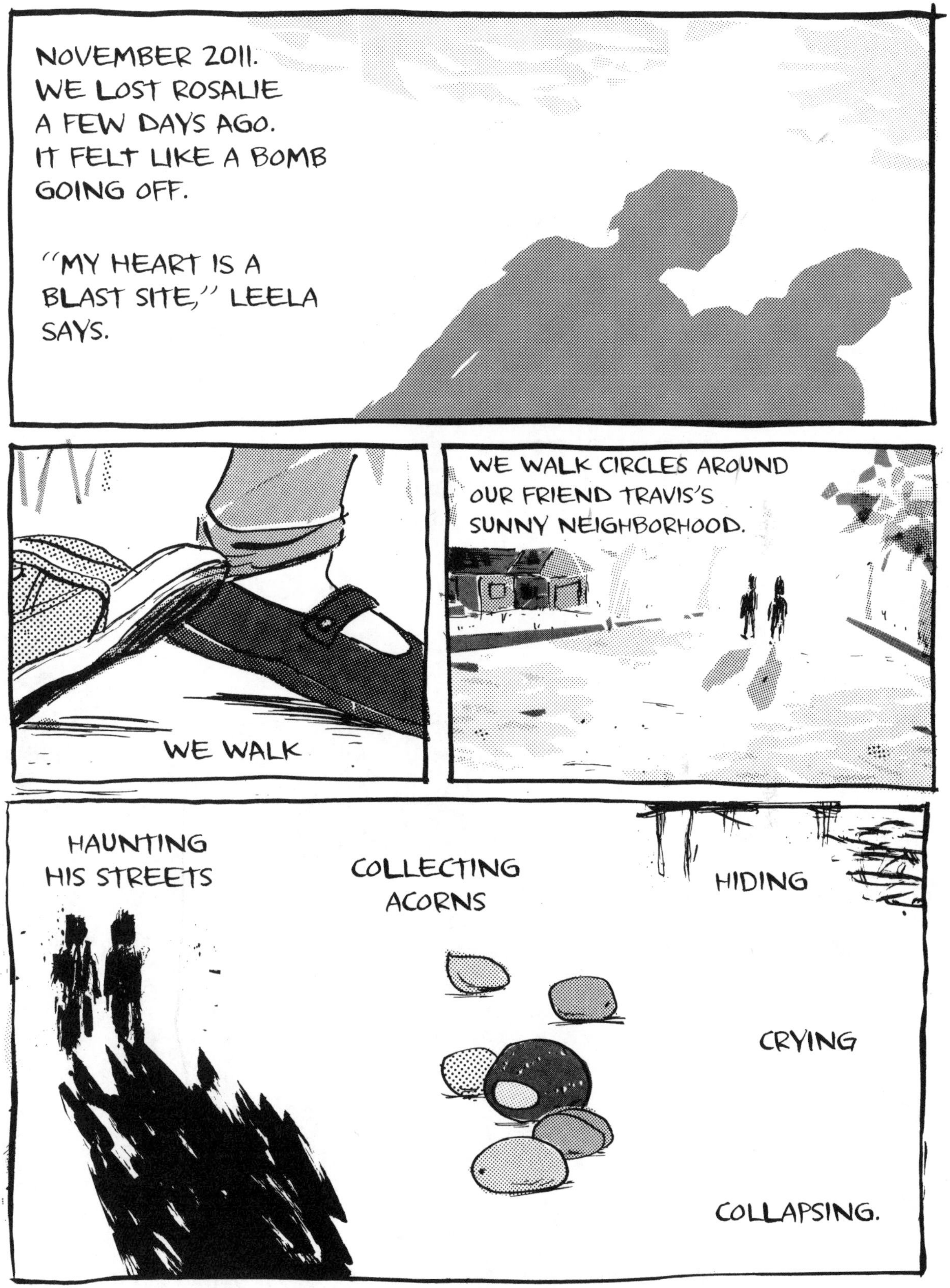
NOVEMBER 2011.
WE LOST ROSALIE
A FEW DAYS AGO.
IT FELT LIKE A BOMB
GOING OFF.
"MY HEART IS A
BLAST SITE," LEELA
SAYS.
WE WALK
WE WALK CIRCLES AROUND
OUR FRIEND TRAVIS'S
SUNNY NEIGHBORHOOD.
HAUNTING
HIS STREETS
COLLECTING
ACORNS
HIDING
CRYING
COLLAPSING.

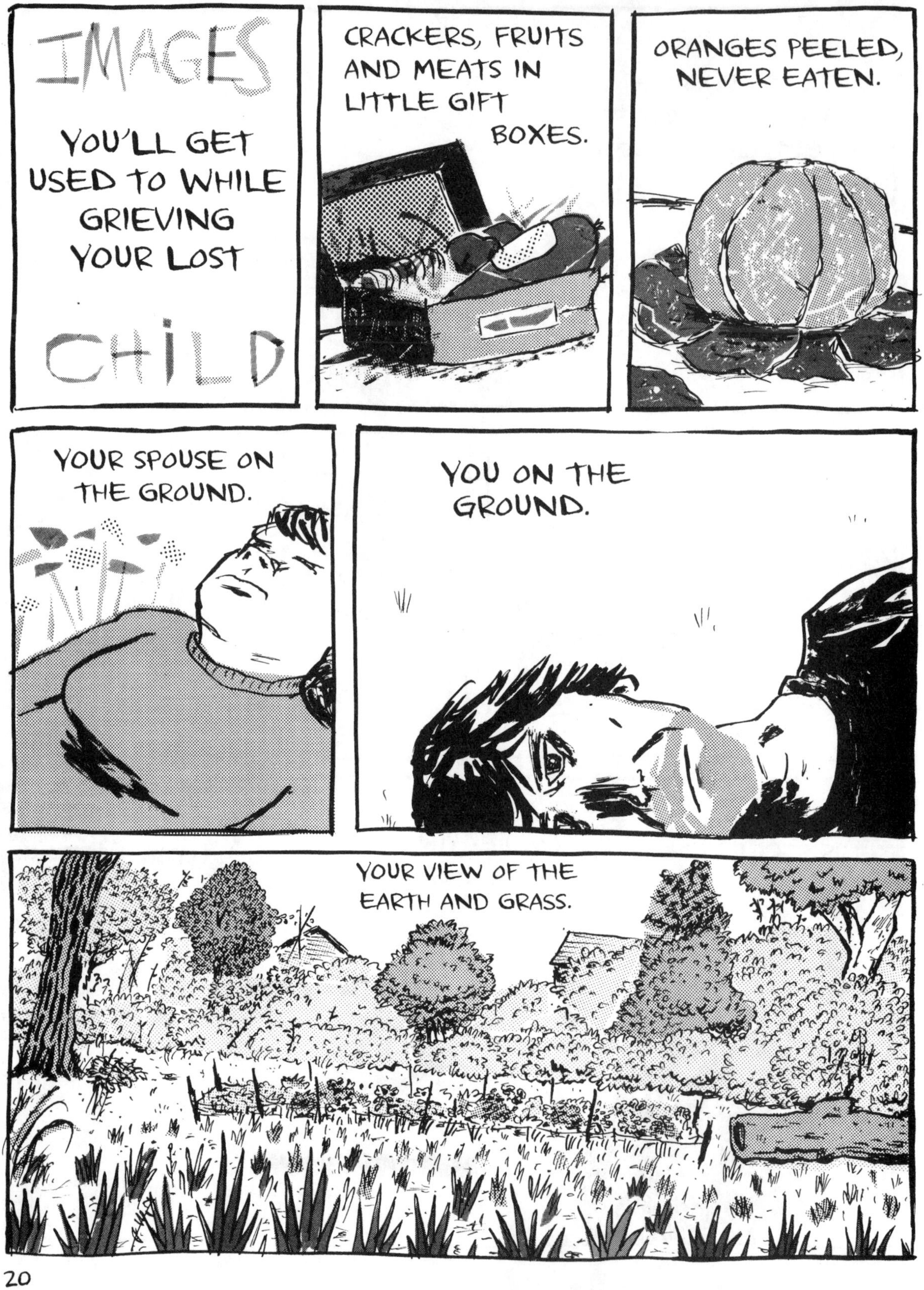
IMAGES
YOU'LL GET USED TO WHILE GRIEVING YOUR LOST
CHILD
CRACKERS, FRUITS AND MEATS IN LITTLE GIFT BOXES.
ORANGES PEELED, NEVER EATEN.
YOUR SPOUSE ON THE GROUND.
YOU ON THE GROUND.
YOUR VIEW OF THE EARTH AND GRASS.

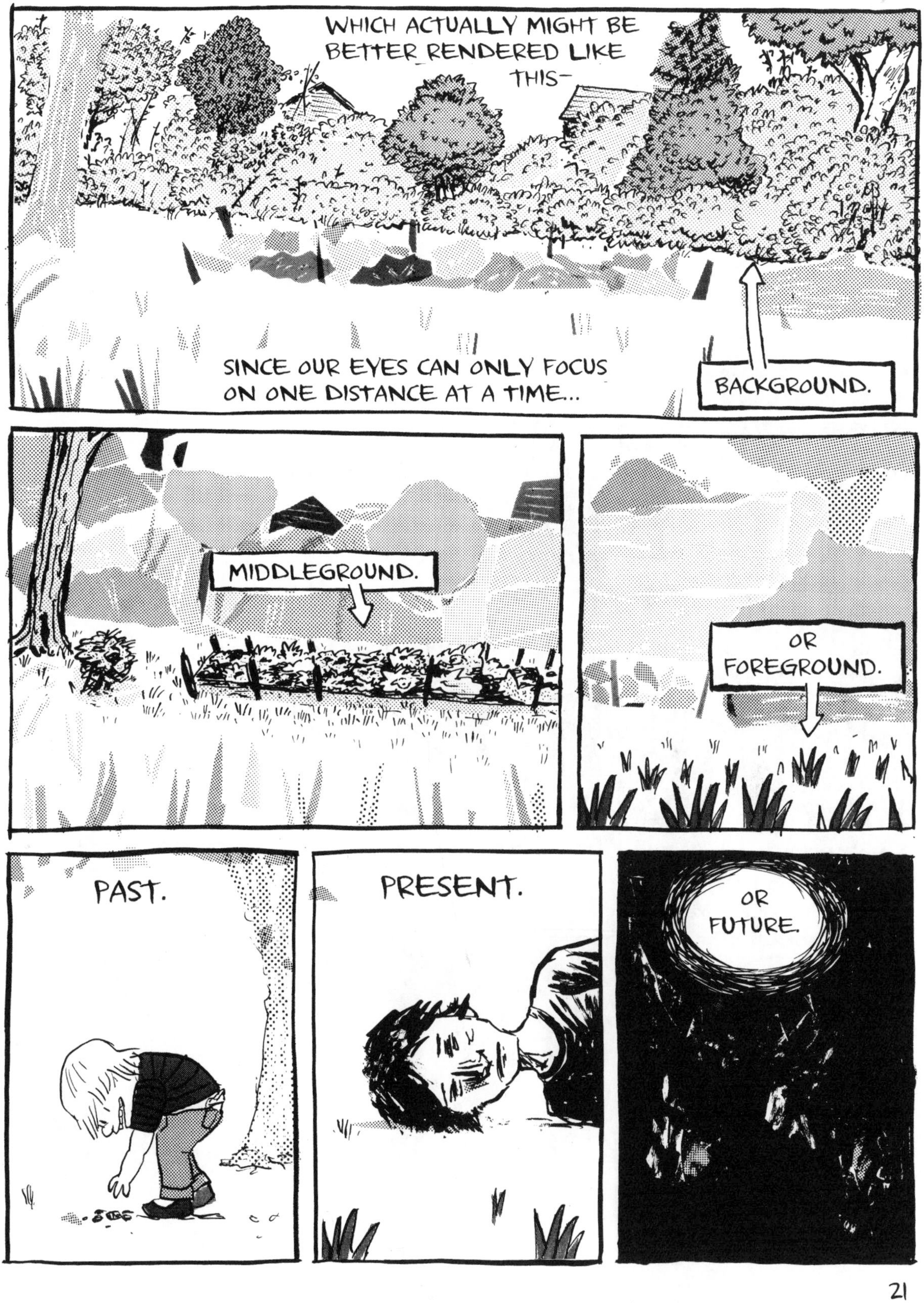
WHICH ACTUALLY MIGHT BE BETTER RENDERED LIKE THIS–
SINCE OUR EYES CAN ONLY FOCUS ON ONE DISTANCE AT A TIME...
BACKGROUND.
MIDDLEGROUND.
OR FOREGROUND.
PAST.
PRESENT.
OR FUTURE.

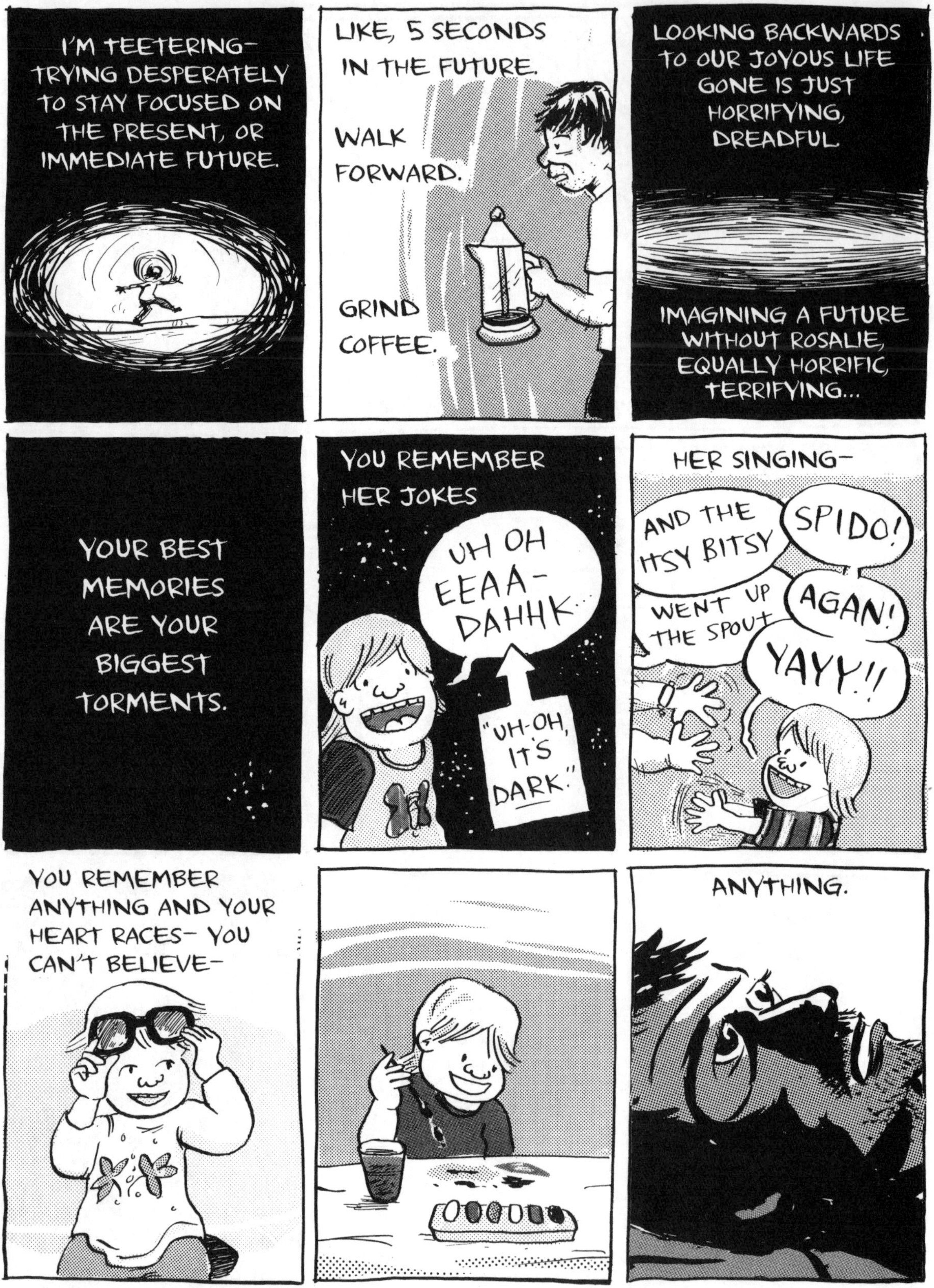
I'M TEETERING- TRYING DESPERATELY TO STAY FOCUSED ON THE PRESENT, OR IMMEDIATE FUTURE.
LIKE, 5 SECONDS IN THE FUTURE.
WALK FORWARD.
GRIND COFFEE.
LOOKING BACKWARDS TO OUR JOYOUS LIFE GONE IS JUST HORRIFYING, DREADFUL.
IMAGINING A FUTURE WITHOUT ROSALIE, EQUALLY HORRIFIC, TERRIFYING...
YOUR BEST MEMORIES ARE YOUR BIGGEST TORMENTS.
YOU REMEMBER HER JOKES
UH OH EEAA-DAHHK...
"UH-OH, IT'S DARK."
HER SINGING-
AND THE ITSY BITSY
SPIDO!
WENT UP THE SPOUT
AGAN!
YAYY!!
YOU REMEMBER ANYTHING AND YOUR HEART RACES- YOU CAN'T BELIEVE-
ANYTHING.

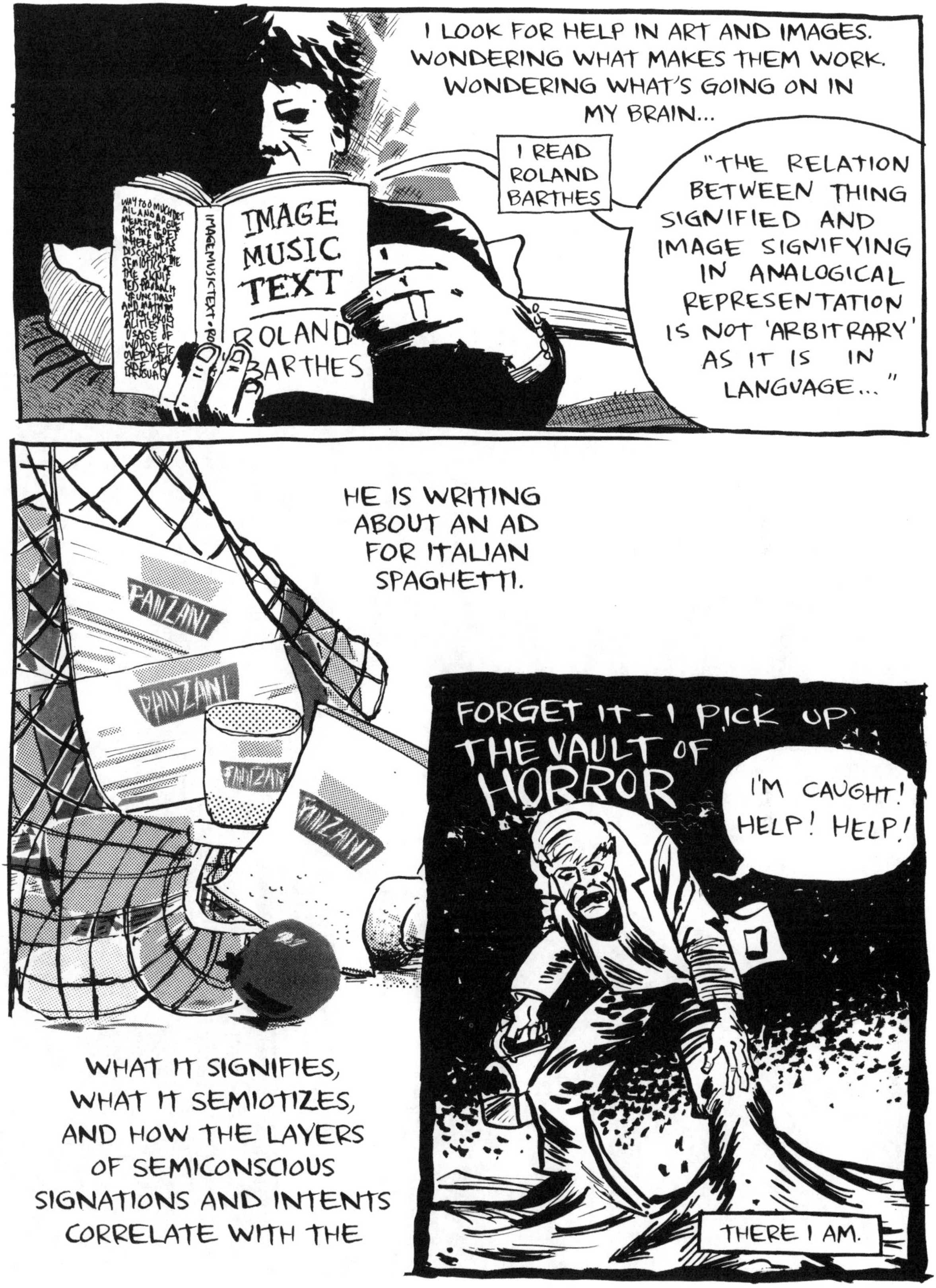
I LOOK FOR HELP IN ART AND IMAGES. WONDERING WHAT MAKES THEM WORK. WONDERING WHAT'S GOING ON IN MY BRAIN...
I READ ROLAND BARTHES
"THE RELATION BETWEEN THING SIGNIFIED AND IMAGE SIGNIFYING IN ANALOGICAL REPRESENTATION IS NOT 'ARBITRARY' AS IT IS IN LANGUAGE..."
IMAGE MUSIC TEXT
ROLAND BARTHES
HE IS WRITING ABOUT AN AD FOR ITALIAN SPAGHETTI.
PANZANI
PANZANI
PANZANI
PANZANI
WHAT IT SIGNIFIES, WHAT IT SEMIOTIZES, AND HOW THE LAYERS OF SEMICONSCIOUS SIGNATIONS AND INTENTS CORRELATE WITH THE
FORGET IT – I PICK UP THE VAULT OF HORROR
I'M CAUGHT! HELP! HELP!
THERE I AM.

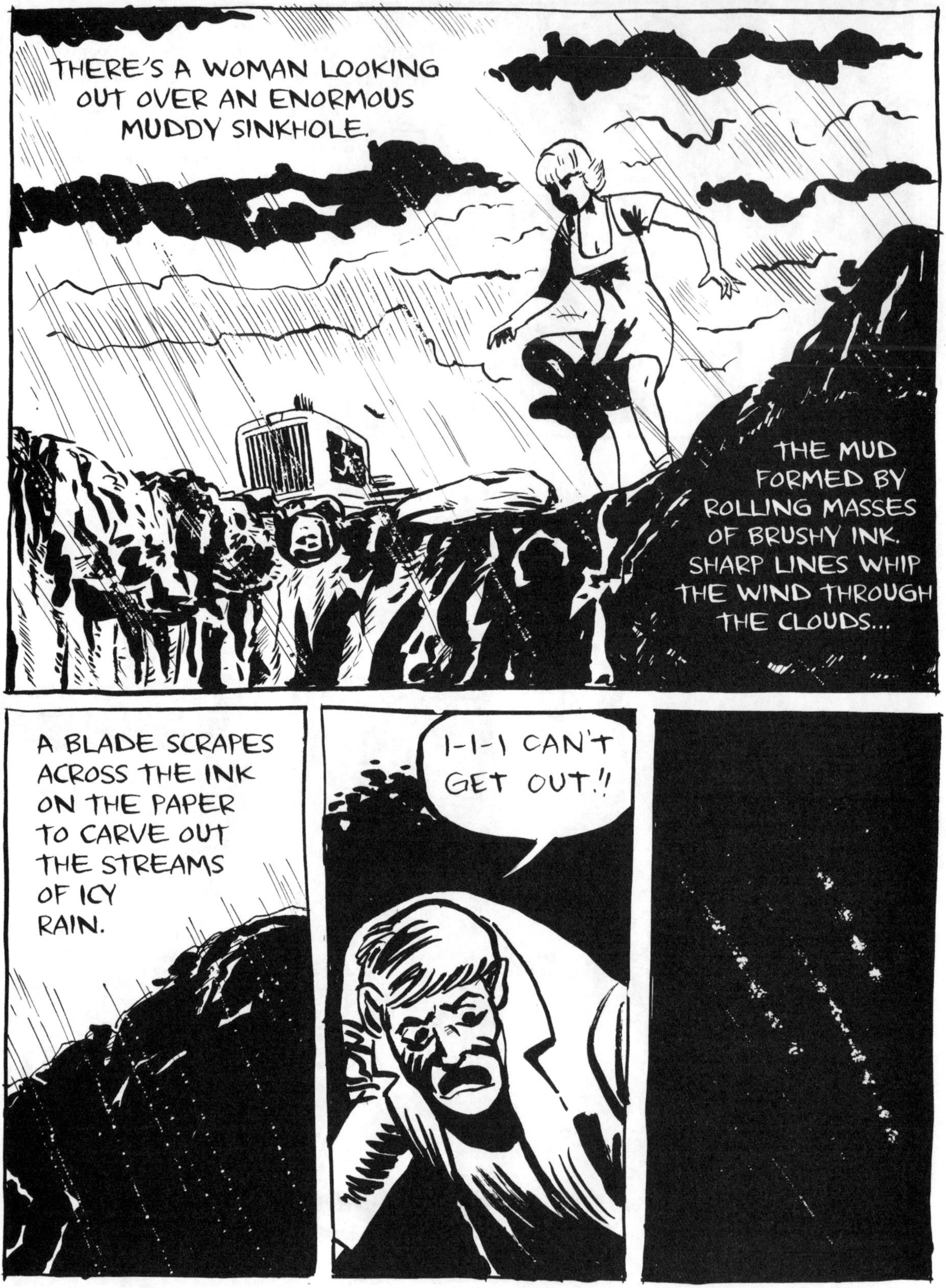
THERE'S A WOMAN LOOKING OUT OVER AN ENORMOUS MUDDY SINKHOLE.
THE MUD FORMED BY ROLLING MASSES OF BRUSHY INK. SHARP LINES WHIP THE WIND THROUGH THE CLOUDS...
A BLADE SCRAPES ACROSS THE INK ON THE PAPER TO CARVE OUT THE STREAMS OF ICY RAIN.
I-I-I CAN'T GET OUT!!

II

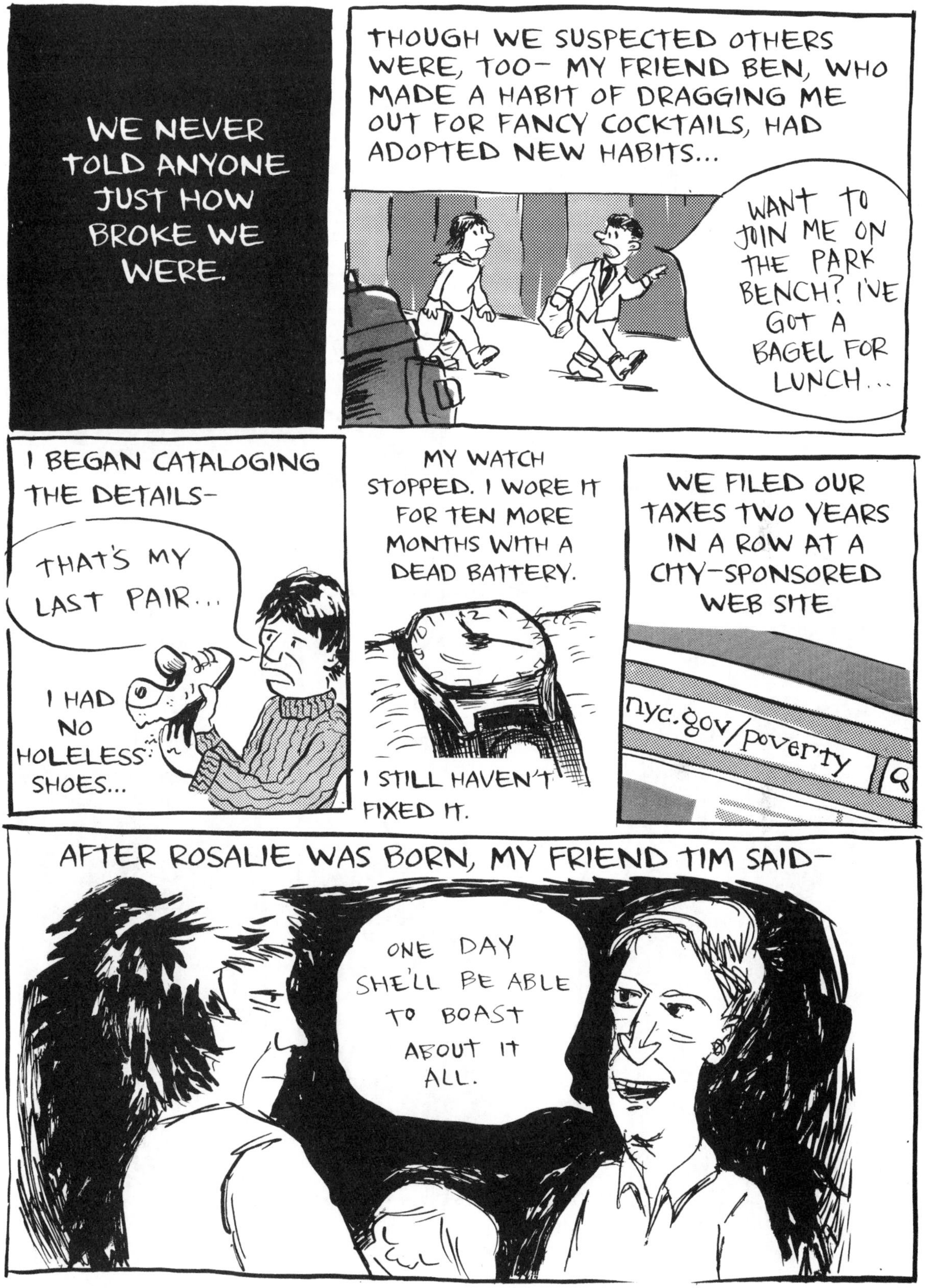
WE NEVER TOLD ANYONE JUST HOW BROKE WE WERE.
THOUGH WE SUSPECTED OTHERS WERE, TOO- MY FRIEND BEN, WHO MADE A HABIT OF DRAGGING ME OUT FOR FANCY COCKTAILS, HAD ADOPTED NEW HABITS...
WANT TO JOIN ME ON THE PARK BENCH? I'VE GOT A BAGEL FOR LUNCH...
I BEGAN CATALOGING THE DETAILS-
THAT'S MY LAST PAIR...
I HAD NO HOLELESS SHOES...
MY WATCH STOPPED. I WORE IT FOR TEN MORE MONTHS WITH A DEAD BATTERY.
I STILL HAVEN'T FIXED IT.
WE FILED OUR TAXES TWO YEARS IN A ROW AT A CITY-SPONSORED WEB SITE
nyc.gov/poverty
AFTER ROSALIE WAS BORN, MY FRIEND TIM SAID-
ONE DAY SHE'LL BE ABLE TO BOAST ABOUT IT ALL.

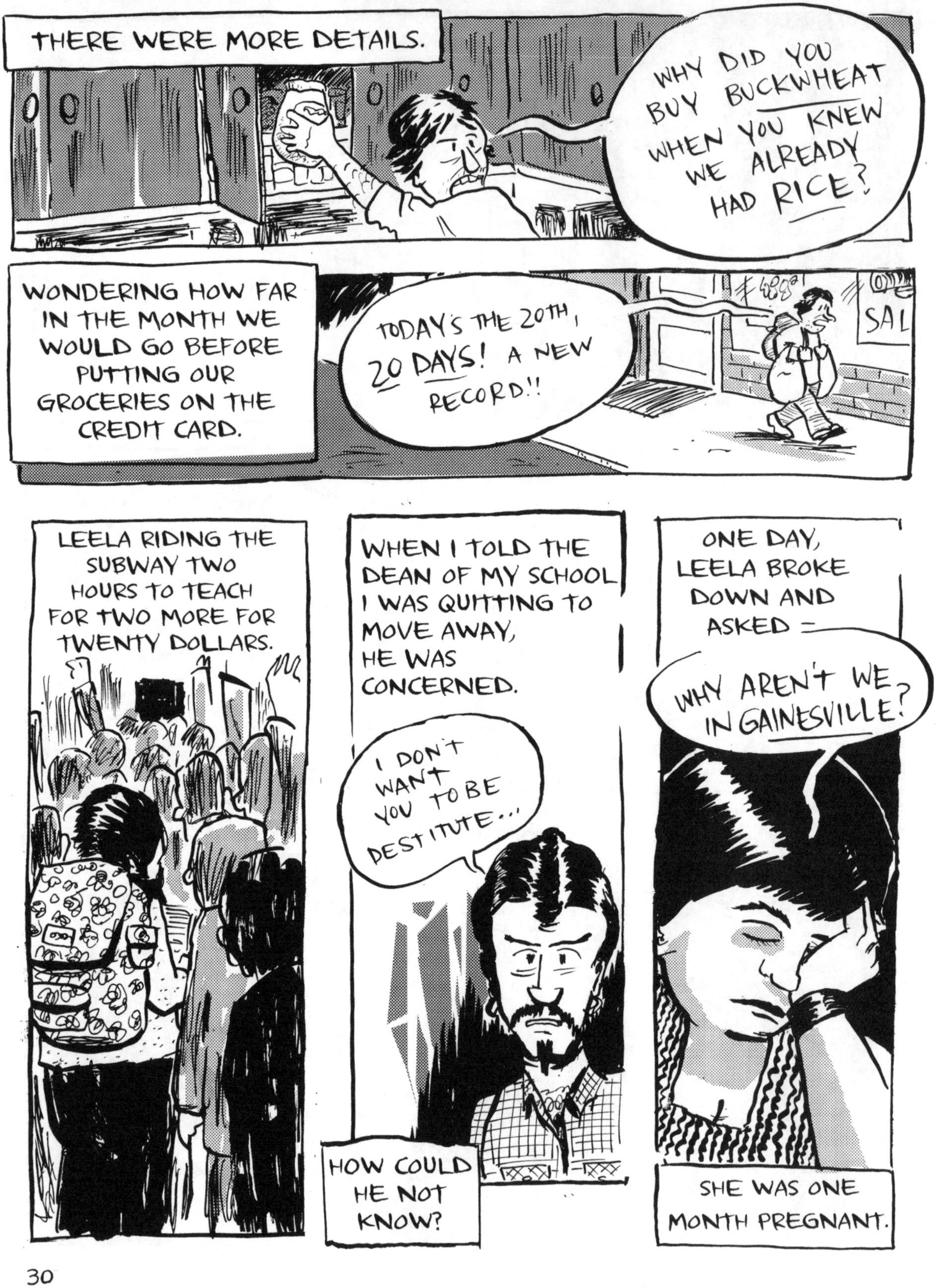
THERE WERE MORE DETAILS.
WHY DID YOU BUY BUCKWHEAT WHEN YOU KNEW WE ALREADY HAD RICE?
WONDERING HOW FAR IN THE MONTH WE WOULD GO BEFORE PUTTING OUR GROCERIES ON THE CREDIT CARD.
TODAY'S THE 20TH, 20 DAYS! A NEW RECORD!!
LEELA RIDING THE SUBWAY TWO HOURS TO TEACH FOR TWO MORE FOR TWENTY DOLLARS.
WHEN I TOLD THE DEAN OF MY SCHOOL I WAS QUITTING TO MOVE AWAY, HE WAS CONCERNED.
I DON'T WANT YOU TO BE DESTITUTE...
HOW COULD HE NOT KNOW?
ONE DAY, LEELA BROKE DOWN AND ASKED —
WHY AREN'T WE IN GAINESVILLE?
SHE WAS ONE MONTH PREGNANT.

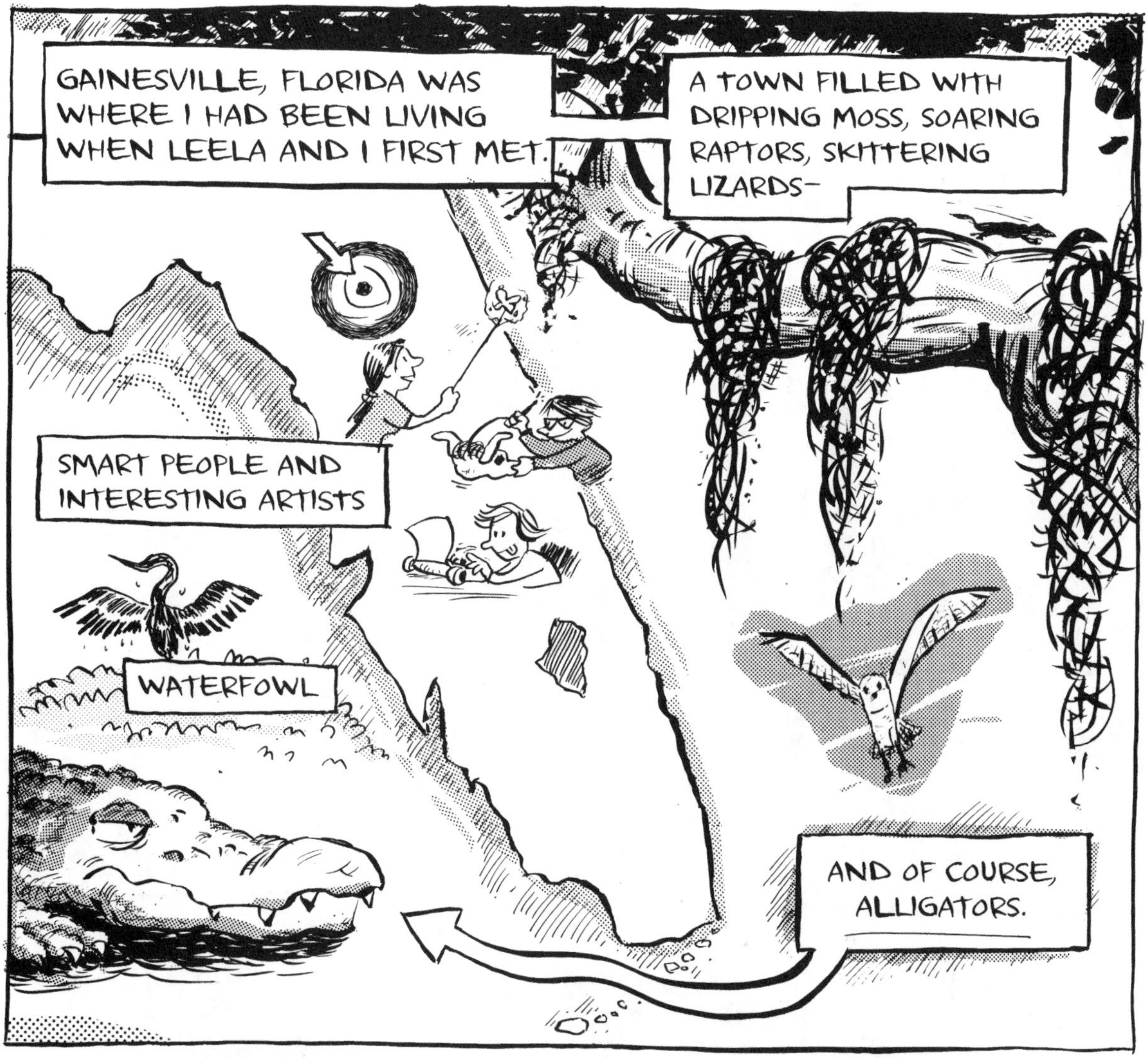
GAINESVILLE, FLORIDA WAS WHERE I HAD BEEN LIVING WHEN LEELA AND I FIRST MET.
A TOWN FILLED WITH DRIPPING MOSS, SOARING RAPTORS, SKITTERING LIZARDS—
SMART PEOPLE AND INTERESTING ARTISTS
WATERFOWL
AND OF COURSE, ALLIGATORS.

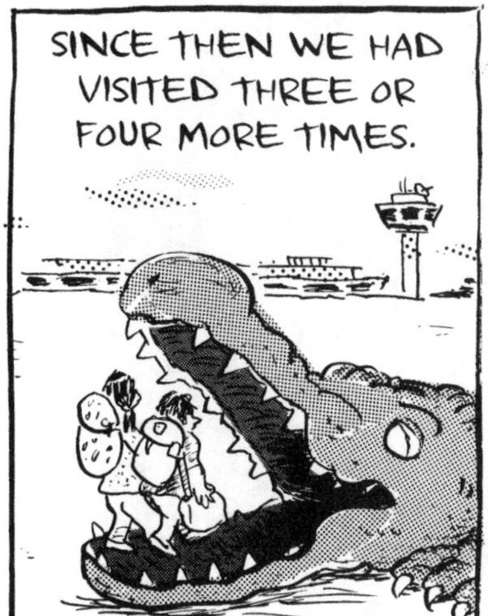
SINCE THEN WE HAD VISITED THREE OR FOUR MORE TIMES.

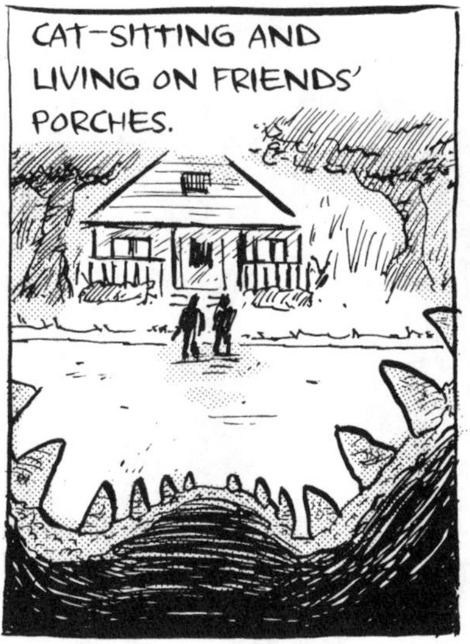
CAT-SITTING AND LIVING ON FRIENDS' PORCHES.

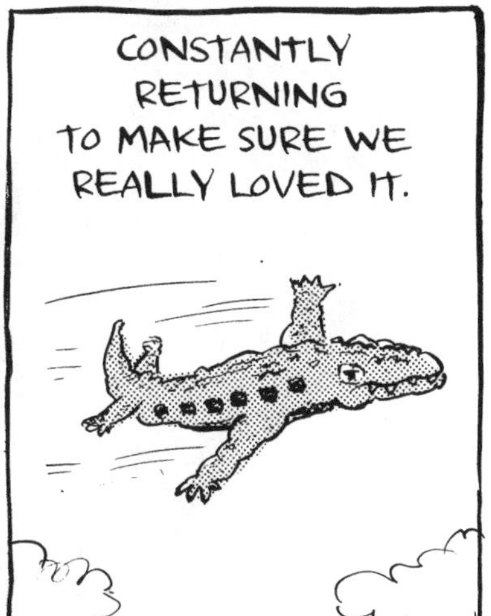
CONSTANTLY RETURNING TO MAKE SURE WE REALLY LOVED IT.

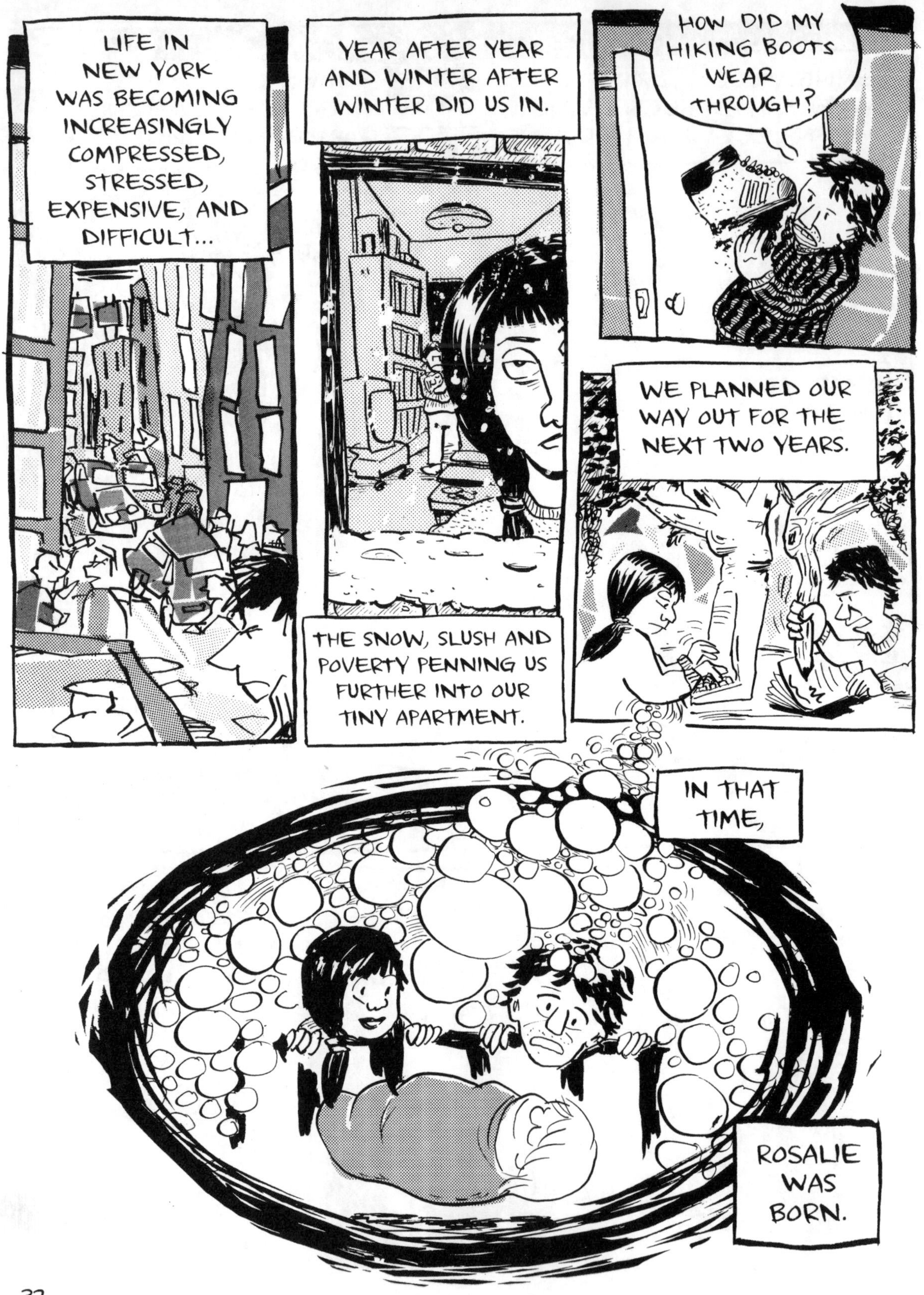
LIFE IN NEW YORK WAS BECOMING INCREASINGLY COMPRESSED, STRESSED, EXPENSIVE, AND DIFFICULT...
YEAR AFTER YEAR AND WINTER AFTER WINTER DID US IN.
THE SNOW, SLUSH AND POVERTY PENNING US FURTHER INTO OUR TINY APARTMENT.
HOW DID MY HIKING BOOTS WEAR THROUGH?
WE PLANNED OUR WAY OUT FOR THE NEXT TWO YEARS.
IN THAT TIME,
ROSALIE WAS BORN.

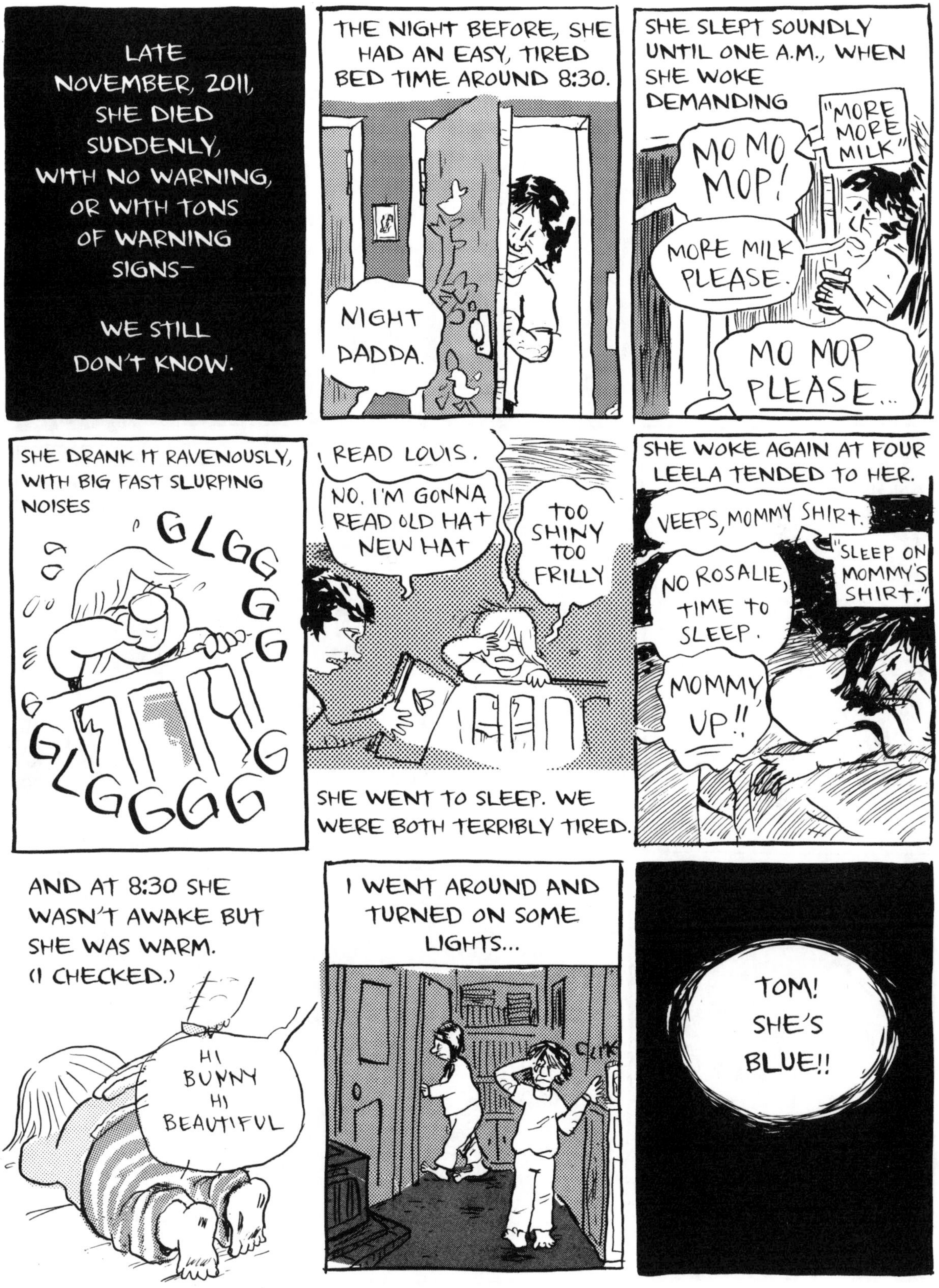
LATE NOVEMBER, 2011, SHE DIED SUDDENLY, WITH NO WARNING, OR WITH TONS OF WARNING SIGNS—
WE STILL DON'T KNOW.
THE NIGHT BEFORE, SHE HAD AN EASY, TIRED BED TIME AROUND 8:30.
NIGHT DADDA.
SHE SLEPT SOUNDLY UNTIL ONE A.M., WHEN SHE WOKE DEMANDING
MO MO MOP!
"MORE MORE MILK"
MORE MILK PLEASE.
MO MOP PLEASE...
SHE DRANK IT RAVENOUSLY, WITH BIG FAST SLURPING NOISES
GLGGGGG
GLGGGGGG
READ LOUIS.
NO. I'M GONNA READ OLD HAT NEW HAT
TOO SHINY TOO FRILLY
SHE WENT TO SLEEP. WE WERE BOTH TERRIBLY TIRED.
SHE WOKE AGAIN AT FOUR LEELA TENDED TO HER.
VEEPS, MOMMY SHIRT.
"SLEEP ON MOMMY'S SHIRT."
NO ROSALIE, TIME TO SLEEP.
MOMMY UP!!
AND AT 8:30 SHE WASN'T AWAKE BUT SHE WAS WARM. (I CHECKED.)
HI BUNNY HI BEAUTIFUL
I WENT AROUND AND TURNED ON SOME LIGHTS...
CLIK
TOM! SHE'S BLUE!!

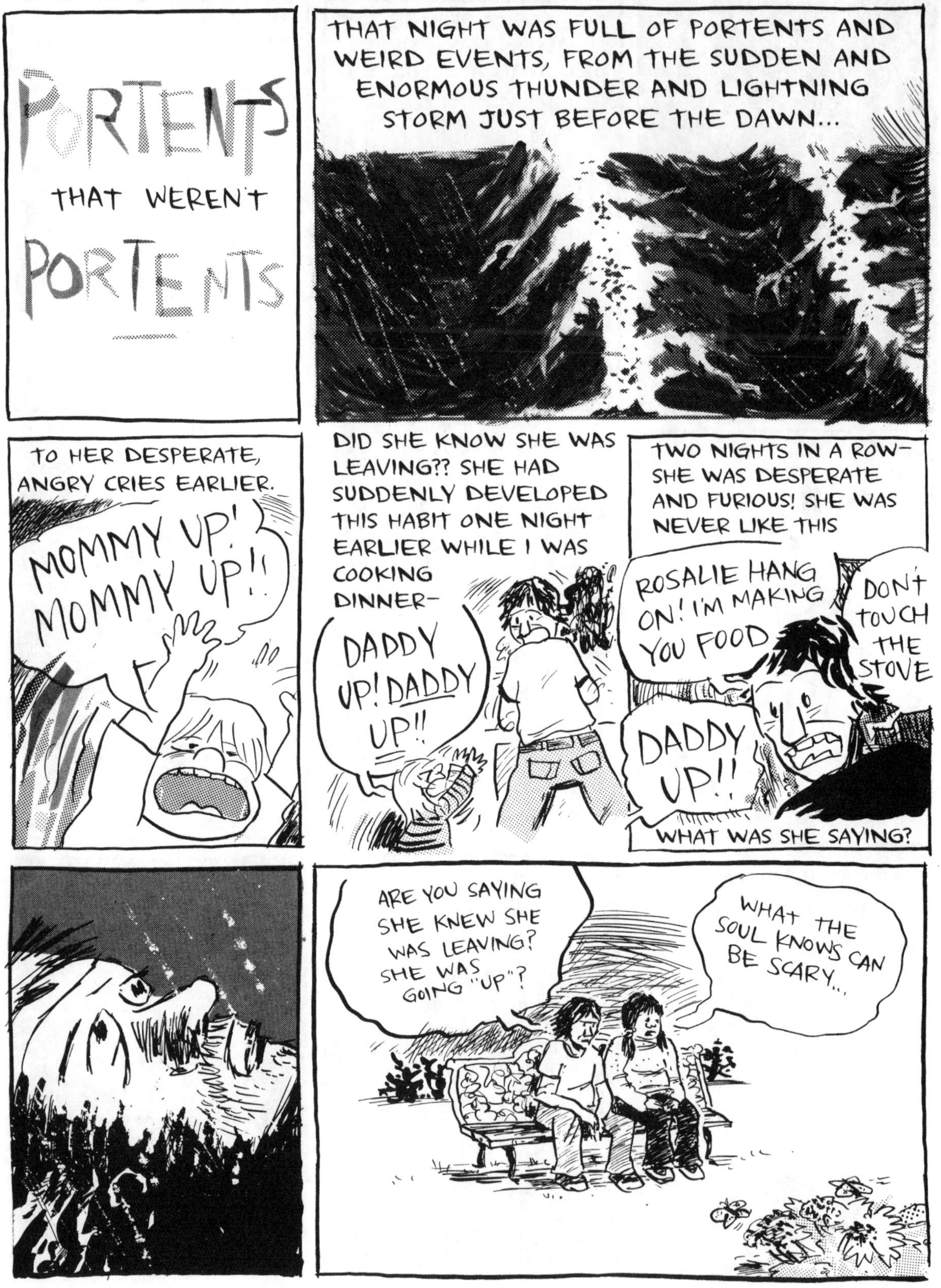
PORTENTS THAT WEREN'T PORTENTS
THAT NIGHT WAS FULL OF PORTENTS AND WEIRD EVENTS, FROM THE SUDDEN AND ENORMOUS THUNDER AND LIGHTNING STORM JUST BEFORE THE DAWN...
TO HER DESPERATE, ANGRY CRIES EARLIER.
MOMMY UP! MOMMY UP!!
DID SHE KNOW SHE WAS LEAVING?? SHE HAD SUDDENLY DEVELOPED THIS HABIT ONE NIGHT EARLIER WHILE I WAS COOKING DINNER-
DADDY UP! DADDY UP!!
TWO NIGHTS IN A ROW- SHE WAS DESPERATE AND FURIOUS! SHE WAS NEVER LIKE THIS
ROSALIE HANG ON! I'M MAKING YOU FOOD
DON'T TOUCH THE STOVE
DADDY UP!!
WHAT WAS SHE SAYING?
ARE YOU SAYING SHE KNEW SHE WAS LEAVING? SHE WAS GOING "UP"?
WHAT THE SOUL KNOWS CAN BE SCARY...

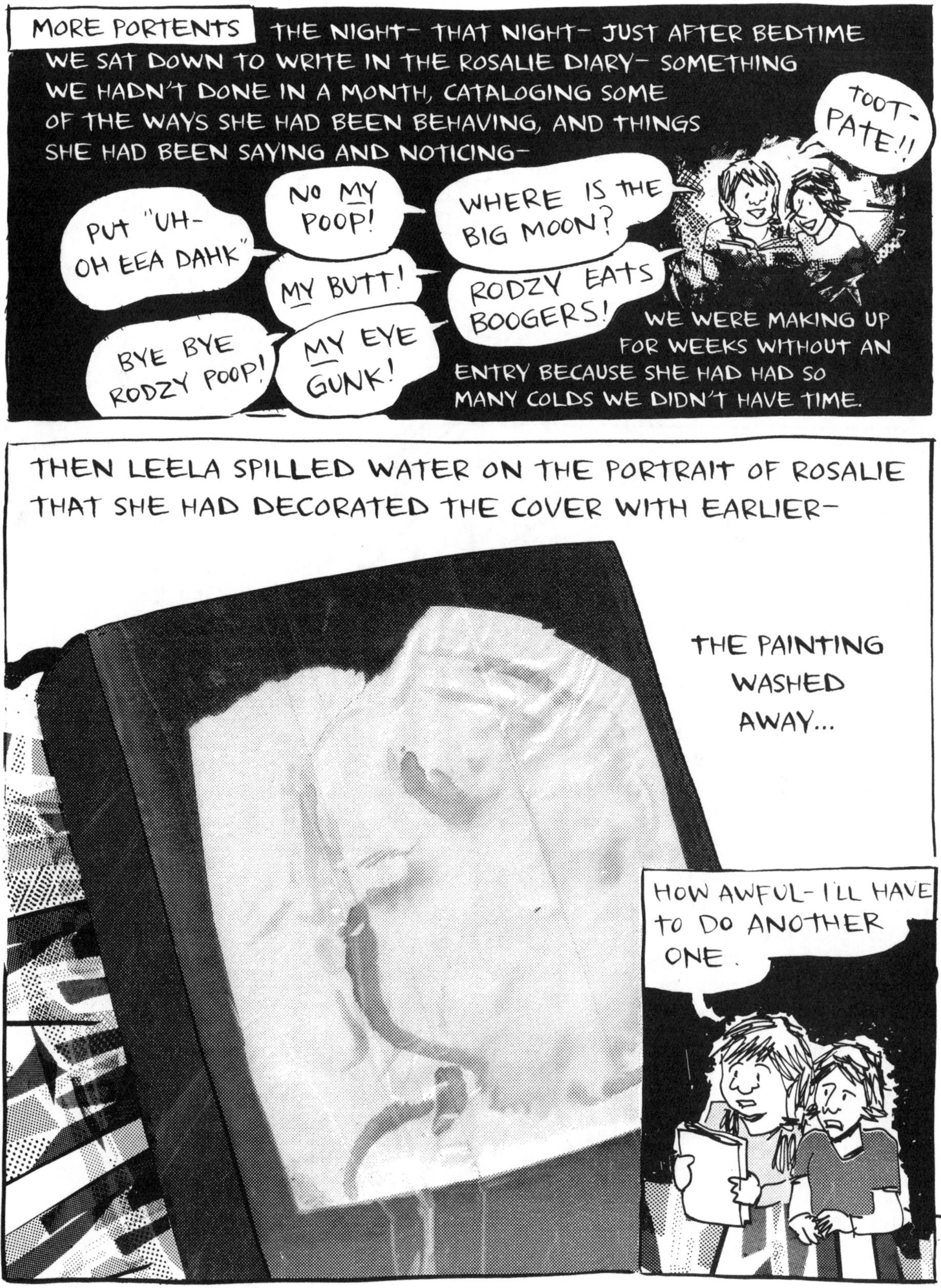
MORE PORTENTS
THE NIGHT— THAT NIGHT— JUST AFTER BEDTIME WE SAT DOWN TO WRITE IN THE ROSALIE DIARY— SOMETHING WE HADN'T DONE IN A MONTH, CATALOGING SOME OF THE WAYS SHE HAD BEEN BEHAVING, AND THINGS SHE HAD BEEN SAYING AND NOTICING—
TOOT-PATE!!
PUT "UH-OH EEA DAHK"
BYE BYE RODZY POOP!
NO MY POOP!
MY BUTT!
MY EYE GUNK!
WHERE IS THE BIG MOON?
RODZY EATS BOOGERS!
WE WERE MAKING UP FOR WEEKS WITHOUT AN ENTRY BECAUSE SHE HAD HAD SO MANY COLDS WE DIDN'T HAVE TIME.
THEN LEELA SPILLED WATER ON THE PORTRAIT OF ROSALIE THAT SHE HAD DECORATED THE COVER WITH EARLIER—
THE PAINTING WASHED AWAY...
HOW AWFUL— I'LL HAVE TO DO ANOTHER ONE.

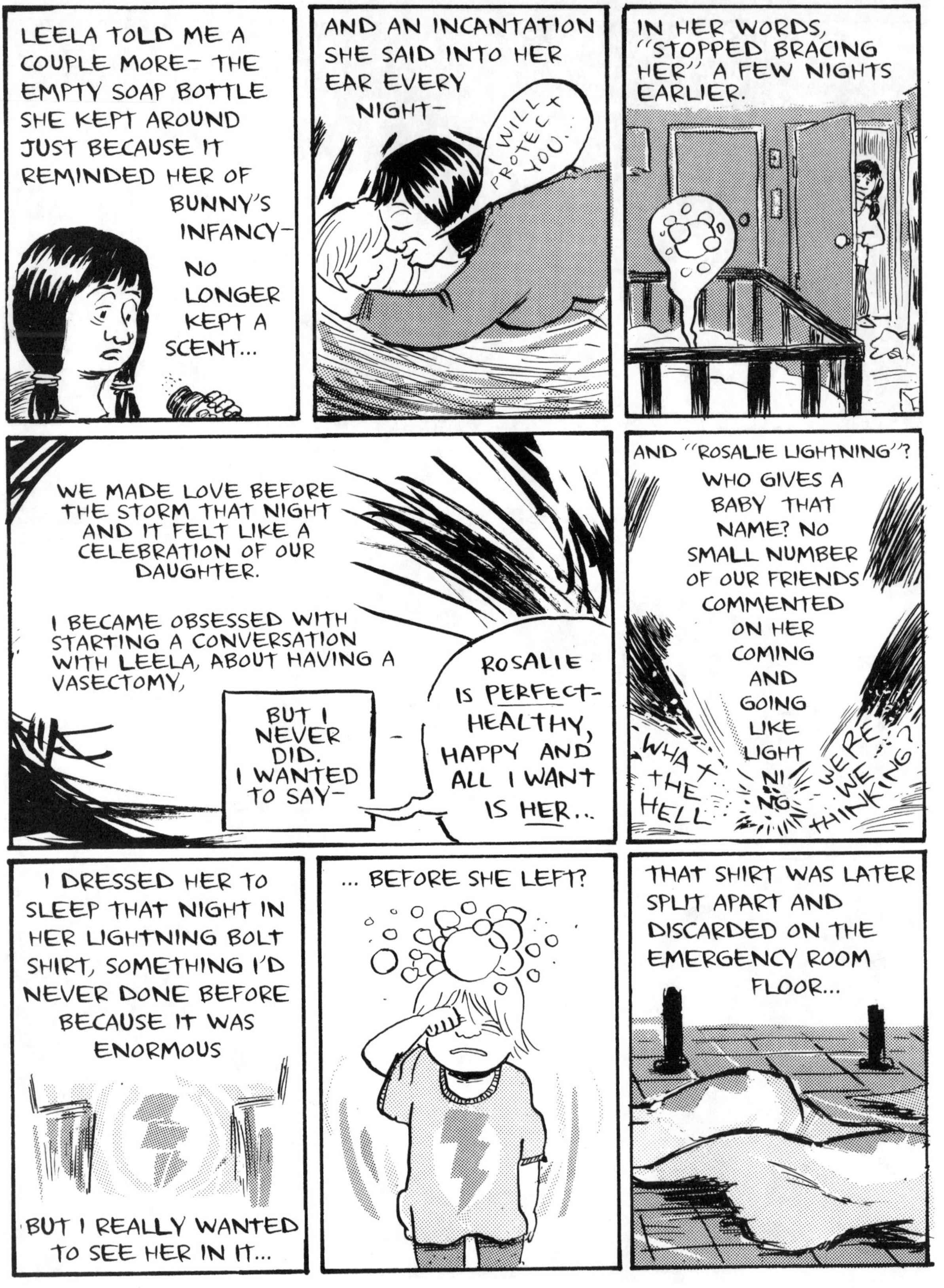
LEELA TOLD ME A COUPLE MORE– THE EMPTY SOAP BOTTLE SHE KEPT AROUND JUST BECAUSE IT REMINDED HER OF BUNNY'S INFANCY–
NO LONGER KEPT A SCENT...
AND AN INCANTATION SHE SAID INTO HER EAR EVERY NIGHT–
I WILL PROTECT YOU...
IN HER WORDS, "STOPPED BRACING HER" A FEW NIGHTS EARLIER.
WE MADE LOVE BEFORE THE STORM THAT NIGHT AND IT FELT LIKE A CELEBRATION OF OUR DAUGHTER.
I BECAME OBSESSED WITH STARTING A CONVERSATION WITH LEELA, ABOUT HAVING A VASECTOMY,
BUT I NEVER DID. I WANTED TO SAY–
ROSALIE IS PERFECT– HEALTHY, HAPPY AND ALL I WANT IS HER...
AND "ROSALIE LIGHTNING"?
WHO GIVES A BABY THAT NAME? NO SMALL NUMBER OF OUR FRIENDS COMMENTED ON HER COMING AND GOING LIKE LIGHT NI NG
WHAT THE HELL
WERE WE THINKING?
I DRESSED HER TO SLEEP THAT NIGHT IN HER LIGHTNING BOLT SHIRT, SOMETHING I'D NEVER DONE BEFORE BECAUSE IT WAS ENORMOUS
BUT I REALLY WANTED TO SEE HER IN IT...
... BEFORE SHE LEFT?
THAT SHIRT WAS LATER SPLIT APART AND DISCARDED ON THE EMERGENCY ROOM FLOOR...

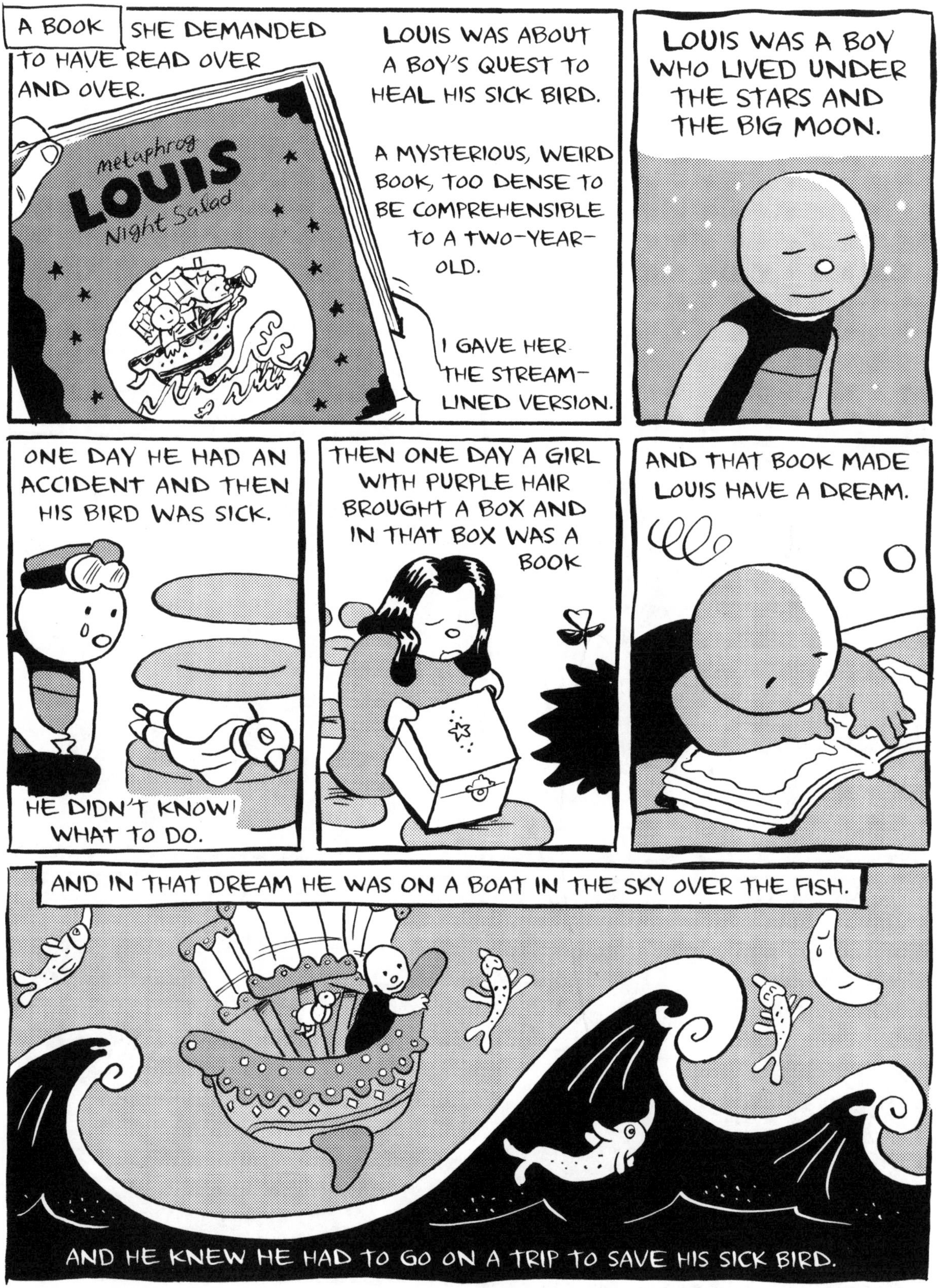
A BOOK SHE DEMANDED TO HAVE READ OVER AND OVER.
metaphrog
LOUIS
Night Salad
LOUIS WAS ABOUT A BOY'S QUEST TO HEAL HIS SICK BIRD.
A MYSTERIOUS, WEIRD BOOK, TOO DENSE TO BE COMPREHENSIBLE TO A TWO-YEAR-OLD.
I GAVE HER THE STREAM-LINED VERSION.
LOUIS WAS A BOY WHO LIVED UNDER THE STARS AND THE BIG MOON.
ONE DAY HE HAD AN ACCIDENT AND THEN HIS BIRD WAS SICK.
HE DIDN'T KNOW WHAT TO DO.
THEN ONE DAY A GIRL WITH PURPLE HAIR BROUGHT A BOX AND IN THAT BOX WAS A BOOK
AND THAT BOOK MADE LOUIS HAVE A DREAM.
AND IN THAT DREAM HE WAS ON A BOAT IN THE SKY OVER THE FISH.
AND HE KNEW HE HAD TO GO ON A TRIP TO SAVE HIS SICK BIRD.

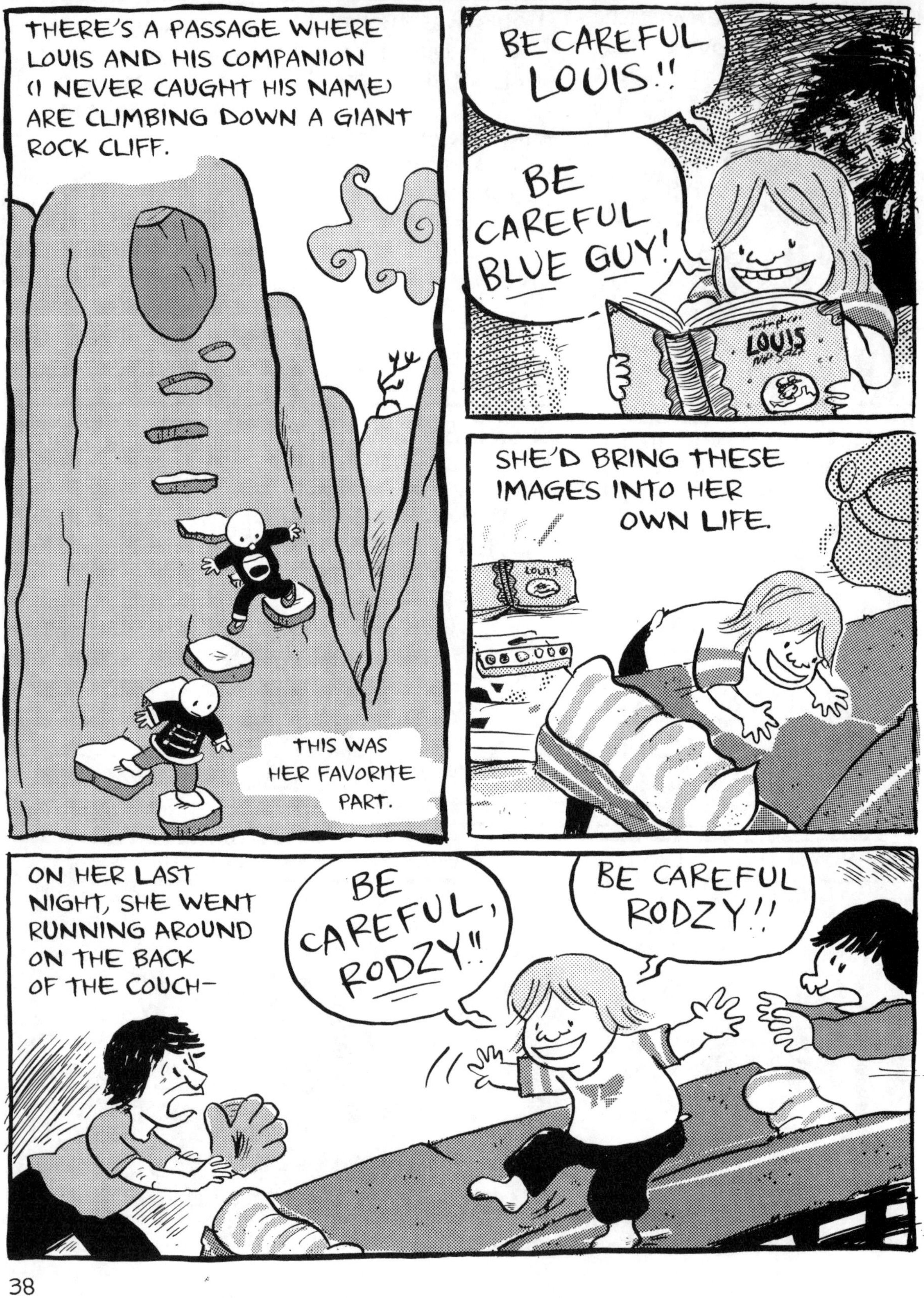

THERE'S A PASSAGE WHERE LOUIS AND HIS COMPANION (I NEVER CAUGHT HIS NAME) ARE CLIMBING DOWN A GIANT ROCK CLIFF.
THIS WAS HER FAVORITE PART.
BE CAREFUL LOUIS!!
BE CAREFUL BLUE GUY!
LOUIS
SHE'D BRING THESE IMAGES INTO HER OWN LIFE.
ON HER LAST NIGHT, SHE WENT RUNNING AROUND ON THE BACK OF THE COUCH—
BE CAREFUL, RODZY!!
BE CAREFUL RODZY!!

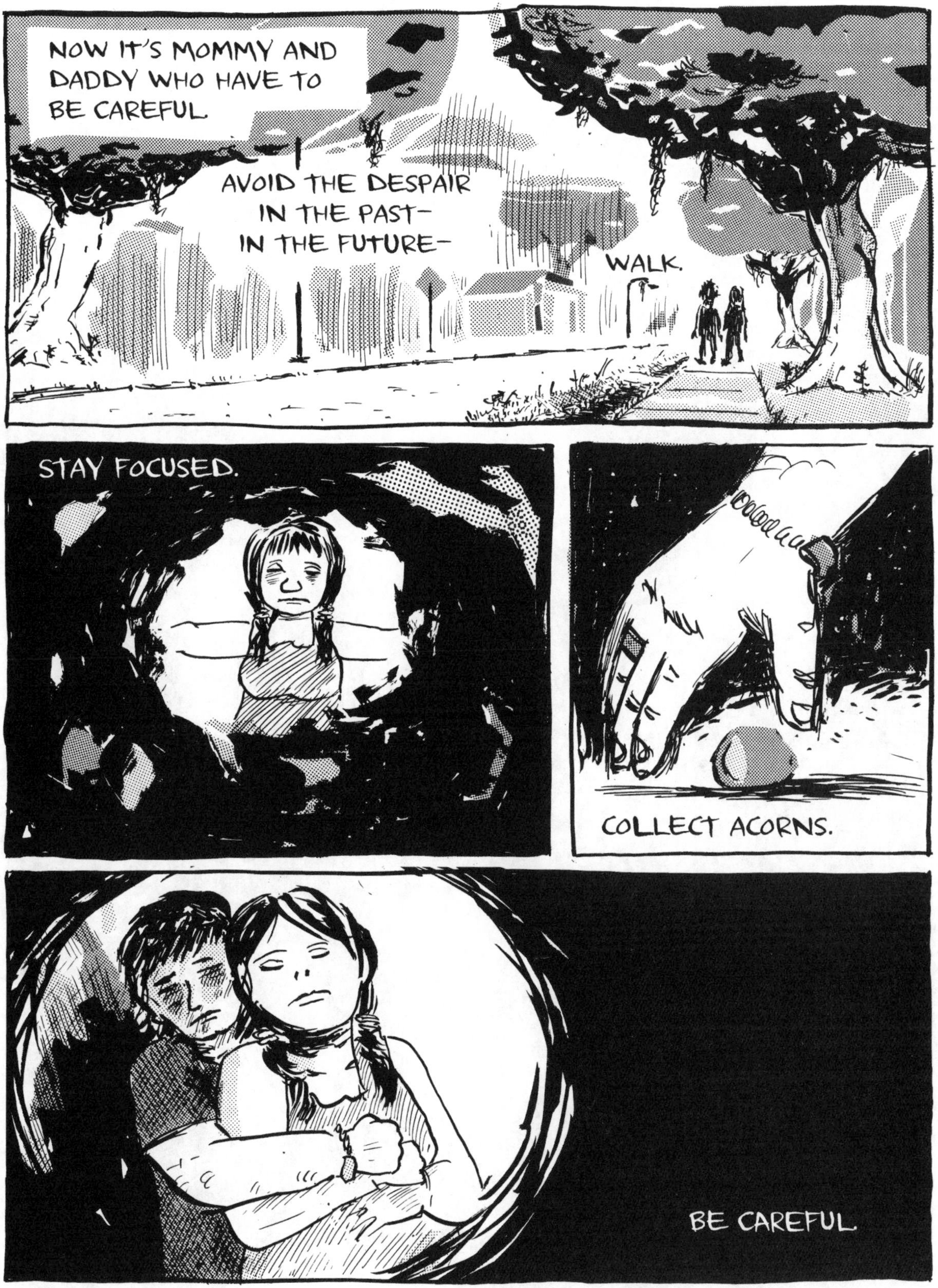
NOW IT'S MOMMY AND DADDY WHO HAVE TO BE CAREFUL.
AVOID THE DESPAIR IN THE PAST— IN THE FUTURE—
WALK.
STAY FOCUSED.
COLLECT ACORNS.
BE CAREFUL.

III

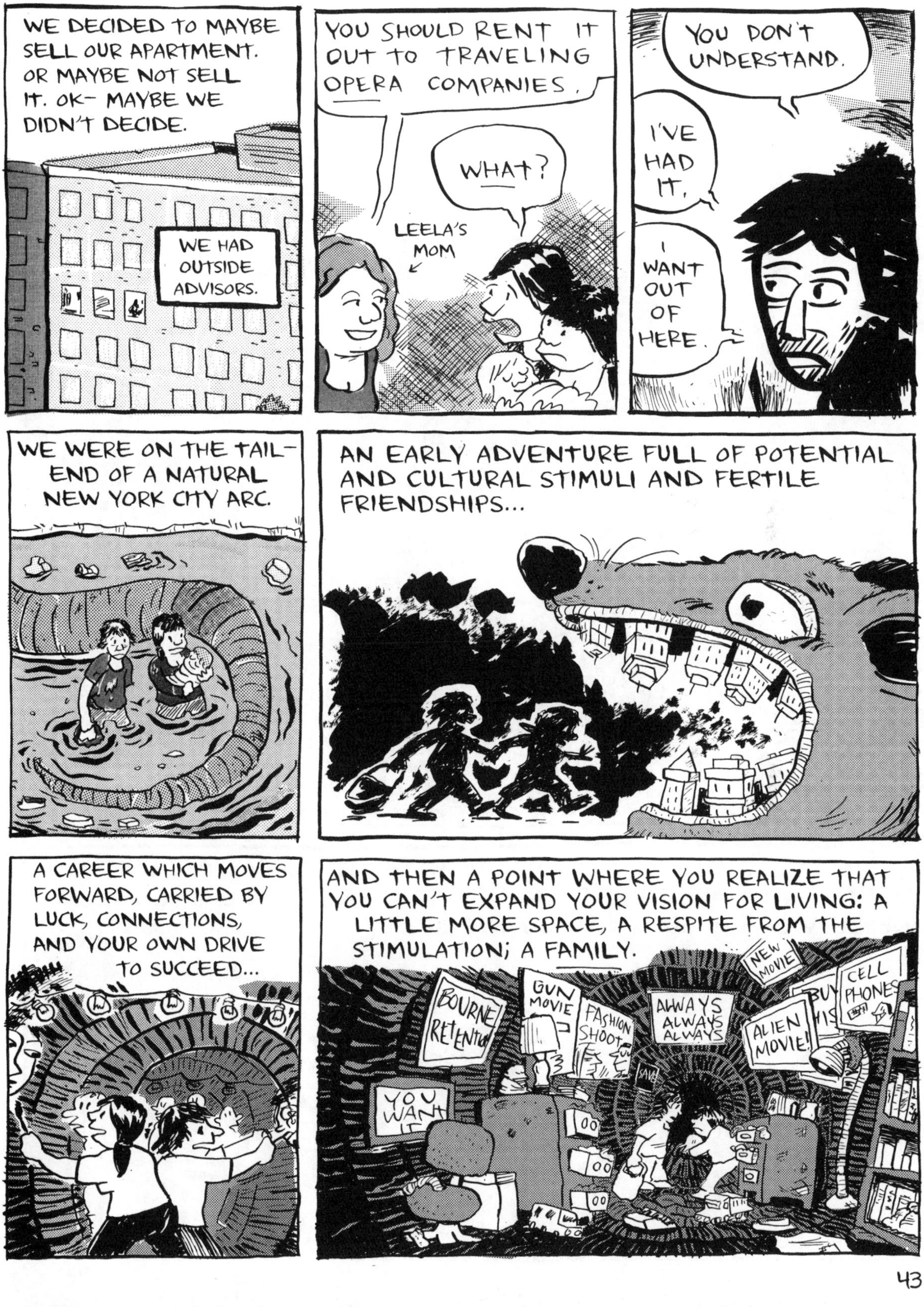
WE DECIDED TO MAYBE SELL OUR APARTMENT. OR MAYBE NOT SELL IT. OK– MAYBE WE DIDN'T DECIDE.
WE HAD OUTSIDE ADVISORS.
YOU SHOULD RENT IT OUT TO TRAVELING OPERA COMPANIES.
WHAT?
LEELA'S MOM
YOU DON'T UNDERSTAND.
I'VE HAD IT.
I WANT OUT OF HERE.
WE WERE ON THE TAIL-END OF A NATURAL NEW YORK CITY ARC.
AN EARLY ADVENTURE FULL OF POTENTIAL AND CULTURAL STIMULI AND FERTILE FRIENDSHIPS...
A CAREER WHICH MOVES FORWARD, CARRIED BY LUCK, CONNECTIONS, AND YOUR OWN DRIVE TO SUCCEED...
AND THEN A POINT WHERE YOU REALIZE THAT YOU CAN'T EXPAND YOUR VISION FOR LIVING: A LITTLE MORE SPACE, A RESPITE FROM THE STIMULATION; A FAMILY.
NEW MOVIE
BOURNE
GUN MOVIE
FASHION SHOOT
ALWAYS ALWAYS ALWAYS
ALIEN MOVIE!
CELL PHONES
SAVE

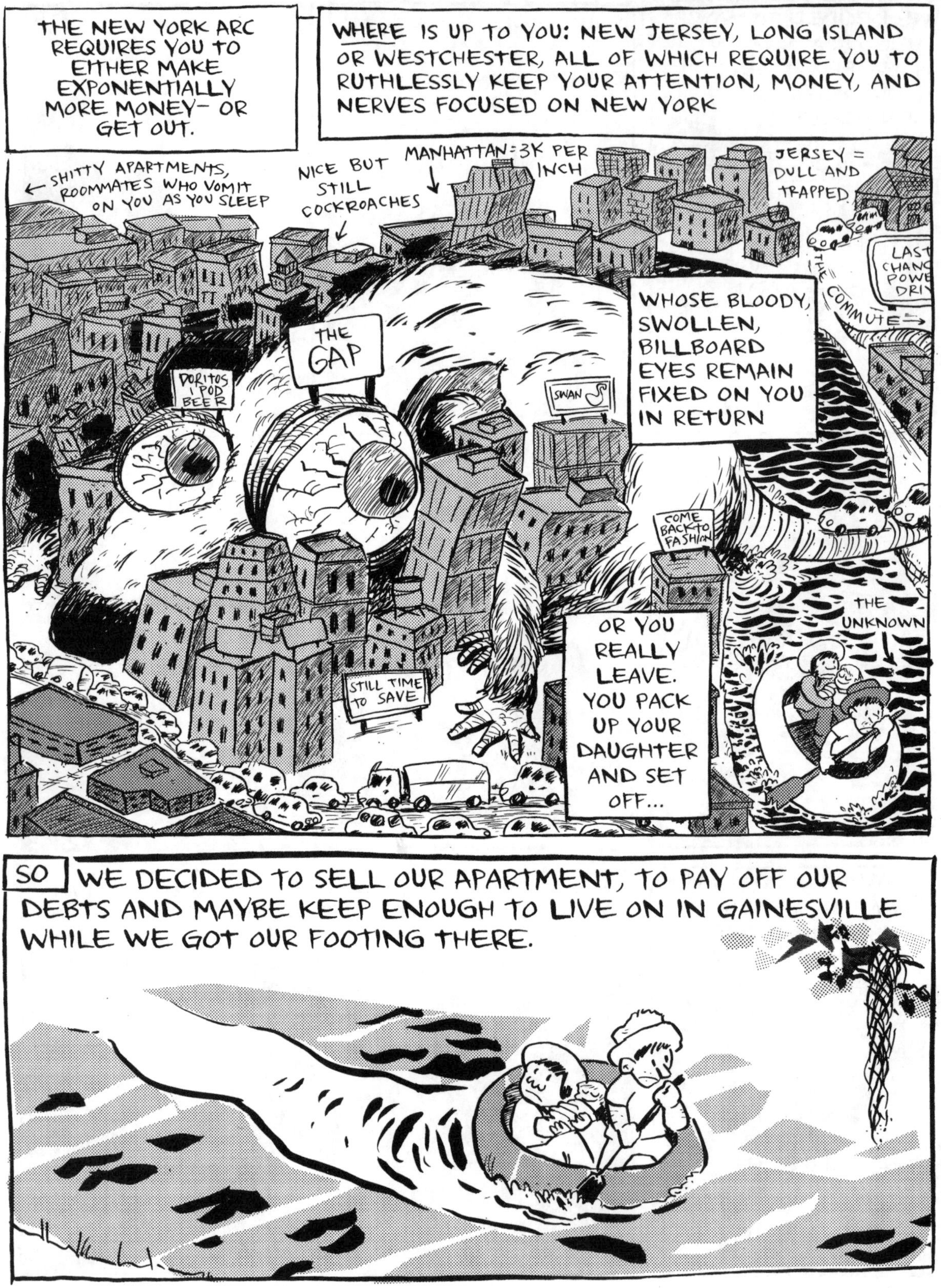

THE NEW YORK ARC REQUIRES YOU TO EITHER MAKE EXPONENTIALLY MORE MONEY– OR GET OUT.
WHERE IS UP TO YOU: NEW JERSEY, LONG ISLAND OR WESTCHESTER, ALL OF WHICH REQUIRE YOU TO RUTHLESSLY KEEP YOUR ATTENTION, MONEY, AND NERVES FOCUSED ON NEW YORK
← SHITTY APARTMENTS, ROOMMATES WHO VOMIT ON YOU AS YOU SLEEP
NICE BUT STILL COCKROACHES
MANHATTAN=3K PER INCH
JERSEY = DULL AND TRAPPED
LAST
THE COMMUTE →
THE GAP
DORITOS IPOD BEER
SWAN
WHOSE BLOODY, SWOLLEN, BILLBOARD EYES REMAIN FIXED ON YOU IN RETURN
COME BACK TO FASHION
THE UNKNOWN
STILL TIME TO SAVE
OR YOU REALLY LEAVE. YOU PACK UP YOUR DAUGHTER AND SET OFF...
SO WE DECIDED TO SELL OUR APARTMENT, TO PAY OFF OUR DEBTS AND MAYBE KEEP ENOUGH TO LIVE ON IN GAINESVILLE WHILE WE GOT OUR FOOTING THERE.

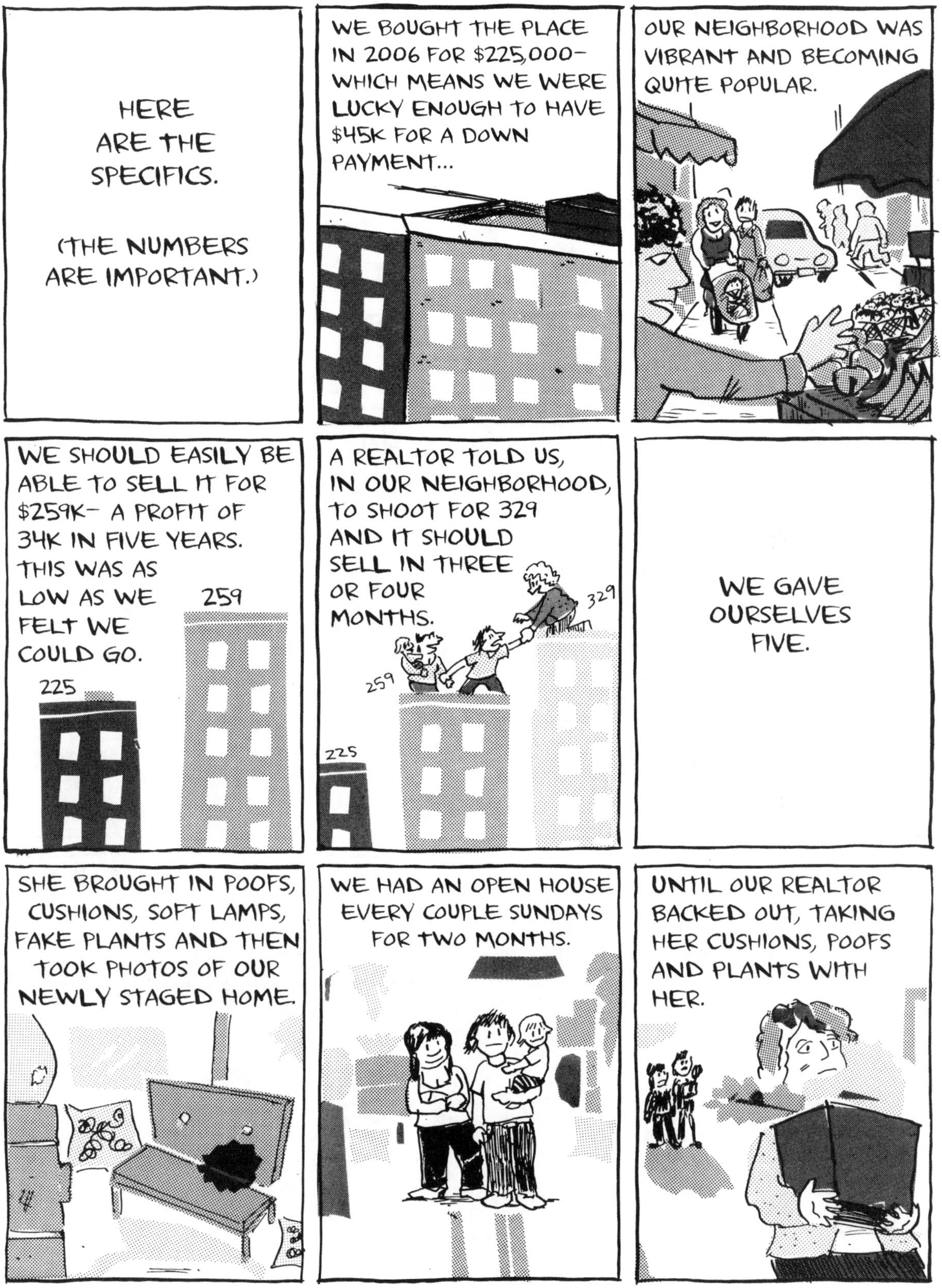
HERE ARE THE SPECIFICS.
(THE NUMBERS ARE IMPORTANT.)
WE BOUGHT THE PLACE IN 2006 FOR $225,000– WHICH MEANS WE WERE LUCKY ENOUGH TO HAVE $45K FOR A DOWN PAYMENT...
OUR NEIGHBORHOOD WAS VIBRANT AND BECOMING QUITE POPULAR.
WE SHOULD EASILY BE ABLE TO SELL IT FOR $259K– A PROFIT OF 34K IN FIVE YEARS. THIS WAS AS LOW AS WE FELT WE COULD GO.
259
225
A REALTOR TOLD US, IN OUR NEIGHBORHOOD, TO SHOOT FOR 329 AND IT SHOULD SELL IN THREE OR FOUR MONTHS.
329
259
225
WE GAVE OURSELVES FIVE.
SHE BROUGHT IN POOFS, CUSHIONS, SOFT LAMPS, FAKE PLANTS AND THEN TOOK PHOTOS OF OUR NEWLY STAGED HOME.
WE HAD AN OPEN HOUSE EVERY COUPLE SUNDAYS FOR TWO MONTHS.
UNTIL OUR REALTOR BACKED OUT, TAKING HER CUSHIONS, POOFS AND PLANTS WITH HER.

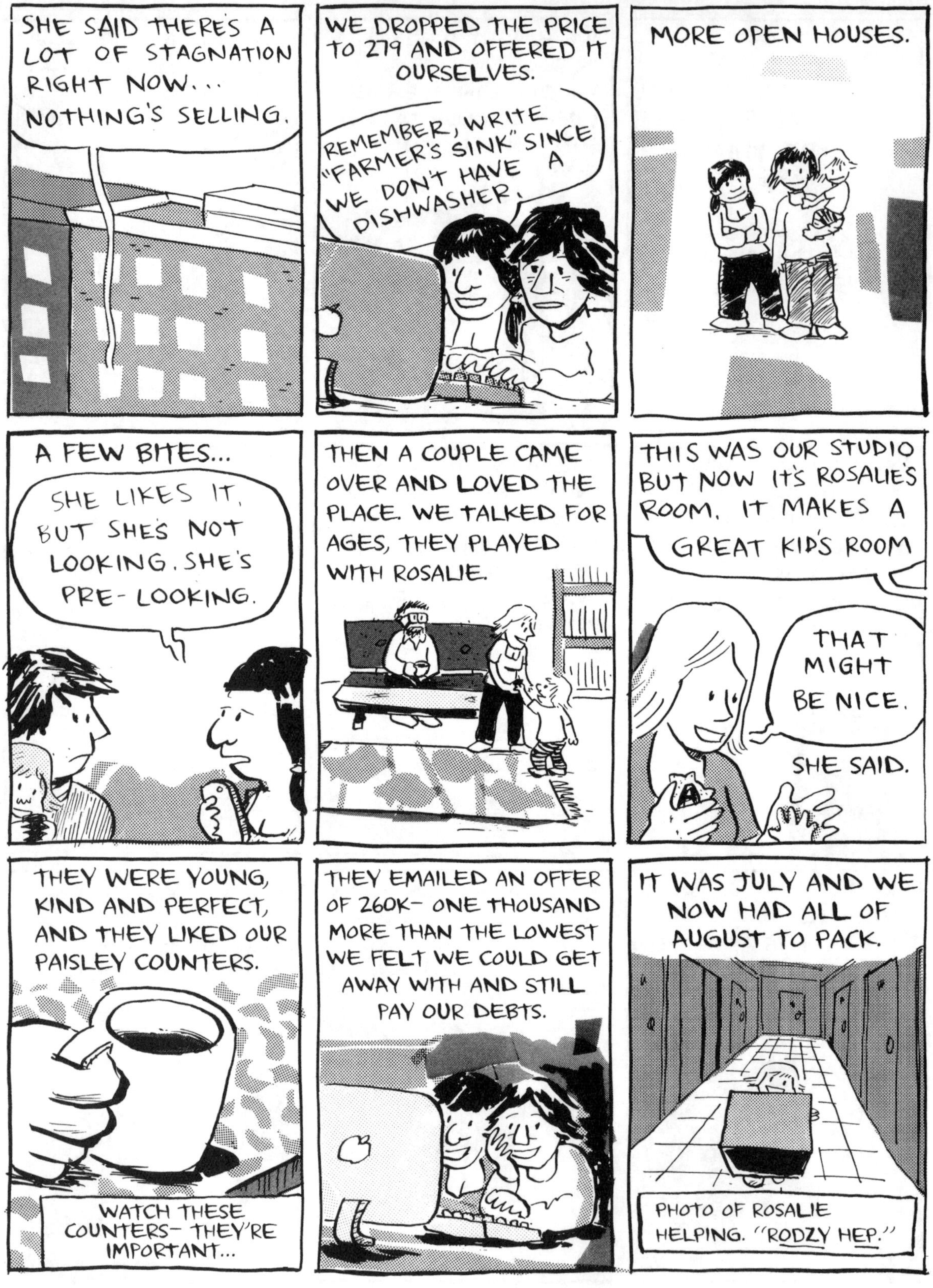
SHE SAID THERE'S A LOT OF STAGNATION RIGHT NOW... NOTHING'S SELLING.
WE DROPPED THE PRICE TO 279 AND OFFERED IT OURSELVES.
REMEMBER, WRITE "FARMER'S SINK" SINCE WE DON'T HAVE A DISHWASHER.
MORE OPEN HOUSES.
A FEW BITES...
SHE LIKES IT, BUT SHE'S NOT LOOKING. SHE'S PRE-LOOKING.
THEN A COUPLE CAME OVER AND LOVED THE PLACE. WE TALKED FOR AGES, THEY PLAYED WITH ROSALIE.
THIS WAS OUR STUDIO BUT NOW IT'S ROSALIE'S ROOM. IT MAKES A GREAT KID'S ROOM
THAT MIGHT BE NICE.
SHE SAID.
THEY WERE YOUNG, KIND AND PERFECT, AND THEY LIKED OUR PAISLEY COUNTERS.
WATCH THESE COUNTERS– THEY'RE IMPORTANT...
THEY EMAILED AN OFFER OF 260K– ONE THOUSAND MORE THAN THE LOWEST WE FELT WE COULD GET AWAY WITH AND STILL PAY OUR DEBTS.
IT WAS JULY AND WE NOW HAD ALL OF AUGUST TO PACK.
PHOTO OF ROSALIE HELPING. "RODZY HEP."

PAPERWORK WAS SUBMITTED TO THE BANKS, OUR CO-OP BOARD AND THE MANY VARIOUS LAWYERS.

AGREEMENT

CONTRACT

ONCE THE CO-OP BOARD APPROVED THE SALE, IT WOULD ALL BE A MATTER OF SIGNING PAPERS AND GETTING OUT OF THERE.

WE PACKED.

MOVED

AND UNPACKED WHAT WE COULD IN FLORIDA.

THERE WILL BE LIGHT!

RODZY BOOK

RODZY HEP.

LEELA HAD A HUGE BOOK DEADLINE WHICH SHE FRANTICALLY HAD TO WORK ON.

AND SLOWLY OTHER THINGS BECAME DIFFICULT...

WHY HASN'T THE BOARD APPROVED THE SALE?

WE CAN'T TELL YOU.

WHY CAN'T YOU TELL US?

THERE ARE COMPLICATIONS WITH THE SALE...

I KNOW THAT. I WANT TO KNOW WHAT THEY ARE.

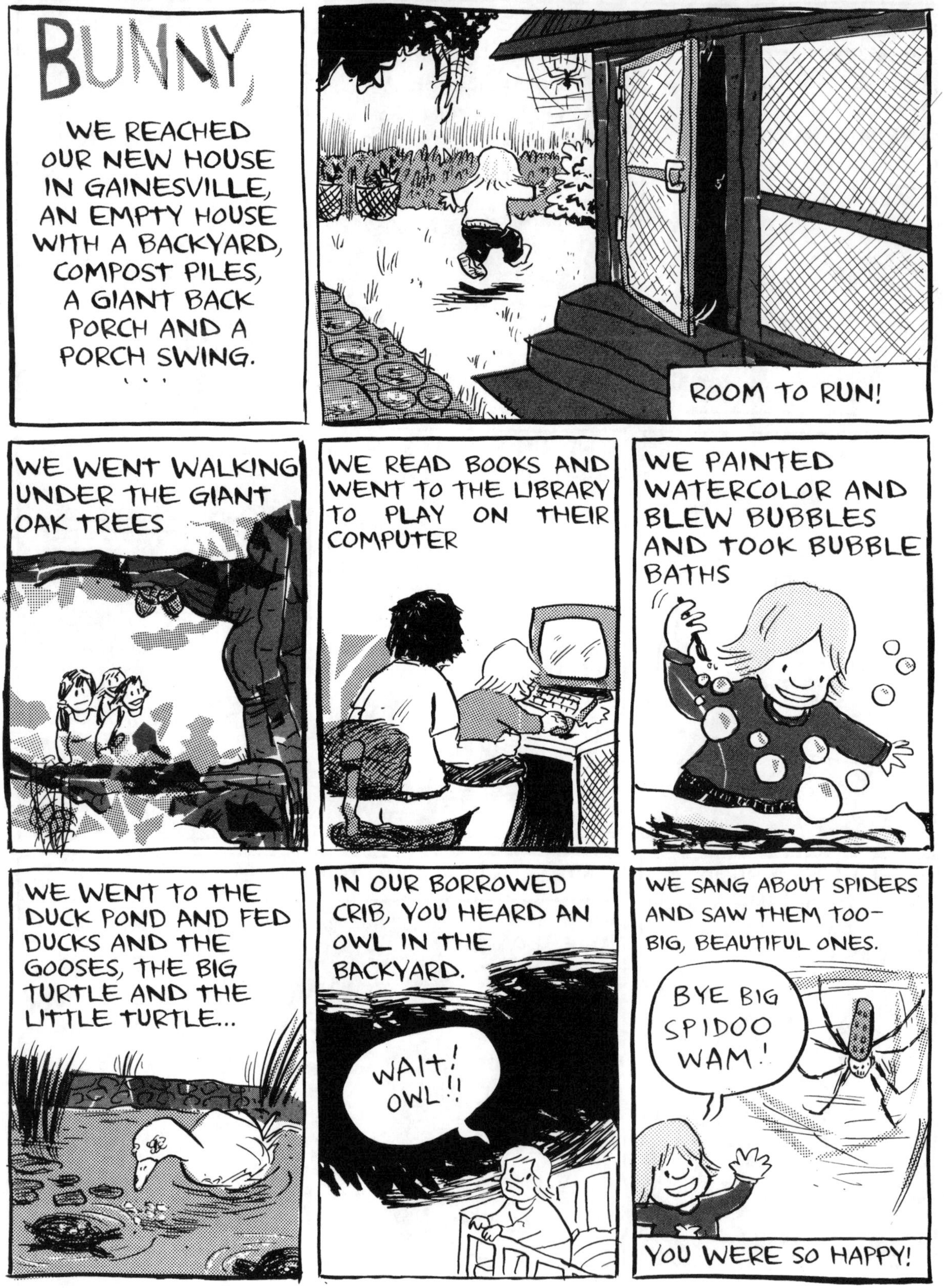
BUNNY,
WE REACHED OUR NEW HOUSE IN GAINESVILLE, AN EMPTY HOUSE WITH A BACKYARD, COMPOST PILES, A GIANT BACK PORCH AND A PORCH SWING. . . .
ROOM TO RUN!
WE WENT WALKING UNDER THE GIANT OAK TREES
WE READ BOOKS AND WENT TO THE LIBRARY TO PLAY ON THEIR COMPUTER
WE PAINTED WATERCOLOR AND BLEW BUBBLES AND TOOK BUBBLE BATHS
WE WENT TO THE DUCK POND AND FED DUCKS AND THE GOOSES, THE BIG TURTLE AND THE LITTLE TURTLE...
IN OUR BORROWED CRIB, YOU HEARD AN OWL IN THE BACKYARD.
WAIT! OWL!!
WE SANG ABOUT SPIDERS AND SAW THEM TOO- BIG, BEAUTIFUL ONES.
BYE BIG SPIDOO WAM!
YOU WERE SO HAPPY!

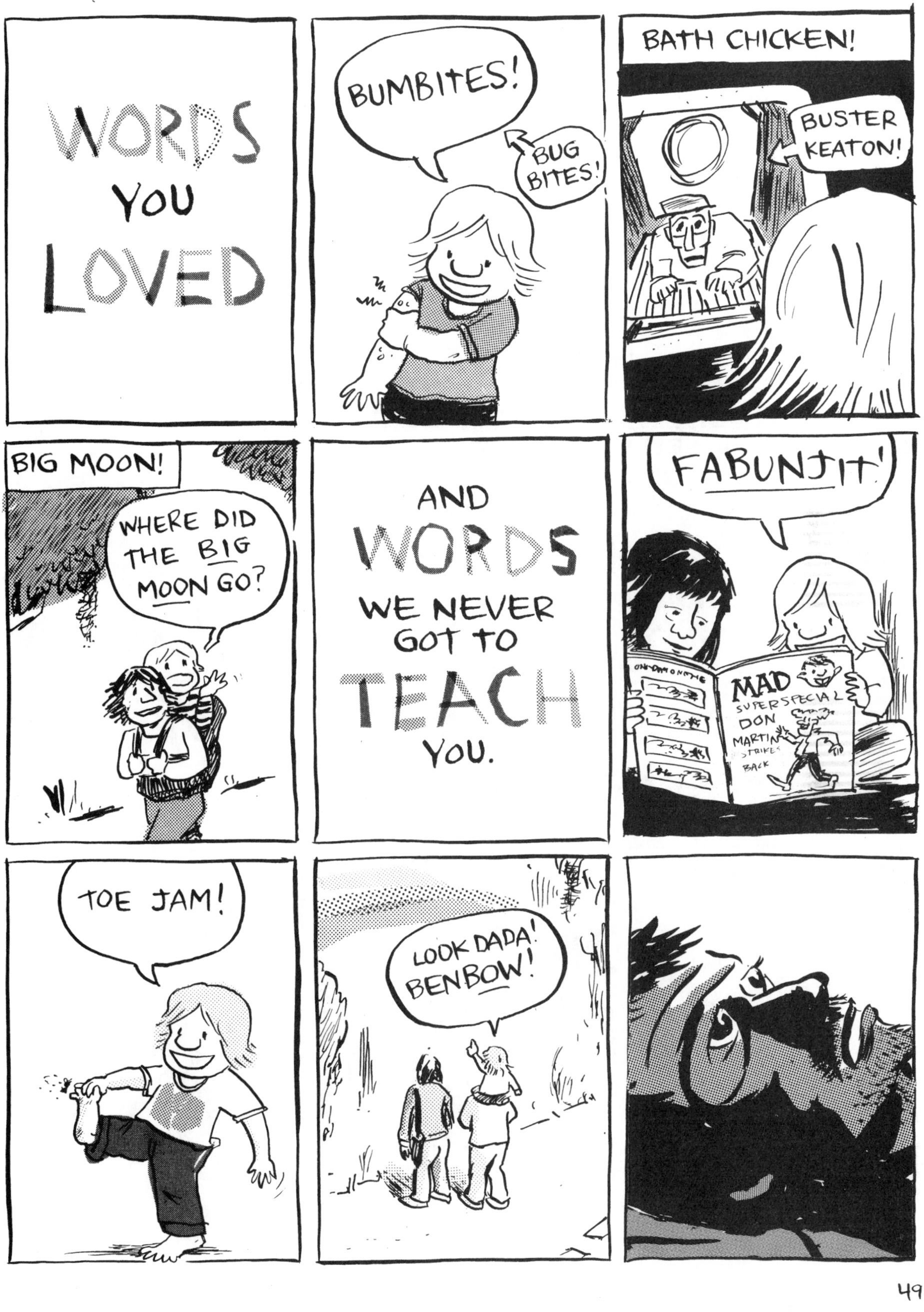
WORDS
YOU
LOVED
BUMBITES!
BUG BITES!
BATH CHICKEN!
BUSTER KEATON!
BIG MOON!
WHERE DID THE BIG MOON GO?
AND
WORDS
WE NEVER GOT TO
TEACH
YOU.
FABUNJIT!
MAD
SUPERSPECIAL
DON MARTIN STRIKES BACK
TOE JAM!
LOOK DADA! BENBOW!

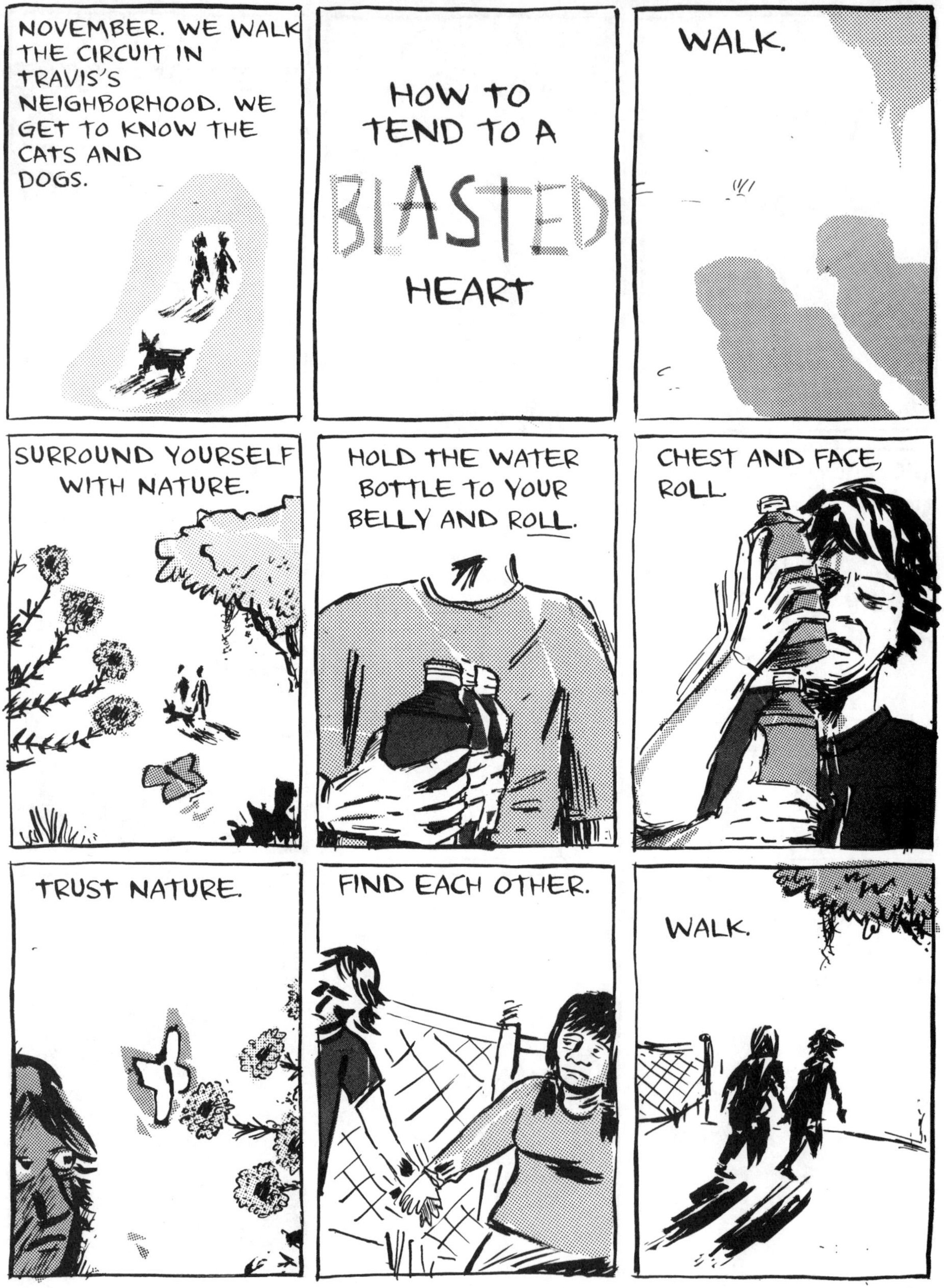
NOVEMBER. WE WALK THE CIRCUIT IN TRAVIS'S NEIGHBORHOOD. WE GET TO KNOW THE CATS AND DOGS.
HOW TO TEND TO A BLASTED HEART
WALK.
SURROUND YOURSELF WITH NATURE.
HOLD THE WATER BOTTLE TO YOUR BELLY AND ROLL.
CHEST AND FACE, ROLL.
TRUST NATURE.
FIND EACH OTHER.
WALK.

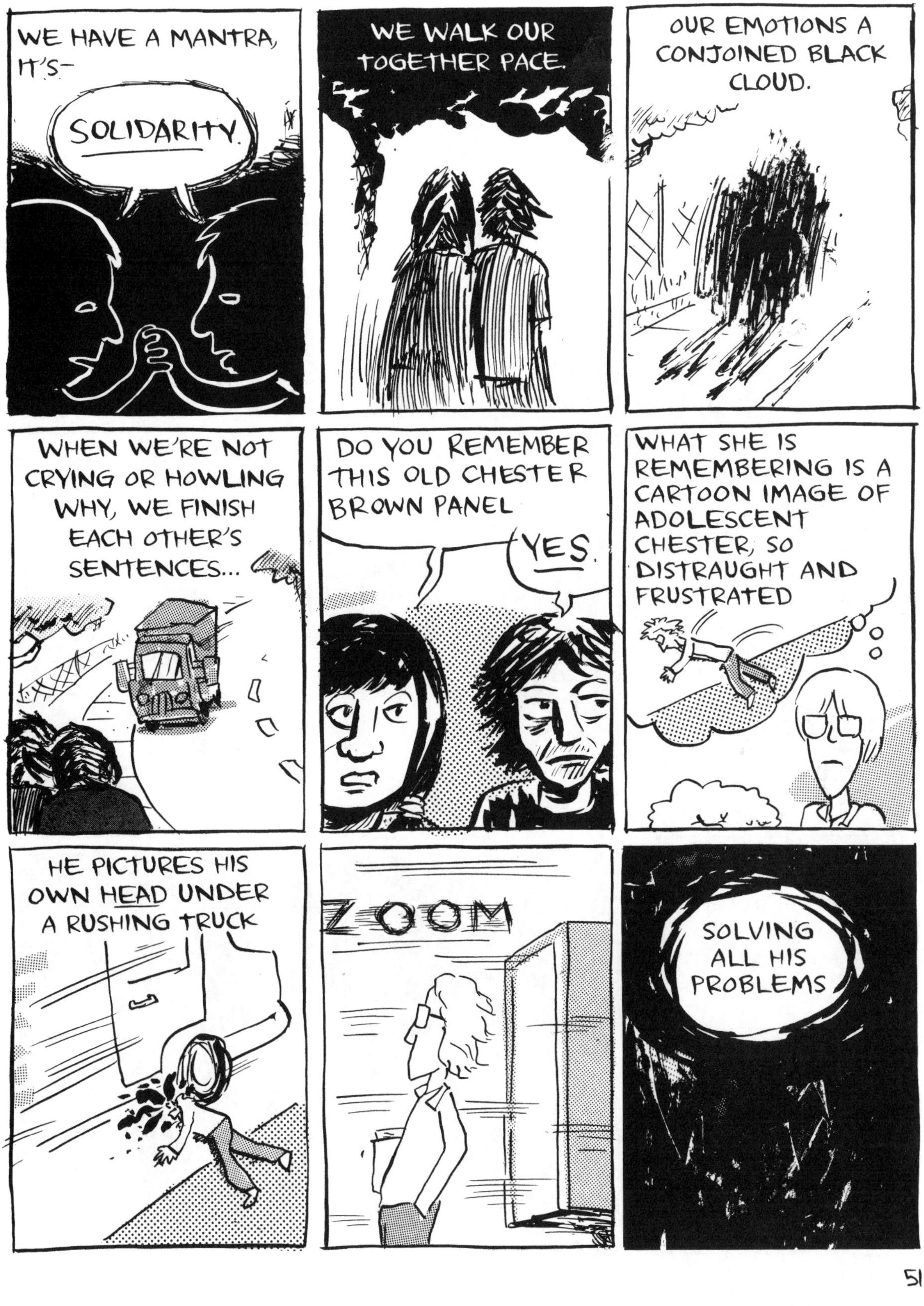
WE HAVE A MANTRA, IT'S–
SOLIDARITY.
WE WALK OUR TOGETHER PACE.
OUR EMOTIONS A CONJOINED BLACK CLOUD.
WHEN WE'RE NOT CRYING OR HOWLING WHY, WE FINISH EACH OTHER'S SENTENCES...
DO YOU REMEMBER THIS OLD CHESTER BROWN PANEL
YES.
WHAT SHE IS REMEMBERING IS A CARTOON IMAGE OF ADOLESCENT CHESTER, SO DISTRAUGHT AND FRUSTRATED
HE PICTURES HIS OWN HEAD UNDER A RUSHING TRUCK
ZOOM
SOLVING ALL HIS PROBLEMS

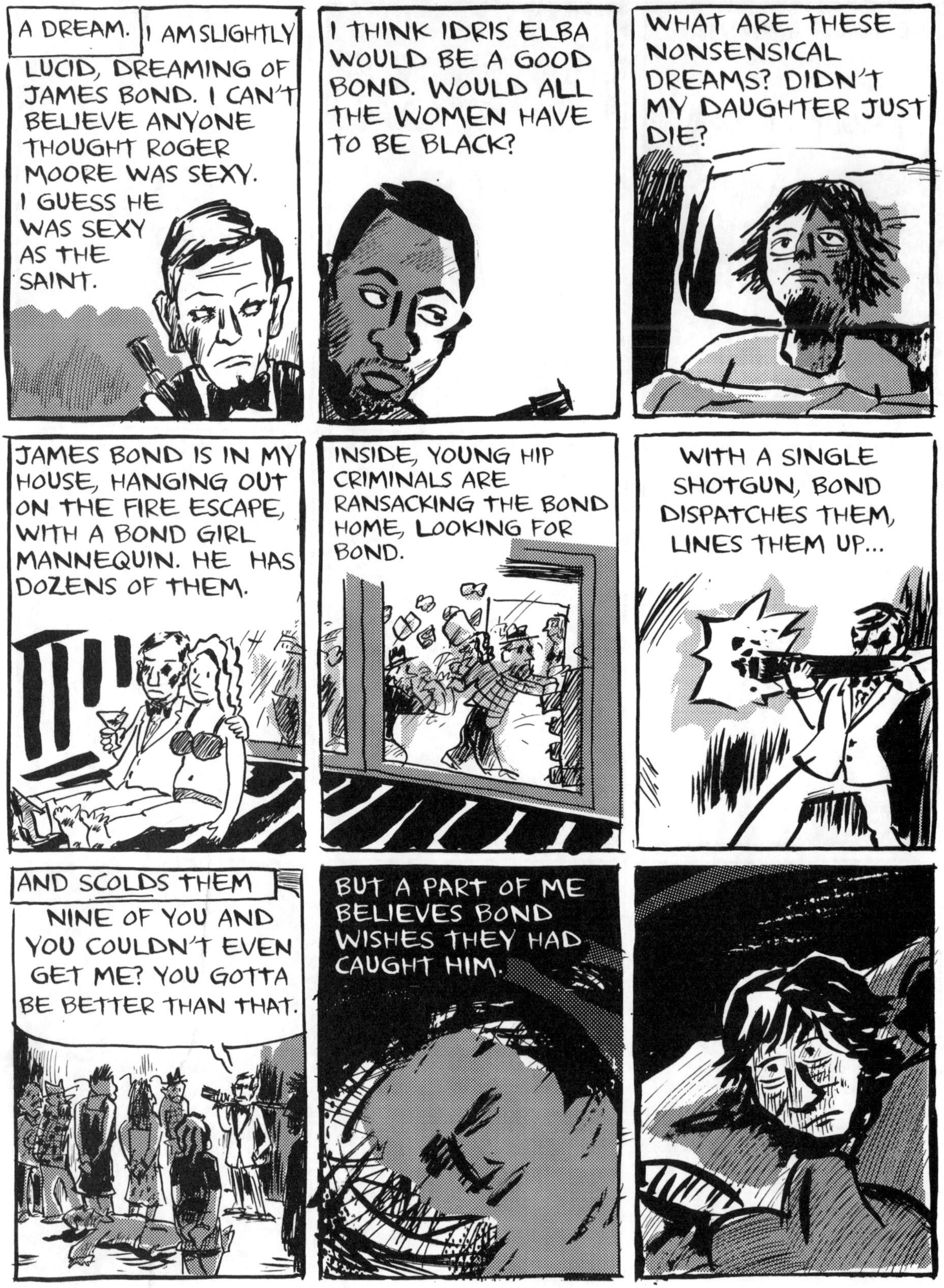
A DREAM.
I AM SLIGHTLY LUCID, DREAMING OF JAMES BOND. I CAN'T BELIEVE ANYONE THOUGHT ROGER MOORE WAS SEXY. I GUESS HE WAS SEXY AS THE SAINT.
I THINK IDRIS ELBA WOULD BE A GOOD BOND. WOULD ALL THE WOMEN HAVE TO BE BLACK?
WHAT ARE THESE NONSENSICAL DREAMS? DIDN'T MY DAUGHTER JUST DIE?
JAMES BOND IS IN MY HOUSE, HANGING OUT ON THE FIRE ESCAPE, WITH A BOND GIRL MANNEQUIN. HE HAS DOZENS OF THEM.
INSIDE, YOUNG HIP CRIMINALS ARE RANSACKING THE BOND HOME, LOOKING FOR BOND.
WITH A SINGLE SHOTGUN, BOND DISPATCHES THEM, LINES THEM UP...
AND SCOLDS THEM
NINE OF YOU AND YOU COULDN'T EVEN GET ME? YOU GOTTA BE BETTER THAN THAT.
BUT A PART OF ME BELIEVES BOND WISHES THEY HAD CAUGHT HIM.

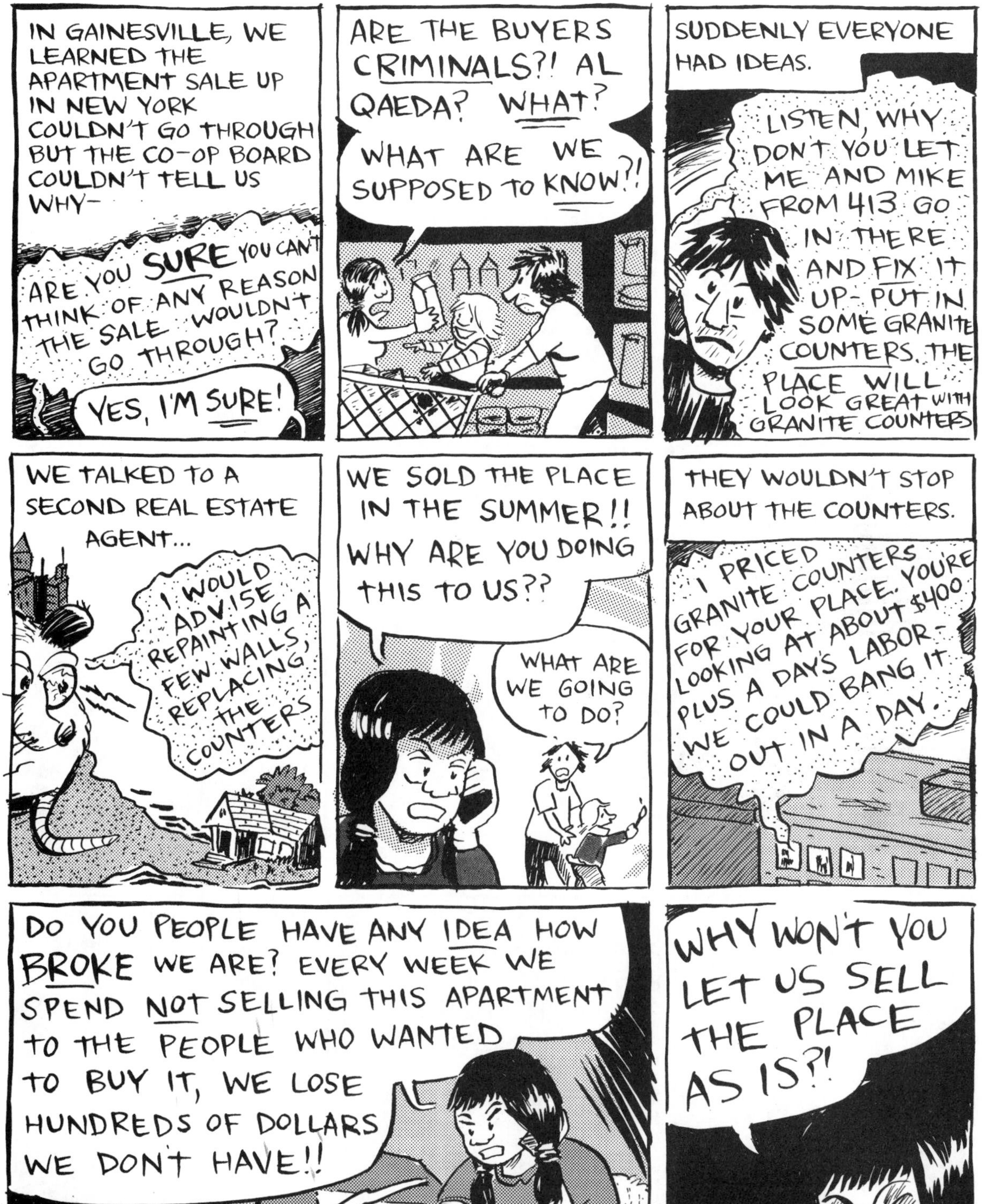
IN GAINESVILLE, WE LEARNED THE APARTMENT SALE UP IN NEW YORK COULDN'T GO THROUGH BUT THE CO-OP BOARD COULDN'T TELL US WHY-
ARE YOU SURE YOU CAN'T THINK OF ANY REASON THE SALE WOULDN'T GO THROUGH?
YES, I'M SURE!
ARE THE BUYERS CRIMINALS?! AL QAEDA? WHAT?
WHAT ARE WE SUPPOSED TO KNOW?!
SUDDENLY EVERYONE HAD IDEAS.
LISTEN, WHY DON'T YOU LET ME AND MIKE FROM 413 GO IN THERE AND FIX IT UP- PUT IN SOME GRANITE COUNTERS. THE PLACE WILL LOOK GREAT WITH GRANITE COUNTERS
WE TALKED TO A SECOND REAL ESTATE AGENT...
I WOULD ADVISE REPAINTING A FEW WALLS, REPLACING THE COUNTERS
WE SOLD THE PLACE IN THE SUMMER!! WHY ARE YOU DOING THIS TO US??
WHAT ARE WE GOING TO DO?
THEY WOULDN'T STOP ABOUT THE COUNTERS.
I PRICED GRANITE COUNTERS FOR YOUR PLACE. YOU'RE LOOKING AT ABOUT $400 PLUS A DAY'S LABOR- WE COULD BANG IT OUT IN A DAY.
DO YOU PEOPLE HAVE ANY IDEA HOW BROKE WE ARE? EVERY WEEK WE SPEND NOT SELLING THIS APARTMENT TO THE PEOPLE WHO WANTED TO BUY IT, WE LOSE HUNDREDS OF DOLLARS WE DON'T HAVE!!
WHY AM I EVEN TALKING ABOUT THIS?!
WHY WON'T YOU LET US SELL THE PLACE AS IS?!

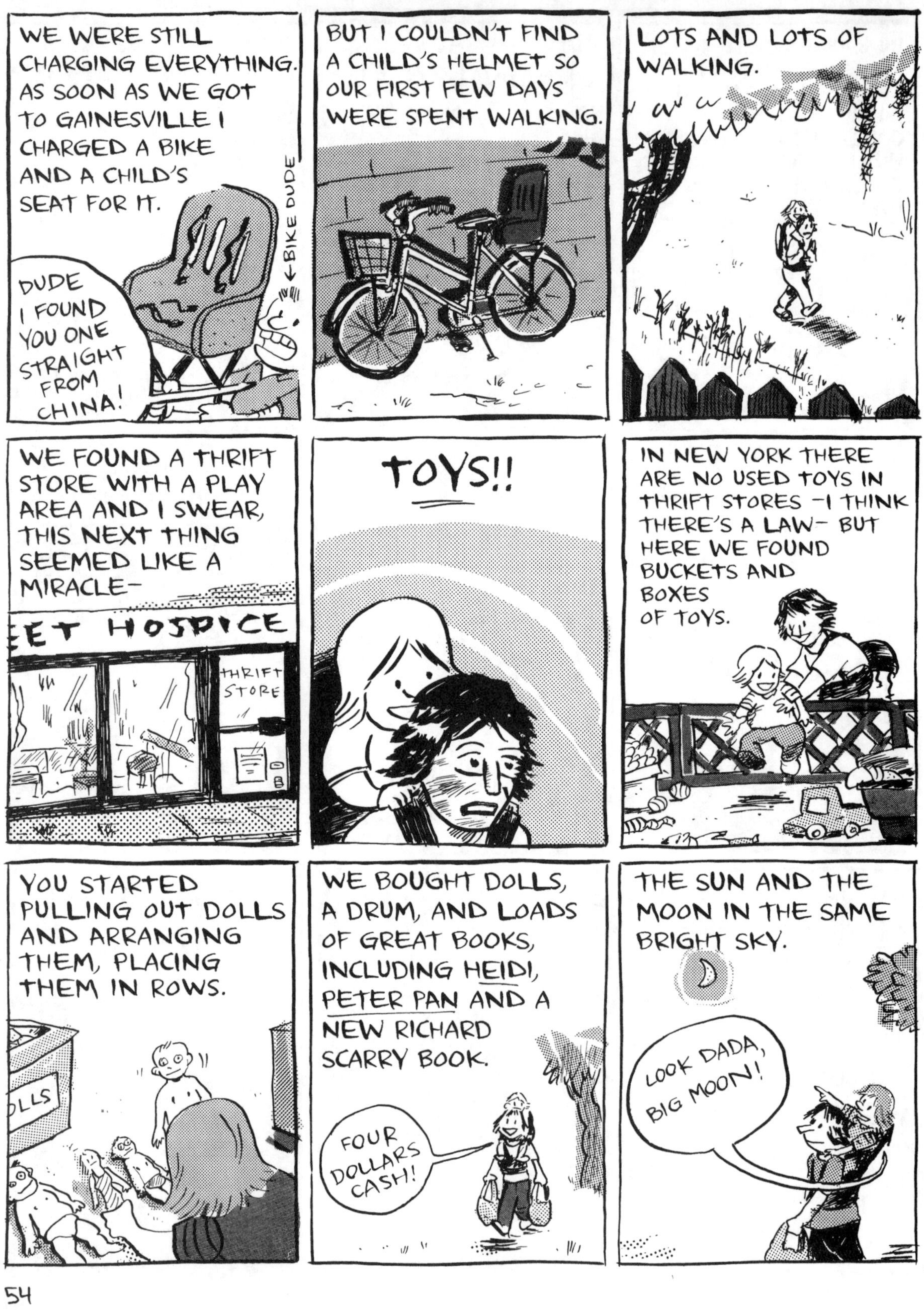
WE WERE STILL CHARGING EVERYTHING. AS SOON AS WE GOT TO GAINESVILLE I CHARGED A BIKE AND A CHILD'S SEAT FOR IT.
DUDE I FOUND YOU ONE STRAIGHT FROM CHINA!
← BIKE DUDE
BUT I COULDN'T FIND A CHILD'S HELMET SO OUR FIRST FEW DAYS WERE SPENT WALKING.
LOTS AND LOTS OF WALKING.
WE FOUND A THRIFT STORE WITH A PLAY AREA AND I SWEAR, THIS NEXT THING SEEMED LIKE A MIRACLE–
EET HOSPICE
THRIFT STORE
TOYS!!
IN NEW YORK THERE ARE NO USED TOYS IN THRIFT STORES –I THINK THERE'S A LAW– BUT HERE WE FOUND BUCKETS AND BOXES OF TOYS.
YOU STARTED PULLING OUT DOLLS AND ARRANGING THEM, PLACING THEM IN ROWS.
DOLLS
WE BOUGHT DOLLS, A DRUM, AND LOADS OF GREAT BOOKS, INCLUDING HEIDI, PETER PAN AND A NEW RICHARD SCARRY BOOK.
FOUR DOLLARS CASH!
THE SUN AND THE MOON IN THE SAME BRIGHT SKY.
LOOK DADA, BIG MOON!

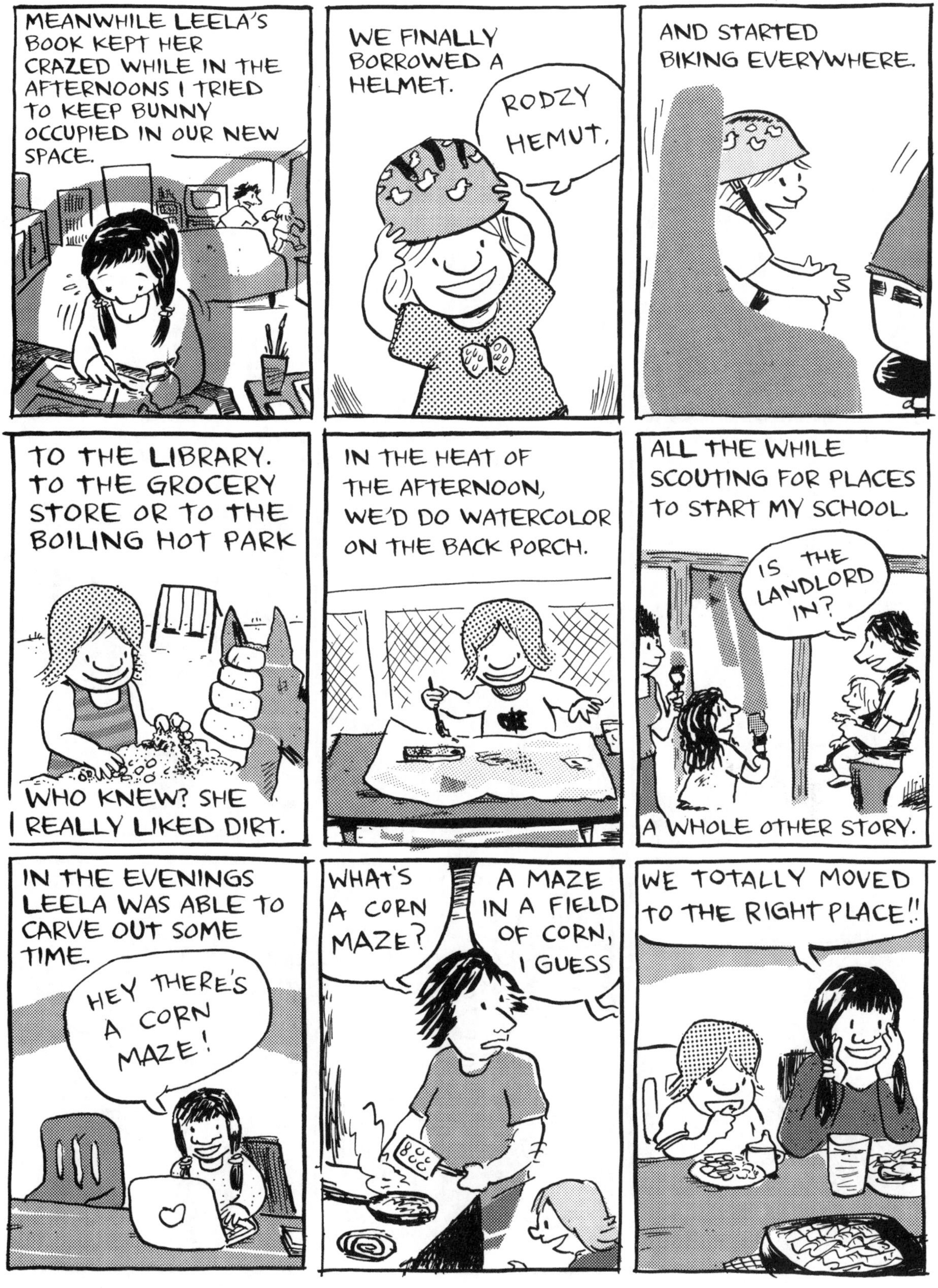
MEANWHILE LEELA'S BOOK KEPT HER CRAZED WHILE IN THE AFTERNOONS I TRIED TO KEEP BUNNY OCCUPIED IN OUR NEW SPACE.
WE FINALLY BORROWED A HELMET.
RODZY HEMUT.
AND STARTED BIKING EVERYWHERE.
TO THE LIBRARY. TO THE GROCERY STORE OR TO THE BOILING HOT PARK
WHO KNEW? SHE REALLY LIKED DIRT.
IN THE HEAT OF THE AFTERNOON, WE'D DO WATERCOLOR ON THE BACK PORCH.
ALL THE WHILE SCOUTING FOR PLACES TO START MY SCHOOL.
IS THE LANDLORD IN?
A WHOLE OTHER STORY.
IN THE EVENINGS LEELA WAS ABLE TO CARVE OUT SOME TIME.
HEY THERE'S A CORN MAZE!
WHAT'S A CORN MAZE?
A MAZE IN A FIELD OF CORN, I GUESS
WE TOTALLY MOVED TO THE RIGHT PLACE!!

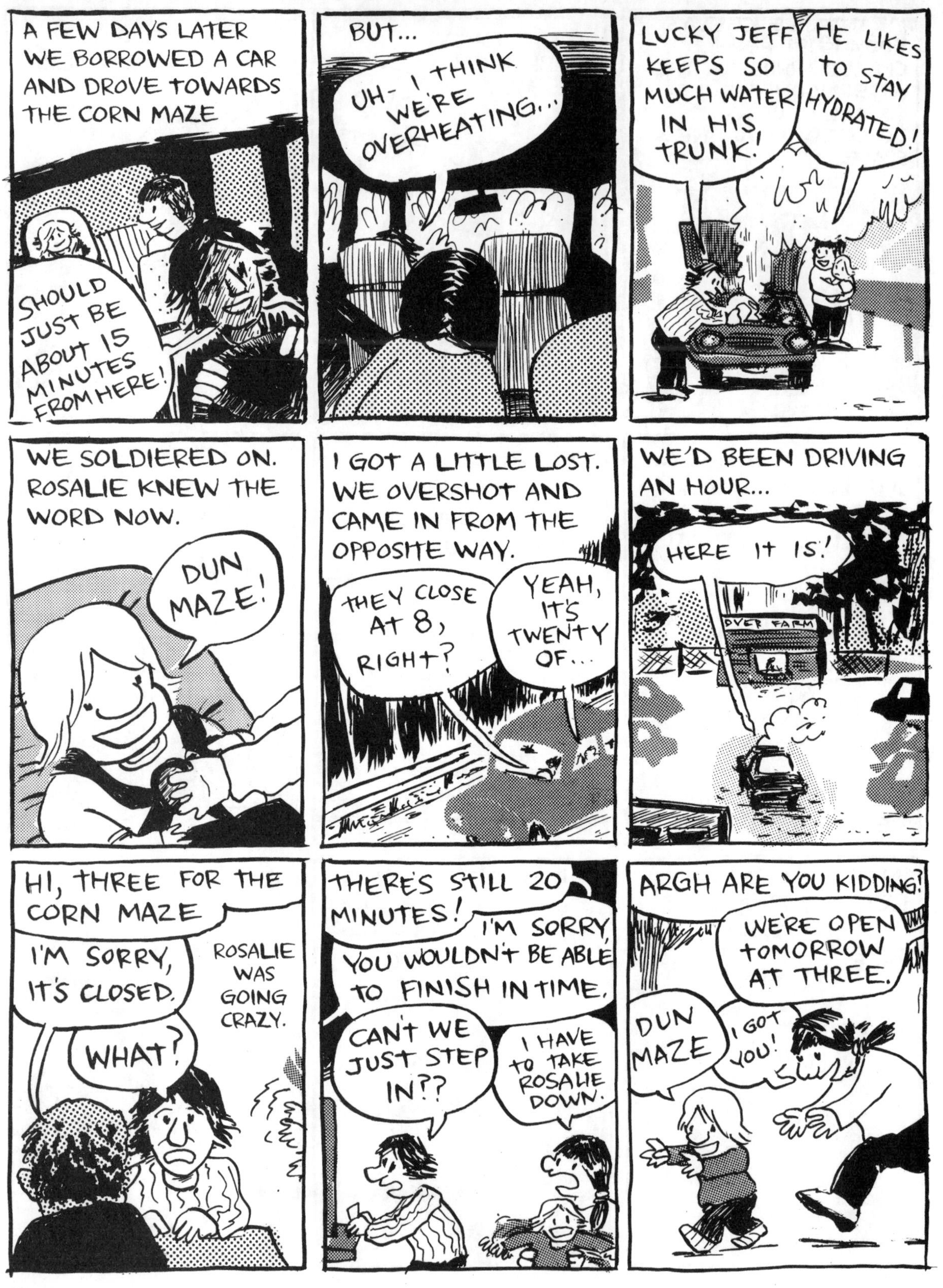
A FEW DAYS LATER WE BORROWED A CAR AND DROVE TOWARDS THE CORN MAZE
SHOULD JUST BE ABOUT 15 MINUTES FROM HERE!
BUT...
UH- I THINK WE'RE OVERHEATING...
LUCKY JEFF KEEPS SO MUCH WATER IN HIS TRUNK!
HE LIKES TO STAY HYDRATED!
WE SOLDIERED ON. ROSALIE KNEW THE WORD NOW.
DUN MAZE!
I GOT A LITTLE LOST. WE OVERSHOT AND CAME IN FROM THE OPPOSITE WAY.
THEY CLOSE AT 8, RIGHT?
YEAH, IT'S TWENTY OF...
WE'D BEEN DRIVING AN HOUR...
HERE IT IS!
OVER FARM
HI, THREE FOR THE CORN MAZE
I'M SORRY, IT'S CLOSED.
ROSALIE WAS GOING CRAZY.
WHAT?
THERE'S STILL 20 MINUTES!
I'M SORRY, YOU WOULDN'T BE ABLE TO FINISH IN TIME.
CAN'T WE JUST STEP IN??
I HAVE TO TAKE ROSALIE DOWN.
ARGH ARE YOU KIDDING?
WE'RE OPEN TOMORROW AT THREE.
DUN MAZE
I GOT YOU!

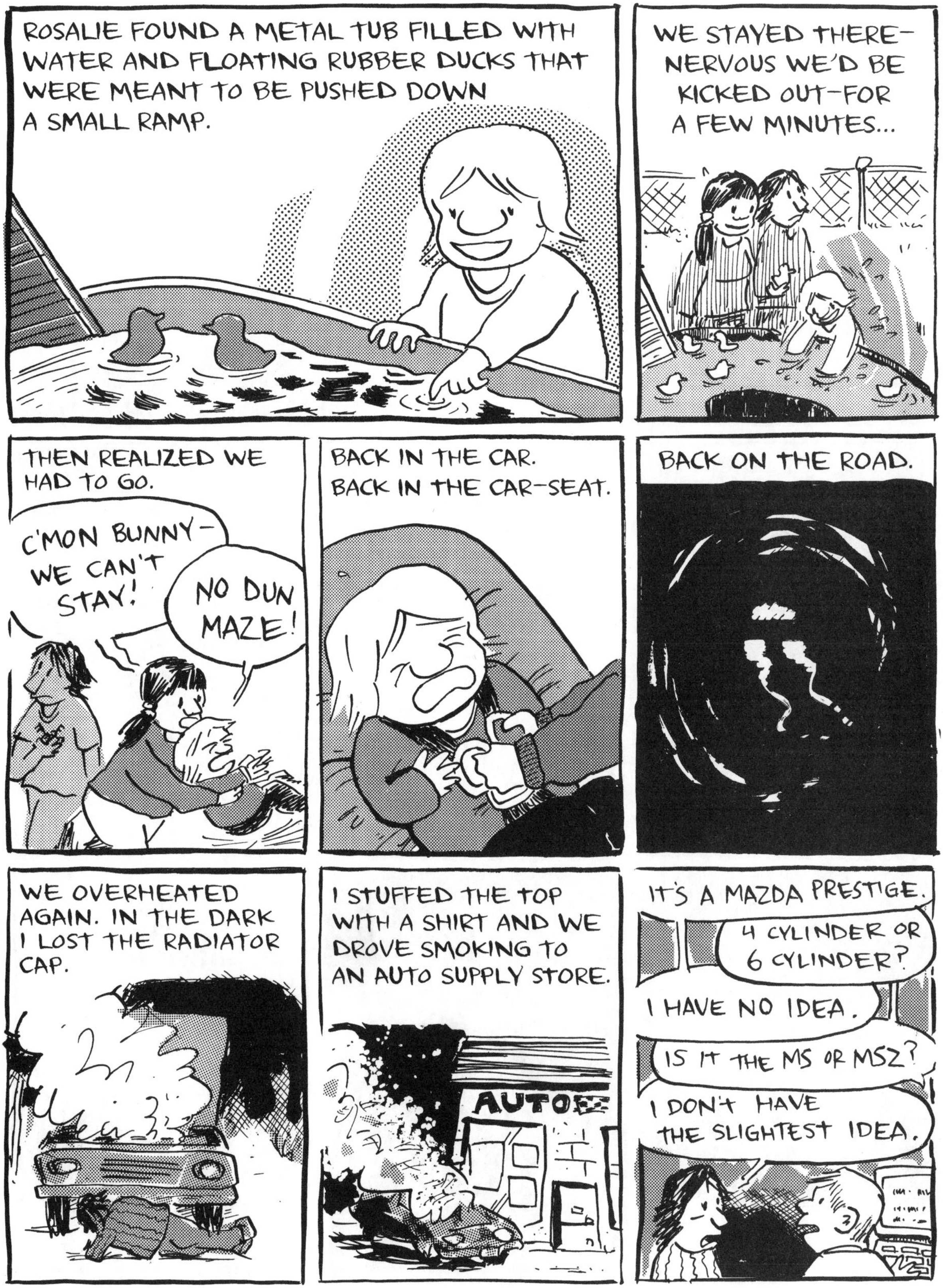
ROSALIE FOUND A METAL TUB FILLED WITH WATER AND FLOATING RUBBER DUCKS THAT WERE MEANT TO BE PUSHED DOWN A SMALL RAMP.
WE STAYED THERE— NERVOUS WE'D BE KICKED OUT—FOR A FEW MINUTES...
THEN REALIZED WE HAD TO GO.
C'MON BUNNY— WE CAN'T STAY!
NO DUN MAZE!
BACK IN THE CAR. BACK IN THE CAR-SEAT.
BACK ON THE ROAD.
WE OVERHEATED AGAIN. IN THE DARK I LOST THE RADIATOR CAP.
I STUFFED THE TOP WITH A SHIRT AND WE DROVE SMOKING TO AN AUTO SUPPLY STORE.
AUTO
IT'S A MAZDA PRESTIGE.
4 CYLINDER OR 6 CYLINDER?
I HAVE NO IDEA.
IS IT THE MS OR MS2?
I DON'T HAVE THE SLIGHTEST IDEA.

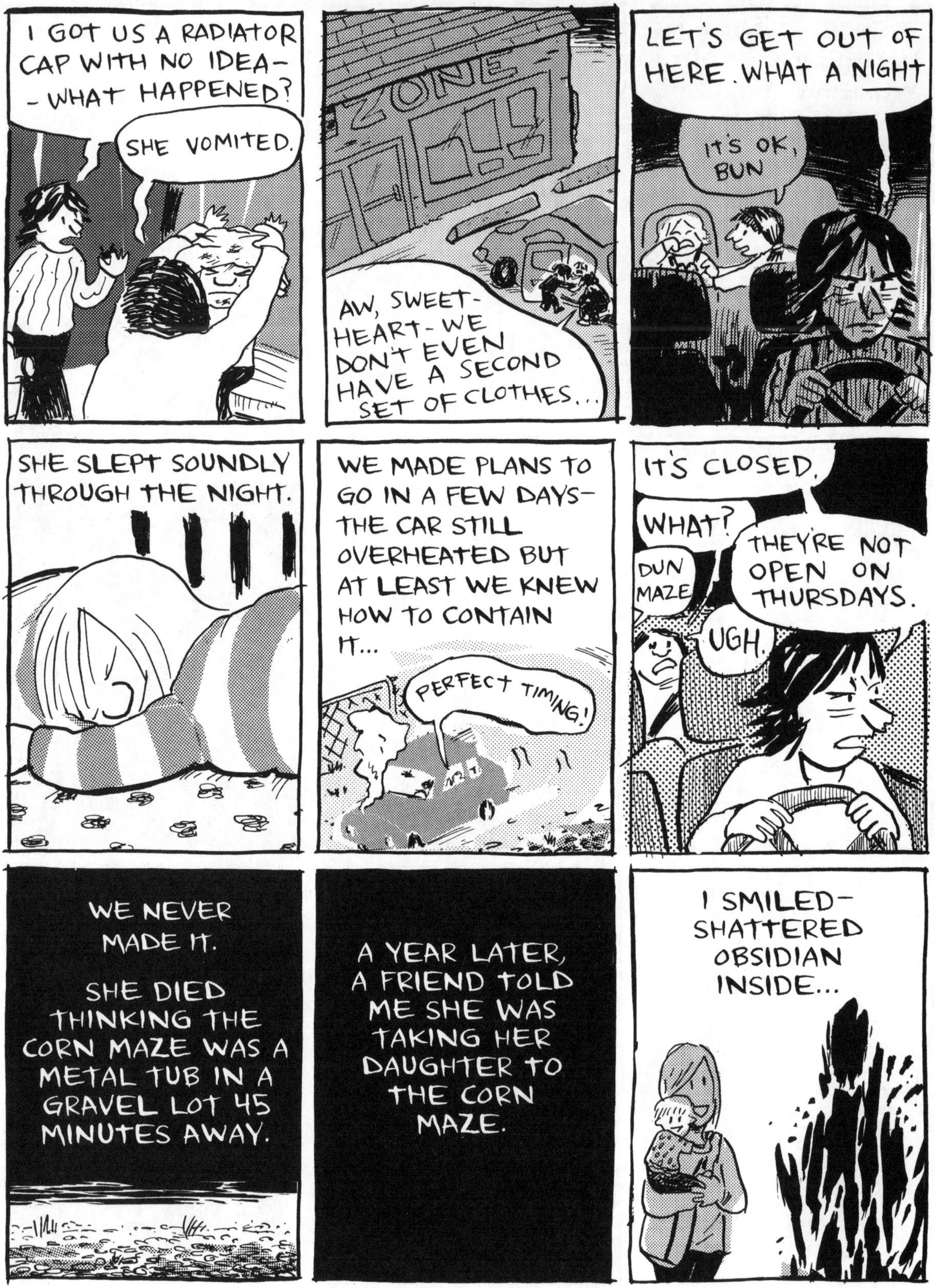
I GOT US A RADIATOR CAP WITH NO IDEA- -WHAT HAPPENED?
SHE VOMITED.
ZONE
AW, SWEET-HEART- WE DON'T EVEN HAVE A SECOND SET OF CLOTHES...
LET'S GET OUT OF HERE. WHAT A NIGHT
IT'S OK, BUN
SHE SLEPT SOUNDLY THROUGH THE NIGHT.
WE MADE PLANS TO GO IN A FEW DAYS- THE CAR STILL OVERHEATED BUT AT LEAST WE KNEW HOW TO CONTAIN IT...
PERFECT TIMING!
IT'S CLOSED.
WHAT?
DUN MAZE
THEY'RE NOT OPEN ON THURSDAYS.
UGH.
WE NEVER MADE IT.
SHE DIED THINKING THE CORN MAZE WAS A METAL TUB IN A GRAVEL LOT 45 MINUTES AWAY.
A YEAR LATER, A FRIEND TOLD ME SHE WAS TAKING HER DAUGHTER TO THE CORN MAZE.
I SMILED- SHATTERED OBSIDIAN INSIDE...

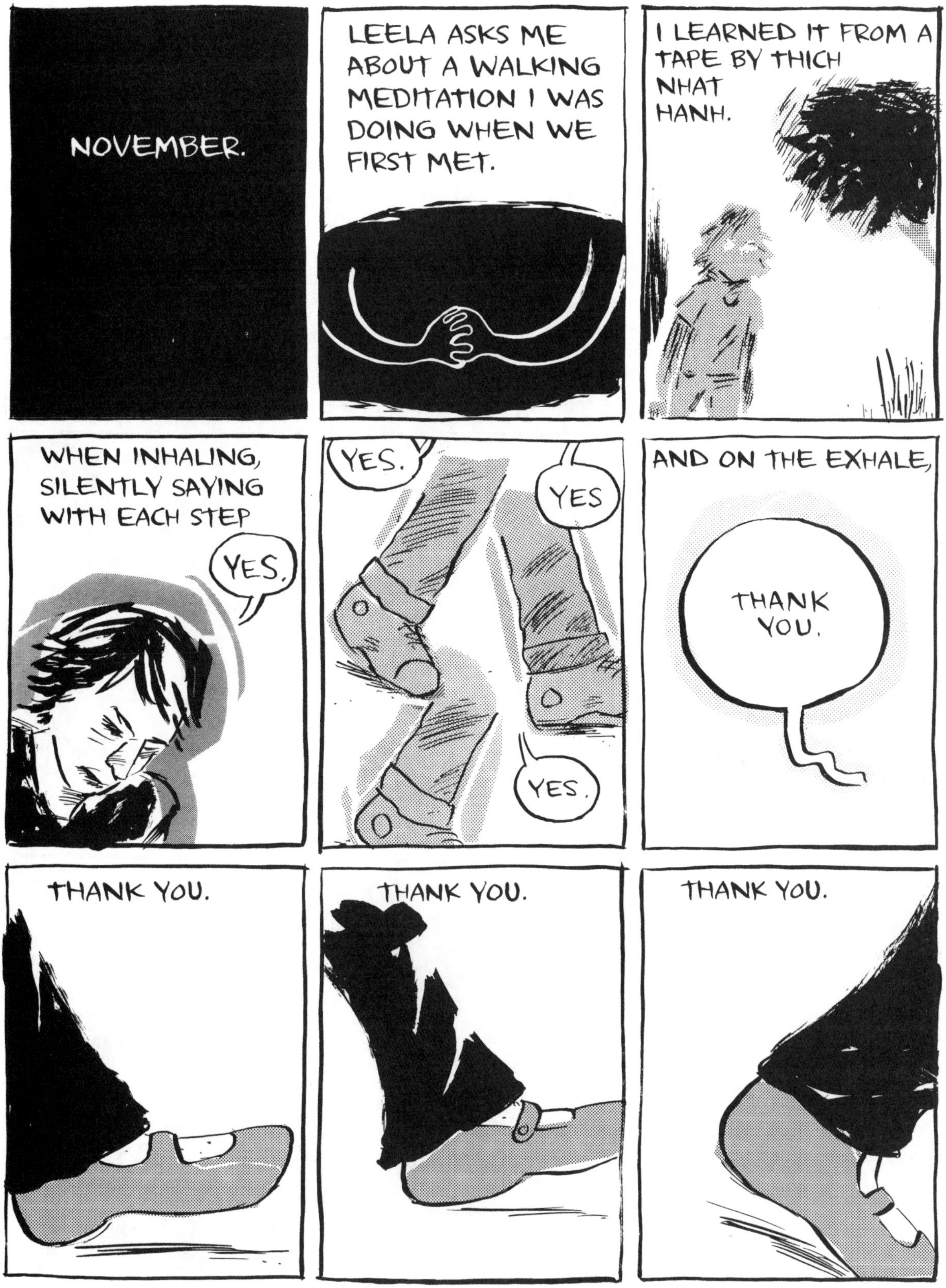
NOVEMBER.
LEELA ASKS ME ABOUT A WALKING MEDITATION I WAS DOING WHEN WE FIRST MET.
I LEARNED IT FROM A TAPE BY THICH NHAT HANH.
WHEN INHALING, SILENTLY SAYING WITH EACH STEP
YES.
YES.
YES
YES.
AND ON THE EXHALE,
THANK YOU.
THANK YOU.
THANK YOU.
THANK YOU.

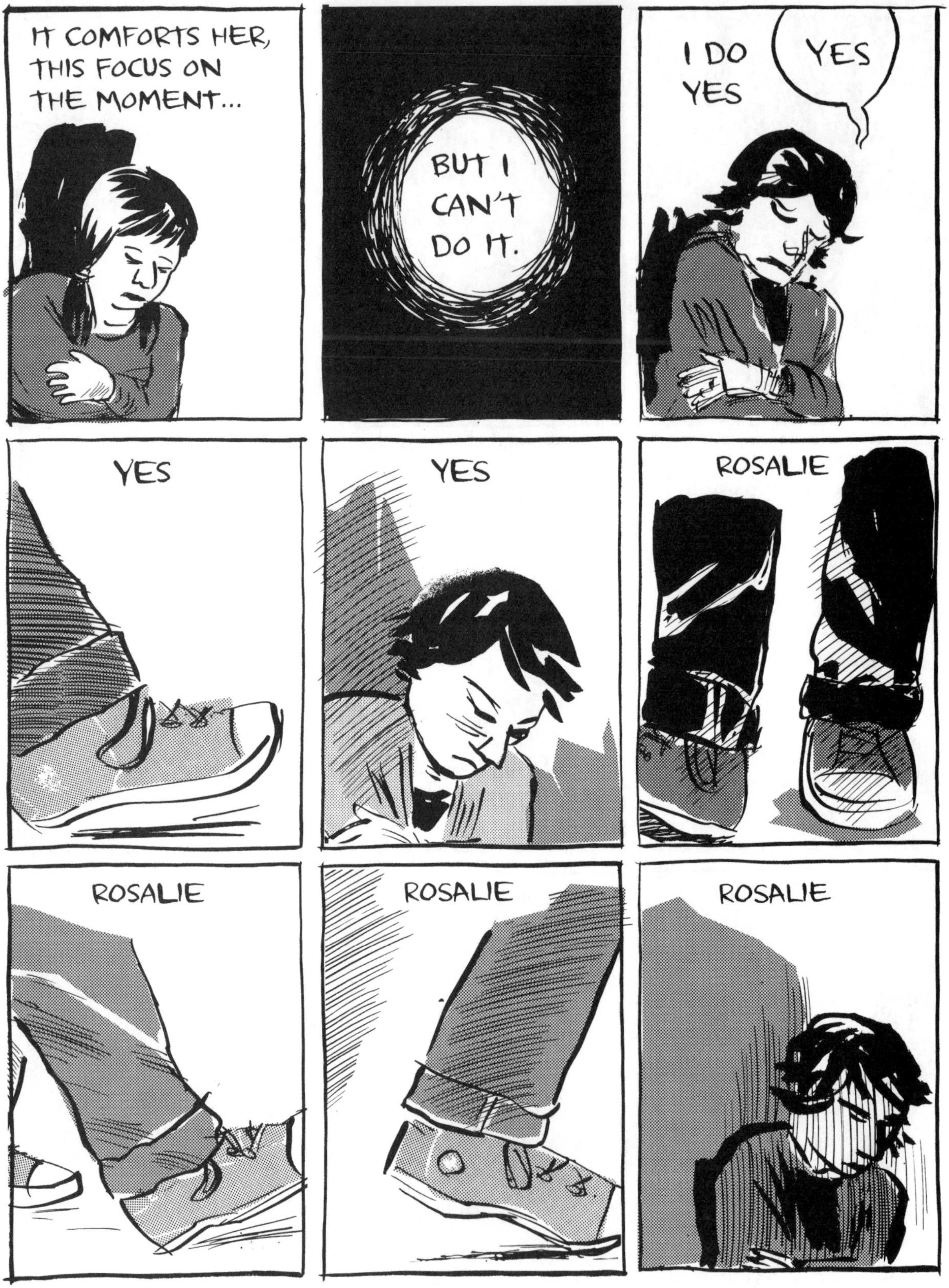
IT COMFORTS HER, THIS FOCUS ON THE MOMENT...
BUT I CAN'T DO IT.
I DO YES
YES
YES
YES
ROSALIE
ROSALIE
ROSALIE
ROSALIE

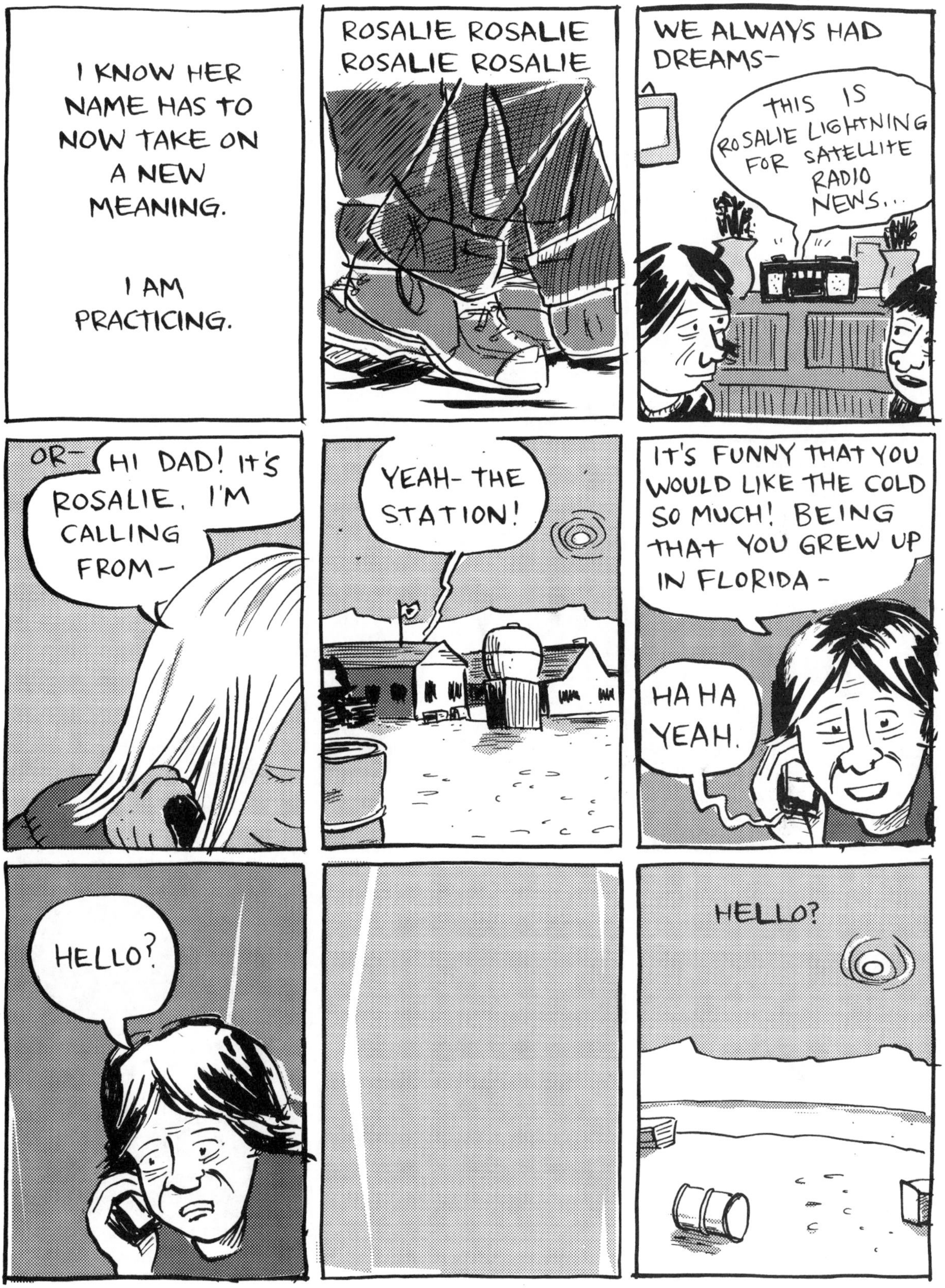
I KNOW HER NAME HAS TO NOW TAKE ON A NEW MEANING.
I AM PRACTICING.
ROSALIE ROSALIE ROSALIE ROSALIE
WE ALWAYS HAD DREAMS-
THIS IS ROSALIE LIGHTNING FOR SATELLITE RADIO NEWS...
OR-
HI DAD! IT'S ROSALIE. I'M CALLING FROM-
YEAH- THE STATION!
IT'S FUNNY THAT YOU WOULD LIKE THE COLD SO MUCH! BEING THAT YOU GREW UP IN FLORIDA-
HA HA YEAH.
HELLO?
HELLO?

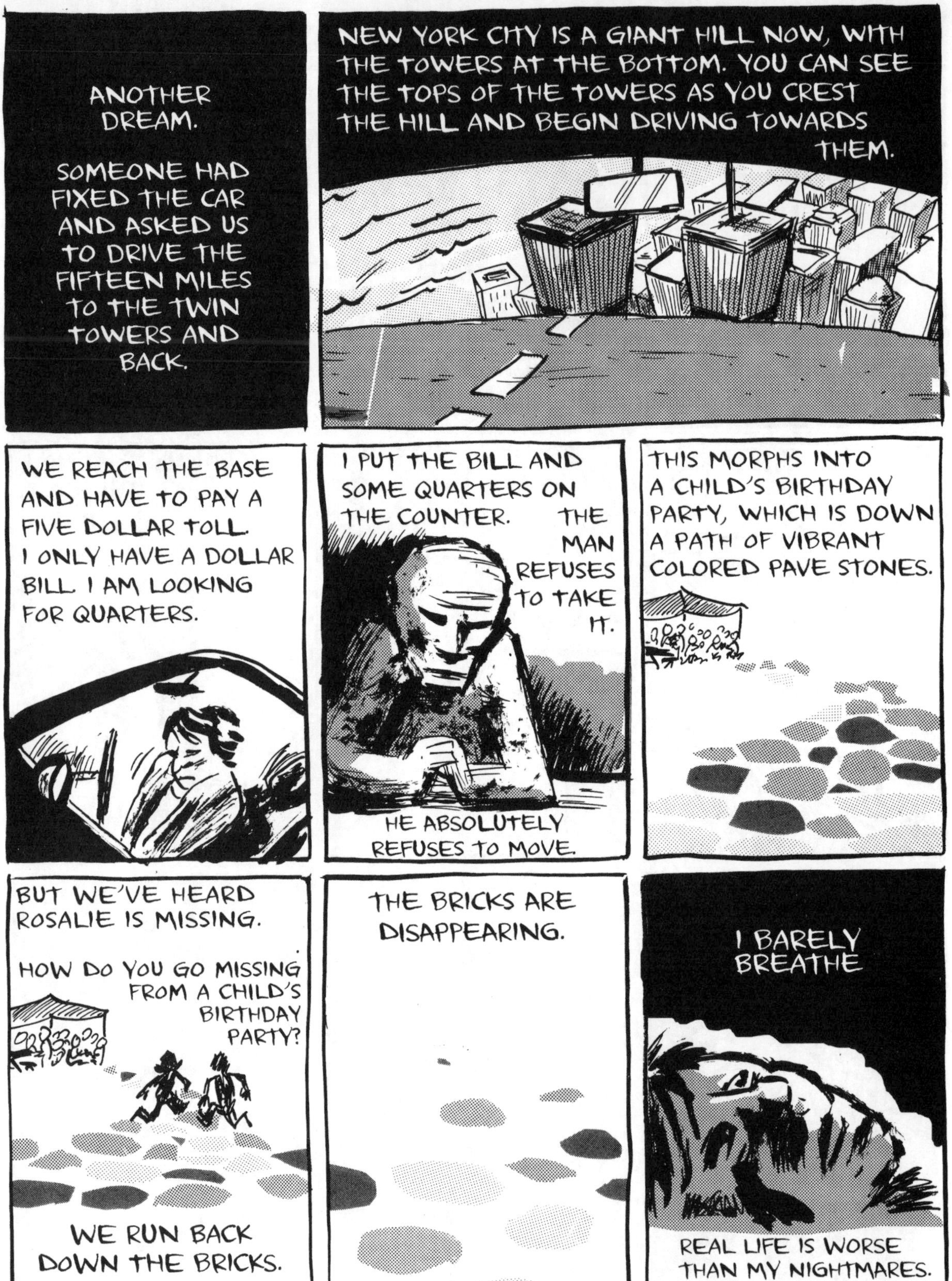
ANOTHER DREAM.
SOMEONE HAD FIXED THE CAR AND ASKED US TO DRIVE THE FIFTEEN MILES TO THE TWIN TOWERS AND BACK.
NEW YORK CITY IS A GIANT HILL NOW, WITH THE TOWERS AT THE BOTTOM. YOU CAN SEE THE TOPS OF THE TOWERS AS YOU CREST THE HILL AND BEGIN DRIVING TOWARDS THEM.
WE REACH THE BASE AND HAVE TO PAY A FIVE DOLLAR TOLL. I ONLY HAVE A DOLLAR BILL. I AM LOOKING FOR QUARTERS.
I PUT THE BILL AND SOME QUARTERS ON THE COUNTER.
THE MAN REFUSES TO TAKE IT.
HE ABSOLUTELY REFUSES TO MOVE.
THIS MORPHS INTO A CHILD'S BIRTHDAY PARTY, WHICH IS DOWN A PATH OF VIBRANT COLORED PAVE STONES.
BUT WE'VE HEARD ROSALIE IS MISSING.
HOW DO YOU GO MISSING FROM A CHILD'S BIRTHDAY PARTY?
WE RUN BACK DOWN THE BRICKS.
THE BRICKS ARE DISAPPEARING.
I BARELY BREATHE
REAL LIFE IS WORSE THAN MY NIGHTMARES.

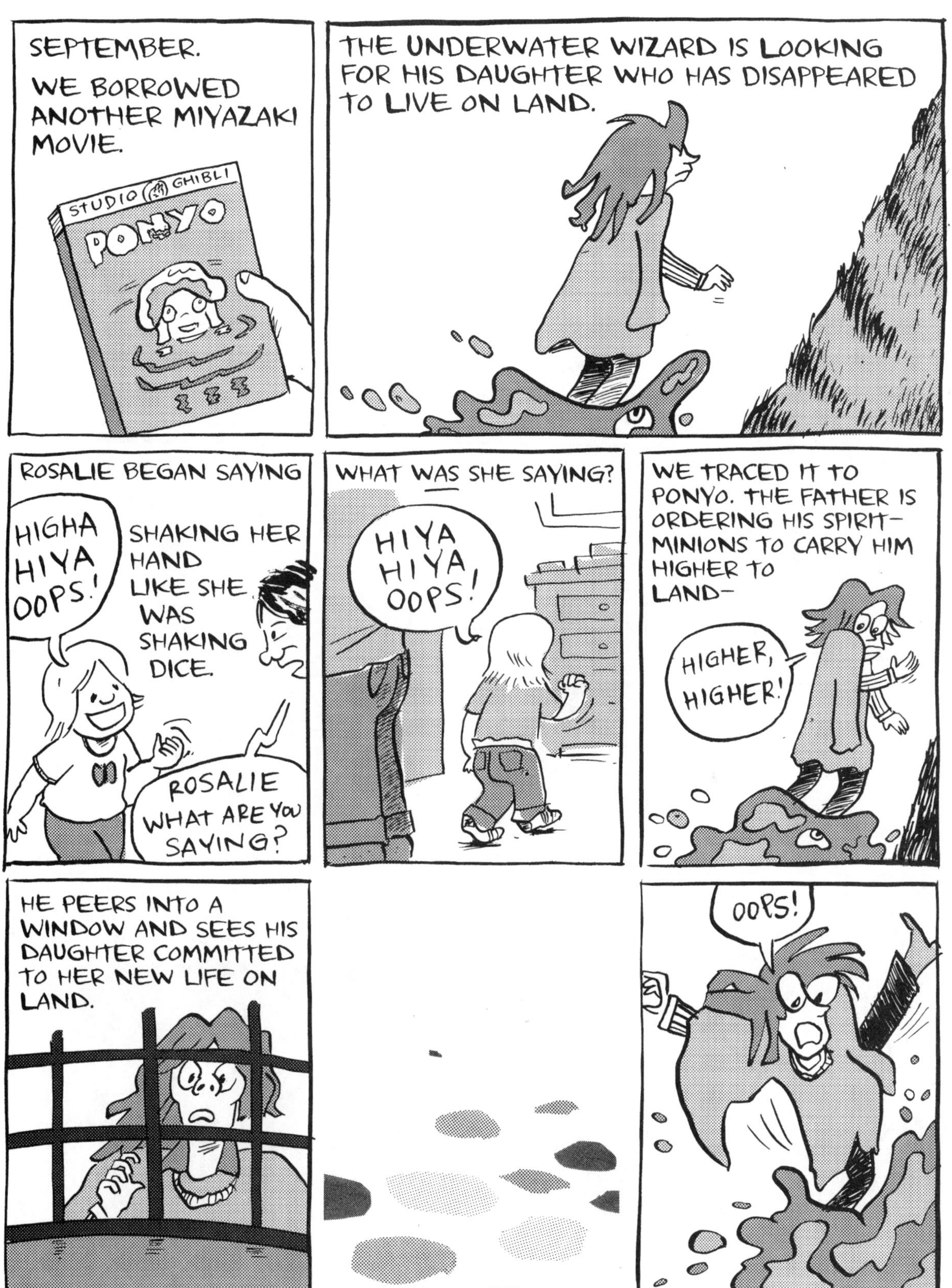
SEPTEMBER.
WE BORROWED ANOTHER MIYAZAKI MOVIE.
STUDIO GHIBLI
PONYO
THE UNDERWATER WIZARD IS LOOKING FOR HIS DAUGHTER WHO HAS DISAPPEARED TO LIVE ON LAND.
ROSALIE BEGAN SAYING
HIGHA HIYA OOPS!
SHAKING HER HAND LIKE SHE WAS SHAKING DICE.
ROSALIE WHAT ARE YOU SAYING?
WHAT WAS SHE SAYING?
HIYA HIYA, OOPS!
WE TRACED IT TO PONYO. THE FATHER IS ORDERING HIS SPIRIT-MINIONS TO CARRY HIM HIGHER TO LAND-
HIGHER, HIGHER!
HE PEERS INTO A WINDOW AND SEES HIS DAUGHTER COMMITTED TO HER NEW LIFE ON LAND.
OOPS!

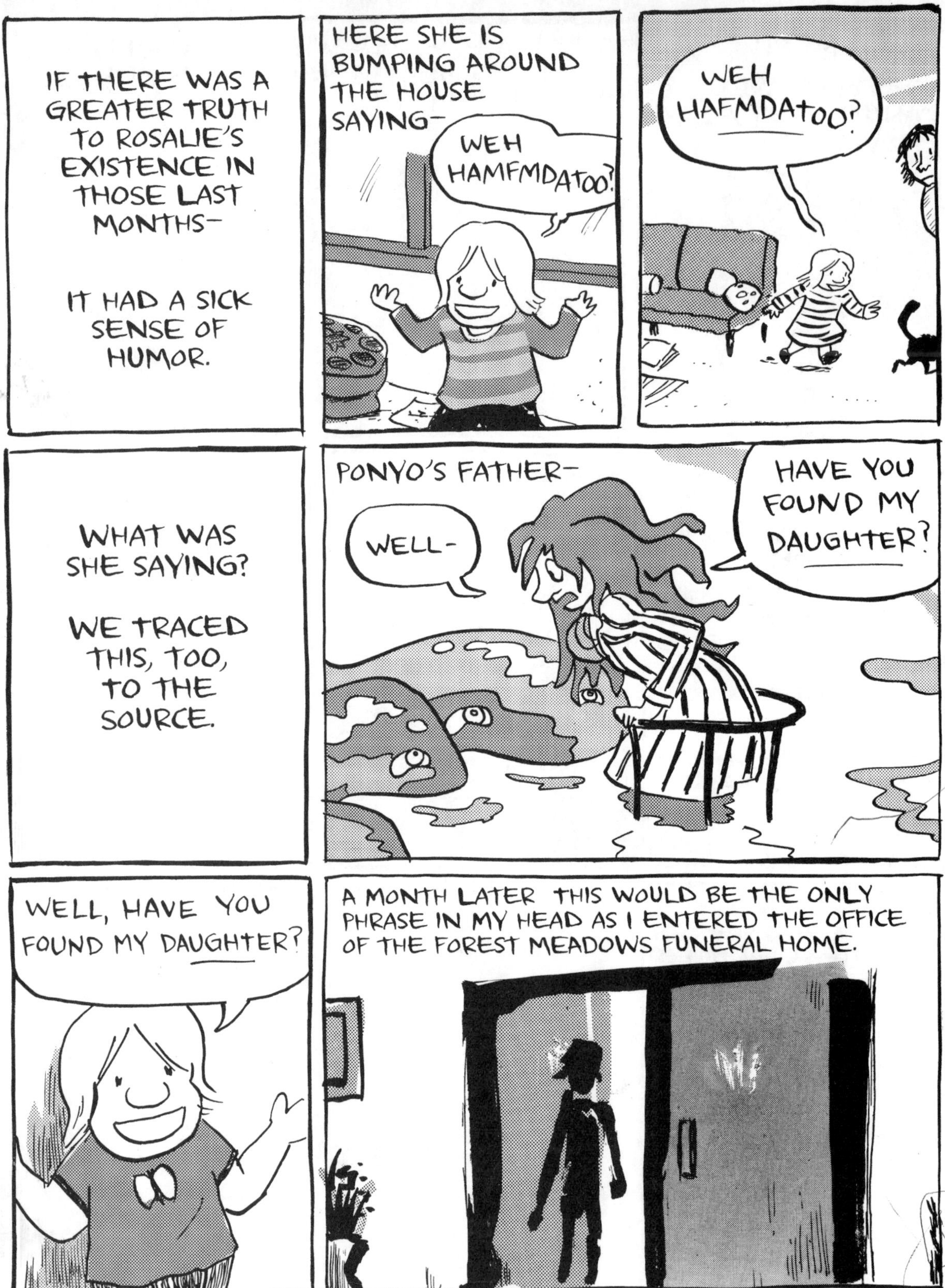
IF THERE WAS A GREATER TRUTH TO ROSALIE'S EXISTENCE IN THOSE LAST MONTHS—
IT HAD A SICK SENSE OF HUMOR.
HERE SHE IS BUMPING AROUND THE HOUSE SAYING—
WEH HAMFMDATOO?
WEH HAFMDATOO?
WHAT WAS SHE SAYING?
WE TRACED THIS, TOO, TO THE SOURCE.
PONYO'S FATHER—
WELL-
HAVE YOU FOUND MY DAUGHTER?
WELL, HAVE YOU FOUND MY DAUGHTER?
A MONTH LATER THIS WOULD BE THE ONLY PHRASE IN MY HEAD AS I ENTERED THE OFFICE OF THE FOREST MEADOWS FUNERAL HOME.

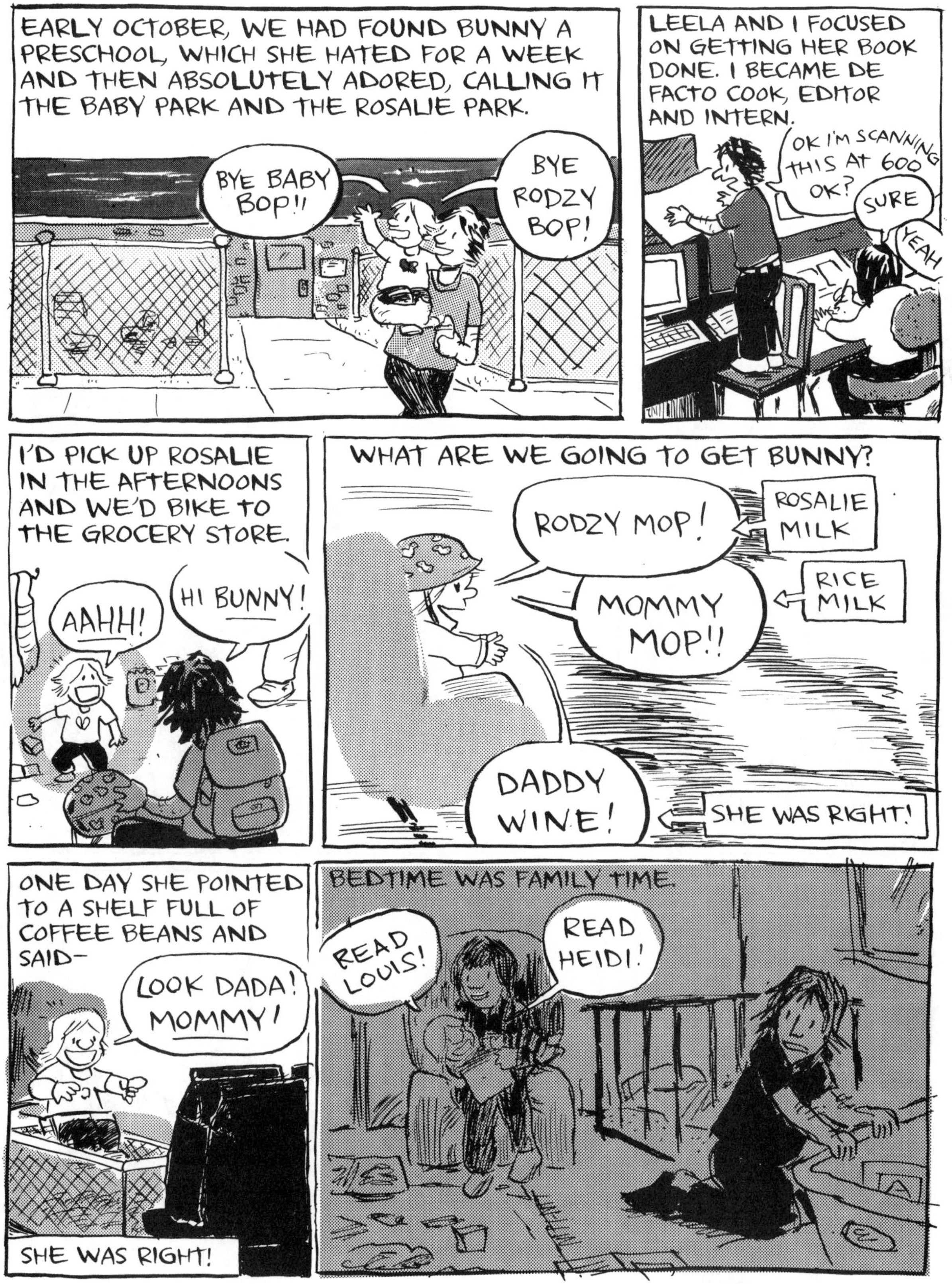

EARLY OCTOBER, WE HAD FOUND BUNNY A PRESCHOOL, WHICH SHE HATED FOR A WEEK AND THEN ABSOLUTELY ADORED, CALLING IT THE BABY PARK AND THE ROSALIE PARK.
BYE BABY BOP!!
BYE RODZY BOP!
LEELA AND I FOCUSED ON GETTING HER BOOK DONE. I BECAME DE FACTO COOK, EDITOR AND INTERN.
OK I'M SCANNING THIS AT 600 OK?
SURE
YEAH
I'D PICK UP ROSALIE IN THE AFTERNOONS AND WE'D BIKE TO THE GROCERY STORE.
AAHH!
HI BUNNY!
WHAT ARE WE GOING TO GET BUNNY?
RODZY MOP!
ROSALIE MILK
MOMMY MOP!!
RICE MILK
DADDY WINE!
SHE WAS RIGHT!
ONE DAY SHE POINTED TO A SHELF FULL OF COFFEE BEANS AND SAID–
LOOK DADA! MOMMY!
SHE WAS RIGHT!
BEDTIME WAS FAMILY TIME.
READ LOUIS!
READ HEIDI!

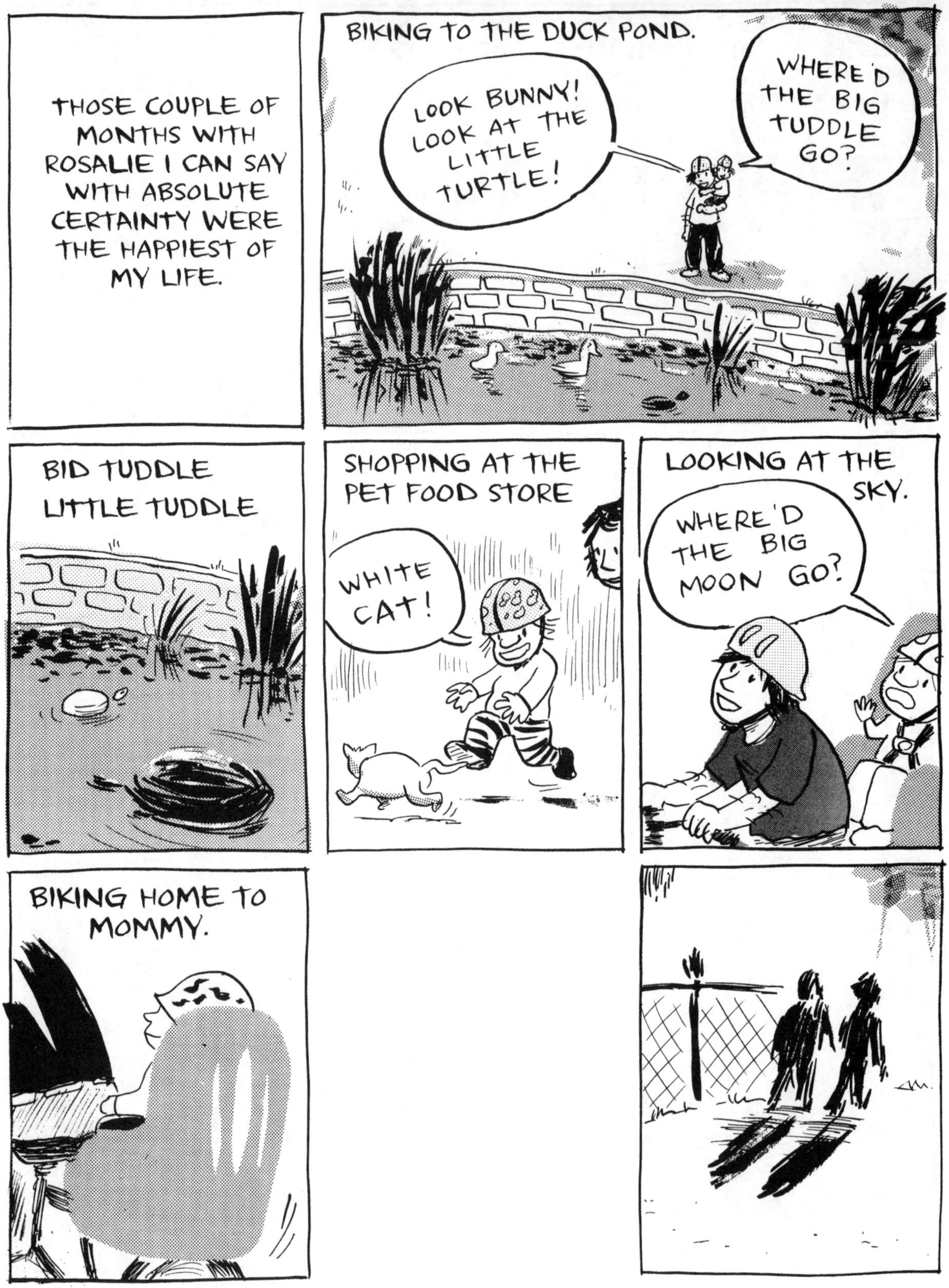
THOSE COUPLE OF MONTHS WITH ROSALIE I CAN SAY WITH ABSOLUTE CERTAINTY WERE THE HAPPIEST OF MY LIFE.
BIKING TO THE DUCK POND.
LOOK BUNNY! LOOK AT THE LITTLE TURTLE!
WHERE'D THE BIG TUDDLE GO?
BID TUDDLE
LITTLE TUDDLE
SHOPPING AT THE PET FOOD STORE
WHITE CAT!
LOOKING AT THE SKY.
WHERE'D THE BIG MOON GO?
BIKING HOME TO MOMMY.

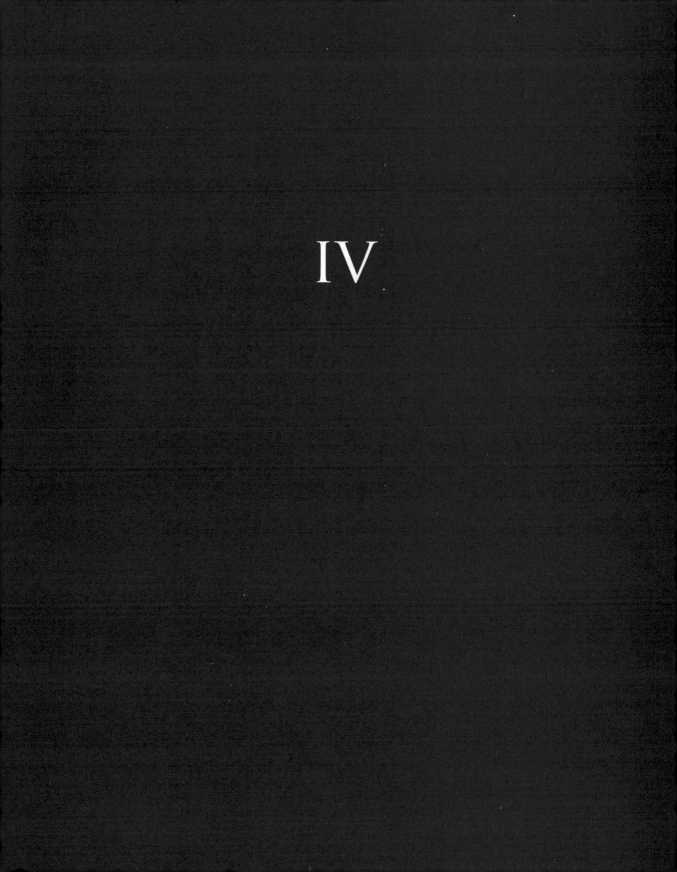

IV

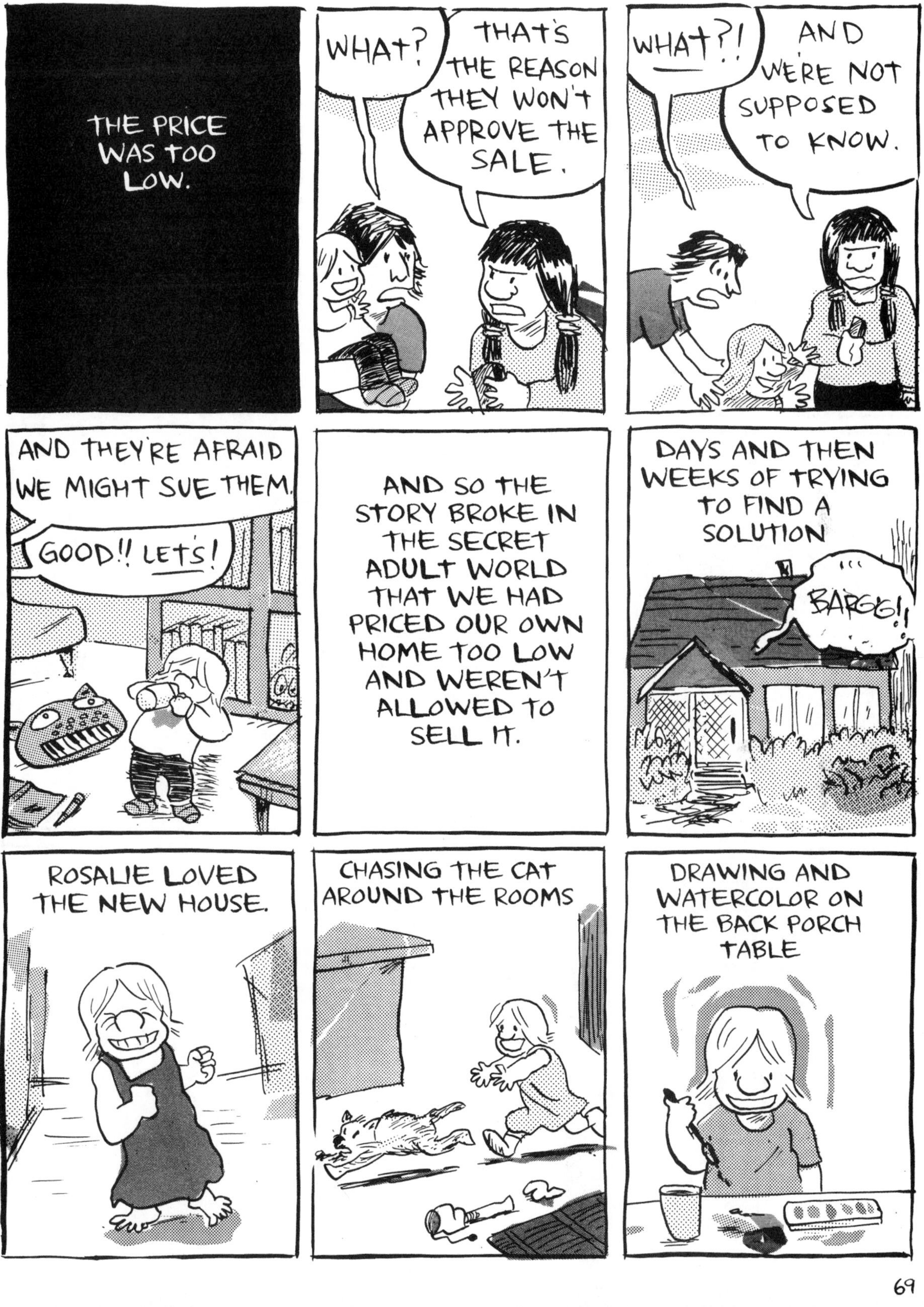
THE PRICE WAS TOO LOW.
WHAT?
THAT'S THE REASON THEY WON'T APPROVE THE SALE.
WHAT?!
AND WE'RE NOT SUPPOSED TO KNOW.
AND THEY'RE AFRAID WE MIGHT SUE THEM.
GOOD!! LET'S!
AND SO THE STORY BROKE IN THE SECRET ADULT WORLD THAT WE HAD PRICED OUR OWN HOME TOO LOW AND WEREN'T ALLOWED TO SELL IT.
DAYS AND THEN WEEKS OF TRYING TO FIND A SOLUTION
BARGG!!
ROSALIE LOVED THE NEW HOUSE.
CHASING THE CAT AROUND THE ROOMS
DRAWING AND WATERCOLOR ON THE BACK PORCH TABLE

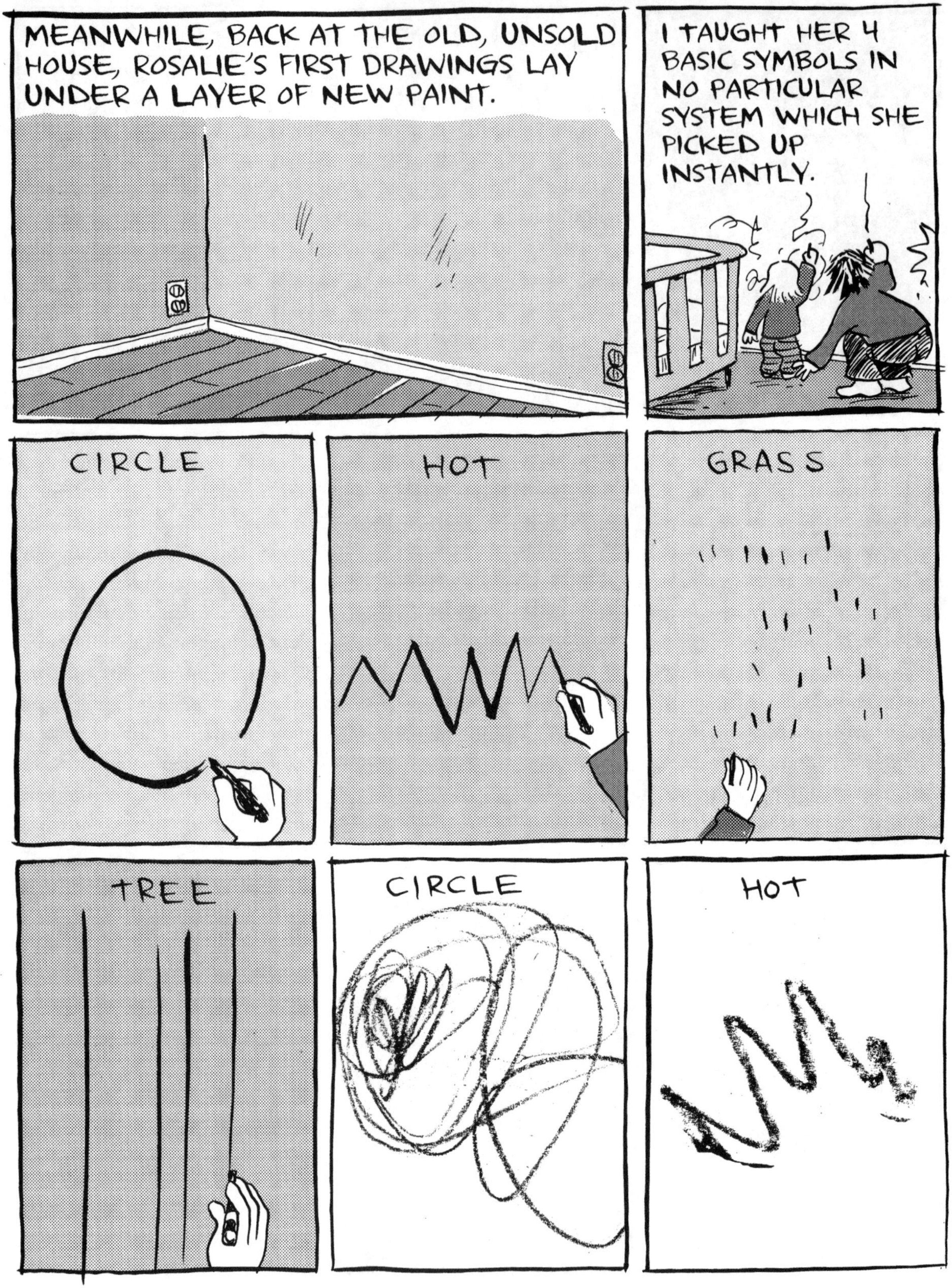
MEANWHILE, BACK AT THE OLD, UNSOLD HOUSE, ROSALIE'S FIRST DRAWINGS LAY UNDER A LAYER OF NEW PAINT.
I TAUGHT HER 4 BASIC SYMBOLS IN NO PARTICULAR SYSTEM WHICH SHE PICKED UP INSTANTLY.
CIRCLE
HOT
GRASS
TREE
CIRCLE
HOT

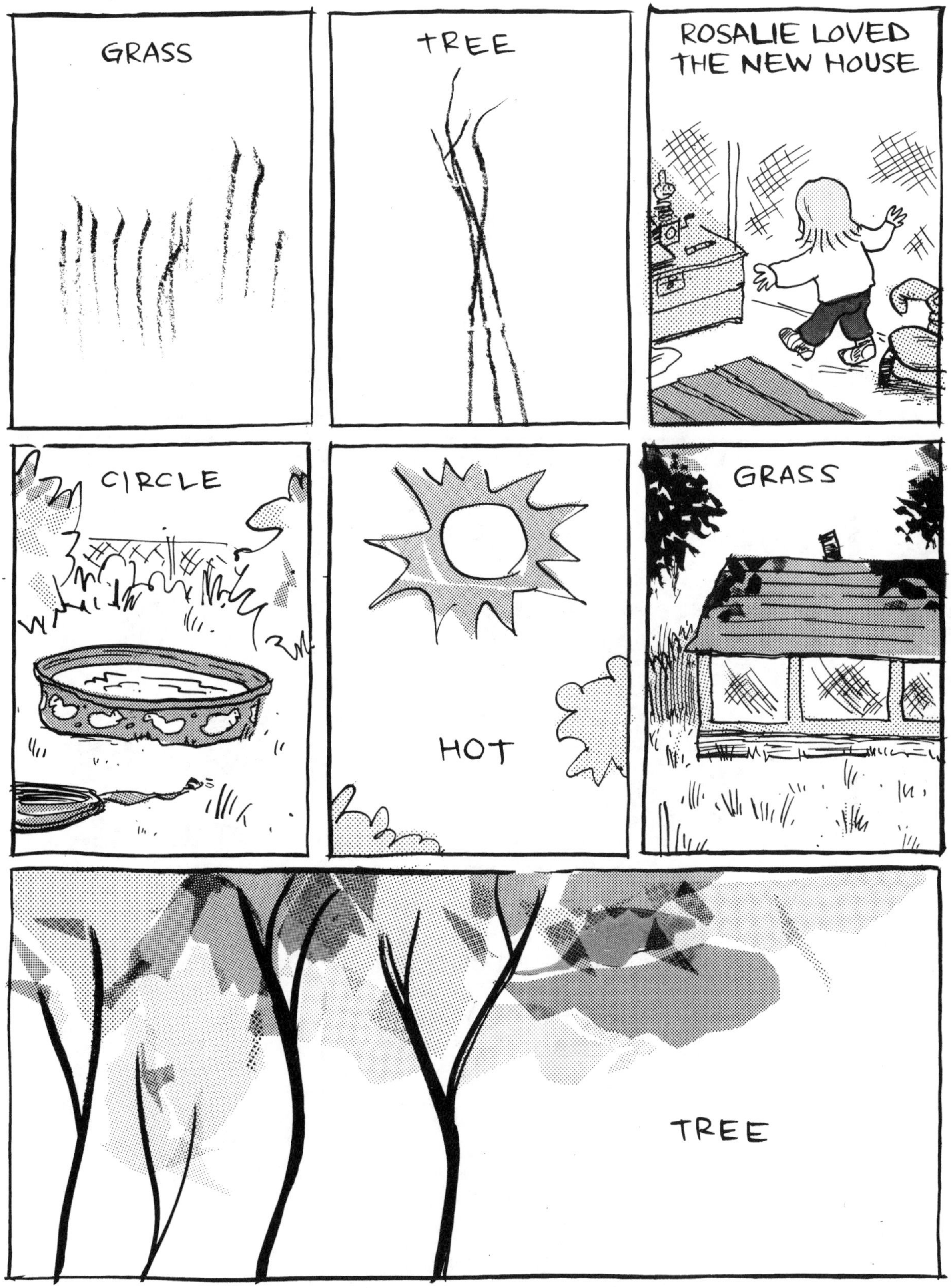
GRASS
TREE
ROSALIE LOVED THE NEW HOUSE
CIRCLE
HOT
GRASS
TREE

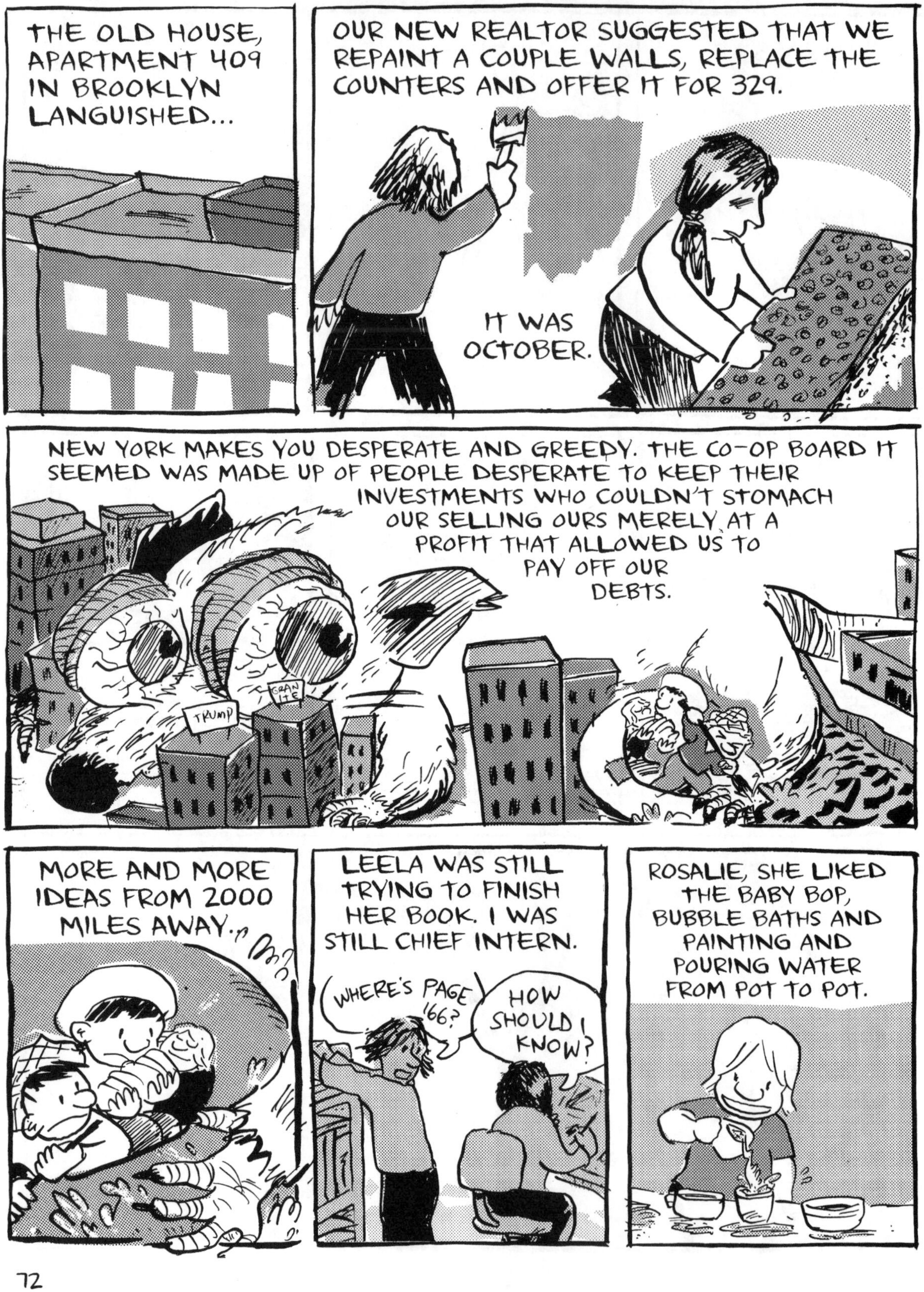
THE OLD HOUSE, APARTMENT 409 IN BROOKLYN LANGUISHED...
OUR NEW REALTOR SUGGESTED THAT WE REPAINT A COUPLE WALLS, REPLACE THE COUNTERS AND OFFER IT FOR 329.
IT WAS OCTOBER.
NEW YORK MAKES YOU DESPERATE AND GREEDY. THE CO-OP BOARD IT SEEMED WAS MADE UP OF PEOPLE DESPERATE TO KEEP THEIR INVESTMENTS WHO COULDN'T STOMACH OUR SELLING OURS MERELY AT A PROFIT THAT ALLOWED US TO PAY OFF OUR DEBTS.
TRUMP
GRANITE
MORE AND MORE IDEAS FROM 2000 MILES AWAY...
LEELA WAS STILL TRYING TO FINISH HER BOOK. I WAS STILL CHIEF INTERN.
WHERE'S PAGE 166?
HOW SHOULD I KNOW?
ROSALIE, SHE LIKED THE BABY BOP, BUBBLE BATHS AND PAINTING AND POURING WATER FROM POT TO POT.

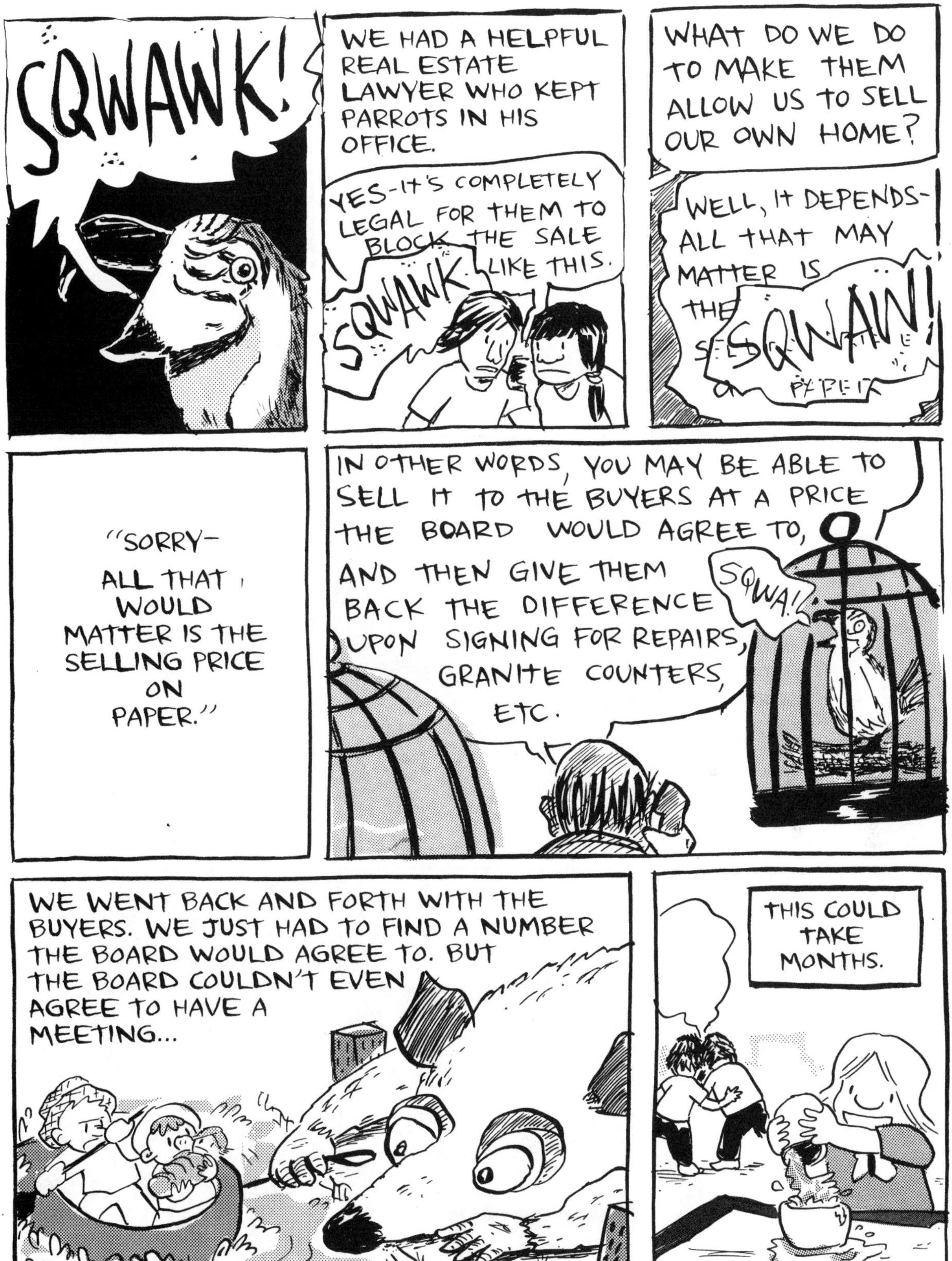
SQWAWK!
WE HAD A HELPFUL REAL ESTATE LAWYER WHO KEPT PARROTS IN HIS OFFICE.
YES-IT'S COMPLETELY LEGAL FOR THEM TO BLOCK THE SALE LIKE THIS.
SQWAWK
WHAT DO WE DO TO MAKE THEM ALLOW US TO SELL OUR OWN HOME?
WELL, IT DEPENDS- ALL THAT MAY MATTER IS THE
SQWAW!
"SORRY- ALL THAT WOULD MATTER IS THE SELLING PRICE ON PAPER."
IN OTHER WORDS, YOU MAY BE ABLE TO SELL IT TO THE BUYERS AT A PRICE THE BOARD WOULD AGREE TO, AND THEN GIVE THEM BACK THE DIFFERENCE UPON SIGNING FOR REPAIRS, GRANITE COUNTERS, ETC.
SQWA!
WE WENT BACK AND FORTH WITH THE BUYERS. WE JUST HAD TO FIND A NUMBER THE BOARD WOULD AGREE TO. BUT THE BOARD COULDN'T EVEN AGREE TO HAVE A MEETING...
THIS COULD TAKE MONTHS.

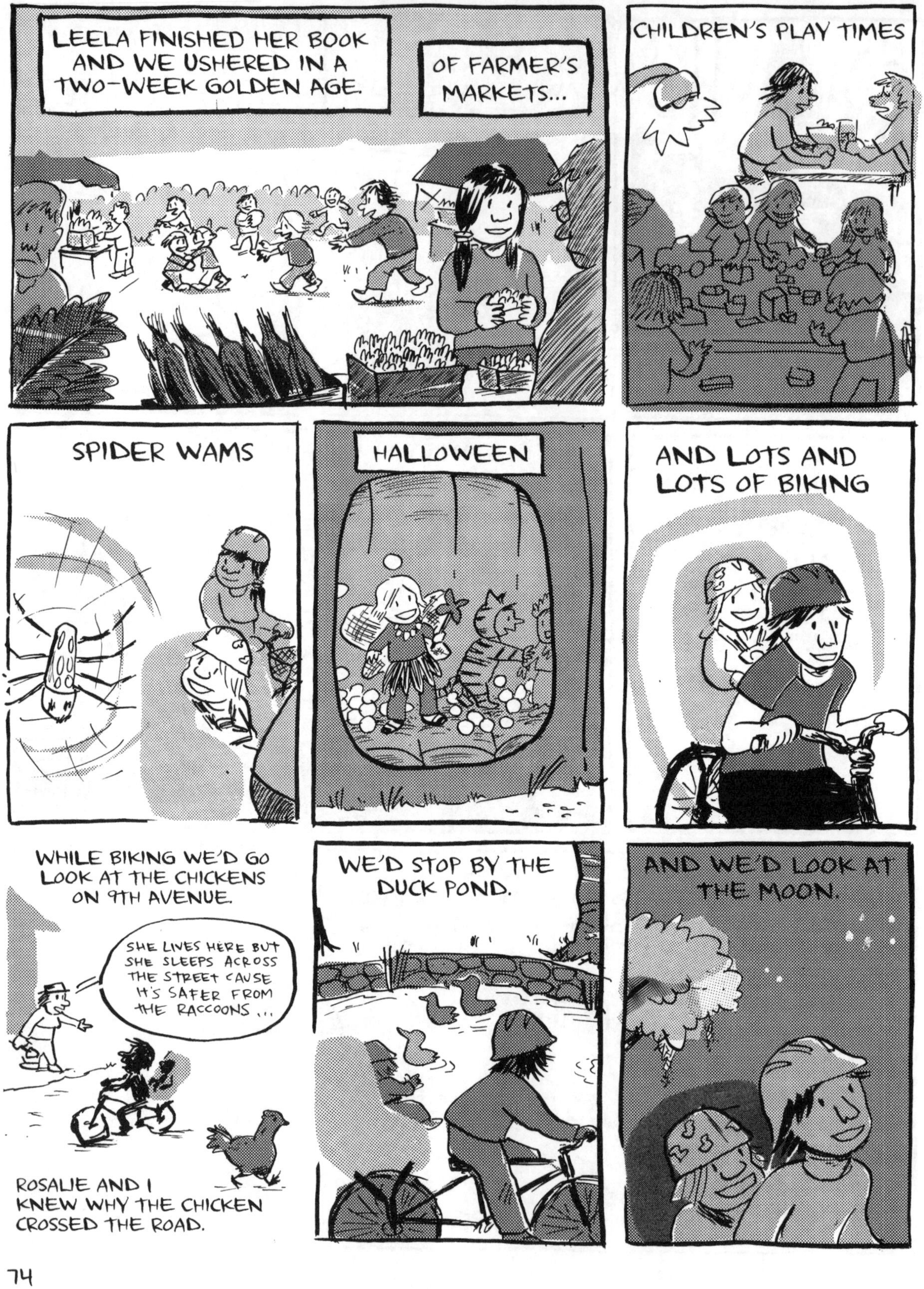
LEELA FINISHED HER BOOK AND WE USHERED IN A TWO-WEEK GOLDEN AGE.
OF FARMER'S MARKETS...
CHILDREN'S PLAY TIMES
SPIDER WAMS
HALLOWEEN
AND LOTS AND LOTS OF BIKING
WHILE BIKING WE'D GO LOOK AT THE CHICKENS ON 9TH AVENUE.
SHE LIVES HERE BUT SHE SLEEPS ACROSS THE STREET CAUSE IT'S SAFER FROM THE RACCOONS...
ROSALIE AND I KNEW WHY THE CHICKEN CROSSED THE ROAD.
WE'D STOP BY THE DUCK POND.
AND WE'D LOOK AT THE MOON.

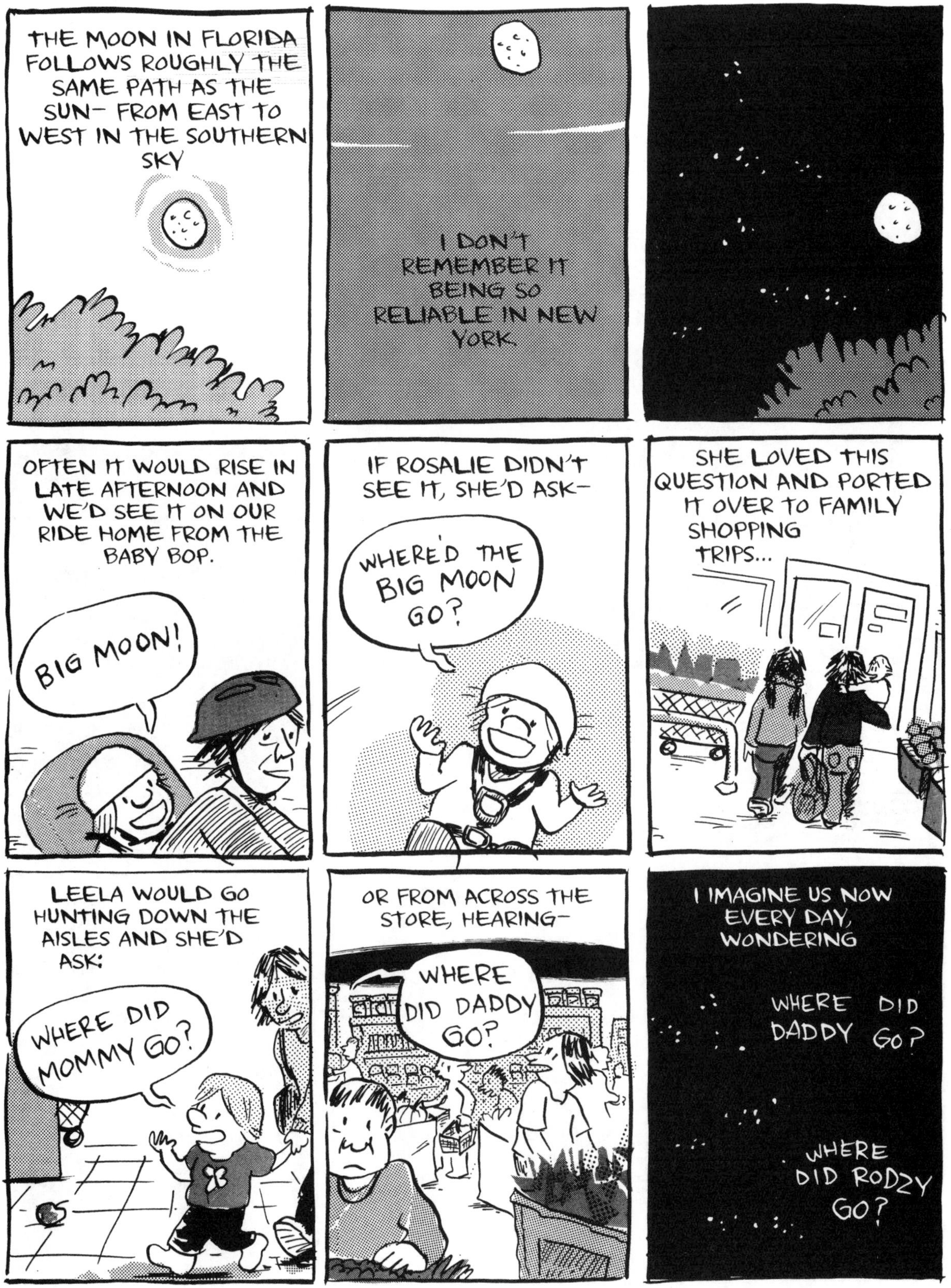
THE MOON IN FLORIDA FOLLOWS ROUGHLY THE SAME PATH AS THE SUN– FROM EAST TO WEST IN THE SOUTHERN SKY
I DON'T REMEMBER IT BEING SO RELIABLE IN NEW YORK.
OFTEN IT WOULD RISE IN LATE AFTERNOON AND WE'D SEE IT ON OUR RIDE HOME FROM THE BABY BOP.
BIG MOON!
IF ROSALIE DIDN'T SEE IT, SHE'D ASK–
WHERE'D THE BIG MOON GO?
SHE LOVED THIS QUESTION AND PORTED IT OVER TO FAMILY SHOPPING TRIPS...
LEELA WOULD GO HUNTING DOWN THE AISLES AND SHE'D ASK:
WHERE DID MOMMY GO?
OR FROM ACROSS THE STORE, HEARING–
WHERE DID DADDY GO?
I IMAGINE US NOW EVERY DAY, WONDERING
WHERE DID DADDY GO?
WHERE DID RODZY GO?

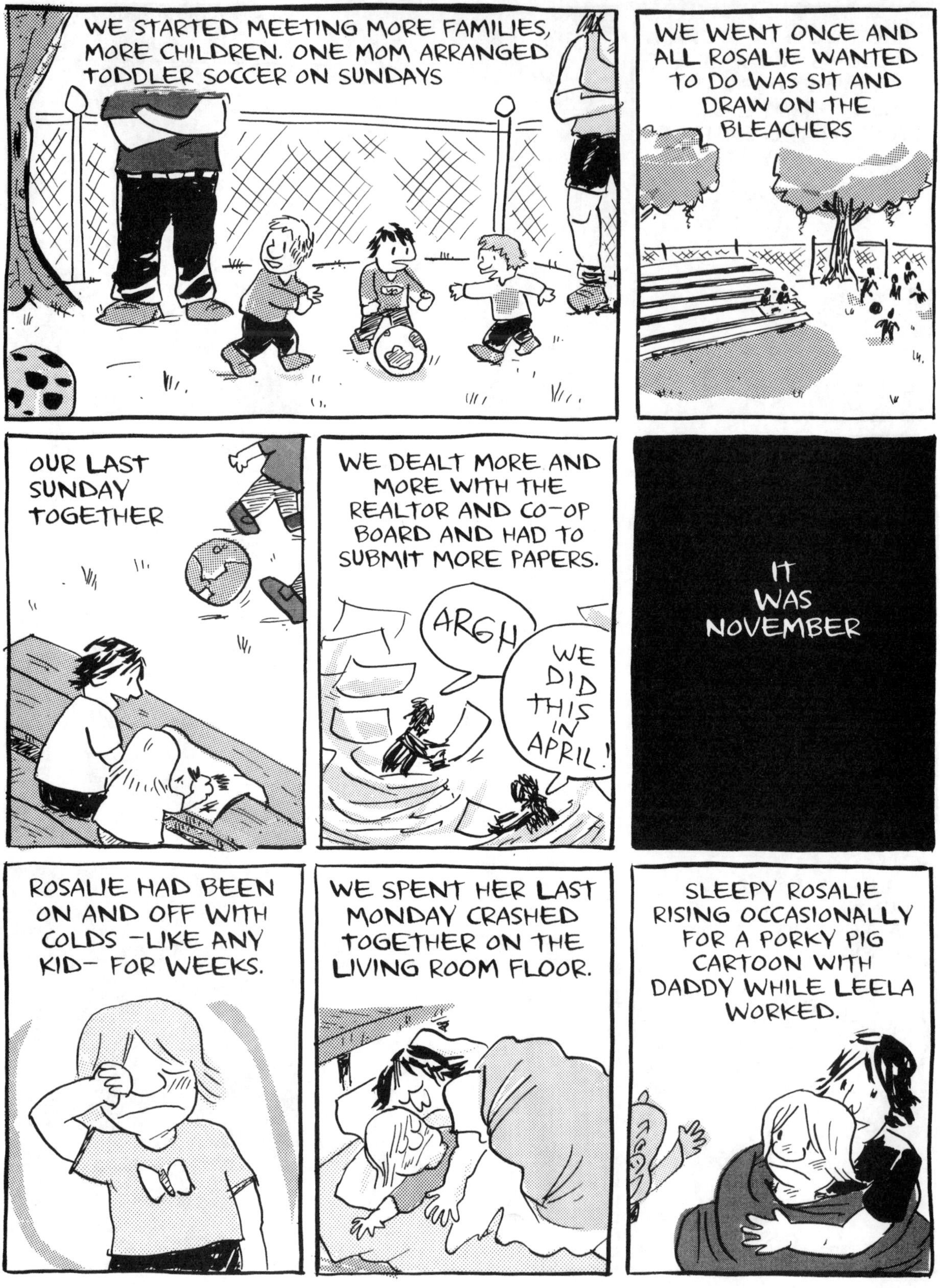
WE STARTED MEETING MORE FAMILIES, MORE CHILDREN. ONE MOM ARRANGED TODDLER SOCCER ON SUNDAYS
WE WENT ONCE AND ALL ROSALIE WANTED TO DO WAS SIT AND DRAW ON THE BLEACHERS
OUR LAST SUNDAY TOGETHER
WE DEALT MORE AND MORE WITH THE REALTOR AND CO-OP BOARD AND HAD TO SUBMIT MORE PAPERS.
ARGH
WE DID THIS IN APRIL!
IT WAS NOVEMBER
ROSALIE HAD BEEN ON AND OFF WITH COLDS -LIKE ANY KID- FOR WEEKS.
WE SPENT HER LAST MONDAY CRASHED TOGETHER ON THE LIVING ROOM FLOOR.
SLEEPY ROSALIE RISING OCCASIONALLY FOR A PORKY PIG CARTOON WITH DADDY WHILE LEELA WORKED.

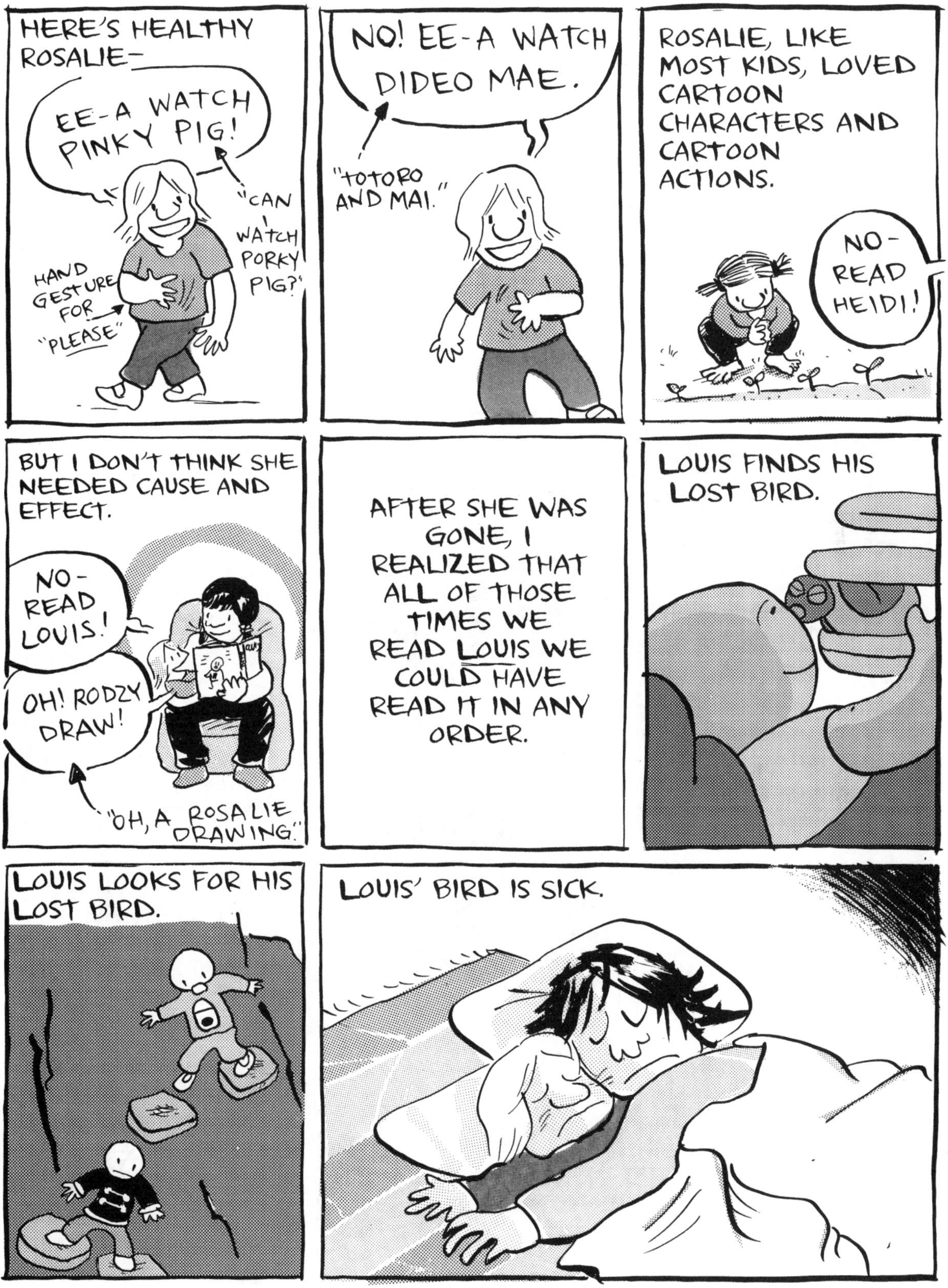
HERE'S HEALTHY ROSALIE–
EE-A WATCH PINKY PIG!
"CAN I WATCH PORKY PIG?"
HAND GESTURE FOR "PLEASE"
NO! EE-A WATCH DIDEO MAE.
"TOTORO AND MAI."
ROSALIE, LIKE MOST KIDS, LOVED CARTOON CHARACTERS AND CARTOON ACTIONS.
NO- READ HEIDI!
BUT I DON'T THINK SHE NEEDED CAUSE AND EFFECT.
NO- READ LOUIS!
OH! RODZY DRAW!
"OH, A ROSALIE DRAWING"
AFTER SHE WAS GONE, I REALIZED THAT ALL OF THOSE TIMES WE READ LOUIS WE COULD HAVE READ IT IN ANY ORDER.
LOUIS FINDS HIS LOST BIRD.
LOUIS LOOKS FOR HIS LOST BIRD.
LOUIS' BIRD IS SICK.

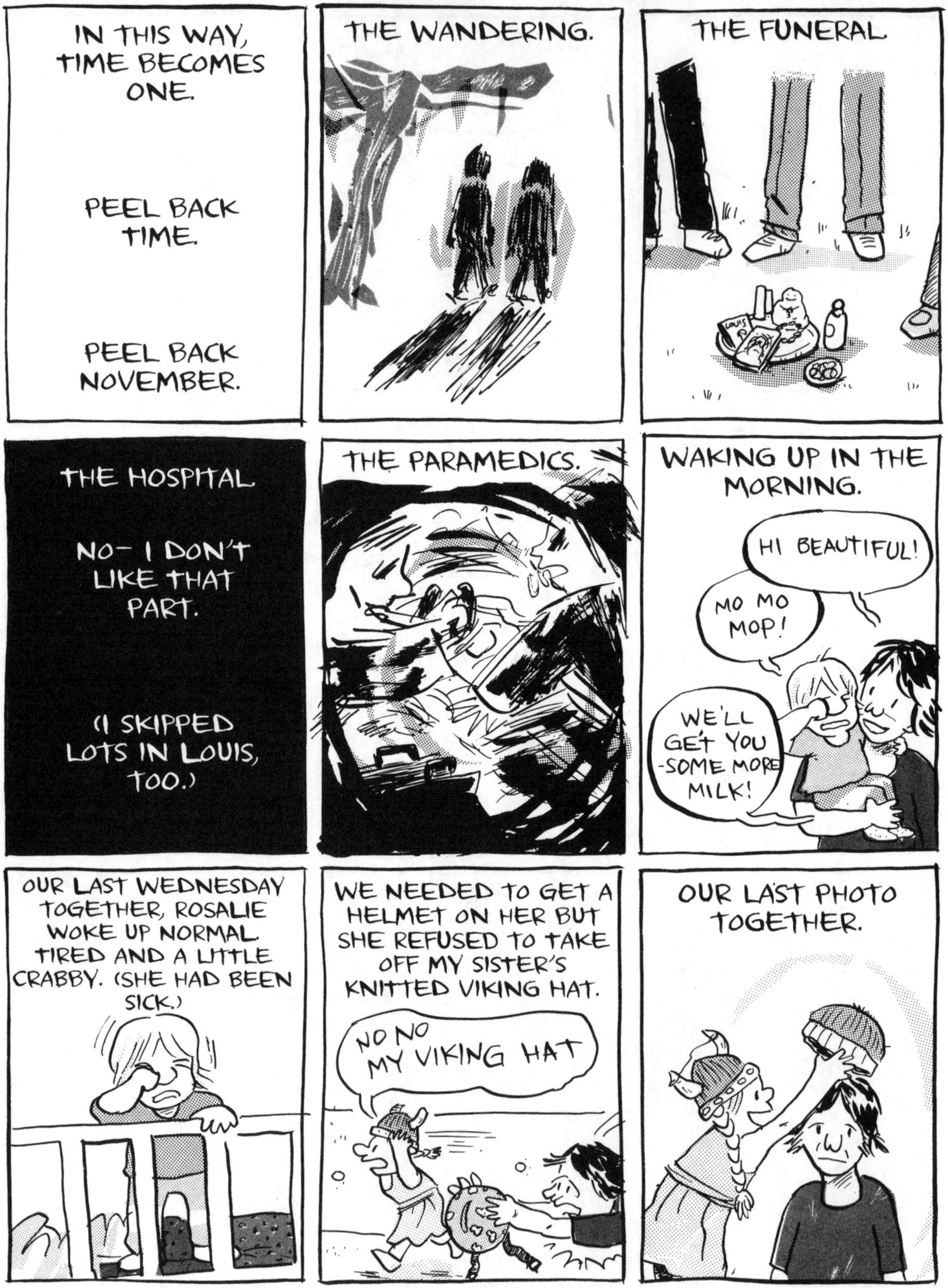
IN THIS WAY, TIME BECOMES ONE.
PEEL BACK TIME.
PEEL BACK NOVEMBER.
THE WANDERING.
THE FUNERAL.
LOUIS
THE HOSPITAL.
NO- I DON'T LIKE THAT PART.
(I SKIPPED LOTS IN LOUIS, TOO.)
THE PARAMEDICS.
WAKING UP IN THE MORNING.
HI BEAUTIFUL!
MO MO MOP!
WE'LL GET YOU -SOME MORE MILK!
OUR LAST WEDNESDAY TOGETHER, ROSALIE WOKE UP NORMAL. TIRED AND A LITTLE CRABBY. (SHE HAD BEEN SICK.)
WE NEEDED TO GET A HELMET ON HER BUT SHE REFUSED TO TAKE OFF MY SISTER'S KNITTED VIKING HAT.
NO NO MY VIKING HAT
OUR LAST PHOTO TOGETHER.

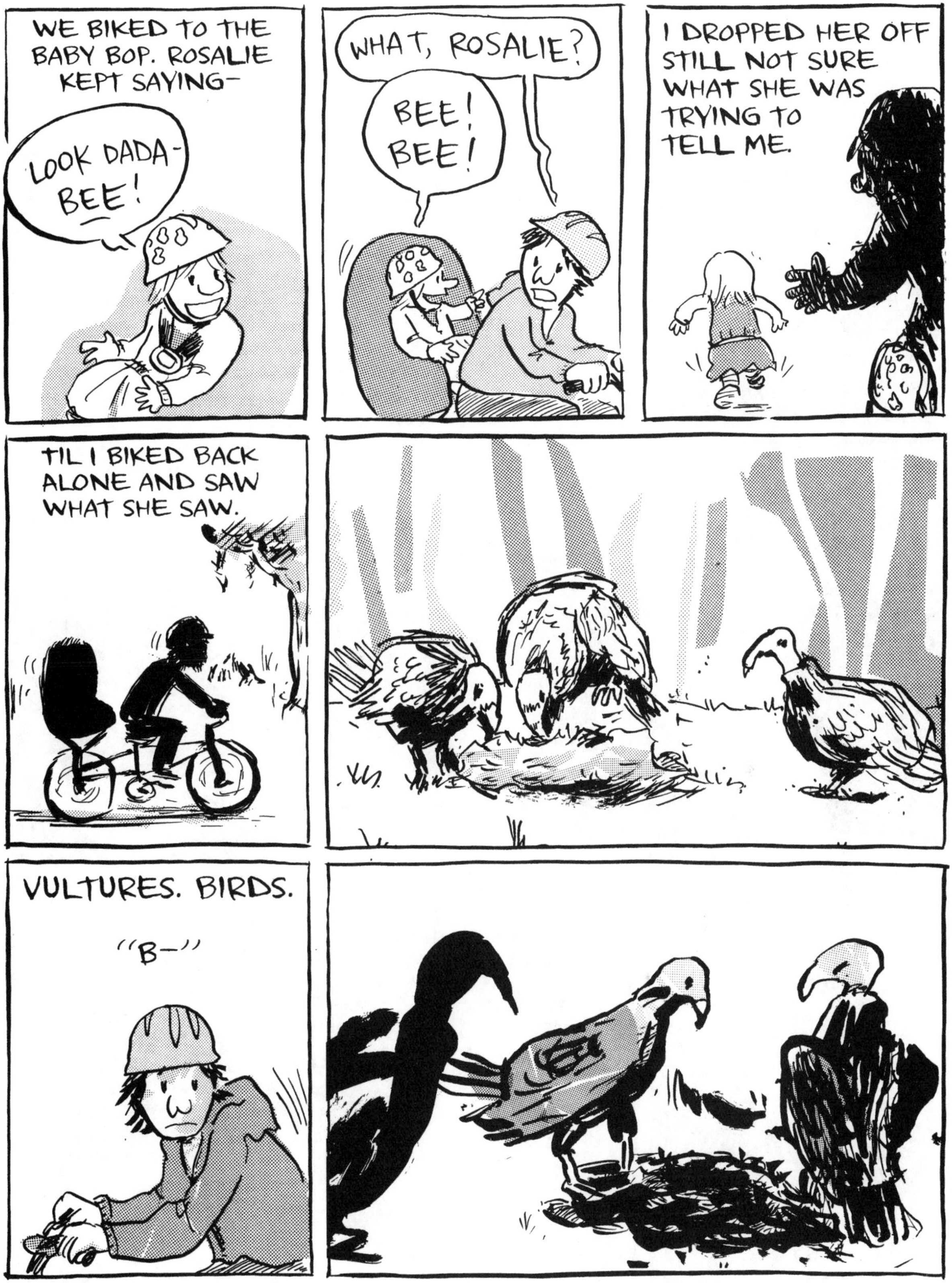
WE BIKED TO THE BABY BOP. ROSALIE KEPT SAYING–
LOOK DADA- BEE!
WHAT, ROSALIE?
BEE! BEE!
I DROPPED HER OFF STILL NOT SURE WHAT SHE WAS TRYING TO TELL ME.
TIL I BIKED BACK ALONE AND SAW WHAT SHE SAW.
VULTURES. BIRDS.
"B–"

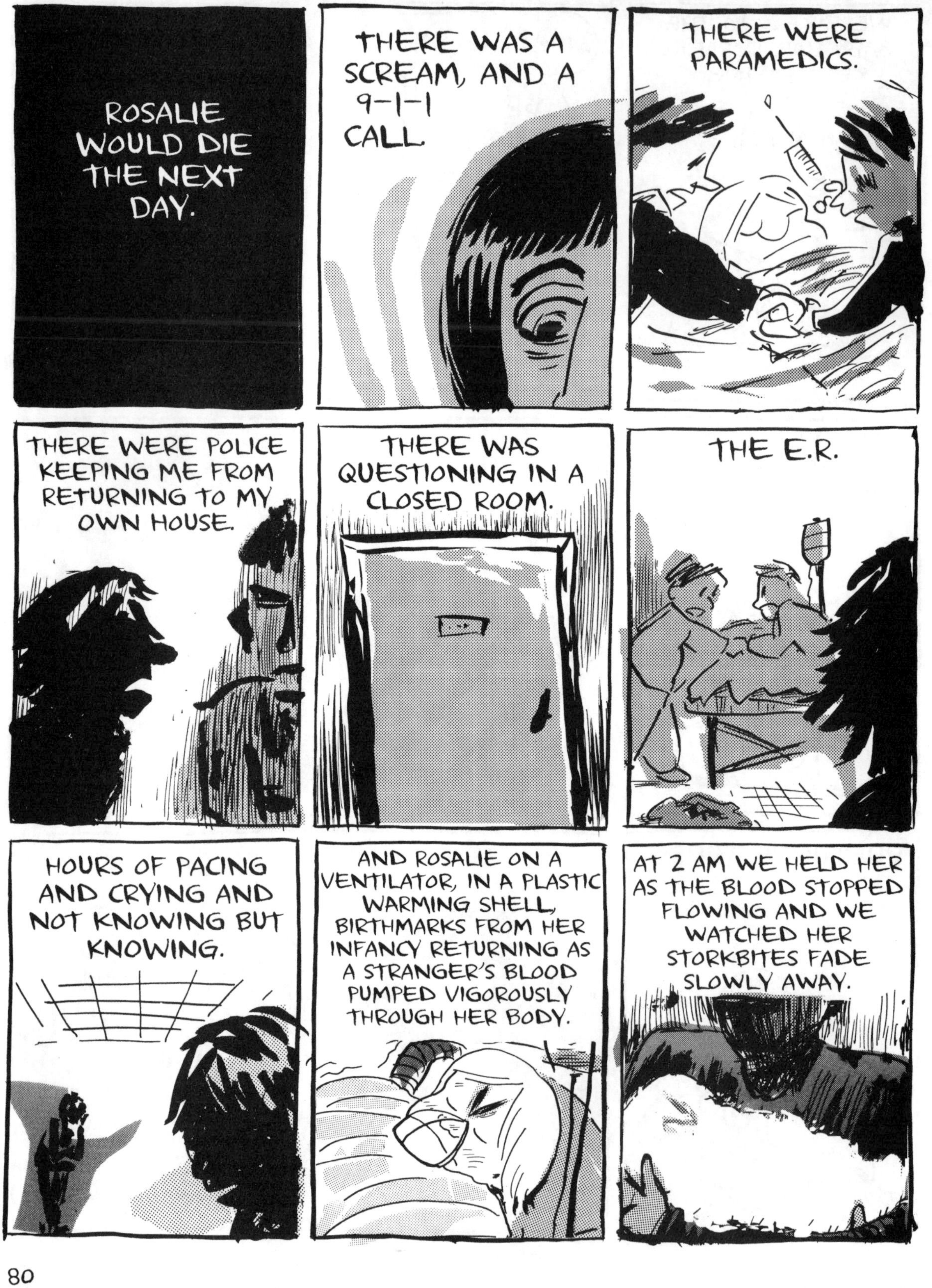
ROSALIE WOULD DIE THE NEXT DAY.
THERE WAS A SCREAM, AND A 9-1-1 CALL.
THERE WERE PARAMEDICS.
THERE WERE POLICE KEEPING ME FROM RETURNING TO MY OWN HOUSE.
THERE WAS QUESTIONING IN A CLOSED ROOM.
THE E.R.
HOURS OF PACING AND CRYING AND NOT KNOWING BUT KNOWING.
AND ROSALIE ON A VENTILATOR, IN A PLASTIC WARMING SHELL, BIRTHMARKS FROM HER INFANCY RETURNING AS A STRANGER'S BLOOD PUMPED VIGOROUSLY THROUGH HER BODY.
AT 2 AM WE HELD HER AS THE BLOOD STOPPED FLOWING AND WE WATCHED HER STORKBITES FADE SLOWLY AWAY.

WHAT DO YOU
DO WHEN
YOUR CHILD DIES?

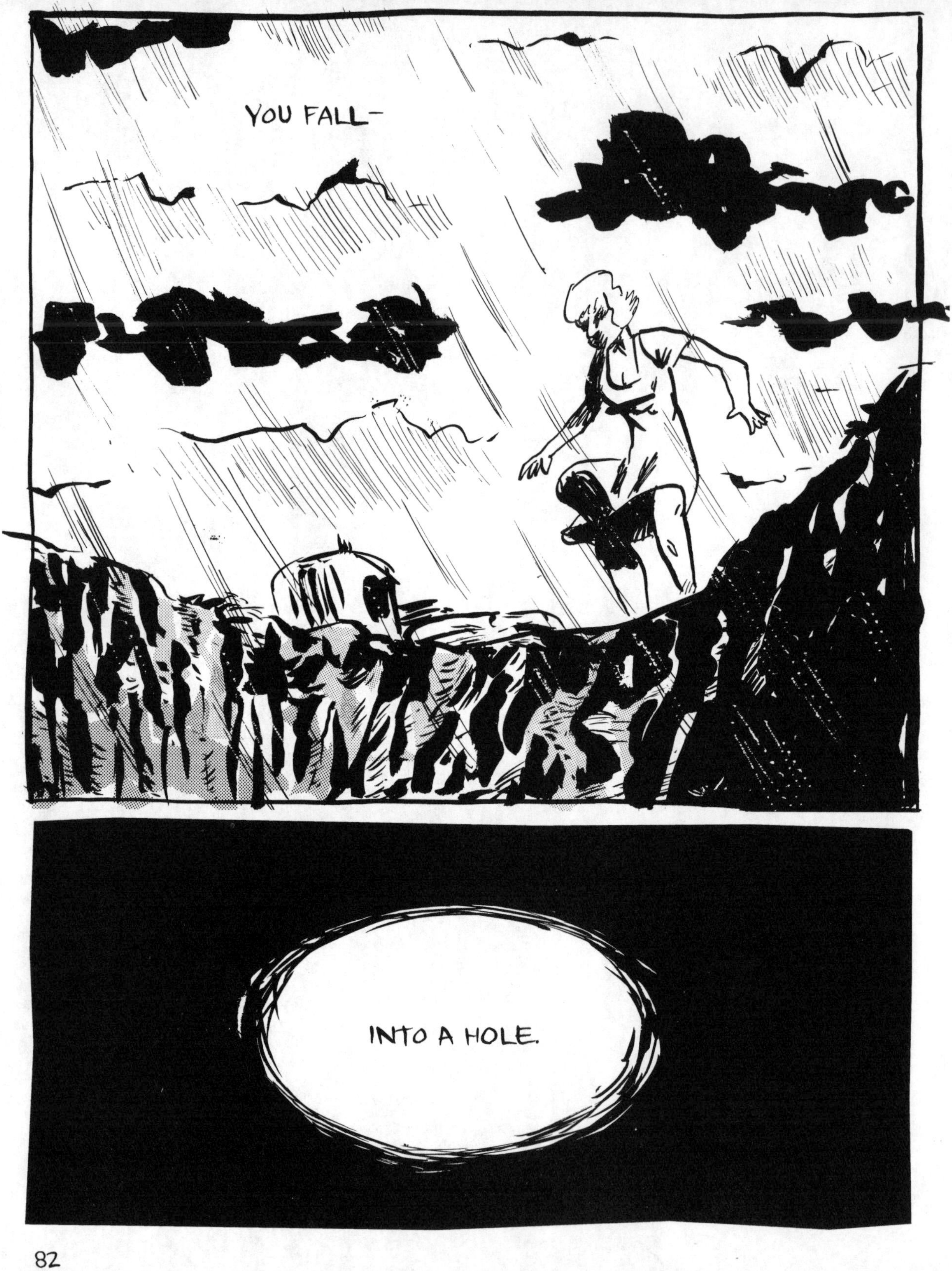
YOU FALL-
INTO A HOLE.

V

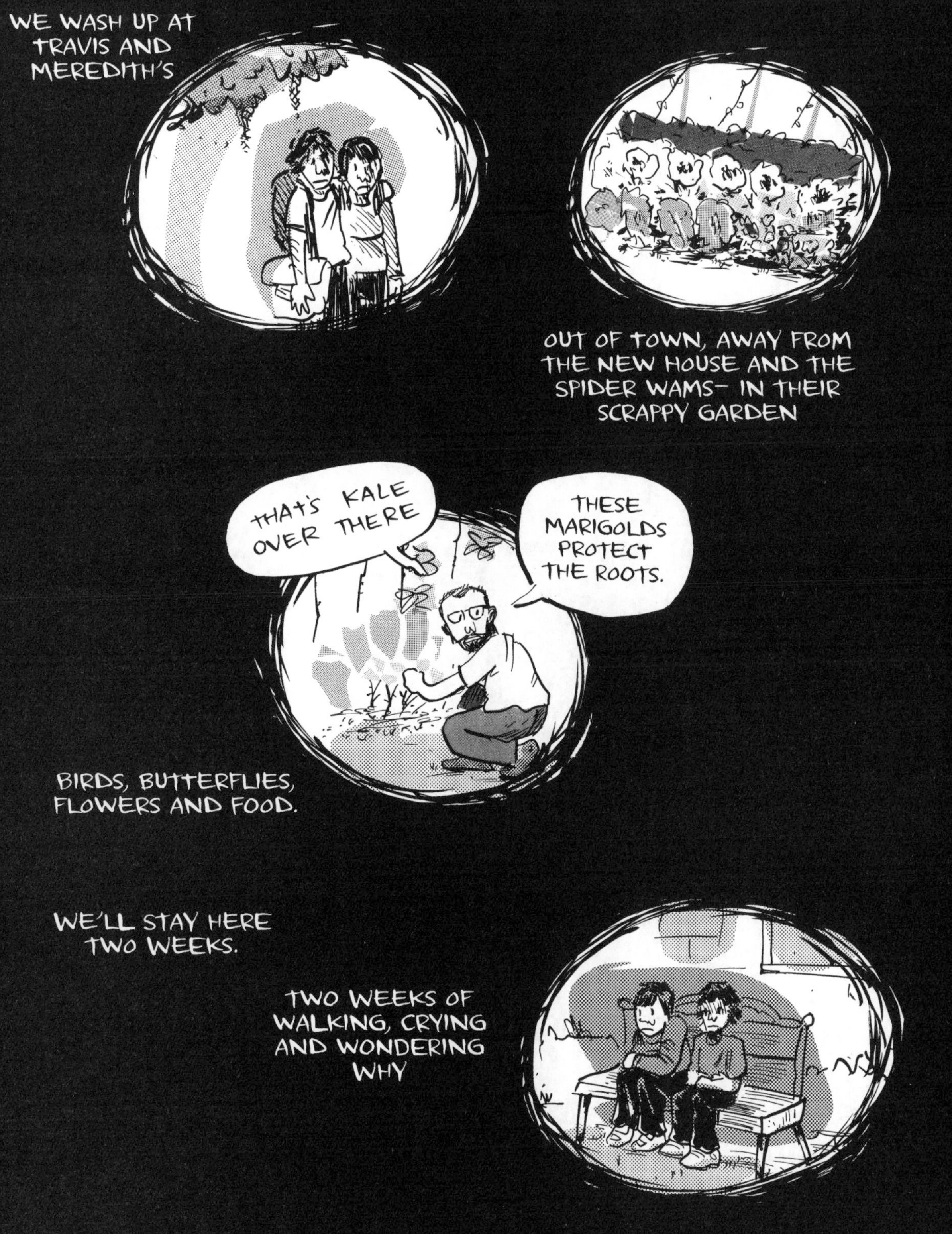
WE WASH UP AT TRAVIS AND MEREDITH'S
OUT OF TOWN, AWAY FROM THE NEW HOUSE AND THE SPIDER WAMS– IN THEIR SCRAPPY GARDEN
THAT'S KALE OVER THERE
THESE MARIGOLDS PROTECT THE ROOTS.
BIRDS, BUTTERFLIES, FLOWERS AND FOOD.
WE'LL STAY HERE TWO WEEKS.
TWO WEEKS OF WALKING, CRYING AND WONDERING WHY

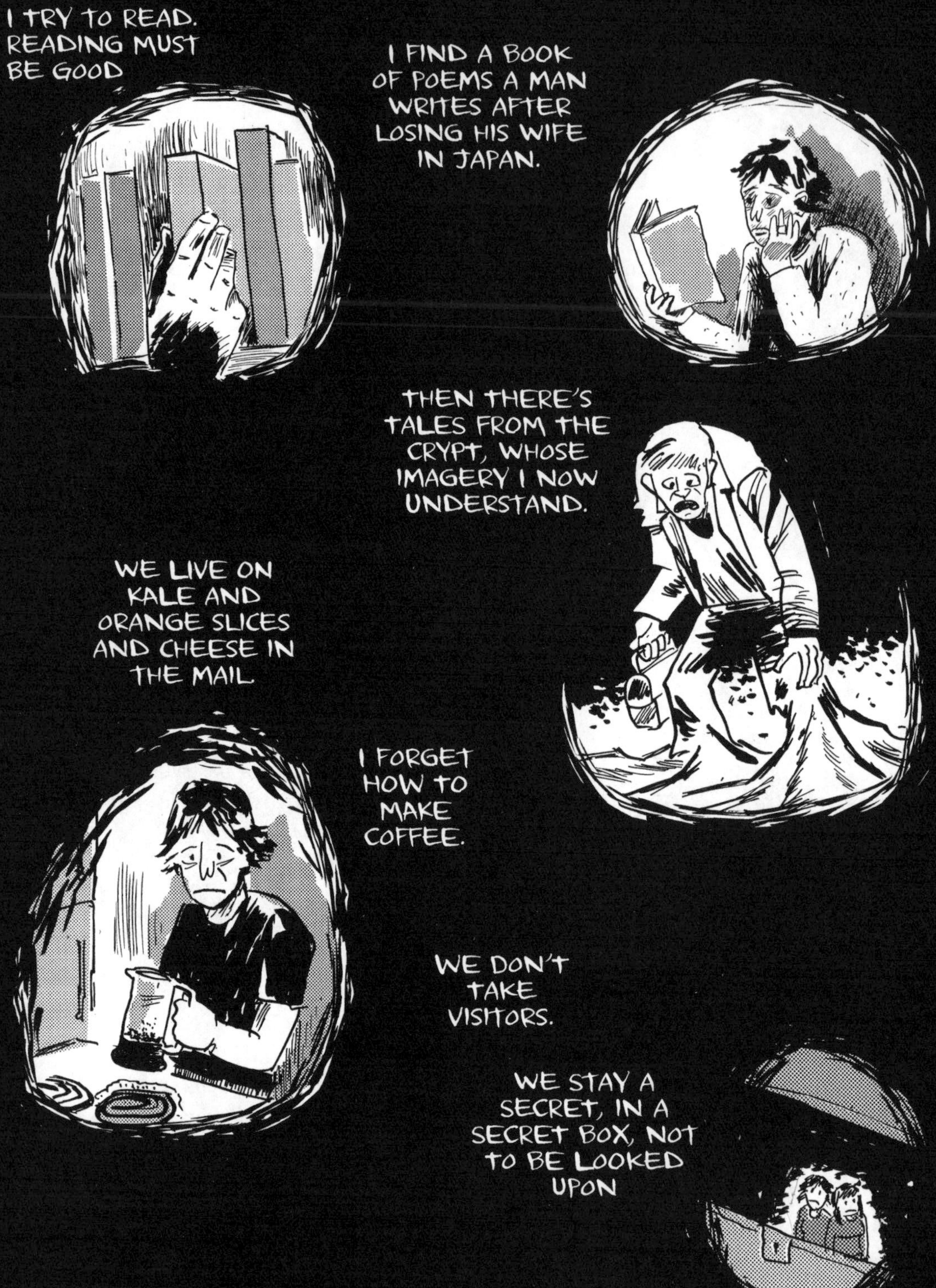
I TRY TO READ. READING MUST BE GOOD
I FIND A BOOK OF POEMS A MAN WRITES AFTER LOSING HIS WIFE IN JAPAN.
THEN THERE'S TALES FROM THE CRYPT, WHOSE IMAGERY I NOW UNDERSTAND.
WE LIVE ON KALE AND ORANGE SLICES AND CHEESE IN THE MAIL.
I FORGET HOW TO MAKE COFFEE.
WE DON'T TAKE VISITORS.
WE STAY A SECRET, IN A SECRET BOX, NOT TO BE LOOKED UPON

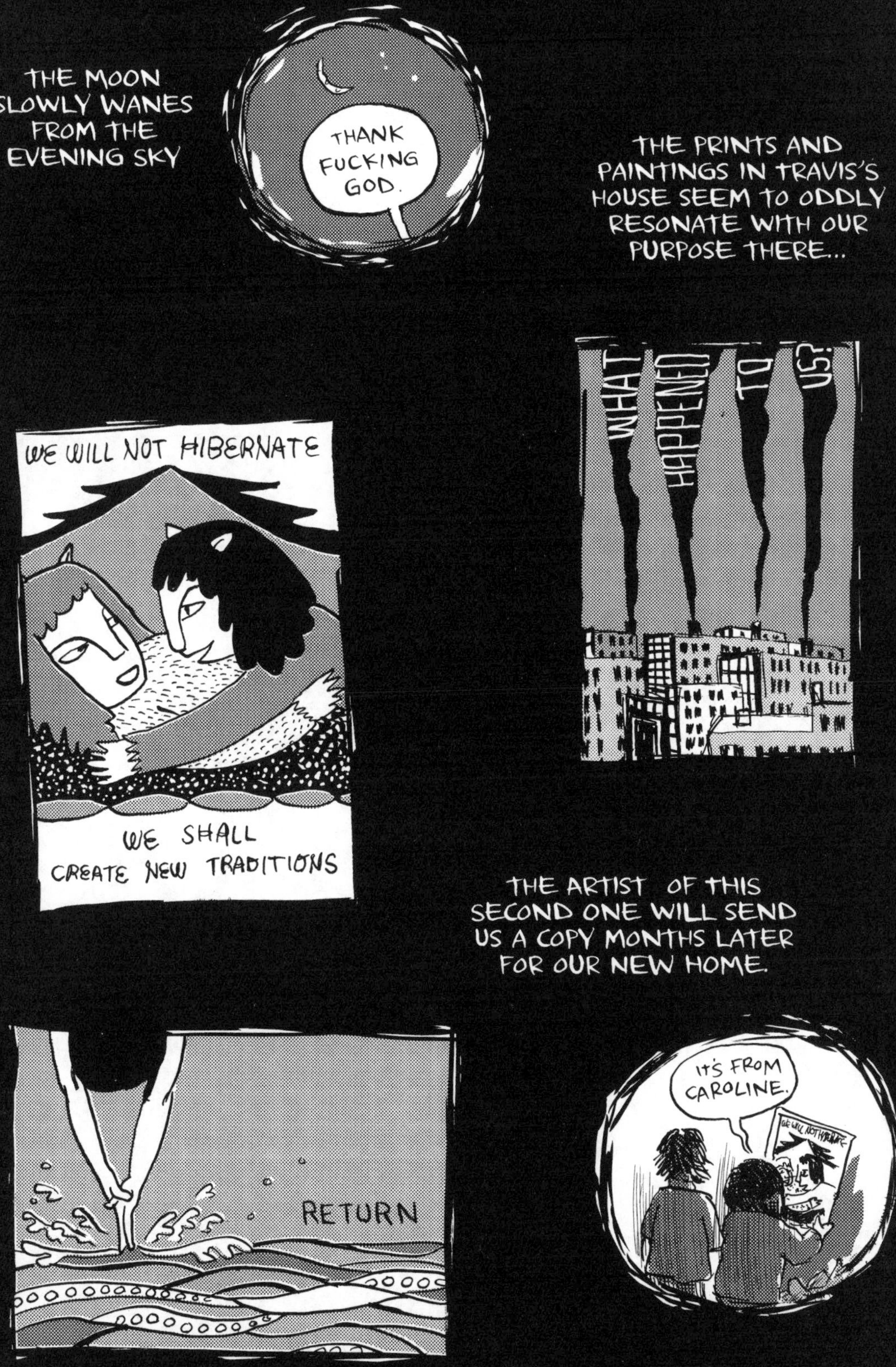
THE MOON SLOWLY WANES FROM THE EVENING SKY
THANK FUCKING GOD.
THE PRINTS AND PAINTINGS IN TRAVIS'S HOUSE SEEM TO ODDLY RESONATE WITH OUR PURPOSE THERE...
WE WILL NOT HIBERNATE
WE SHALL CREATE NEW TRADITIONS
WHAT HAPPENED TO US?
THE ARTIST OF THIS SECOND ONE WILL SEND US A COPY MONTHS LATER FOR OUR NEW HOME.
RETURN
IT'S FROM CAROLINE.

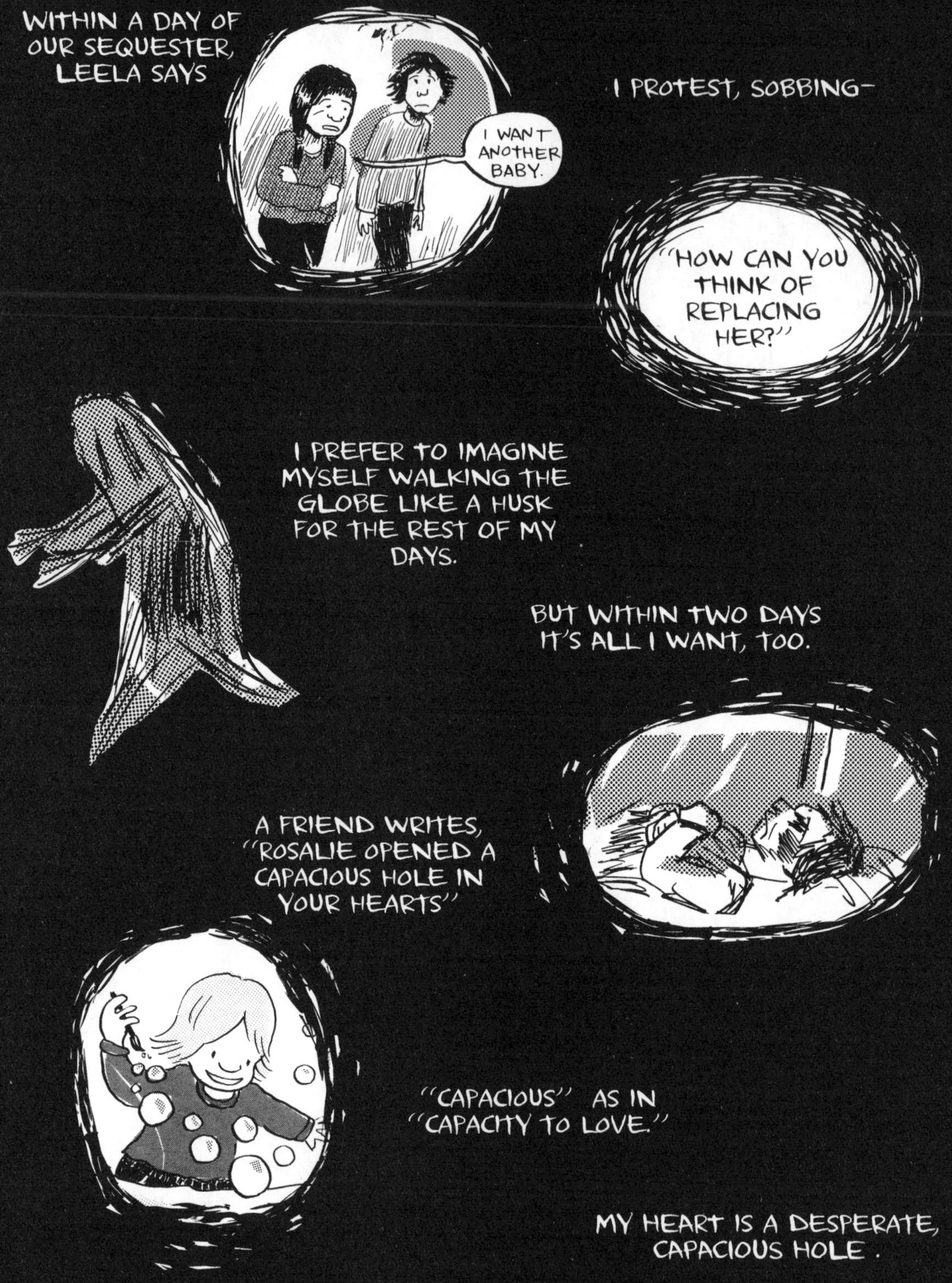
WITHIN A DAY OF OUR SEQUESTER, LEELA SAYS
I WANT ANOTHER BABY.
I PROTEST, SOBBING–
"HOW CAN YOU THINK OF REPLACING HER?"
I PREFER TO IMAGINE MYSELF WALKING THE GLOBE LIKE A HUSK FOR THE REST OF MY DAYS.
BUT WITHIN TWO DAYS IT'S ALL I WANT, TOO.
A FRIEND WRITES, "ROSALIE OPENED A CAPACIOUS HOLE IN YOUR HEARTS"
"CAPACIOUS" AS IN "CAPACITY TO LOVE."
MY HEART IS A DESPERATE, CAPACIOUS HOLE.

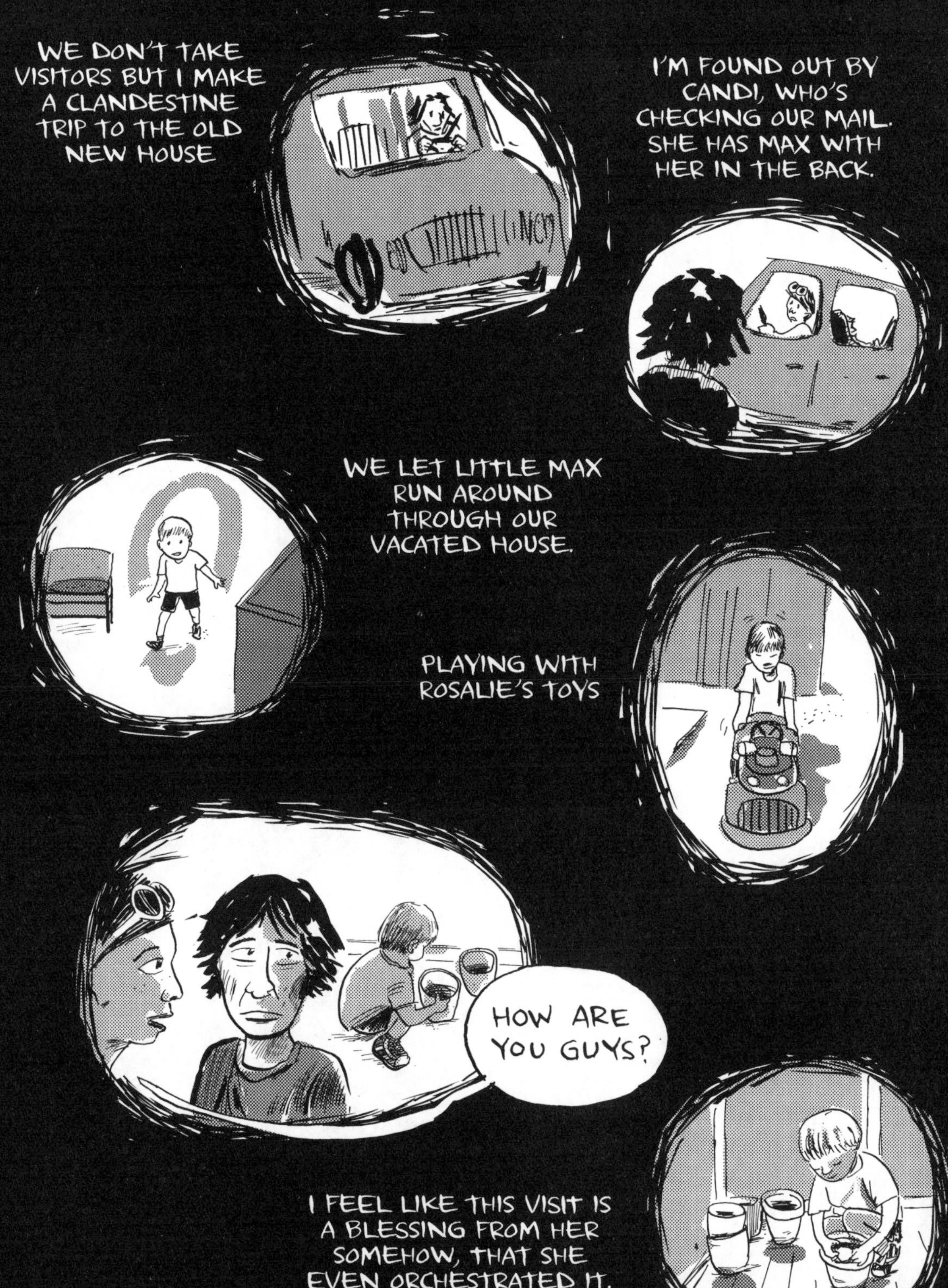
WE DON'T TAKE VISITORS BUT I MAKE A CLANDESTINE TRIP TO THE OLD NEW HOUSE
I'M FOUND OUT BY CANDI, WHO'S CHECKING OUR MAIL. SHE HAS MAX WITH HER IN THE BACK.
WE LET LITTLE MAX RUN AROUND THROUGH OUR VACATED HOUSE.
PLAYING WITH ROSALIE'S TOYS
HOW ARE YOU GUYS?
I FEEL LIKE THIS VISIT IS A BLESSING FROM HER SOMEHOW, THAT SHE EVEN ORCHESTRATED IT.

WHEN WE WALK THE NEIGHBORHOOD

I SEE IMAGES EVERYWHERE

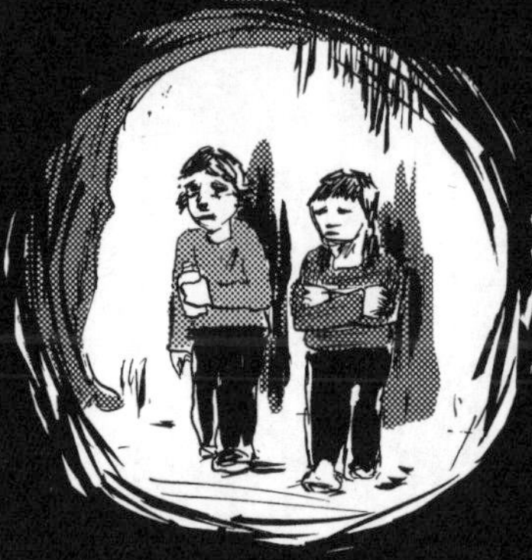

THIS SEWAGE DRAIN IS MY BROKEN RIB CAGE

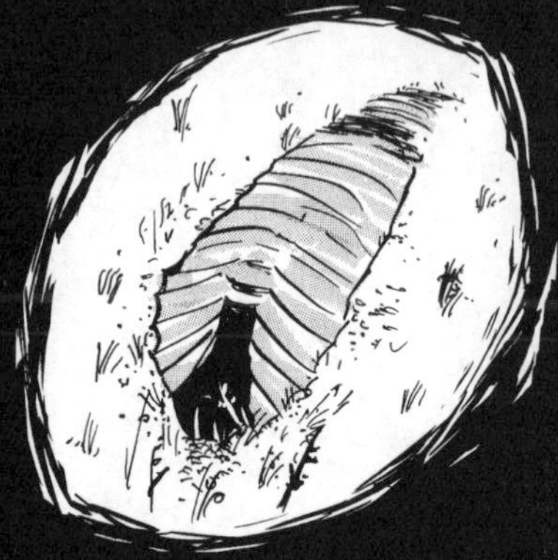

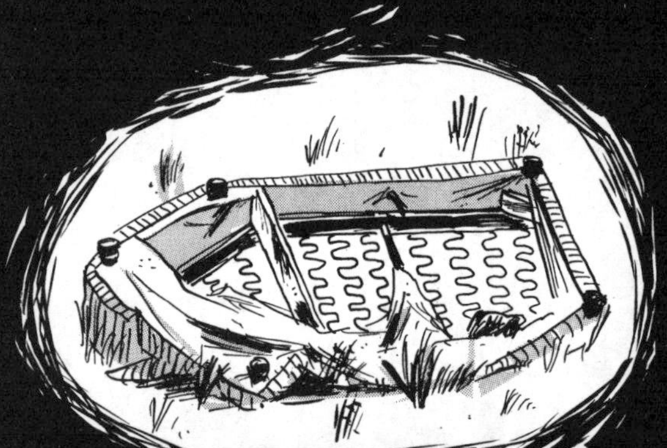

I WALK BY THIS OVERTURNED SOFA THREE TIMES BEFORE I REALIZE IT'S NOT A BROKEN BOAT

EVERY SIGN TAKES ON A NEW MEANING

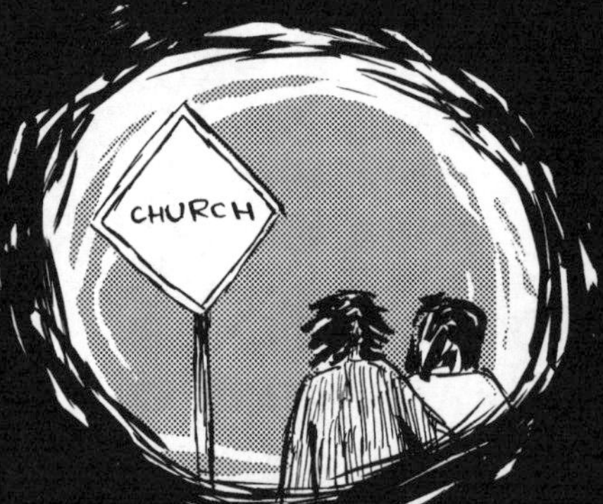
CHURCH

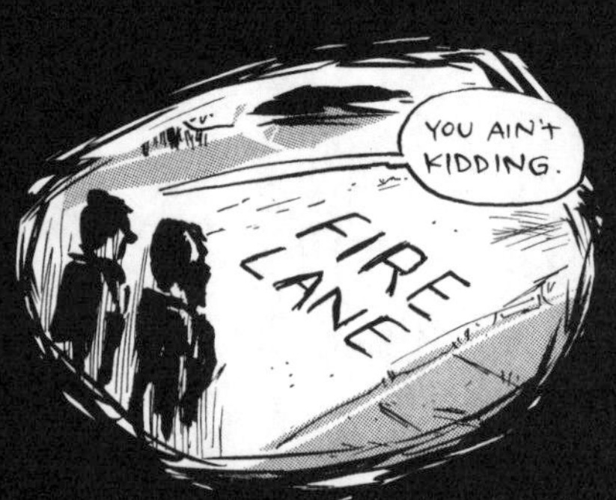
YOU AIN'T KIDDING.
FIRE LANE

OTHER IMAGES, CLIPPED FROM RANDOM JAPANESE COMIC STORIES FALL OUT OF MY NOTEBOOK. I TRY TO DECIPHER THEM.

THIS ONE, A WOMAN IN A SWIMMING LANE.

I REDRAW IT. SHE LOOKS HORRIFIED.

IT TAKES ME AGES TO REALIZE THIS THING ON THE RIGHT ISN'T SOME MALEVOLENT PIECE OF MACHINERY EMERGING FROM THE DEPTHS,

IT'S JUST A LANE MARKER.

AND OVER HER HEAD, IS A TWO.

NOT SOME GIANT QUESTION MARK LIKE THE ONE THAT HOVERS OVER OURS.

THEN A PHOTOGRAPH OF A LOST BOY.

A DETECTIVE STORY? A LOST LOVER? A CHILDHOOD PHOTO? I HAVE NO IDEA WHAT THE KANJI AND KATAKANA SAYS

THEN I REALIZE:

WHY DID I ASSUME THIS BOY WAS LOST?

WHY WAS I CARRYING THESE PICTURES AROUND?

I'M LOOKING FOR CLUES, MORE PORTENTS.

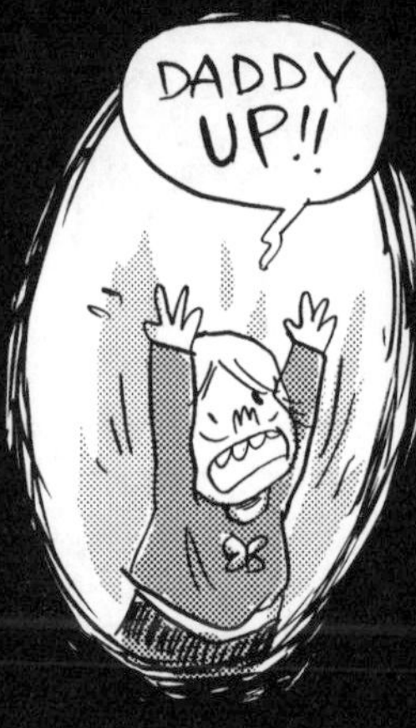
DADDY UP!!

SHOULD I HAVE KNOWN SHE WAS GOING?

ANOTHER IMAGE APPEARS. AN ABORTED CARTOON DAYDREAM.

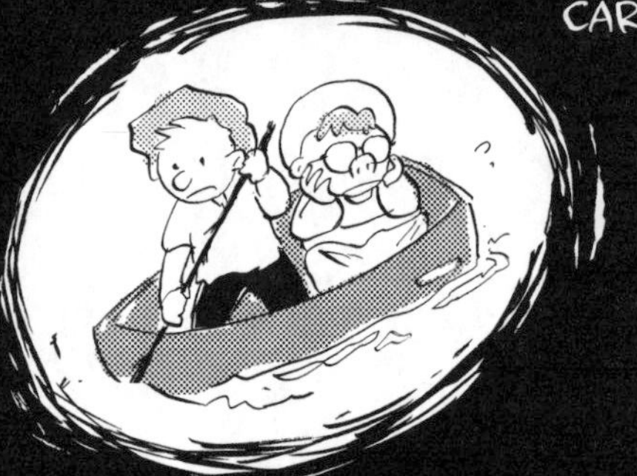

A MAN AND A WOMAN ADRIFT ON A RAFT, MAKING THEIR SLOW WAY TO–

SOMEWHERE...

I'VE BEEN DOODLING THIS FOR YEARS, NEVER KNOWING WHAT IT'S ABOUT. NEVER KNOWING WHERE THEY ARE GOING.

NOW I KNOW THEY AREN'T GOING ANYWHERE.

THEY'RE JUST LEAVING. FLEEING.

MOVING FORWARD FROM SOME HORRIBLE LOSS.

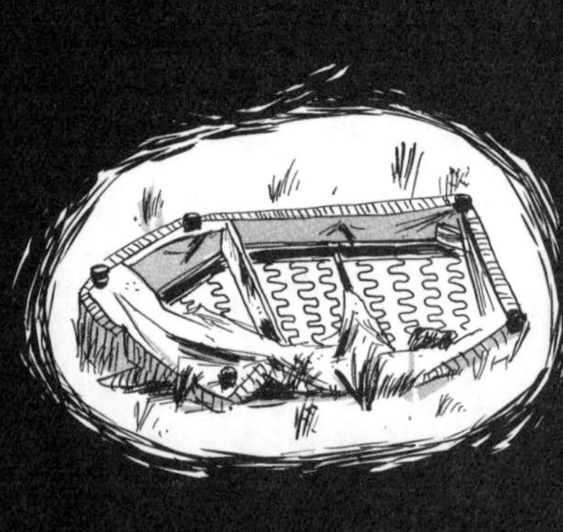

AND THEN A SERIES OF CATASTROPHES

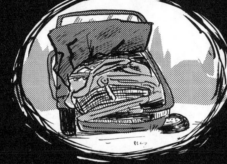

TOM, JEFF'S BEEN IN A BAD CAR ACCIDENT. HE'S GOT A HOLE IN HIS ABDOMEN.

THERE'S LOTS OF INTERNAL BLEEDING. HIS WIFE IS AWAY AT SCHOOL FOR 3 MONTHS.

WE'LL MOVE IN WITH HIM SOON. DAYS LATER WE'LL SEE THE CAR.

I GET MY FRIEND SARAH ON THE PHONE. SHE REMINDS ME THAT HER OWN BROTHER DIED WHEN SHE WAS 13.

I ASK HER LOTS OF QUESTIONS.

WAS IT HARD?

HOW DID YOU DO IT?

DO YOU STILL FEEL IT?

AGHHHH!

I THINK I HAVE TO GO CHECK ON LEELA.

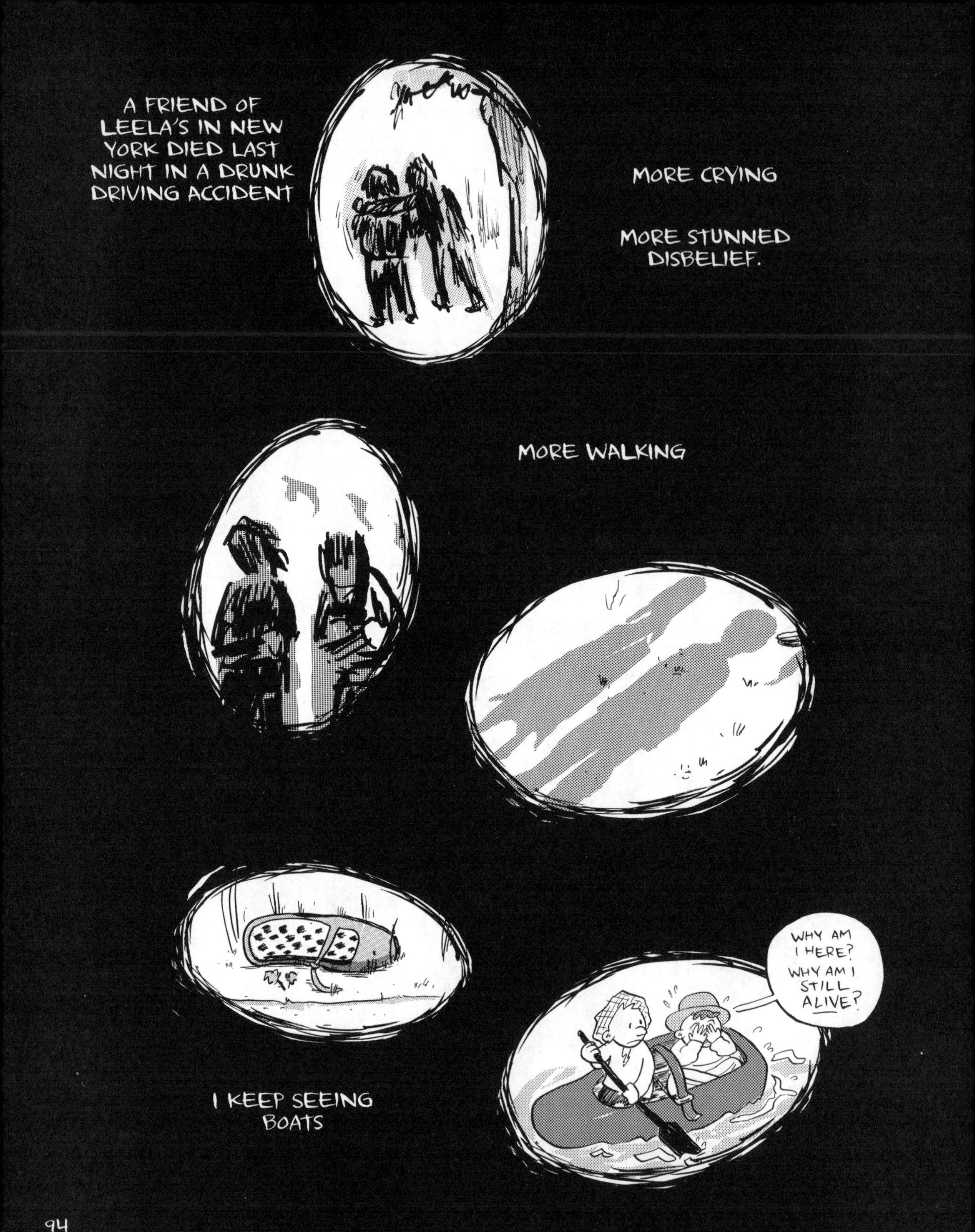
A FRIEND OF LEELA'S IN NEW YORK DIED LAST NIGHT IN A DRUNK DRIVING ACCIDENT
MORE CRYING
MORE STUNNED DISBELIEF.
MORE WALKING
I KEEP SEEING BOATS
WHY AM I HERE? WHY AM I STILL ALIVE?

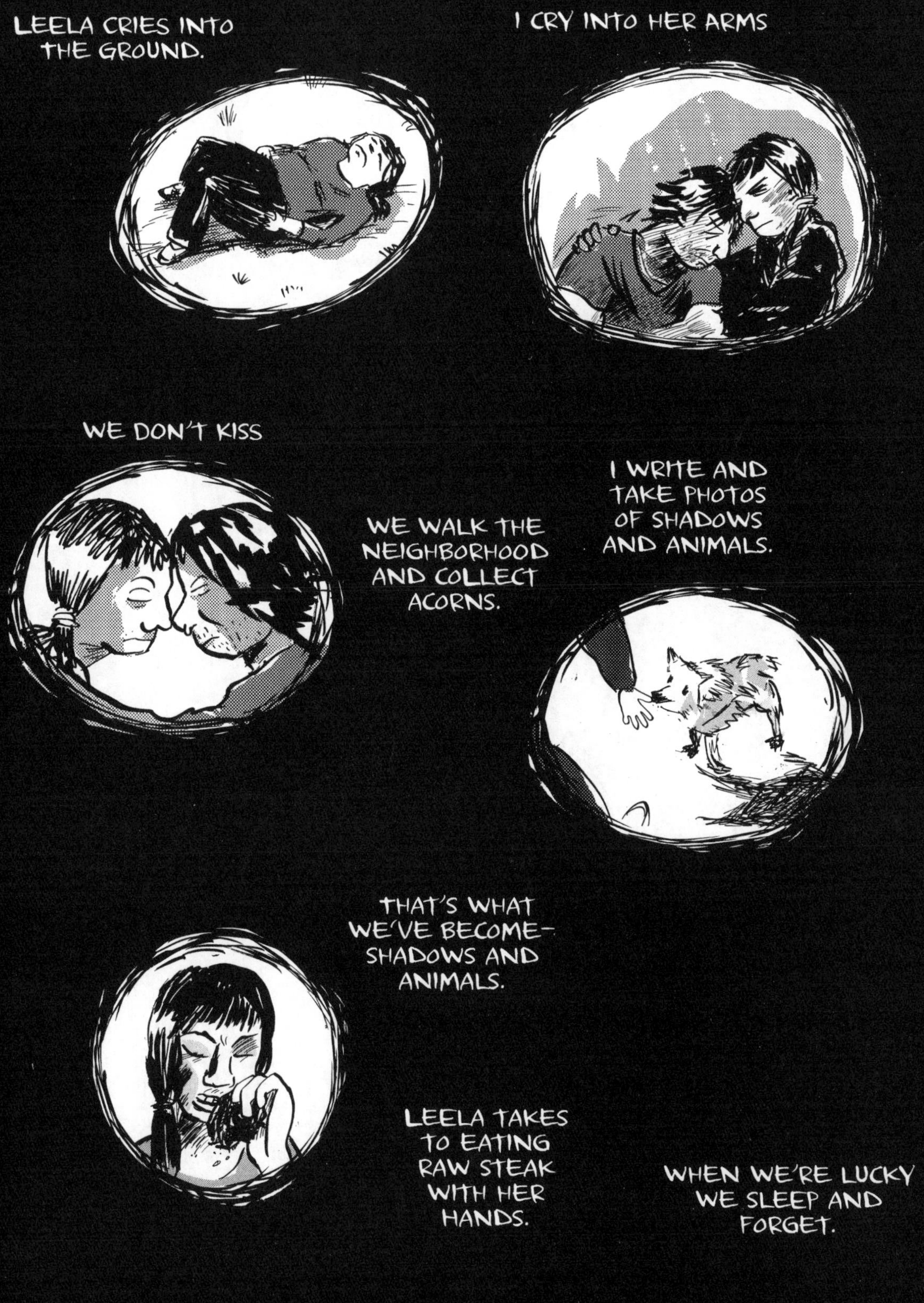
LEELA CRIES INTO THE GROUND.
I CRY INTO HER ARMS
WE DON'T KISS
WE WALK THE NEIGHBORHOOD AND COLLECT ACORNS.
I WRITE AND TAKE PHOTOS OF SHADOWS AND ANIMALS.
THAT'S WHAT WE'VE BECOME- SHADOWS AND ANIMALS.
LEELA TAKES TO EATING RAW STEAK WITH HER HANDS.
WHEN WE'RE LUCKY WE SLEEP AND FORGET.

OR SLEEP AND
REMEMBER.

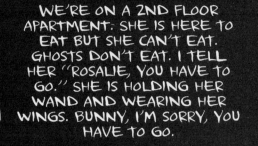

WE'RE ON A 2ND FLOOR
APARTMENT. SHE IS HERE TO
EAT BUT SHE CAN'T EAT.
GHOSTS DON'T EAT. I TELL
HER "ROSALIE, YOU HAVE TO
GO." SHE IS HOLDING HER
WAND AND WEARING HER
WINGS. BUNNY, I'M SORRY, YOU
HAVE TO GO.

SHE KNOWS IT TOO.

WE SLEEP
TOGETHER, ROSALIE
AND ME. PEOPLE
THINK IT'S WEIRD.
SHE IS FULL GROWN.
WE SLEEP
STANDING IN A
LUCITE BOX.

MY FRIEND TIM, STANDING
IN THE STREET, HOLDING HIS INFANT
SELF. I'M COMPARING THEIR SKIN,
LOOKING AT BIRTHMARKS AND SCARS.
COMPREHENDING HOW WE
GROW TO ADULTHOOD.

HER ALIVE, IN
MANY ROOMS OF A
HOUSE....

AND US GOING ON A
TRIP ON A ROCKET. HER
LEADING THE WAY.

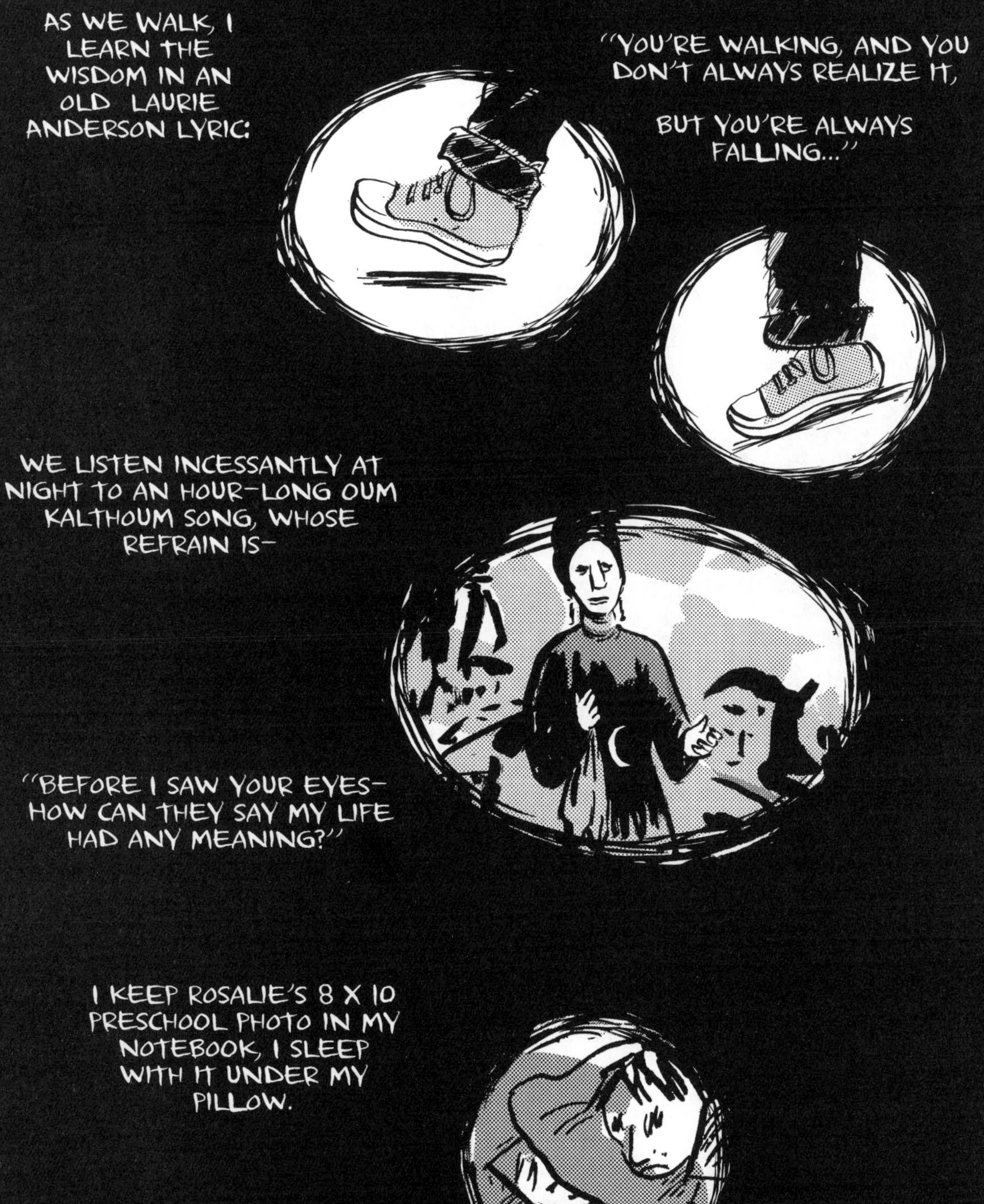
AS WE WALK, I LEARN THE WISDOM IN AN OLD LAURIE ANDERSON LYRIC:
"YOU'RE WALKING, AND YOU DON'T ALWAYS REALIZE IT,
BUT YOU'RE ALWAYS FALLING..."
WE LISTEN INCESSANTLY AT NIGHT TO AN HOUR-LONG OUM KALTHOUM SONG, WHOSE REFRAIN IS-
"BEFORE I SAW YOUR EYES- HOW CAN THEY SAY MY LIFE HAD ANY MEANING?"
I KEEP ROSALIE'S 8 X 10 PRESCHOOL PHOTO IN MY NOTEBOOK, I SLEEP WITH IT UNDER MY PILLOW.
YOUR EYES, BUNNY

LAURIE ANDERSON'S SONG HAS ONE OTHER REFRAIN:

"I WAS LOOKING FOR YOU BUT I COULDN'T FIND YOU

I WAS LOOKING FOR YOU ALL DAY..."

AND LATER,

"YOUR EYES— IT'S A DAY'S WORK

JUST LOOKING INTO THEM."

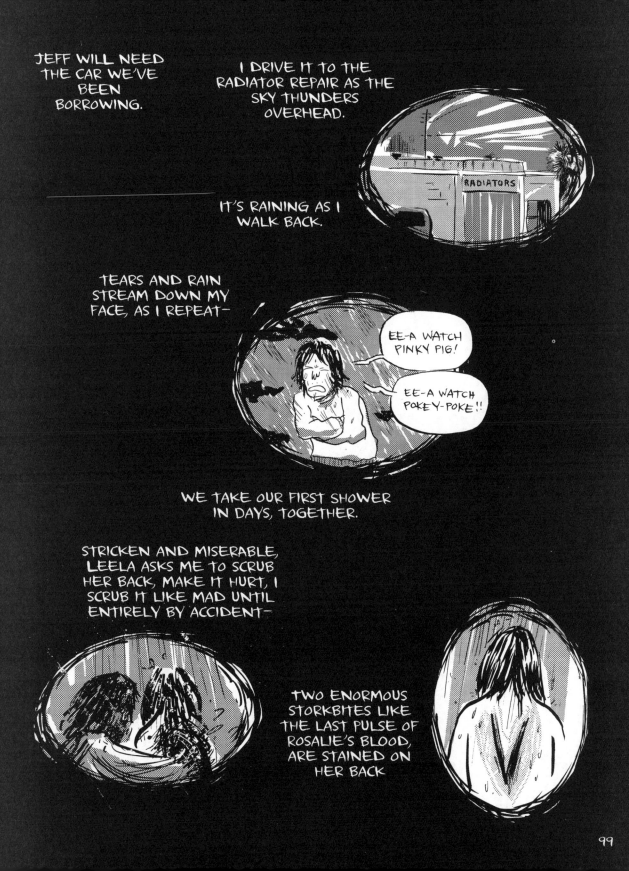

JEFF WILL NEED THE CAR WE'VE BEEN BORROWING.

I DRIVE IT TO THE RADIATOR REPAIR AS THE SKY THUNDERS OVERHEAD.

IT'S RAINING AS I WALK BACK.

TEARS AND RAIN STREAM DOWN MY FACE, AS I REPEAT—

EE-A WATCH PINKY PIG!

EE-A WATCH POKEY-POKE!!

WE TAKE OUR FIRST SHOWER IN DAYS, TOGETHER.

STRICKEN AND MISERABLE, LEELA ASKS ME TO SCRUB HER BACK, MAKE IT HURT, I SCRUB IT LIKE MAD UNTIL ENTIRELY BY ACCIDENT—

TWO ENORMOUS STORKBITES LIKE THE LAST PULSE OF ROSALIE'S BLOOD, ARE STAINED ON HER BACK

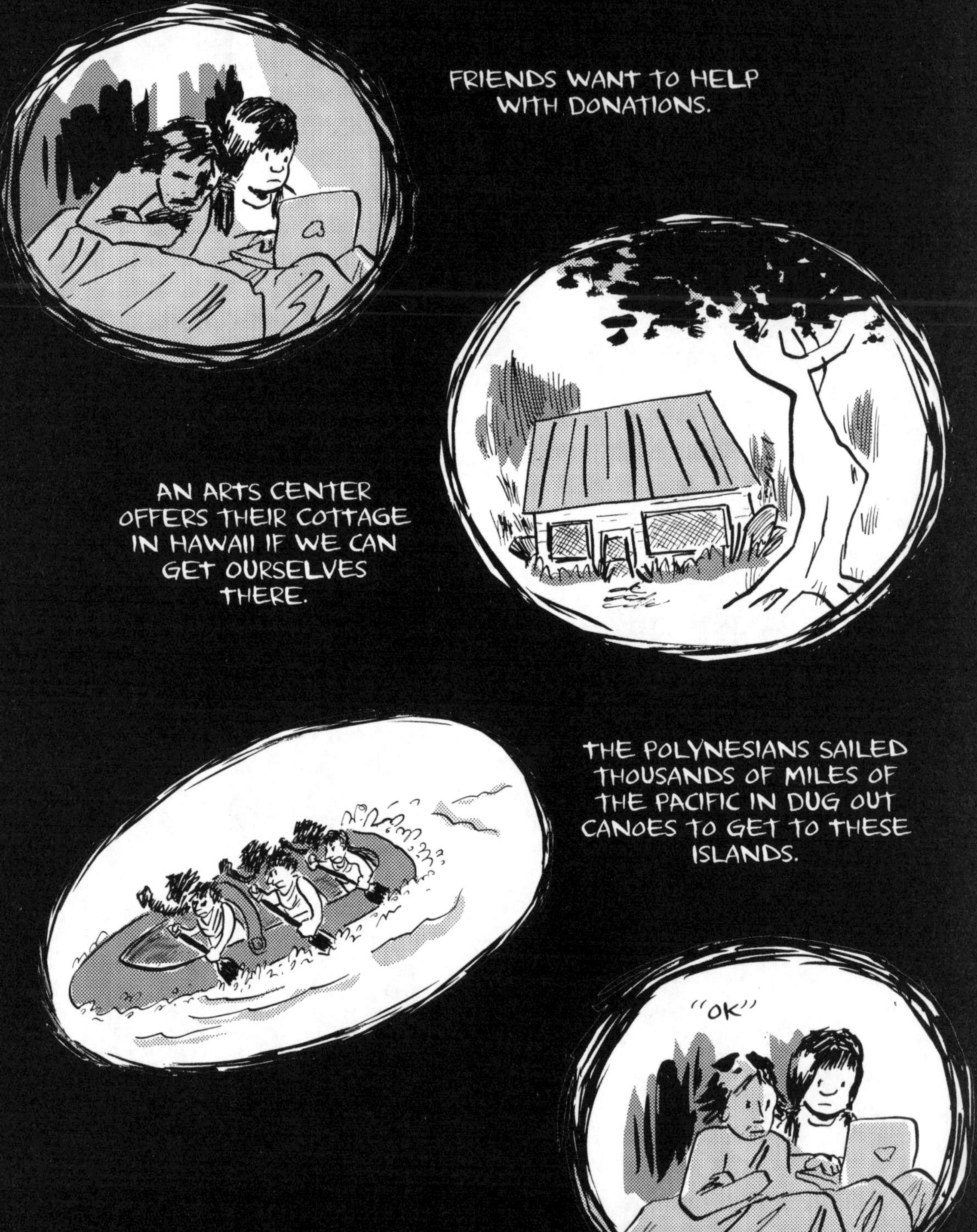
FRIENDS WANT TO HELP WITH DONATIONS.
AN ARTS CENTER OFFERS THEIR COTTAGE IN HAWAII IF WE CAN GET OURSELVES THERE.
THE POLYNESIANS SAILED THOUSANDS OF MILES OF THE PACIFIC IN DUG OUT CANOES TO GET TO THESE ISLANDS.
"OK"

I'M TRAINED TO SEE EVERYTHING IN STORY AND MYTHIC JOURNEYS.

I KNOW THAT BROKEN AND TROUBLED CHARACTERS MUST TRAVEL TO NEW WORLDS TO HEAL AND OVERCOME. VENTURE TO THE UNDERWORLD AND THE SUBCONSCIOUS WHERE TRUTHS ARE MET.

LEELA HAS HEARD OF A PLACE IN NEW MEXICO, A "GRIEF RETREAT."

THE FOUNDER LOST HIS BROTHER, WIFE, MOTHER-IN-LAW AND TWO YOUNG CHILDREN IN A SERIES OF SUCCESSIVE CATASTROPHES.

AFTER BOTTOMING OUT, HE SET UP THIS PLACE FOR PEOPLE WHO'VE LOST LOVED ONES TO CONFRONT AND GRIEVE THEIR LOSSES.

WE'VE BEEN MARKED AND WE'VE BEEN RAINED ON.

WE CRAWL OUT OF THE SCRAPPY GARDEN.

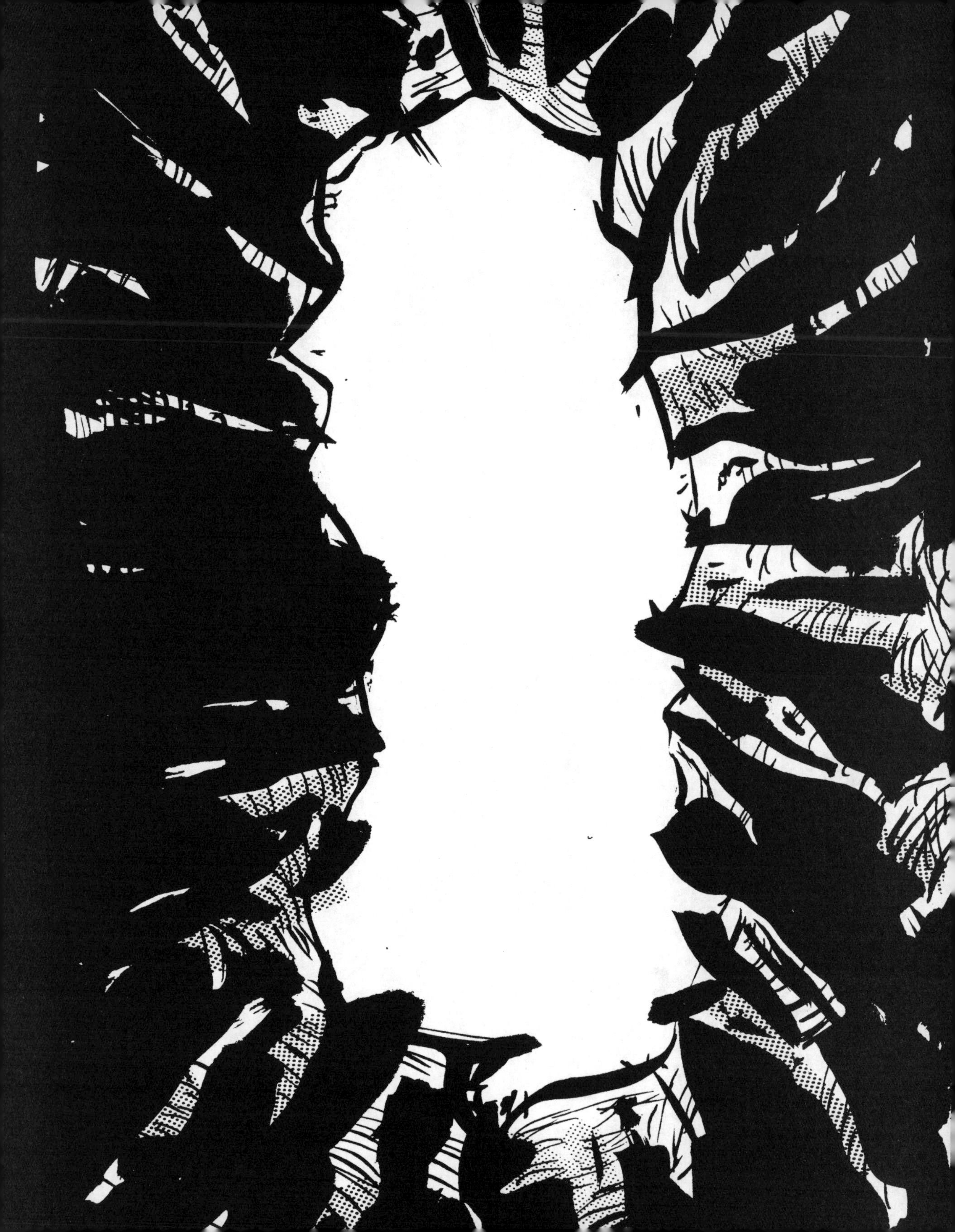

VI

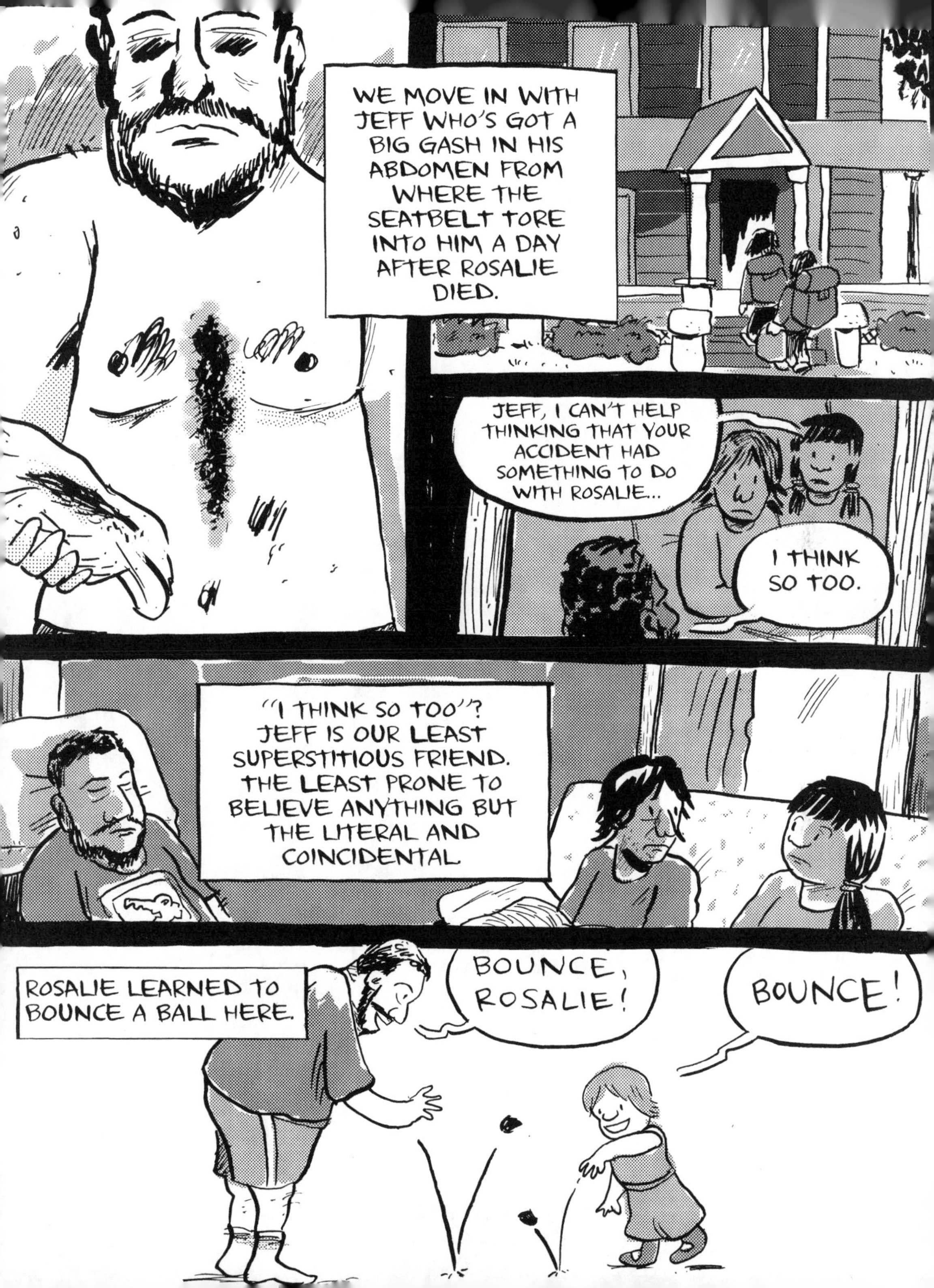
WE MOVE IN WITH JEFF WHO'S GOT A BIG GASH IN HIS ABDOMEN FROM WHERE THE SEATBELT TORE INTO HIM A DAY AFTER ROSALIE DIED.
JEFF, I CAN'T HELP THINKING THAT YOUR ACCIDENT HAD SOMETHING TO DO WITH ROSALIE...
I THINK SO TOO.
"I THINK SO TOO"? JEFF IS OUR LEAST SUPERSTITIOUS FRIEND. THE LEAST PRONE TO BELIEVE ANYTHING BUT THE LITERAL AND COINCIDENTAL.
ROSALIE LEARNED TO BOUNCE A BALL HERE.
BOUNCE, ROSALIE!
BOUNCE!

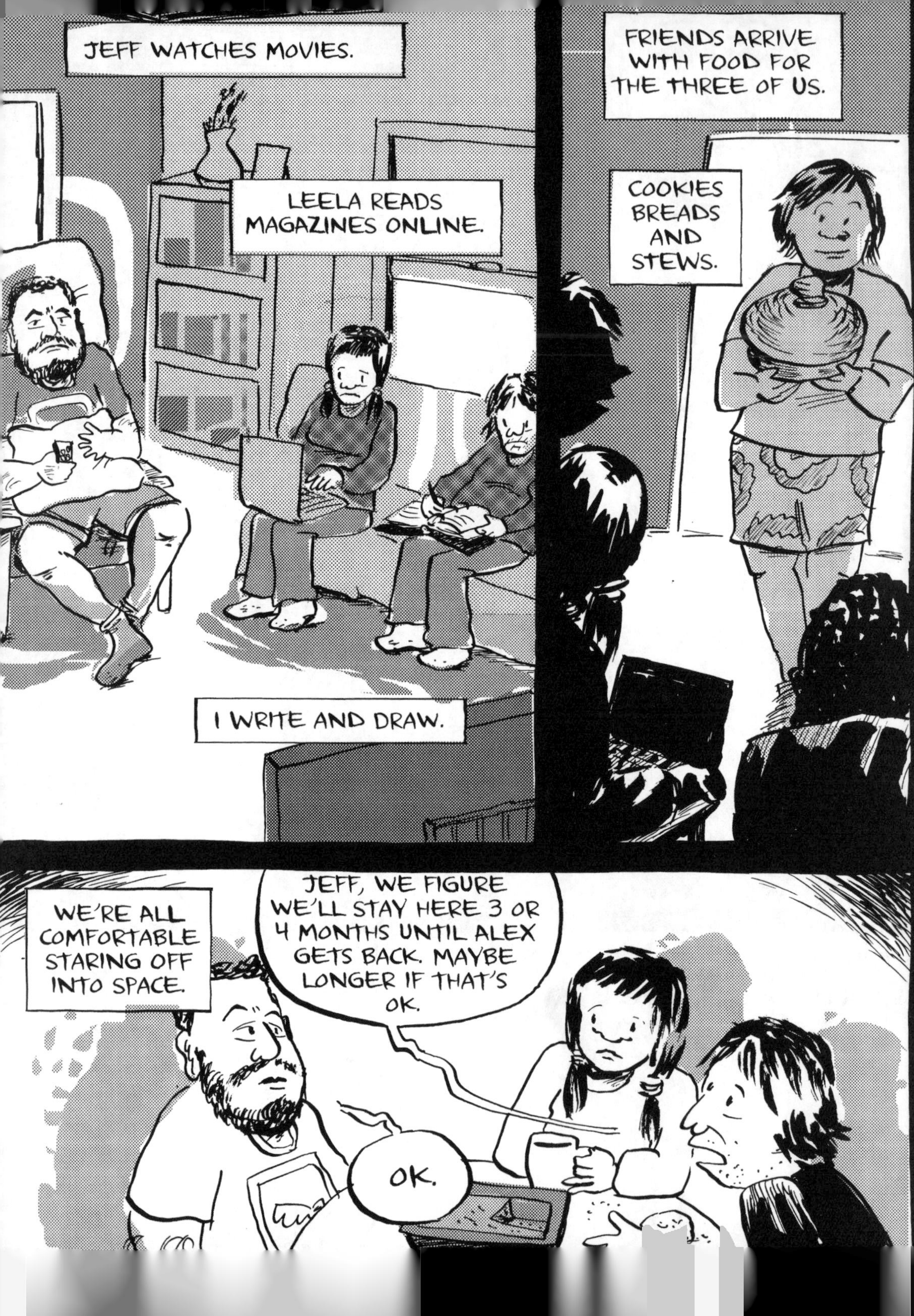
JEFF WATCHES MOVIES.
LEELA READS MAGAZINES ONLINE.
I WRITE AND DRAW.
FRIENDS ARRIVE WITH FOOD FOR THE THREE OF US.
COOKIES BREADS AND STEWS.
WE'RE ALL COMFORTABLE STARING OFF INTO SPACE.
JEFF, WE FIGURE WE'LL STAY HERE 3 OR 4 MONTHS UNTIL ALEX GETS BACK. MAYBE LONGER IF THAT'S OK.
OK.

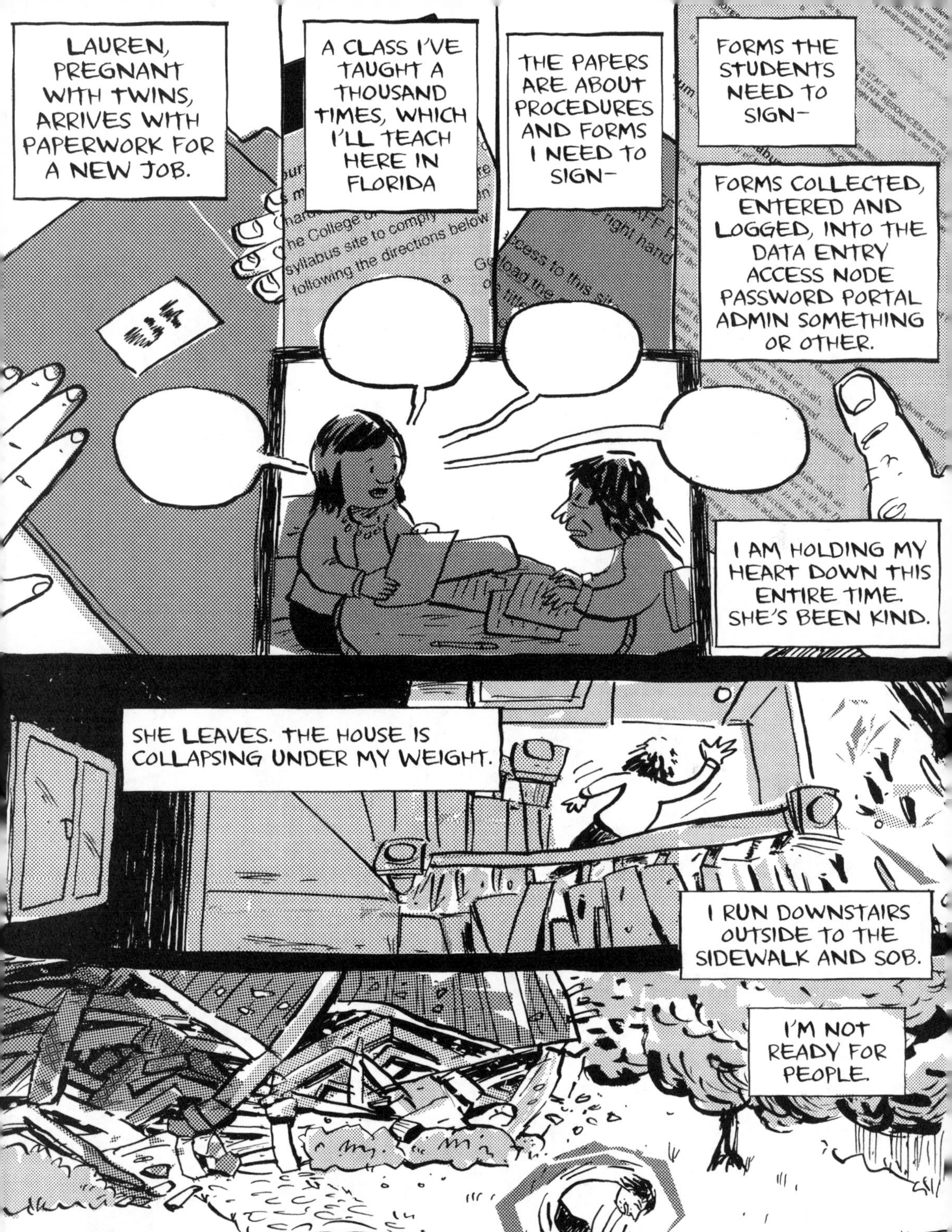
LAUREN, PREGNANT WITH TWINS, ARRIVES WITH PAPERWORK FOR A NEW JOB.
A CLASS I'VE TAUGHT A THOUSAND TIMES, WHICH I'LL TEACH HERE IN FLORIDA
THE PAPERS ARE ABOUT PROCEDURES AND FORMS I NEED TO SIGN–
FORMS THE STUDENTS NEED TO SIGN–
FORMS COLLECTED, ENTERED AND LOGGED, INTO THE DATA ENTRY ACCESS NODE PASSWORD PORTAL ADMIN SOMETHING OR OTHER.
I AM HOLDING MY HEART DOWN THIS ENTIRE TIME. SHE'S BEEN KIND.
SHE LEAVES. THE HOUSE IS COLLAPSING UNDER MY WEIGHT.
I RUN DOWNSTAIRS OUTSIDE TO THE SIDEWALK AND SOB.
I'M NOT READY FOR PEOPLE.

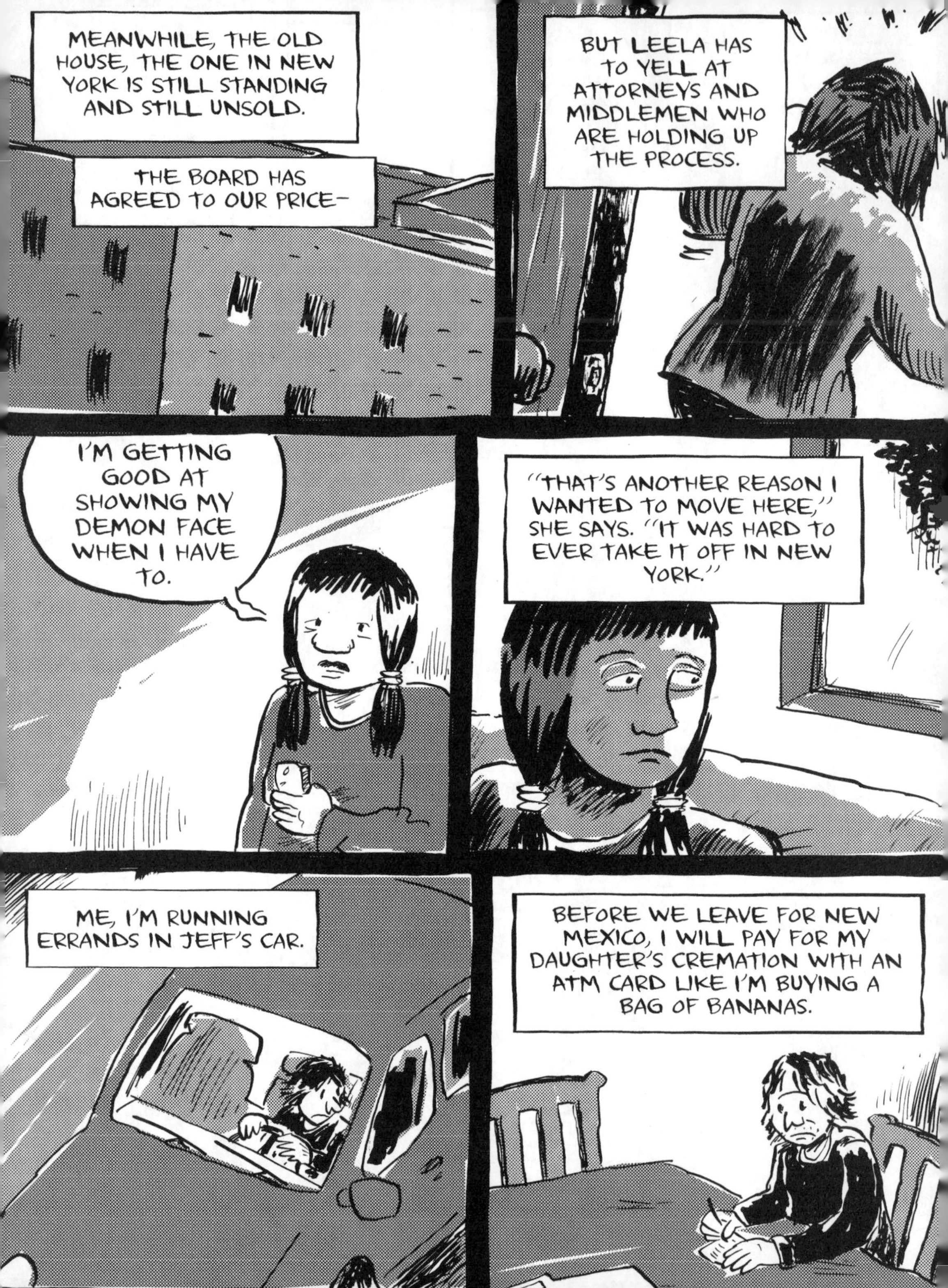
MEANWHILE, THE OLD HOUSE, THE ONE IN NEW YORK IS STILL STANDING AND STILL UNSOLD.
THE BOARD HAS AGREED TO OUR PRICE–
BUT LEELA HAS TO YELL AT ATTORNEYS AND MIDDLEMEN WHO ARE HOLDING UP THE PROCESS.
I'M GETTING GOOD AT SHOWING MY DEMON FACE WHEN I HAVE TO.
"THAT'S ANOTHER REASON I WANTED TO MOVE HERE," SHE SAYS. "IT WAS HARD TO EVER TAKE IT OFF IN NEW YORK."
ME, I'M RUNNING ERRANDS IN JEFF'S CAR.
BEFORE WE LEAVE FOR NEW MEXICO, I WILL PAY FOR MY DAUGHTER'S CREMATION WITH AN ATM CARD LIKE I'M BUYING A BAG OF BANANAS.

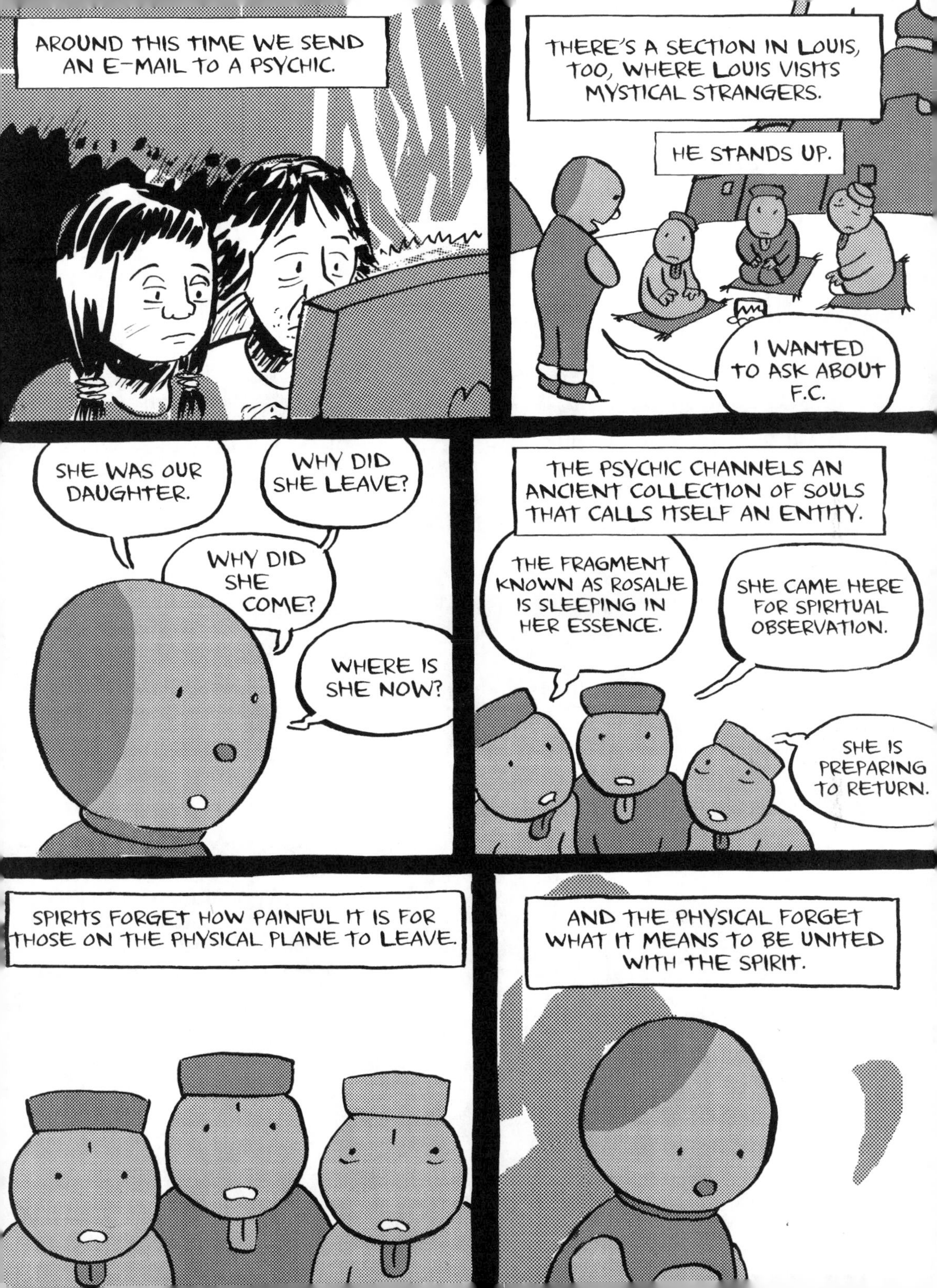
AROUND THIS TIME WE SEND AN E-MAIL TO A PSYCHIC.
THERE'S A SECTION IN LOUIS, TOO, WHERE LOUIS VISITS MYSTICAL STRANGERS.
HE STANDS UP.
I WANTED TO ASK ABOUT F.C.
SHE WAS OUR DAUGHTER.
WHY DID SHE LEAVE?
WHY DID SHE COME?
WHERE IS SHE NOW?
THE PSYCHIC CHANNELS AN ANCIENT COLLECTION OF SOULS THAT CALLS ITSELF AN ENTITY.
THE FRAGMENT KNOWN AS ROSALIE IS SLEEPING IN HER ESSENCE.
SHE CAME HERE FOR SPIRITUAL OBSERVATION.
SHE IS PREPARING TO RETURN.
SPIRITS FORGET HOW PAINFUL IT IS FOR THOSE ON THE PHYSICAL PLANE TO LEAVE.
AND THE PHYSICAL FORGET WHAT IT MEANS TO BE UNITED WITH THE SPIRIT.

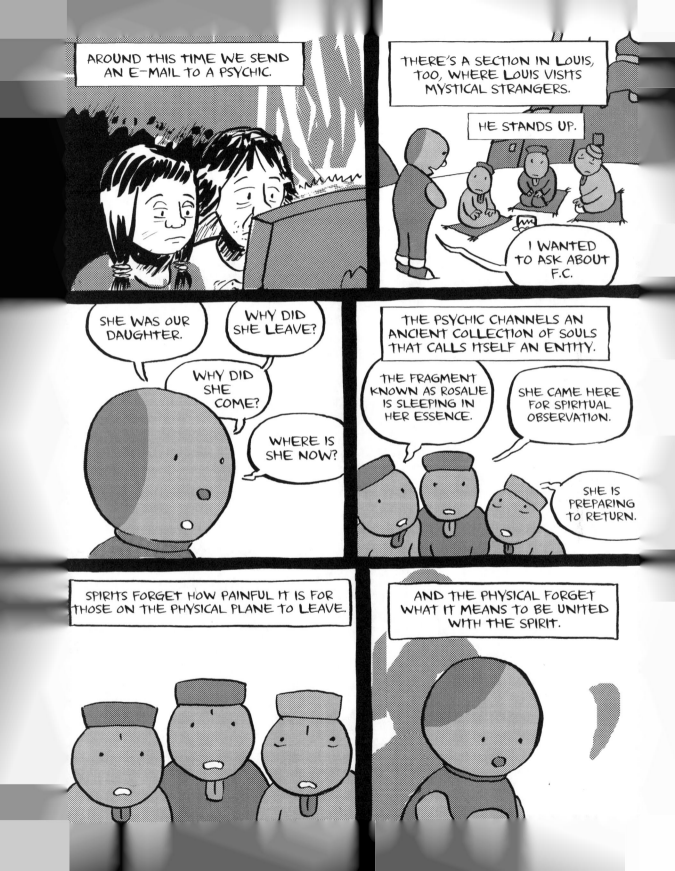

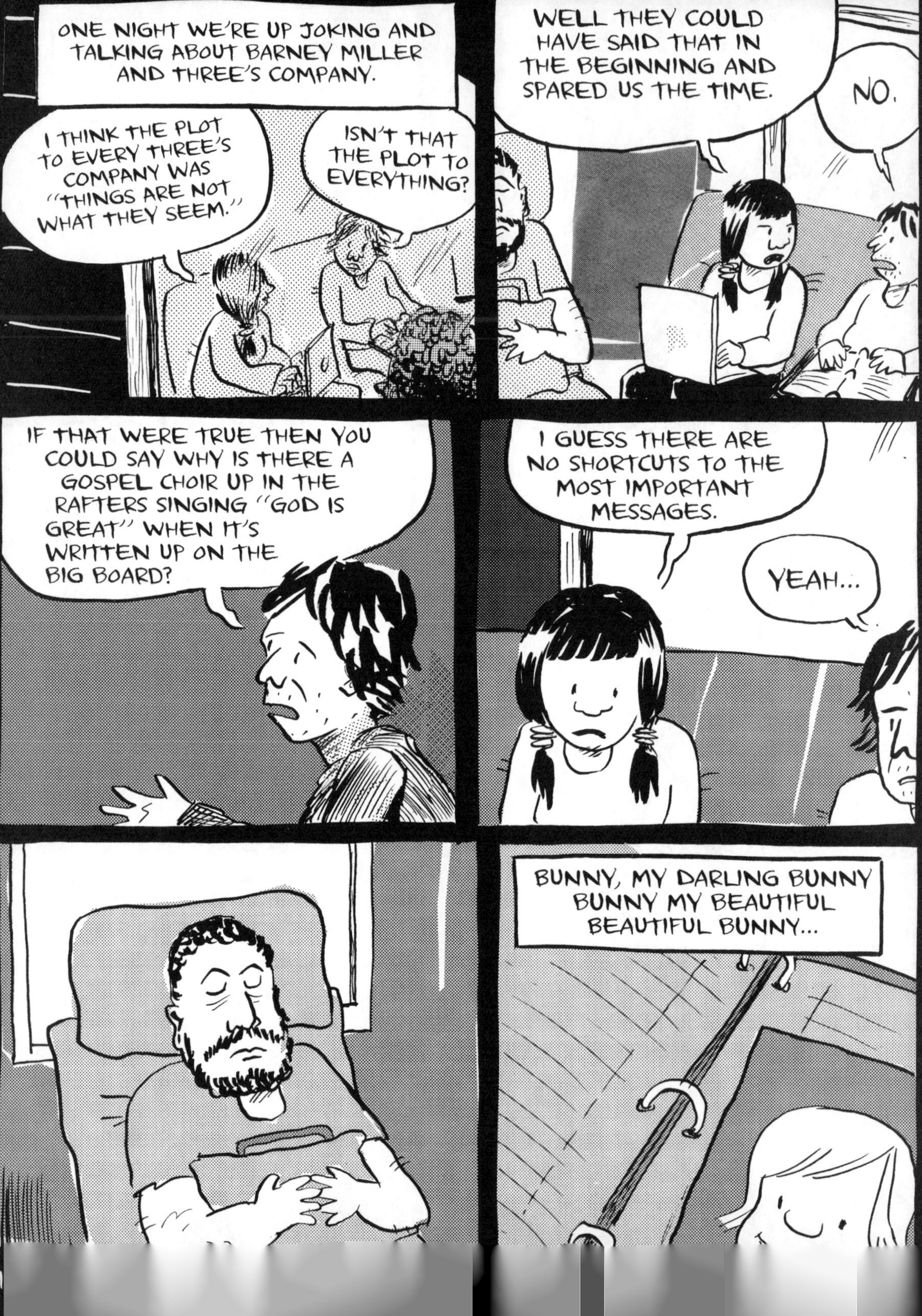
ONE NIGHT WE'RE UP JOKING AND TALKING ABOUT BARNEY MILLER AND THREE'S COMPANY.
I THINK THE PLOT TO EVERY THREE'S COMPANY WAS "THINGS ARE NOT WHAT THEY SEEM."
ISN'T THAT THE PLOT TO EVERYTHING?
WELL THEY COULD HAVE SAID THAT IN THE BEGINNING AND SPARED US THE TIME.
NO.
IF THAT WERE TRUE THEN YOU COULD SAY WHY IS THERE A GOSPEL CHOIR UP IN THE RAFTERS SINGING "GOD IS GREAT" WHEN IT'S WRITTEN UP ON THE BIG BOARD?
I GUESS THERE ARE NO SHORTCUTS TO THE MOST IMPORTANT MESSAGES.
YEAH...
BUNNY, MY DARLING BUNNY BUNNY MY BEAUTIFUL BEAUTIFUL BUNNY...

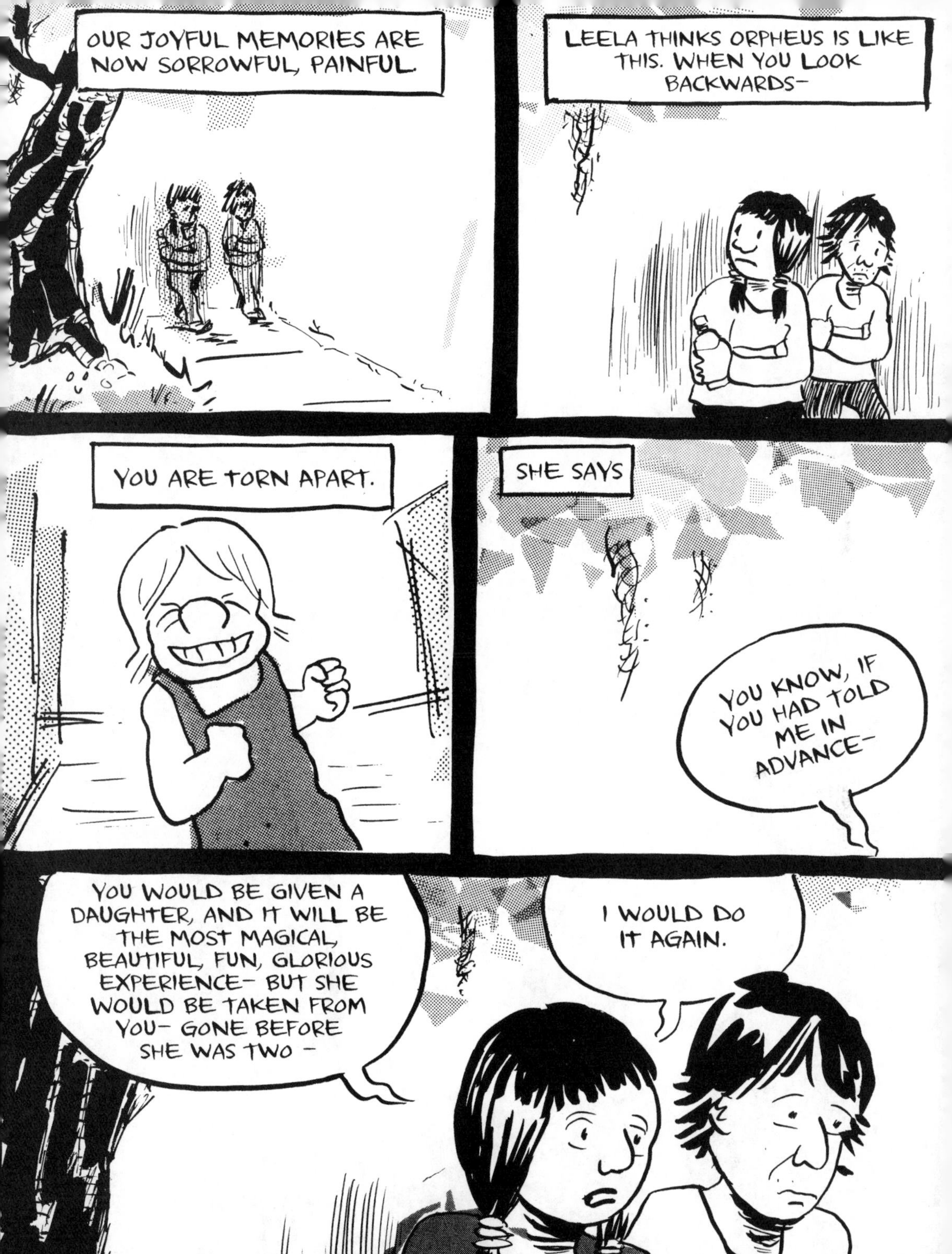
OUR JOYFUL MEMORIES ARE NOW SORROWFUL, PAINFUL.
LEELA THINKS ORPHEUS IS LIKE THIS. WHEN YOU LOOK BACKWARDS-
YOU ARE TORN APART.
SHE SAYS
YOU KNOW, IF YOU HAD TOLD ME IN ADVANCE-
YOU WOULD BE GIVEN A DAUGHTER, AND IT WILL BE THE MOST MAGICAL, BEAUTIFUL, FUN, GLORIOUS EXPERIENCE- BUT SHE WOULD BE TAKEN FROM YOU- GONE BEFORE SHE WAS TWO -
I WOULD DO IT AGAIN.

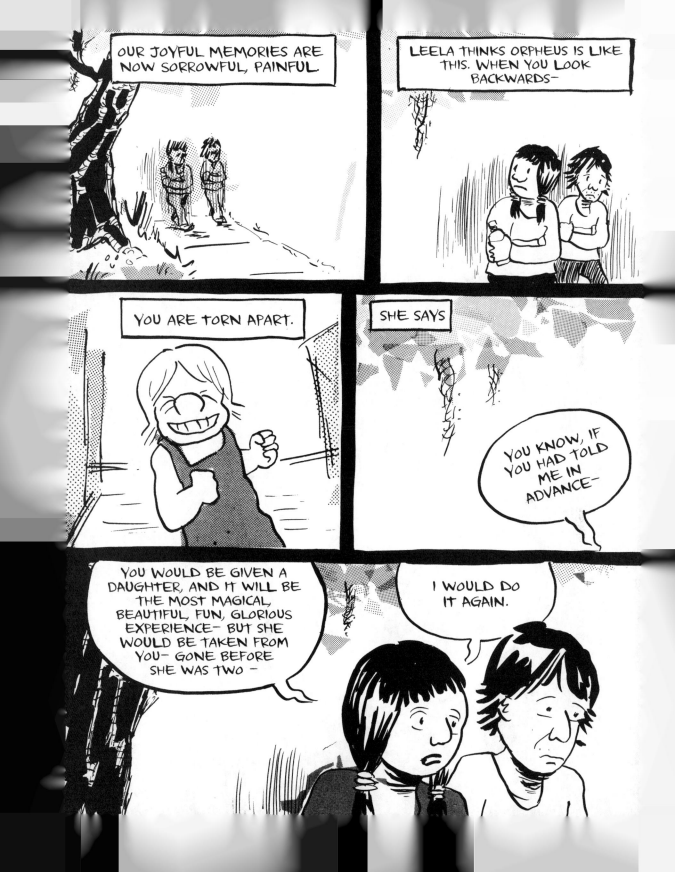

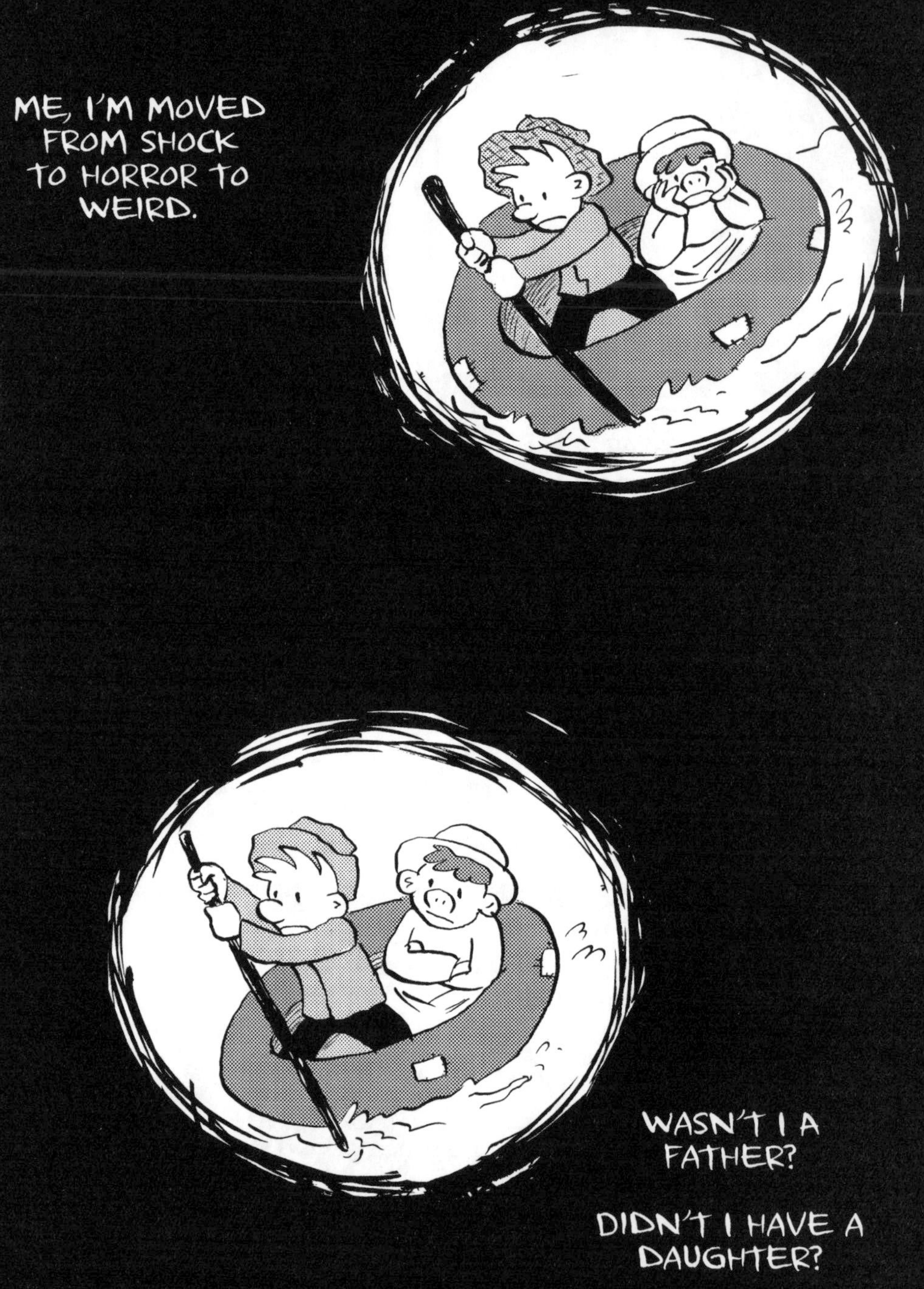
ME, I'M MOVED
FROM SHOCK
TO HORROR TO
WEIRD.
WASN'T I A
FATHER?
DIDN'T I HAVE A
DAUGHTER?

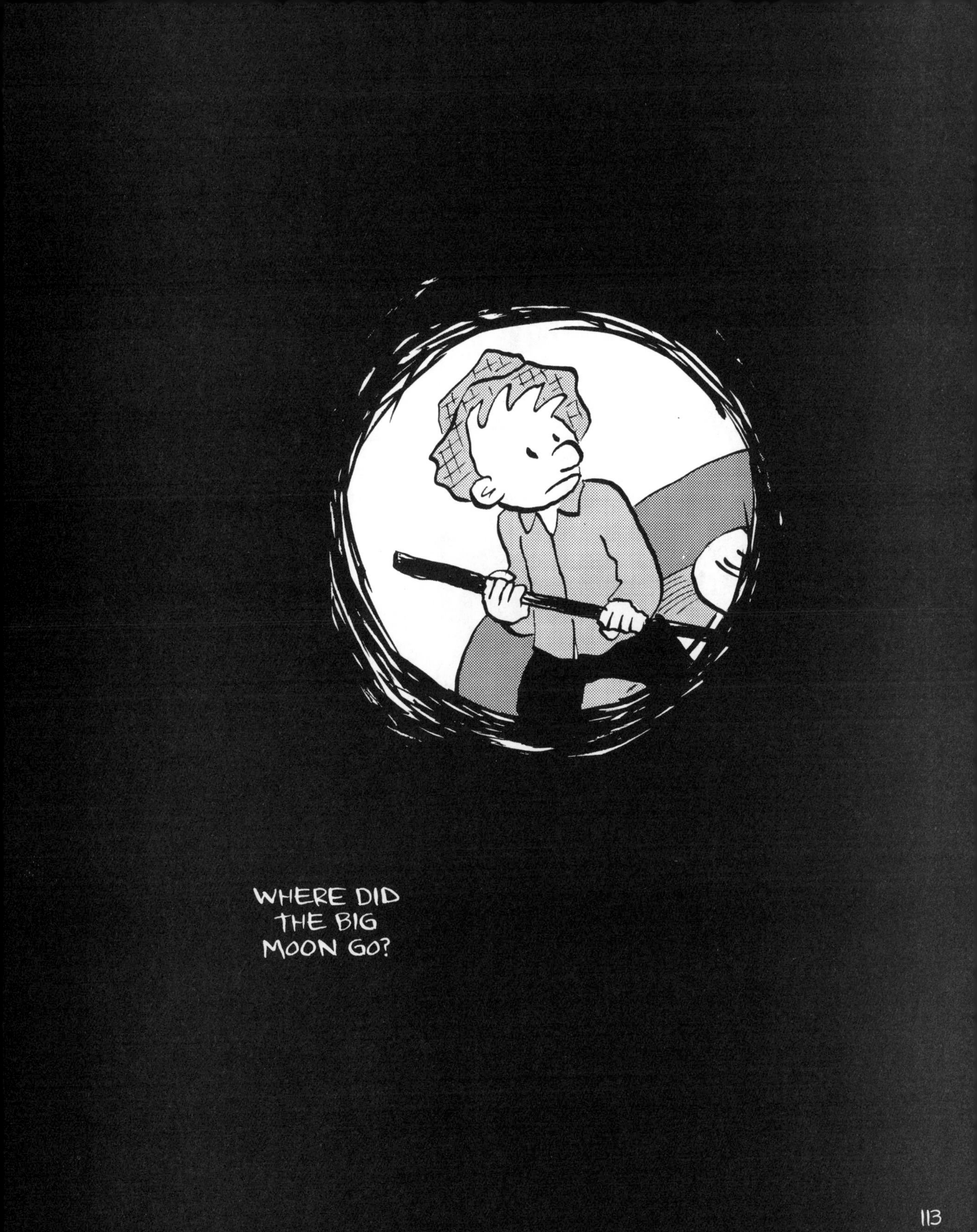
WHERE DID THE BIG MOON GO?

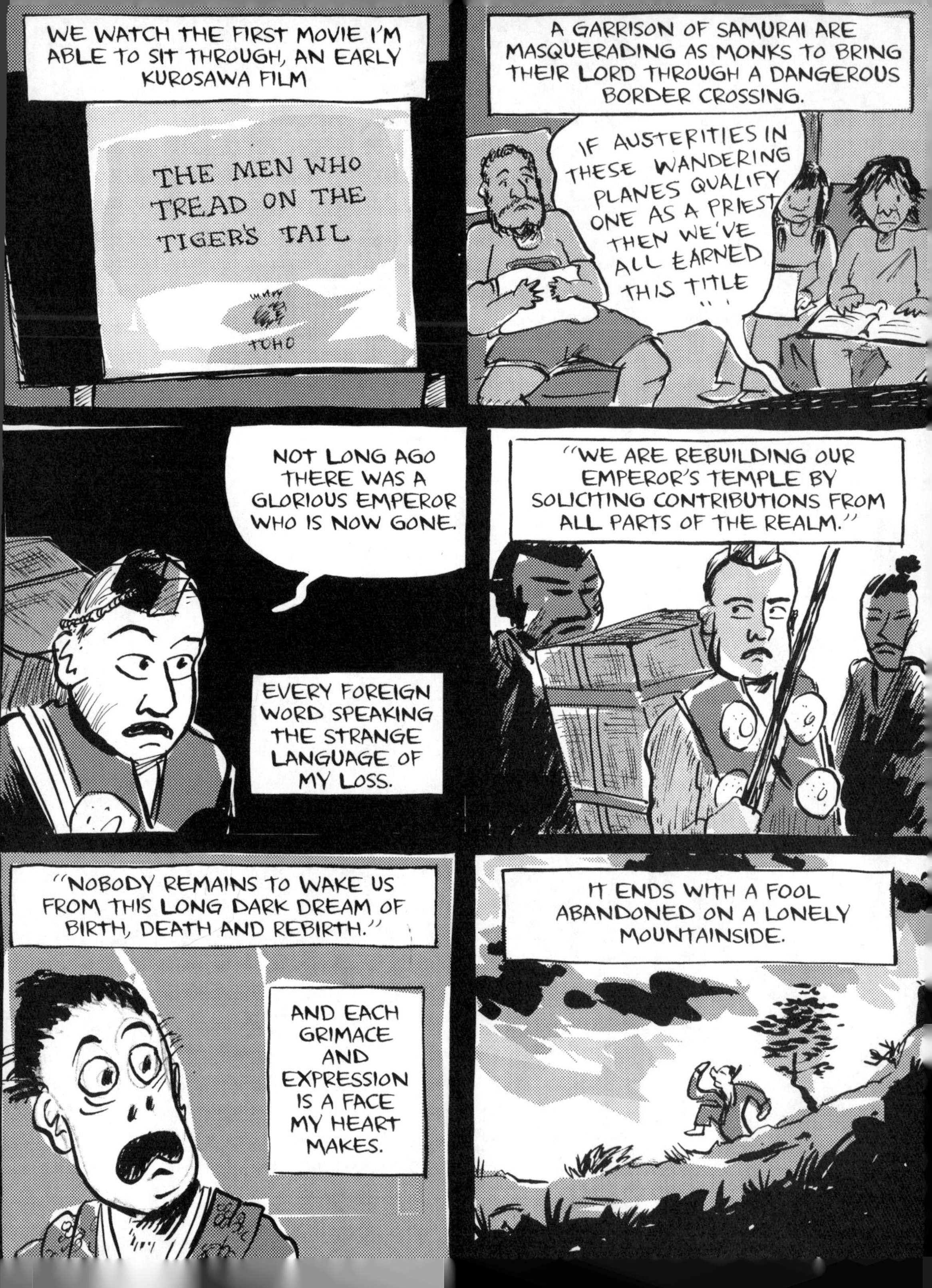
WE WATCH THE FIRST MOVIE I'M ABLE TO SIT THROUGH, AN EARLY KUROSAWA FILM
THE MEN WHO TREAD ON THE TIGER'S TAIL
TOHO
A GARRISON OF SAMURAI ARE MASQUERADING AS MONKS TO BRING THEIR LORD THROUGH A DANGEROUS BORDER CROSSING.
IF AUSTERITIES IN THESE WANDERING PLANES QUALIFY ONE AS A PRIEST THEN WE'VE ALL EARNED THIS TITLE . . .
NOT LONG AGO THERE WAS A GLORIOUS EMPEROR WHO IS NOW GONE.
EVERY FOREIGN WORD SPEAKING THE STRANGE LANGUAGE OF MY LOSS.
"WE ARE REBUILDING OUR EMPEROR'S TEMPLE BY SOLICITING CONTRIBUTIONS FROM ALL PARTS OF THE REALM."
"NOBODY REMAINS TO WAKE US FROM THIS LONG DARK DREAM OF BIRTH, DEATH AND REBIRTH."
AND EACH GRIMACE AND EXPRESSION IS A FACE MY HEART MAKES.
IT ENDS WITH A FOOL ABANDONED ON A LONELY MOUNTAINSIDE.

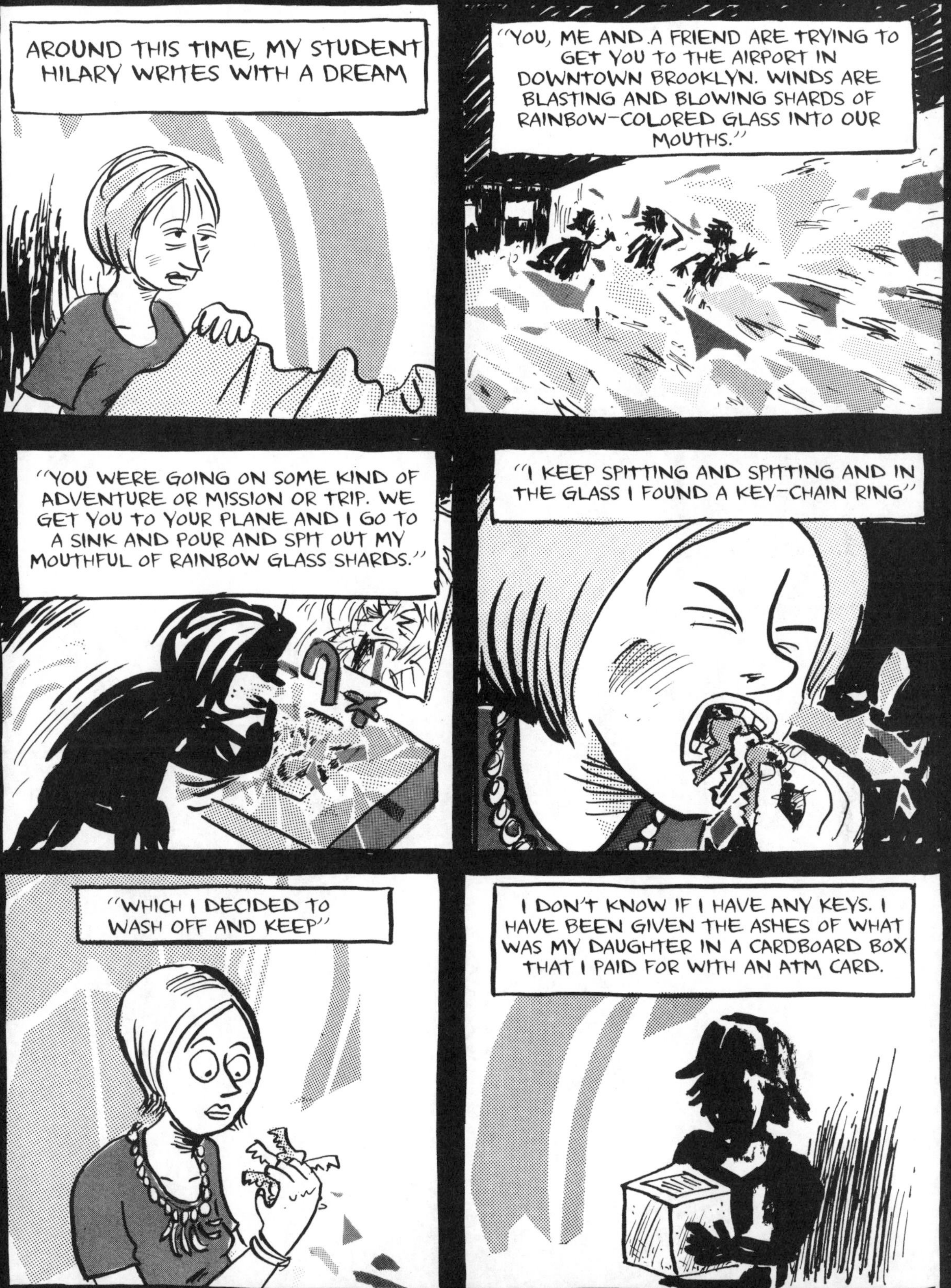
AROUND THIS TIME, MY STUDENT HILARY WRITES WITH A DREAM
"YOU, ME AND A FRIEND ARE TRYING TO GET YOU TO THE AIRPORT IN DOWNTOWN BROOKLYN. WINDS ARE BLASTING AND BLOWING SHARDS OF RAINBOW-COLORED GLASS INTO OUR MOUTHS."
"YOU WERE GOING ON SOME KIND OF ADVENTURE OR MISSION OR TRIP. WE GET YOU TO YOUR PLANE AND I GO TO A SINK AND POUR AND SPIT OUT MY MOUTHFUL OF RAINBOW GLASS SHARDS."
"I KEEP SPITTING AND SPITTING AND IN THE GLASS I FOUND A KEY-CHAIN RING"
"WHICH I DECIDED TO WASH OFF AND KEEP"
I DON'T KNOW IF I HAVE ANY KEYS. I HAVE BEEN GIVEN THE ASHES OF WHAT WAS MY DAUGHTER IN A CARDBOARD BOX THAT I PAID FOR WITH AN ATM CARD.

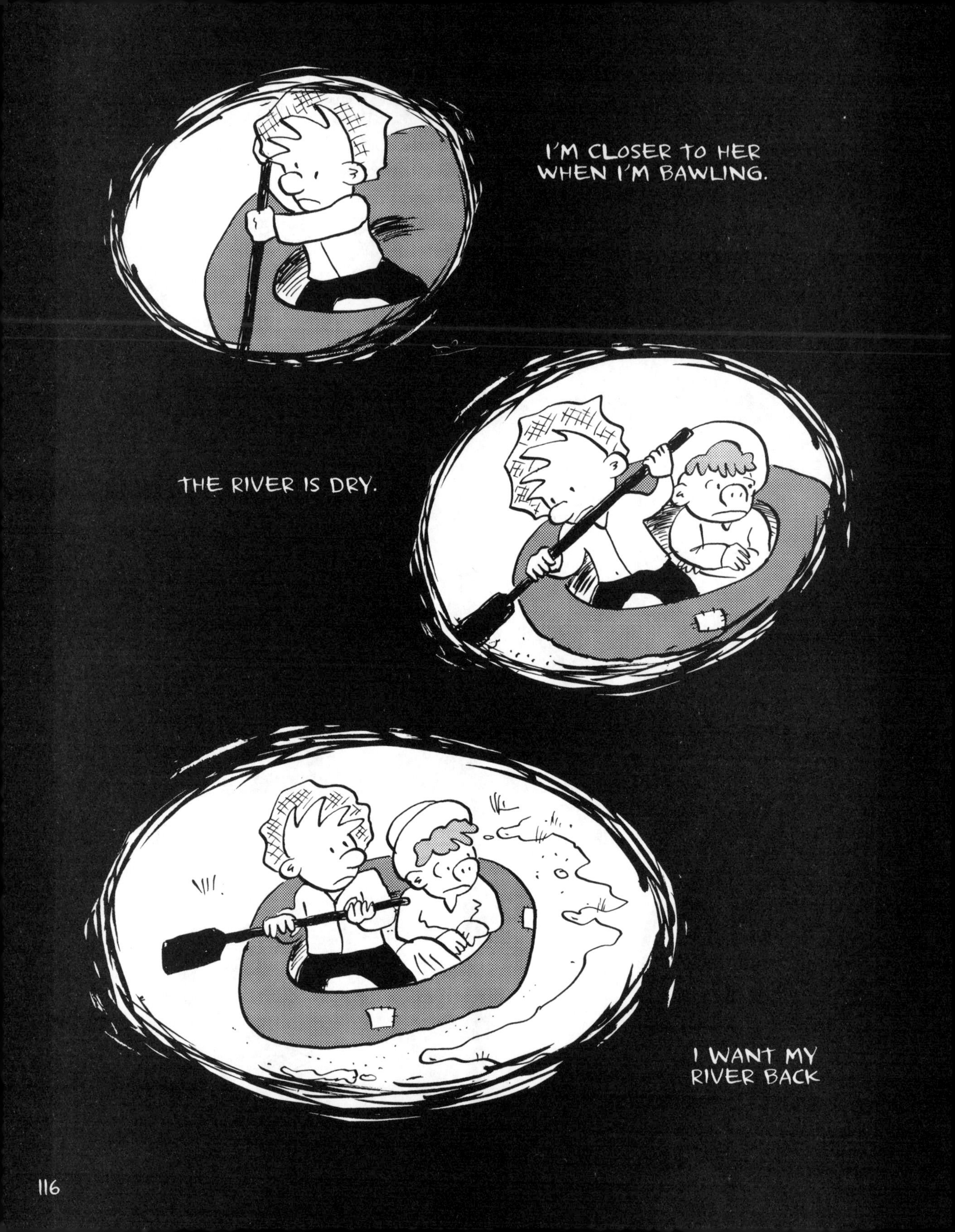
I'M CLOSER TO HER
WHEN I'M BAWLING.
THE RIVER IS DRY.
I WANT MY
RIVER BACK

VII

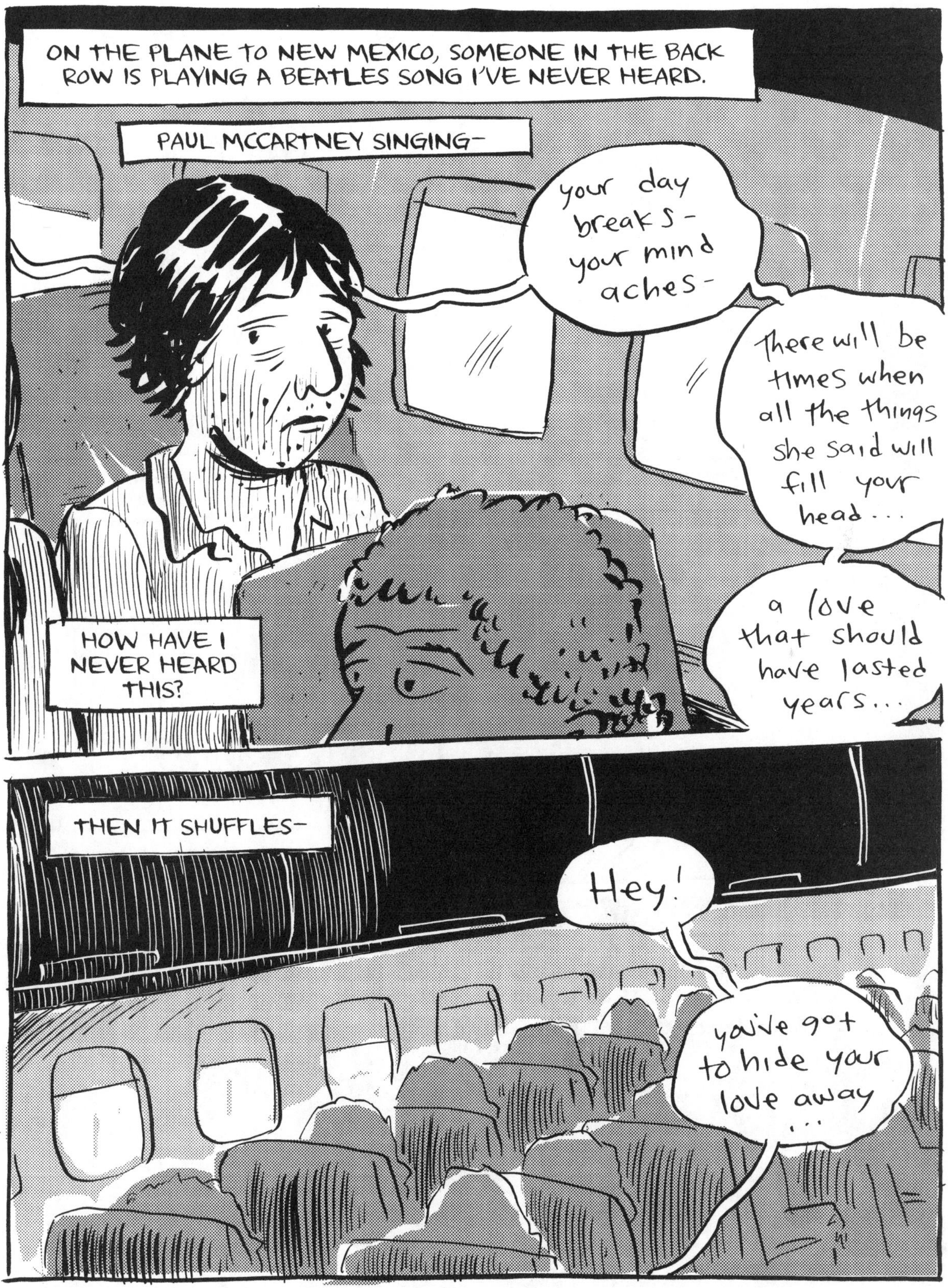
ON THE PLANE TO NEW MEXICO, SOMEONE IN THE BACK ROW IS PLAYING A BEATLES SONG I'VE NEVER HEARD.
PAUL MCCARTNEY SINGING–
your day breaks- your mind aches-
there will be times when all the things she said will fill your head...
HOW HAVE I NEVER HEARD THIS?
a love that should have lasted years...
THEN IT SHUFFLES–
Hey!
you've got to hide your love away ...

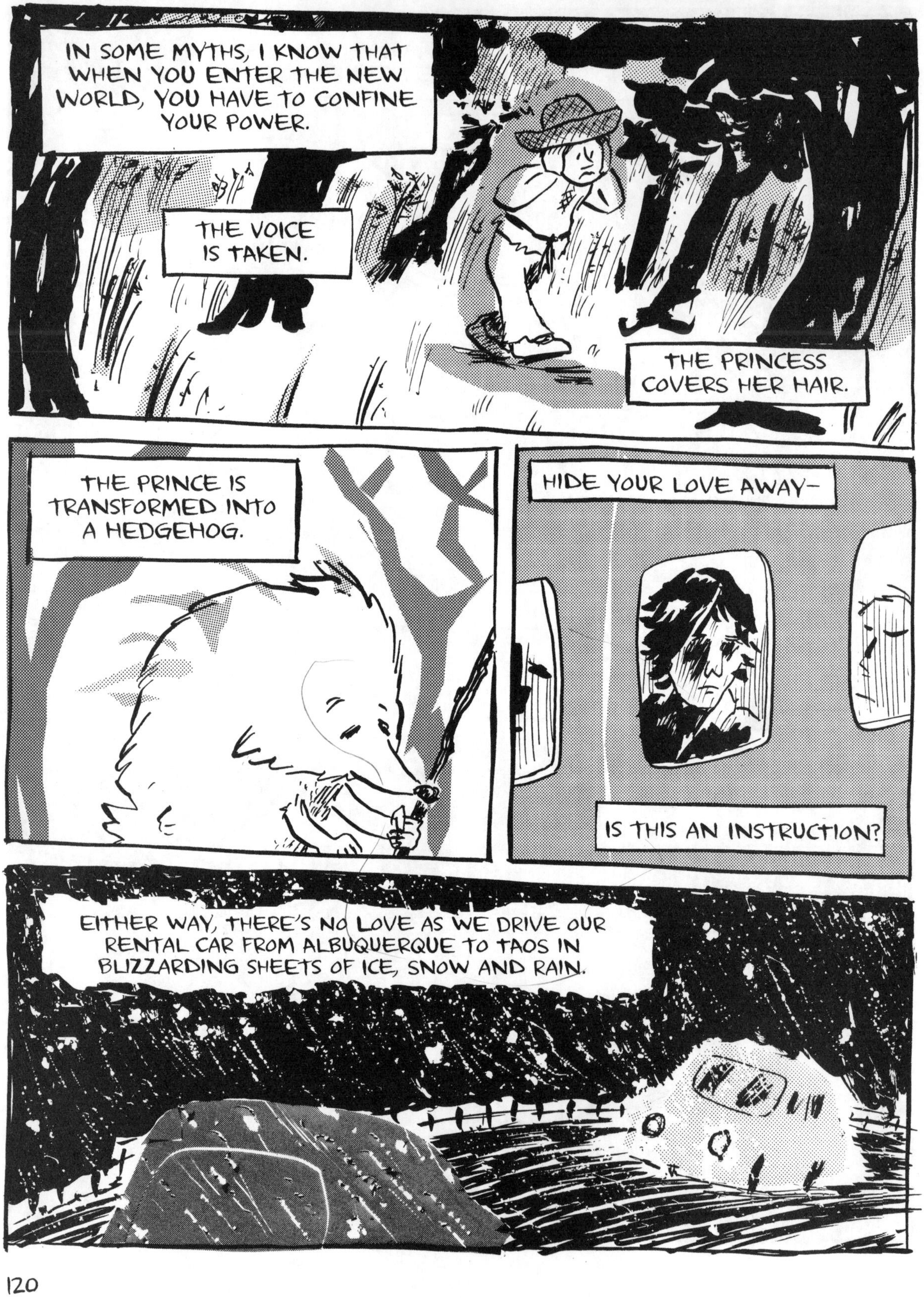
IN SOME MYTHS, I KNOW THAT WHEN YOU ENTER THE NEW WORLD, YOU HAVE TO CONFINE YOUR POWER.
THE VOICE IS TAKEN.
THE PRINCESS COVERS HER HAIR.
THE PRINCE IS TRANSFORMED INTO A HEDGEHOG.
HIDE YOUR LOVE AWAY-
IS THIS AN INSTRUCTION?
EITHER WAY, THERE'S NO LOVE AS WE DRIVE OUR RENTAL CAR FROM ALBUQUERQUE TO TAOS IN BLIZZARDING SHEETS OF ICE, SNOW AND RAIN.

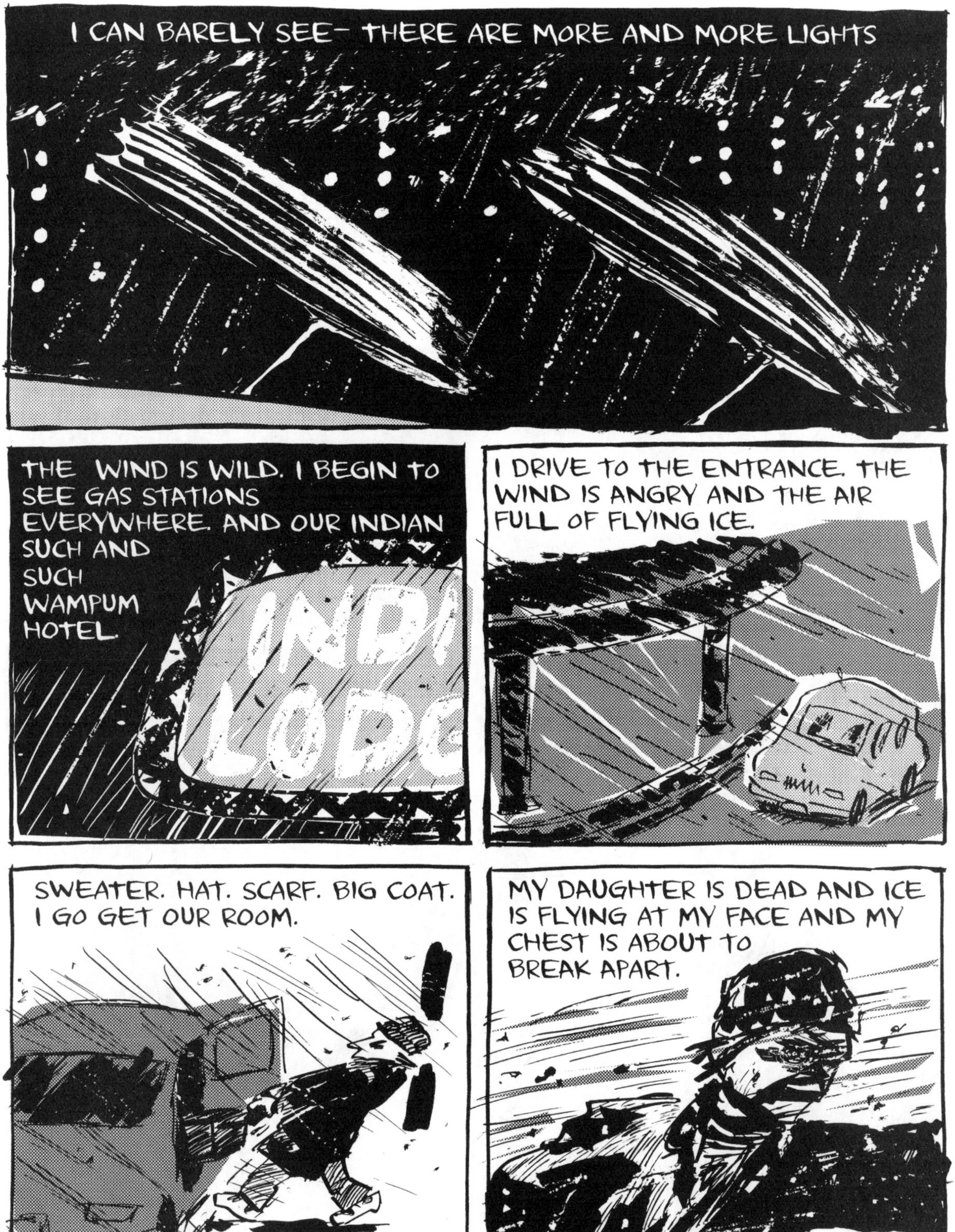
I CAN BARELY SEE- THERE ARE MORE AND MORE LIGHTS
THE WIND IS WILD. I BEGIN TO SEE GAS STATIONS EVERYWHERE. AND OUR INDIAN SUCH AND SUCH WAMPUM HOTEL.
I DRIVE TO THE ENTRANCE. THE WIND IS ANGRY AND THE AIR FULL OF FLYING ICE.
SWEATER. HAT. SCARF. BIG COAT. I GO GET OUR ROOM.
MY DAUGHTER IS DEAD AND ICE IS FLYING AT MY FACE AND MY CHEST IS ABOUT TO BREAK APART.

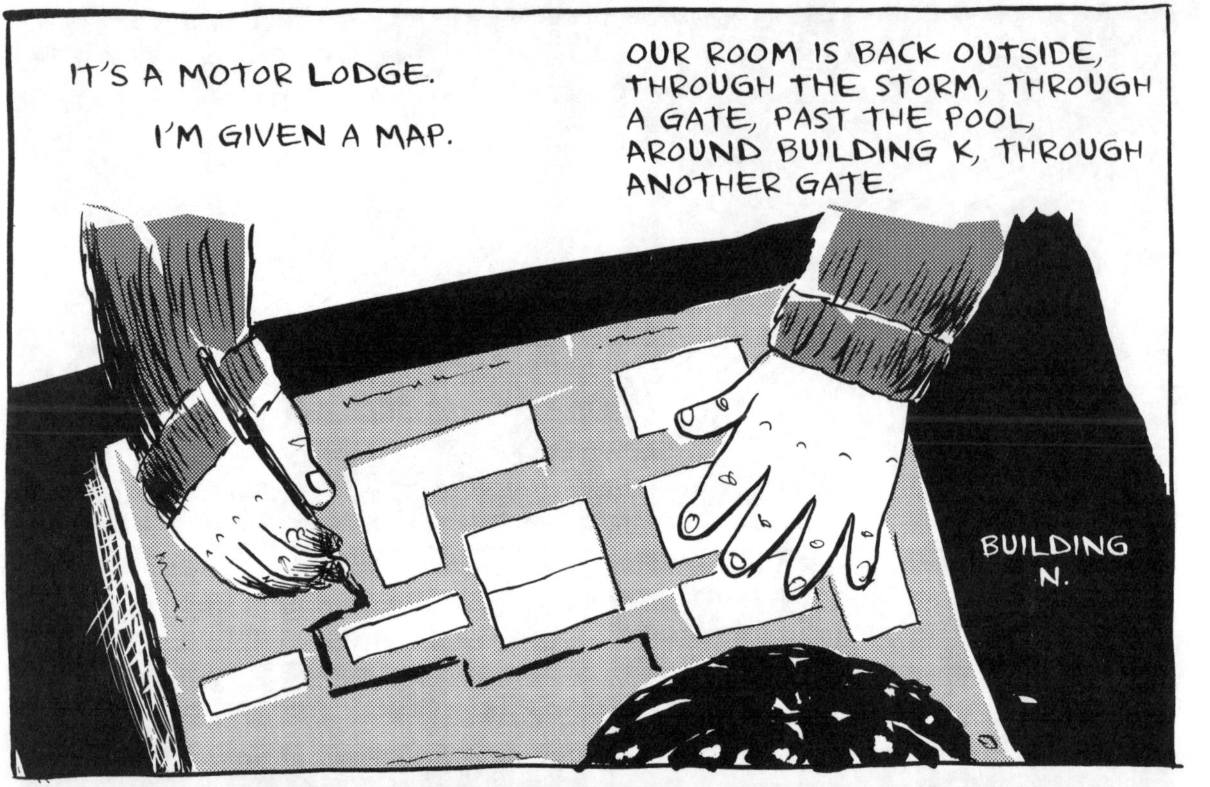
IT'S A MOTOR LODGE.
I'M GIVEN A MAP.
OUR ROOM IS BACK OUTSIDE, THROUGH THE STORM, THROUGH A GATE, PAST THE POOL, AROUND BUILDING K, THROUGH ANOTHER GATE.
BUILDING N.

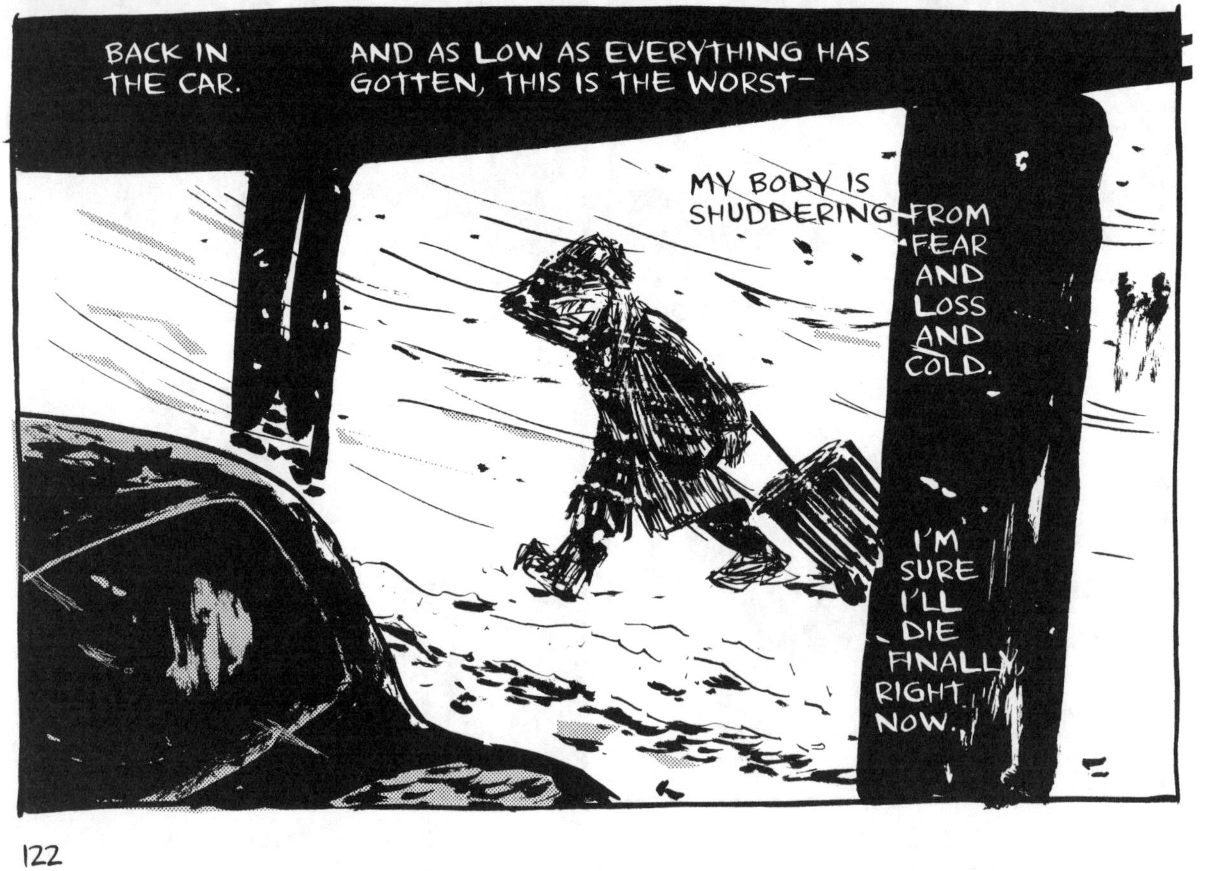
BACK IN THE CAR.
AND AS LOW AS EVERYTHING HAS GOTTEN, THIS IS THE WORST—
MY BODY IS SHUDDERING FROM FEAR AND LOSS AND COLD.
I'M SURE I'LL DIE FINALLY, RIGHT NOW.

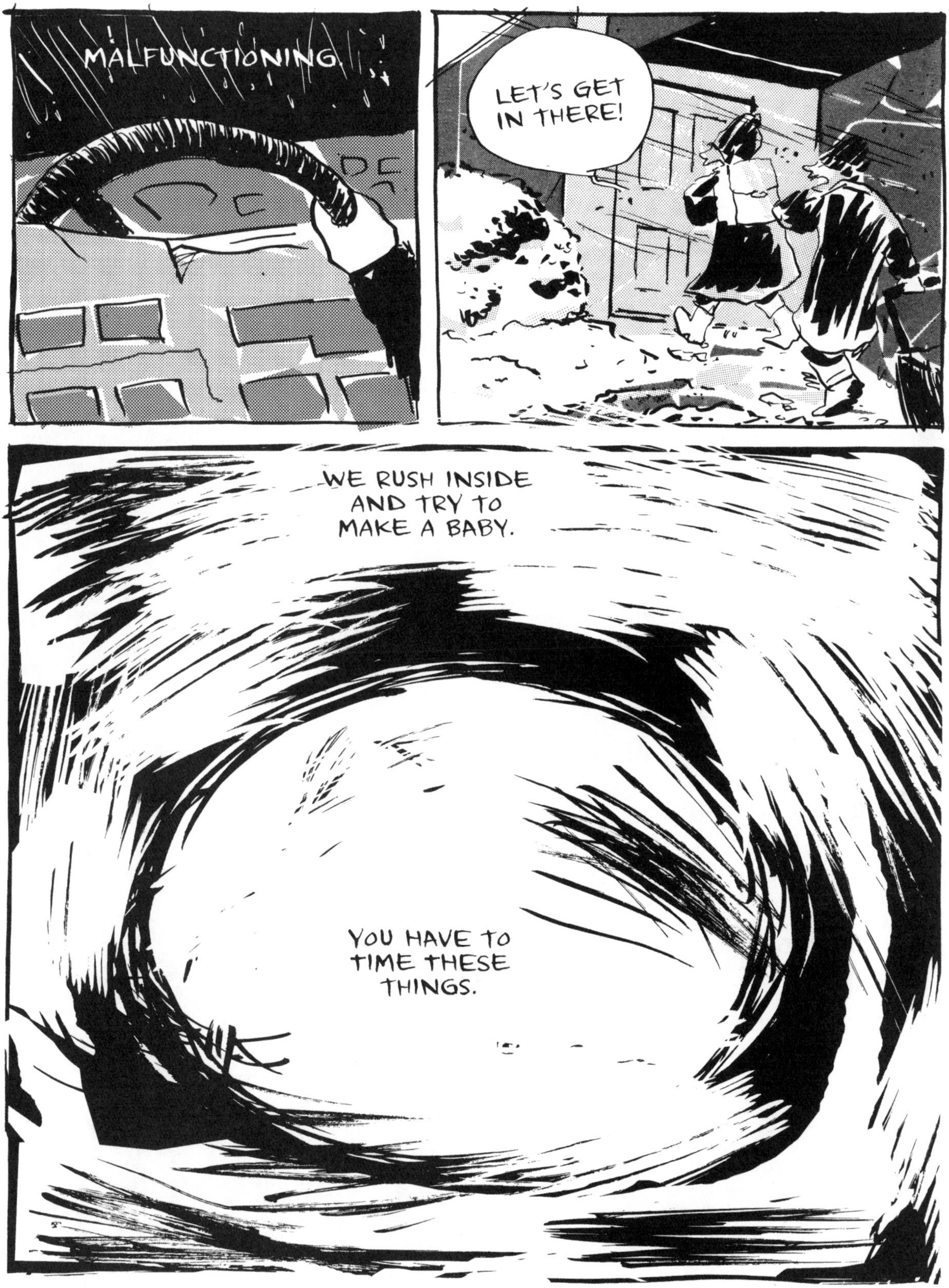
MALFUNCTIONING.
LET'S GET IN THERE!
WE RUSH INSIDE AND TRY TO MAKE A BABY.
YOU HAVE TO TIME THESE THINGS.

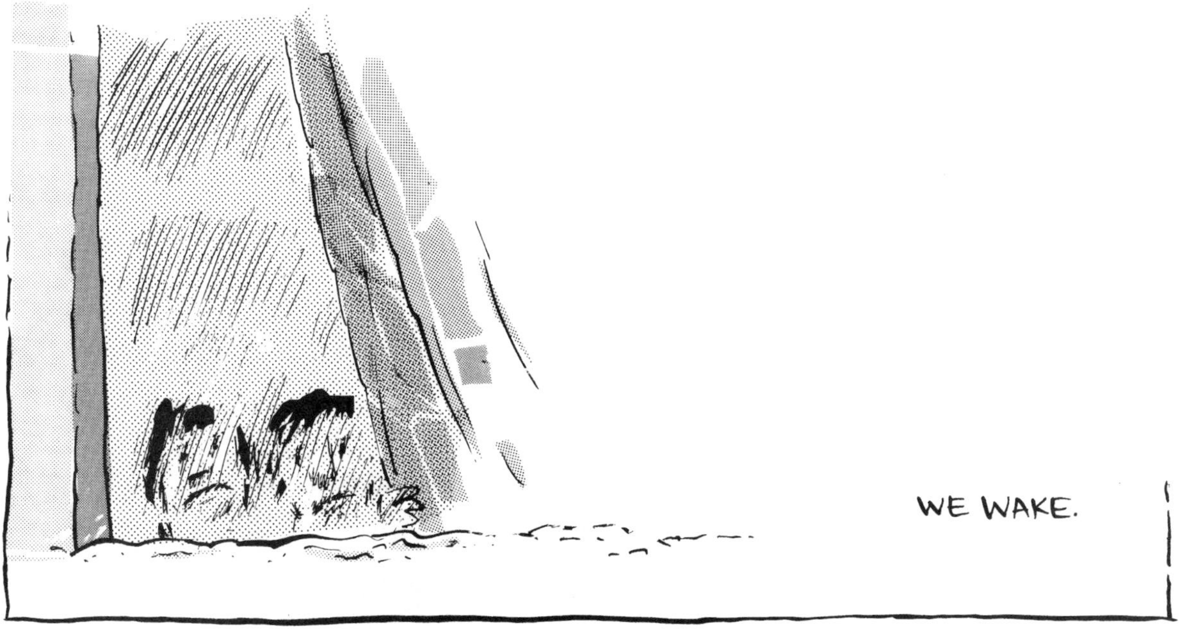
WE WAKE.
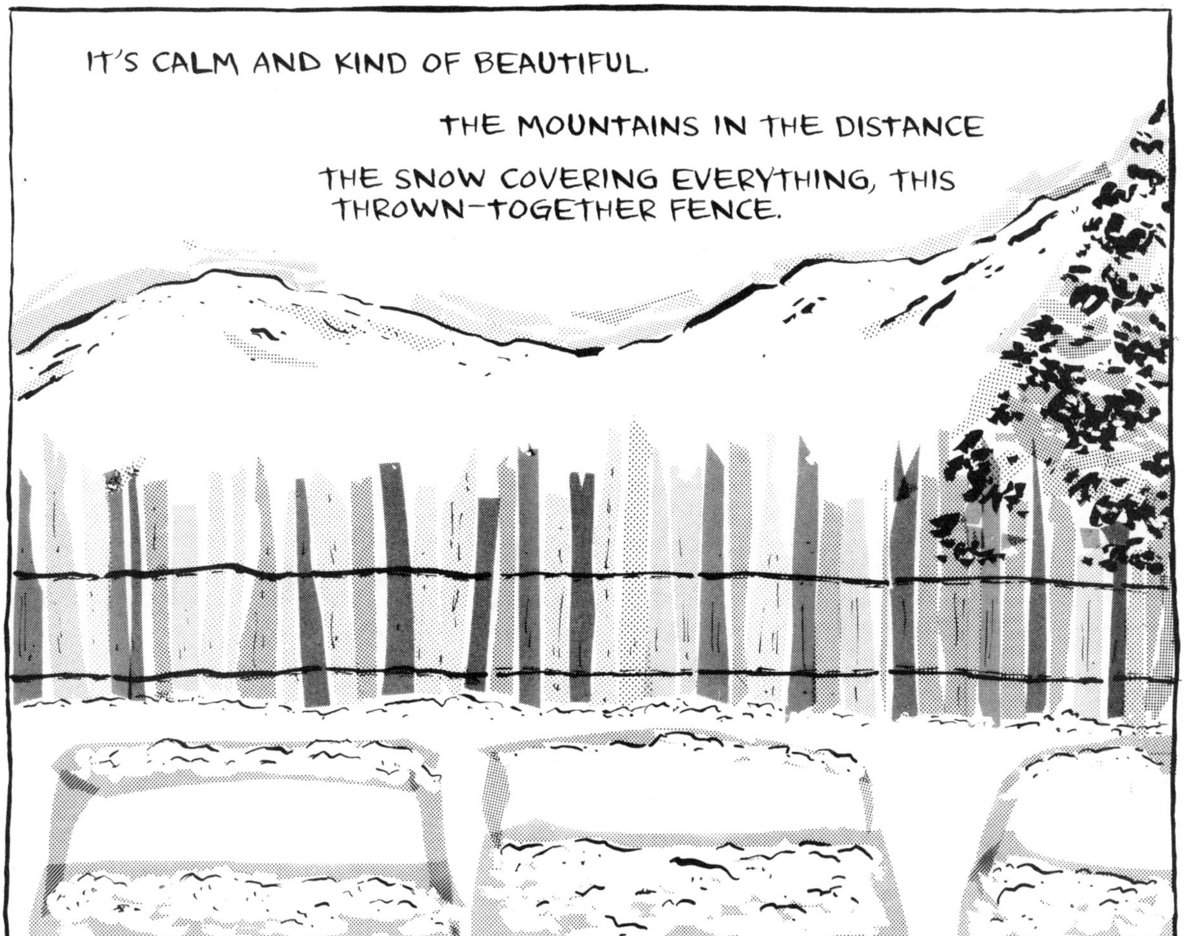
IT'S CALM AND KIND OF BEAUTIFUL.
THE MOUNTAINS IN THE DISTANCE
THE SNOW COVERING EVERYTHING, THIS THROWN-TOGETHER FENCE.

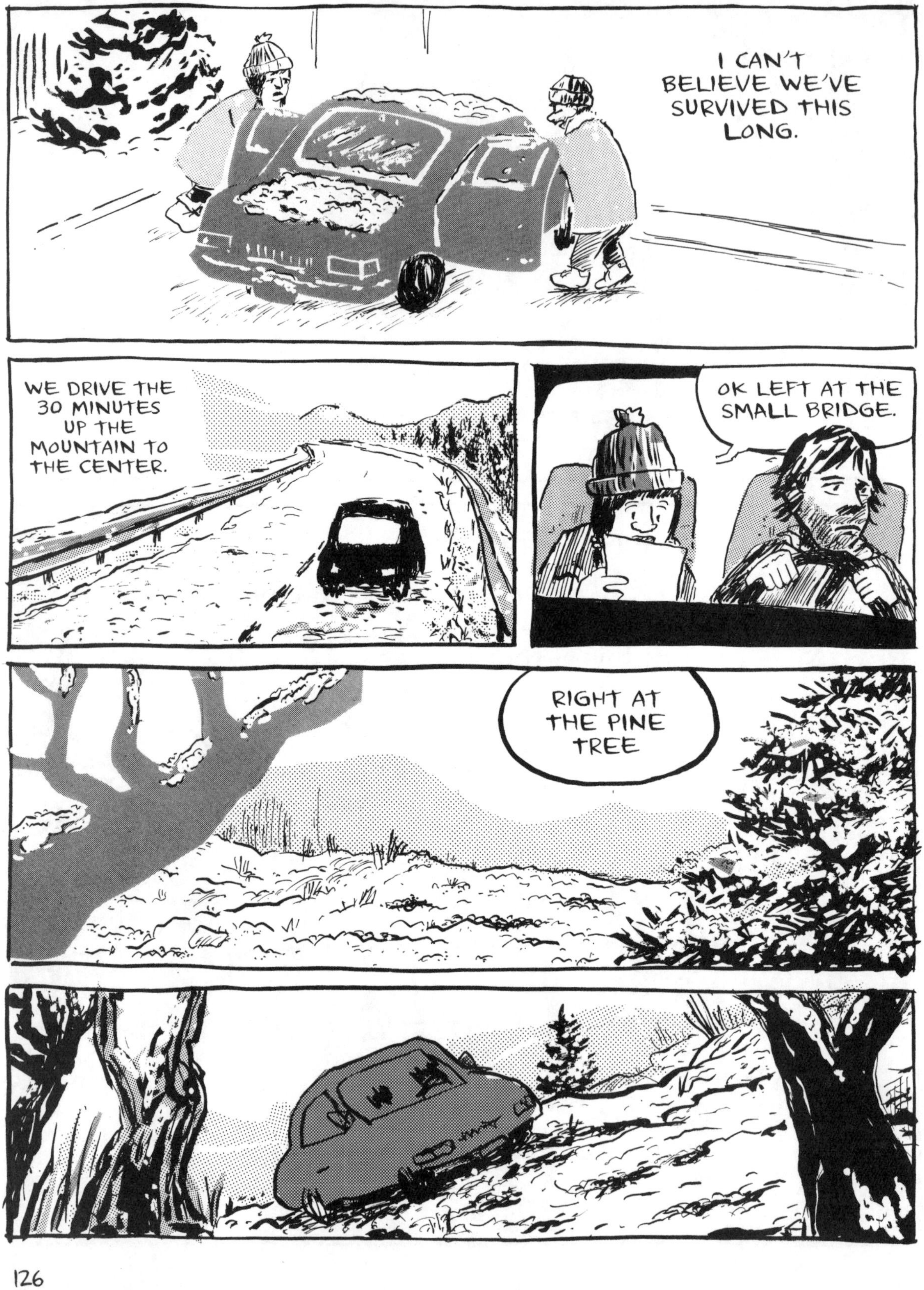
I CAN'T BELIEVE WE'VE SURVIVED THIS LONG.
WE DRIVE THE 30 MINUTES UP THE MOUNTAIN TO THE CENTER.
OK LEFT AT THE SMALL BRIDGE.
RIGHT AT THE PINE TREE

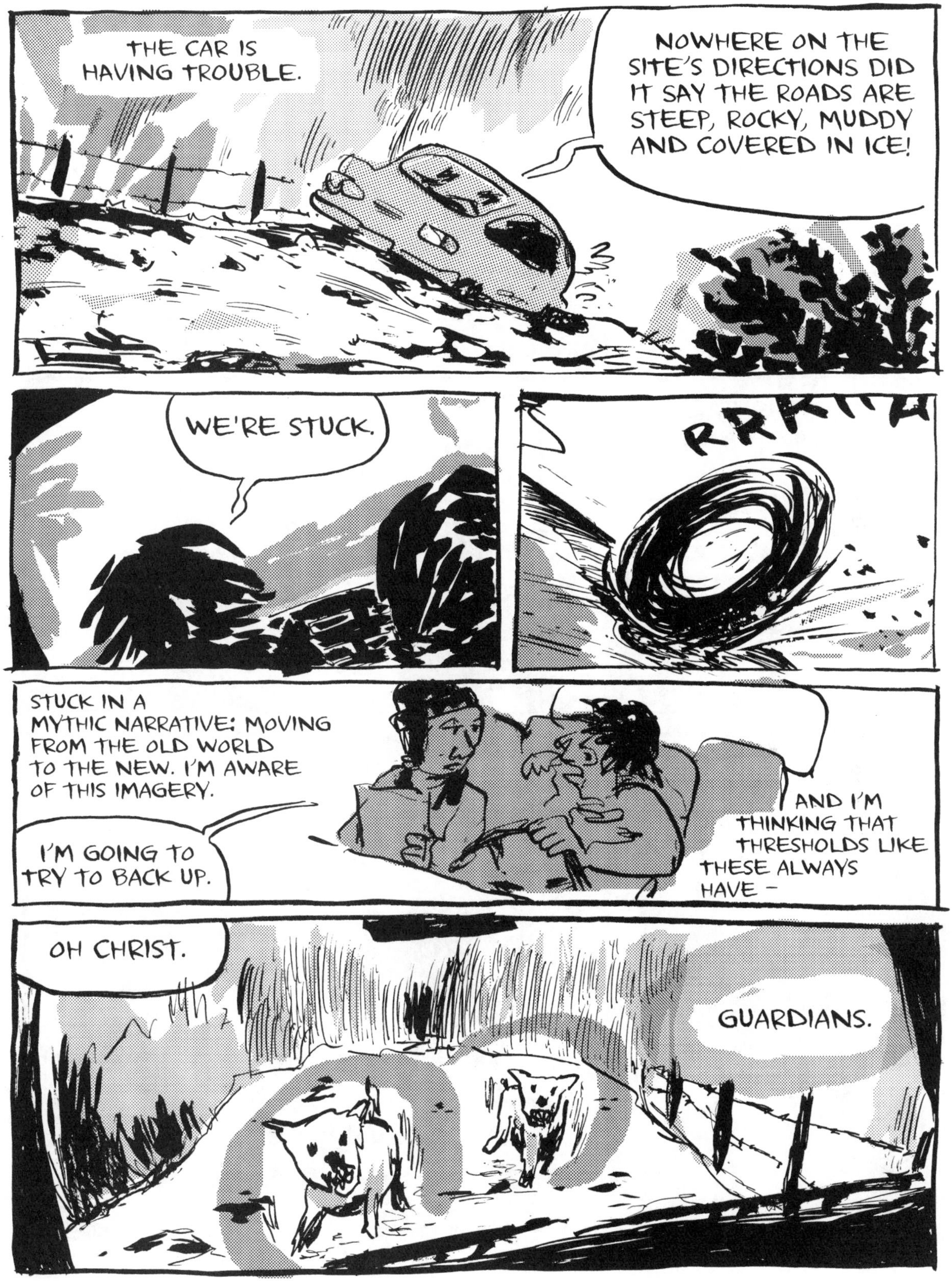
THE CAR IS HAVING TROUBLE.
NOWHERE ON THE SITE'S DIRECTIONS DID IT SAY THE ROADS ARE STEEP, ROCKY, MUDDY AND COVERED IN ICE!
WE'RE STUCK.
RRRRRR
STUCK IN A MYTHIC NARRATIVE: MOVING FROM THE OLD WORLD TO THE NEW. I'M AWARE OF THIS IMAGERY.
I'M GOING TO TRY TO BACK UP.
AND I'M THINKING THAT THRESHOLDS LIKE THESE ALWAYS HAVE –
OH CHRIST.
GUARDIANS.

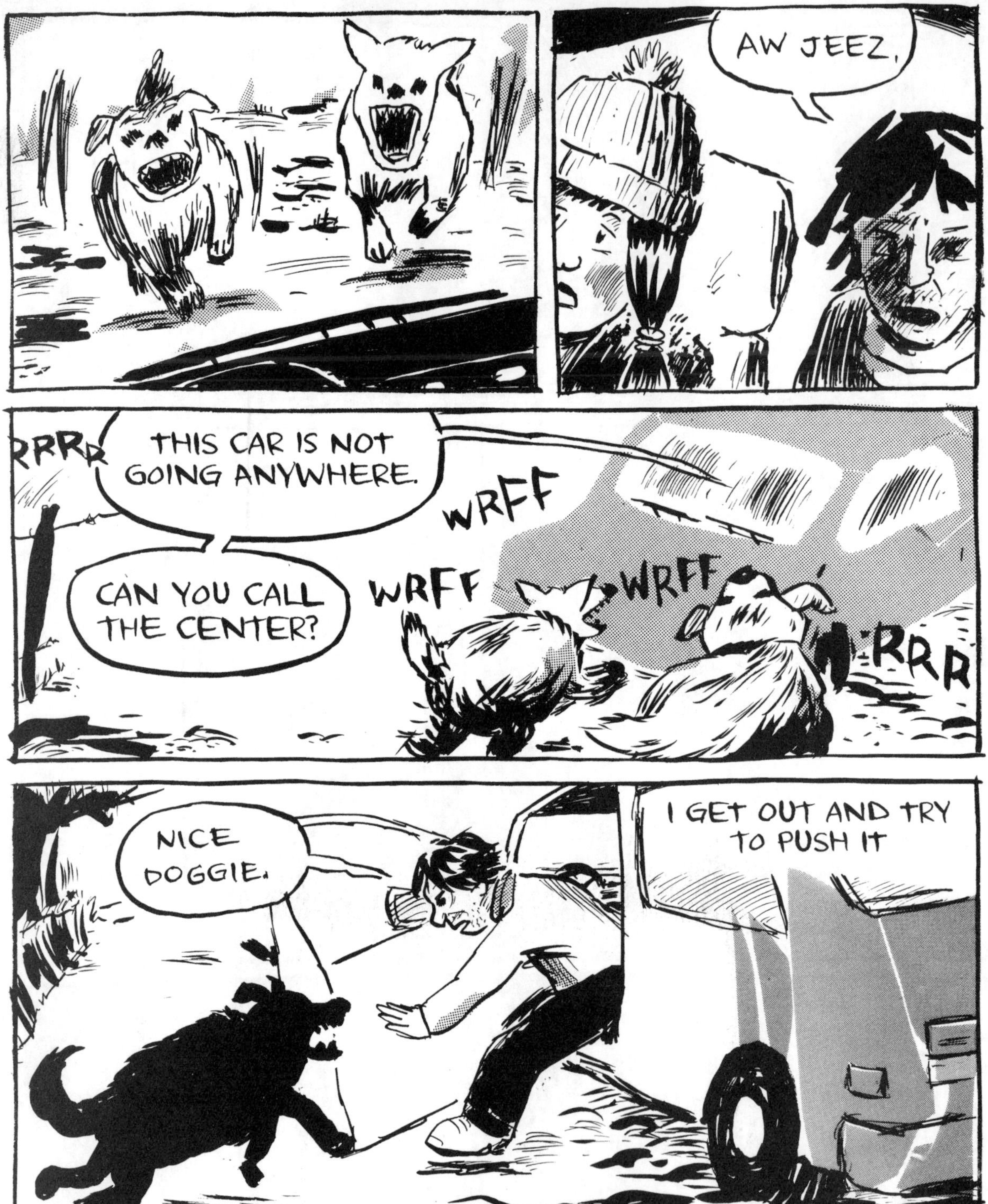
AW JEEZ.
RRRR
THIS CAR IS NOT GOING ANYWHERE.
WRFF
CAN YOU CALL THE CENTER?
WRFF
WRFF
RRRR
NICE DOGGIE.
I GET OUT AND TRY TO PUSH IT

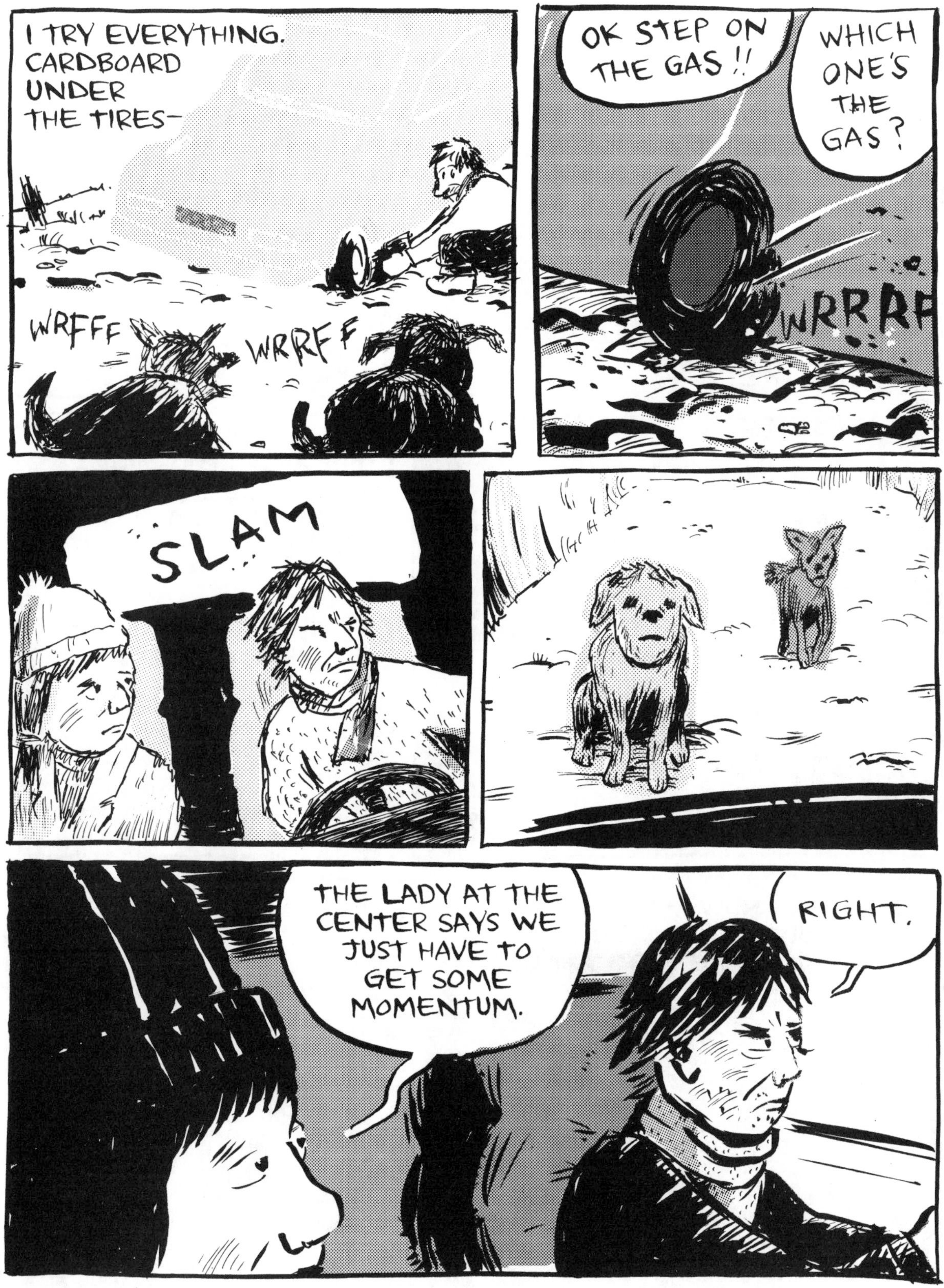

I TRY EVERYTHING. CARDBOARD UNDER THE TIRES–
WRFFF
WRRFF
OK STEP ON THE GAS !!
WHICH ONE'S THE GAS ?
WRRRP
SLAM
THE LADY AT THE CENTER SAYS WE JUST HAVE TO GET SOME MOMENTUM.
RIGHT.

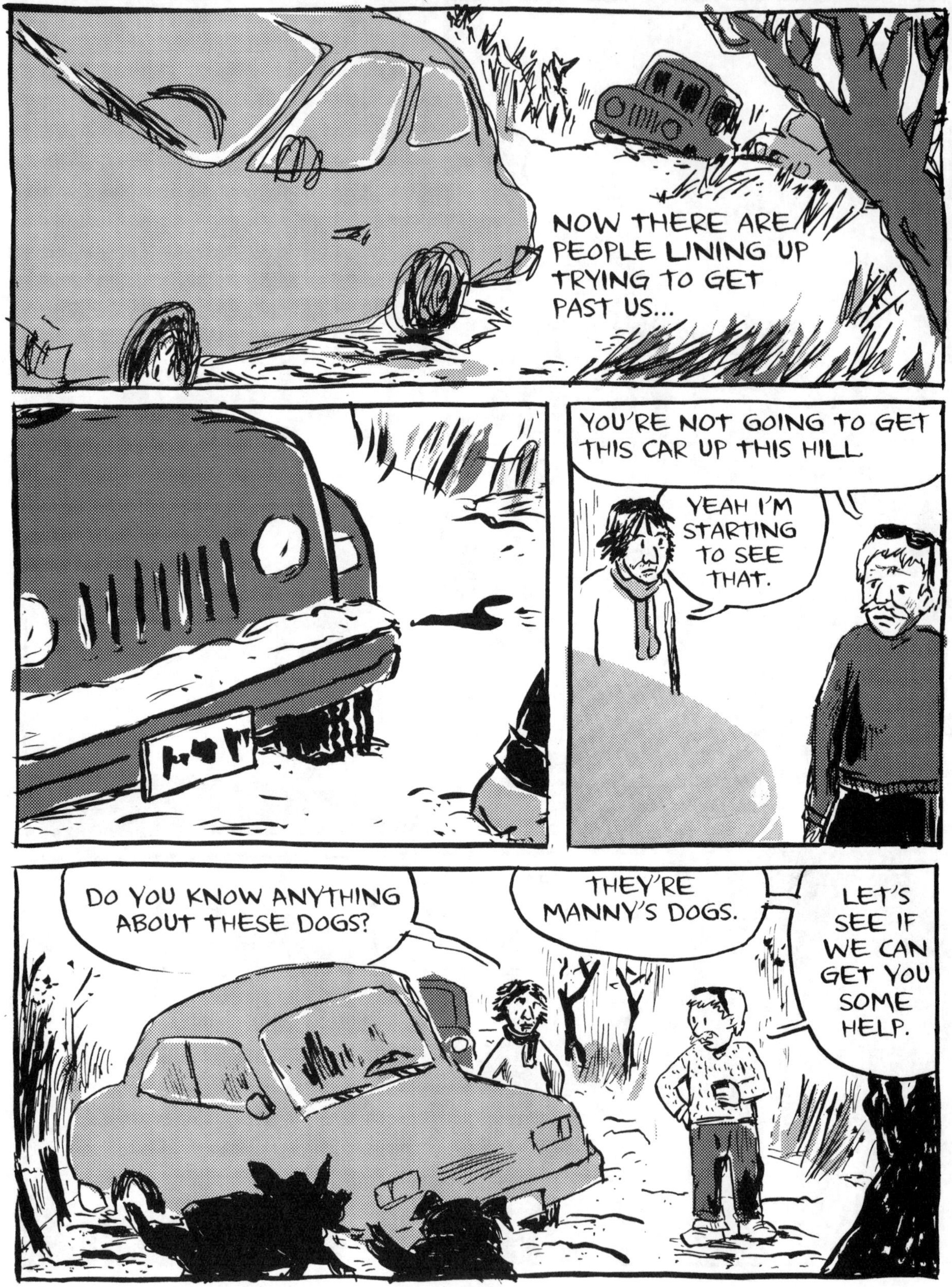
NOW THERE ARE PEOPLE LINING UP TRYING TO GET PAST US...
YOU'RE NOT GOING TO GET THIS CAR UP THIS HILL.
YEAH I'M STARTING TO SEE THAT.
DO YOU KNOW ANYTHING ABOUT THESE DOGS?
THEY'RE MANNY'S DOGS.
LET'S SEE IF WE CAN GET YOU SOME HELP.

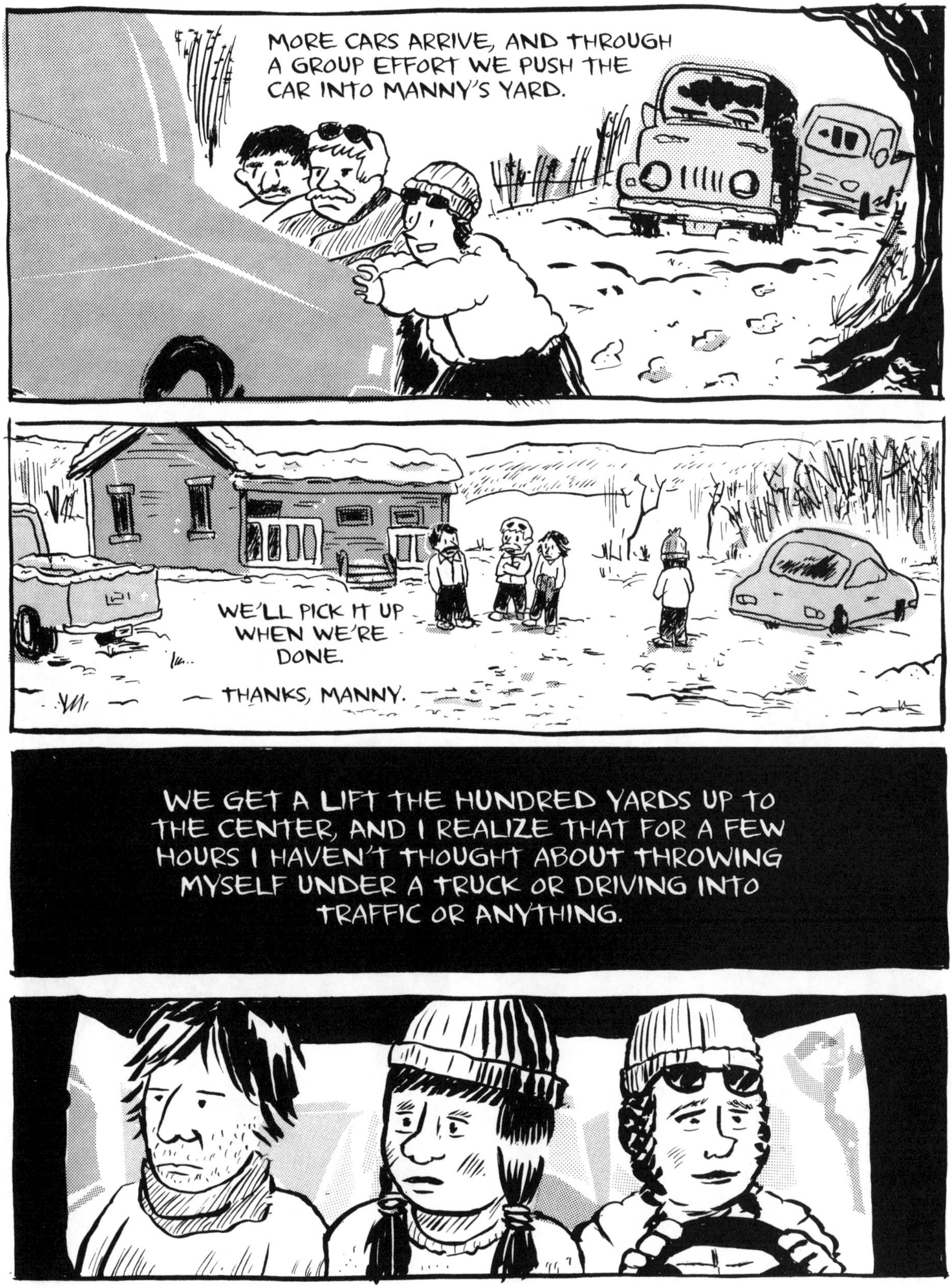
MORE CARS ARRIVE, AND THROUGH A GROUP EFFORT WE PUSH THE CAR INTO MANNY'S YARD.
WE'LL PICK IT UP WHEN WE'RE DONE.
THANKS, MANNY.
WE GET A LIFT THE HUNDRED YARDS UP TO THE CENTER, AND I REALIZE THAT FOR A FEW HOURS I HAVEN'T THOUGHT ABOUT THROWING MYSELF UNDER A TRUCK OR DRIVING INTO TRAFFIC OR ANYTHING.

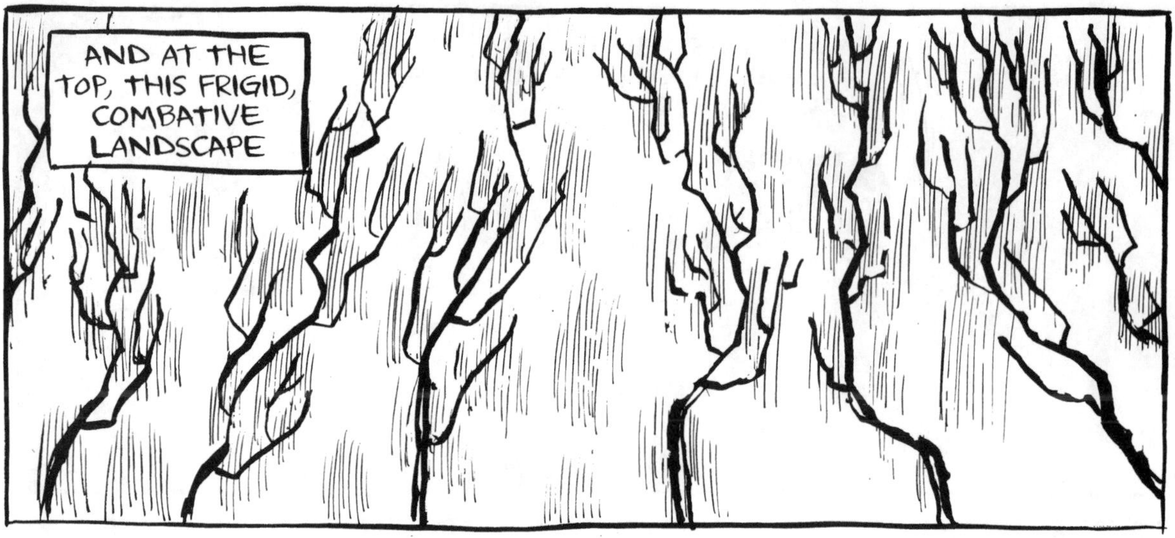
AND AT THE TOP, THIS FRIGID, COMBATIVE LANDSCAPE

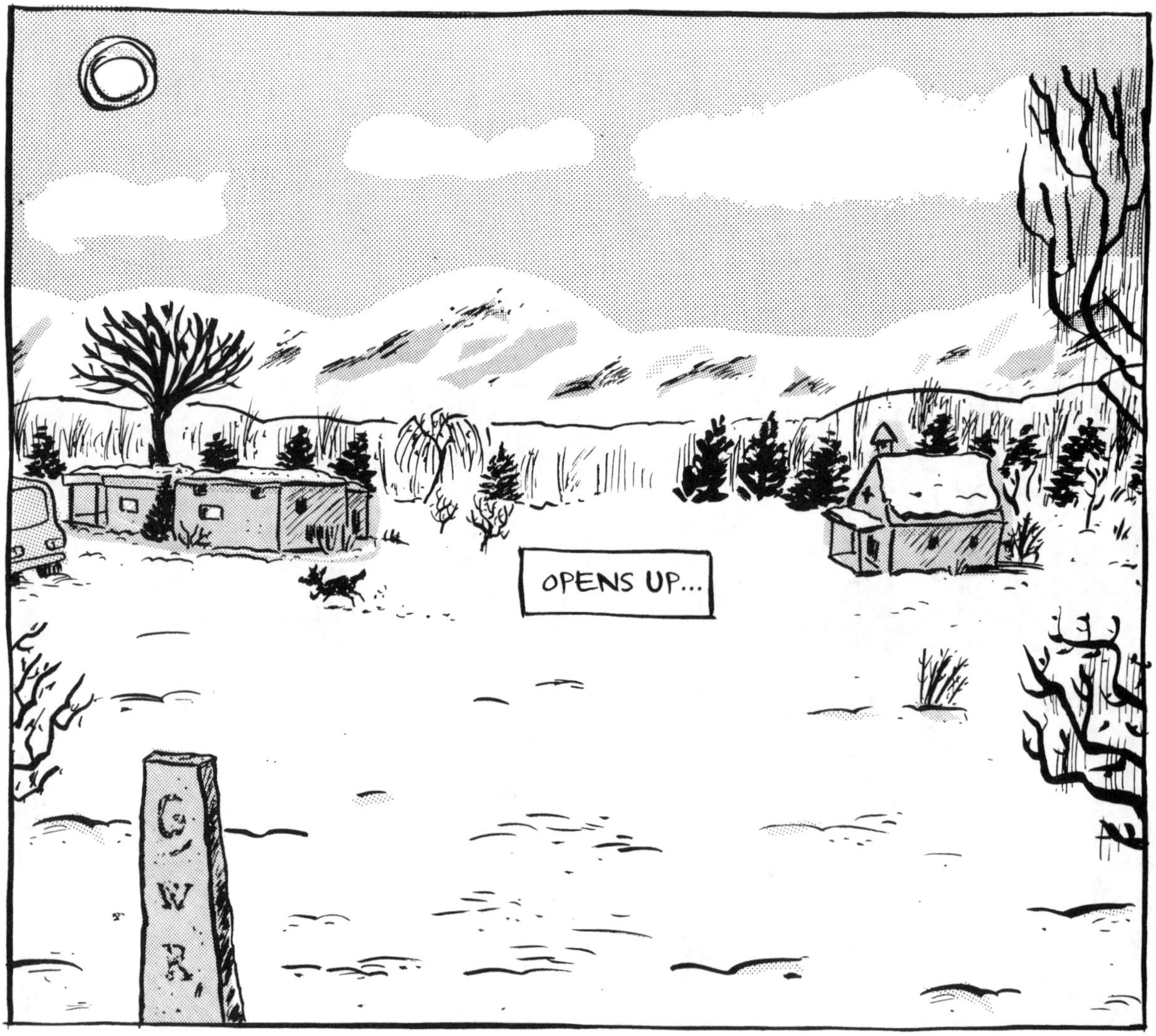
OPENS UP...
G W R

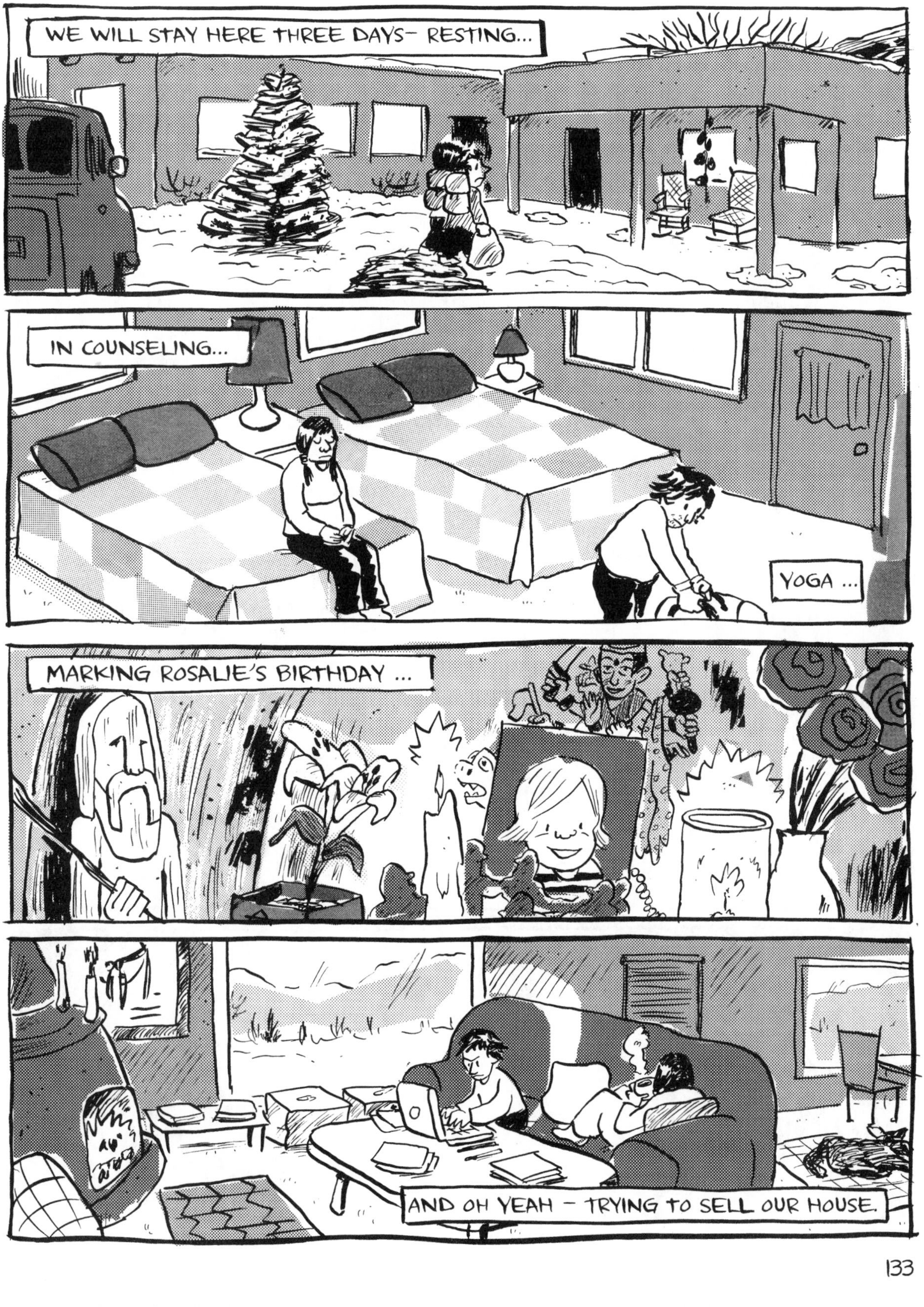
WE WILL STAY HERE THREE DAYS– RESTING...
IN COUNSELING...
YOGA ...
MARKING ROSALIE'S BIRTHDAY ...
AND OH YEAH – TRYING TO SELL OUR HOUSE.

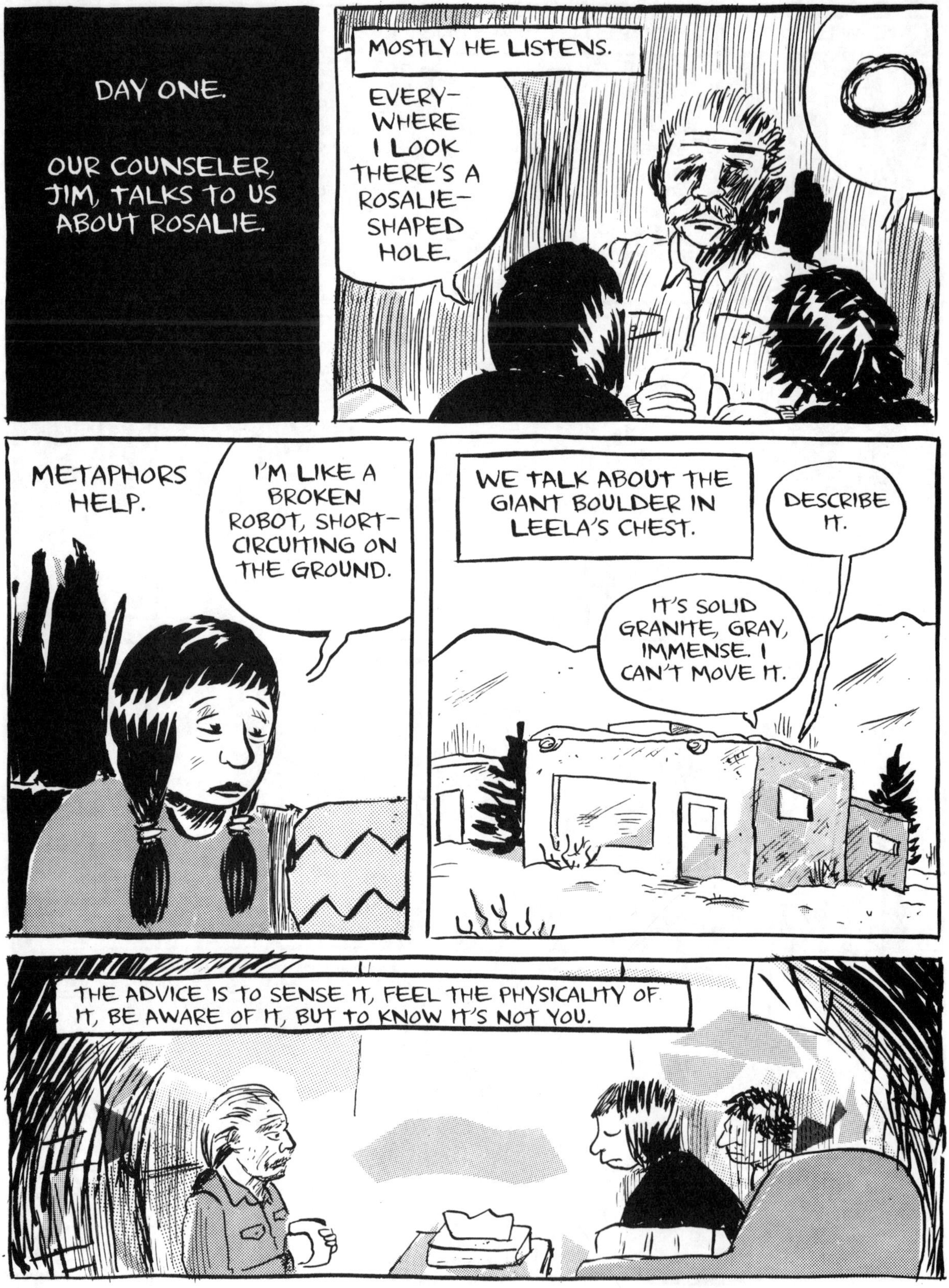
DAY ONE.
OUR COUNSELER, JIM, TALKS TO US ABOUT ROSALIE.
MOSTLY HE LISTENS.
EVERYWHERE I LOOK THERE'S A ROSALIE-SHAPED HOLE.
METAPHORS HELP.
I'M LIKE A BROKEN ROBOT, SHORT-CIRCUITING ON THE GROUND.
WE TALK ABOUT THE GIANT BOULDER IN LEELA'S CHEST.
DESCRIBE IT.
IT'S SOLID GRANITE, GRAY, IMMENSE. I CAN'T MOVE IT.
THE ADVICE IS TO SENSE IT, FEEL THE PHYSICALITY OF IT, BE AWARE OF IT, BUT TO KNOW IT'S NOT YOU.

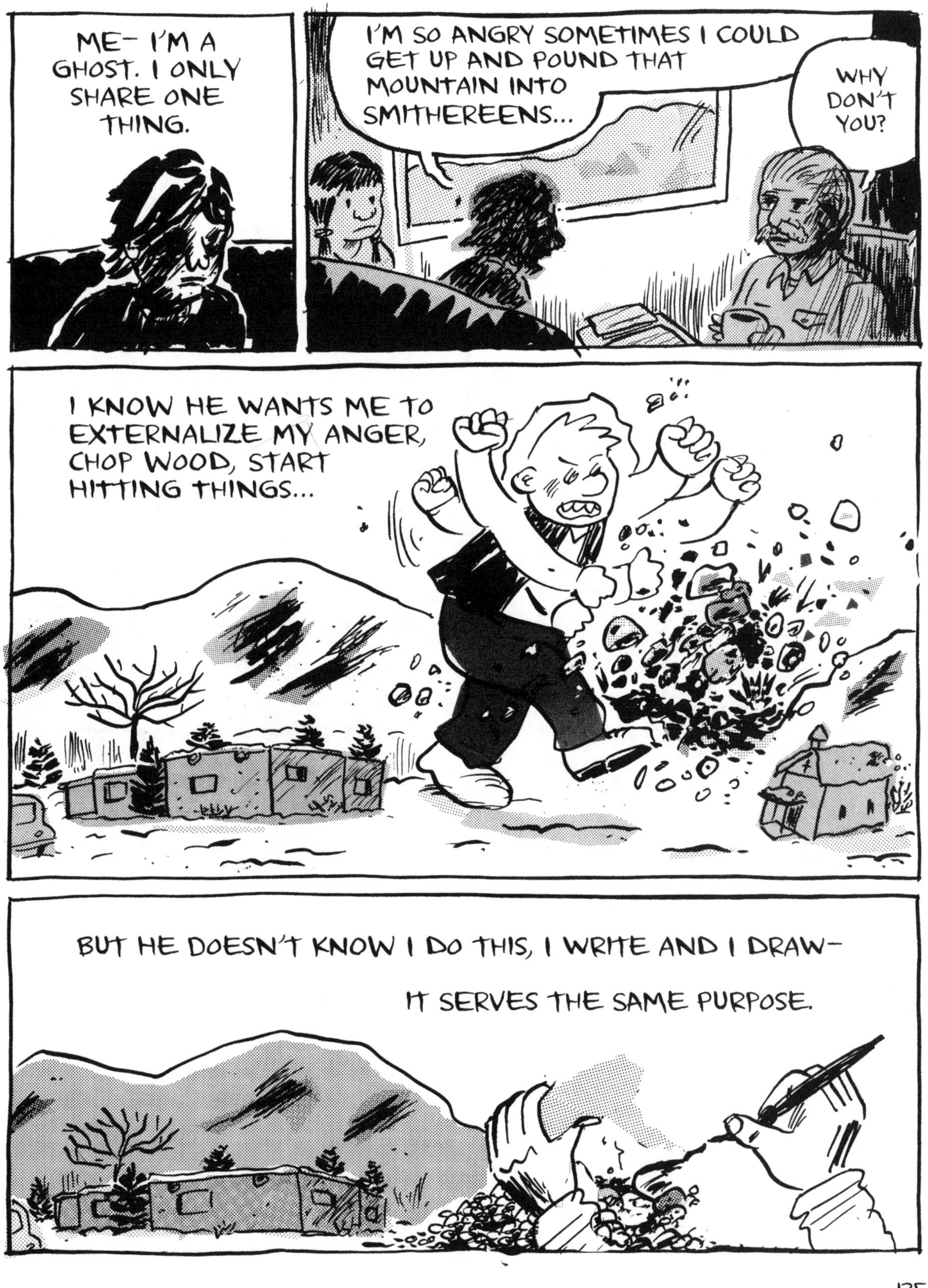
ME- I'M A GHOST. I ONLY SHARE ONE THING.
I'M SO ANGRY SOMETIMES I COULD GET UP AND POUND THAT MOUNTAIN INTO SMITHEREENS...
WHY DON'T YOU?
I KNOW HE WANTS ME TO EXTERNALIZE MY ANGER, CHOP WOOD, START HITTING THINGS...
BUT HE DOESN'T KNOW I DO THIS, I WRITE AND I DRAW-
IT SERVES THE SAME PURPOSE.

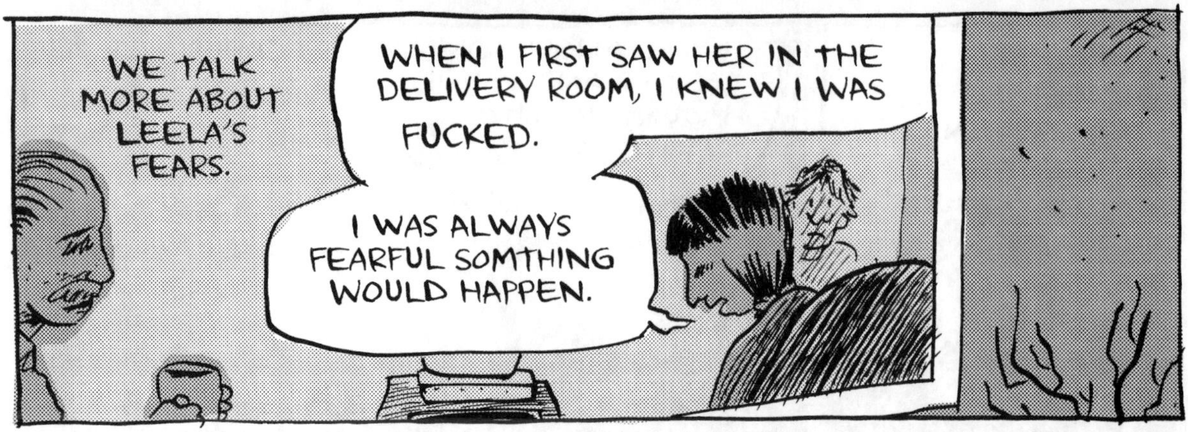
WE TALK MORE ABOUT LEELA'S FEARS.
WHEN I FIRST SAW HER IN THE DELIVERY ROOM, I KNEW I WAS FUCKED.
I WAS ALWAYS FEARFUL SOMTHING WOULD HAPPEN.

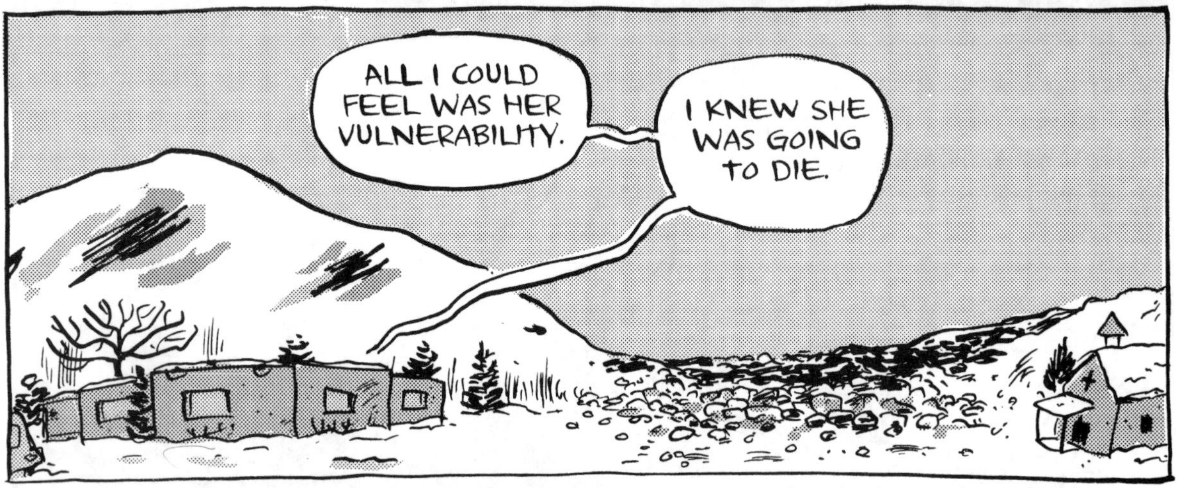
ALL I COULD FEEL WAS HER VULNERABILITY.
I KNEW SHE WAS GOING TO DIE.

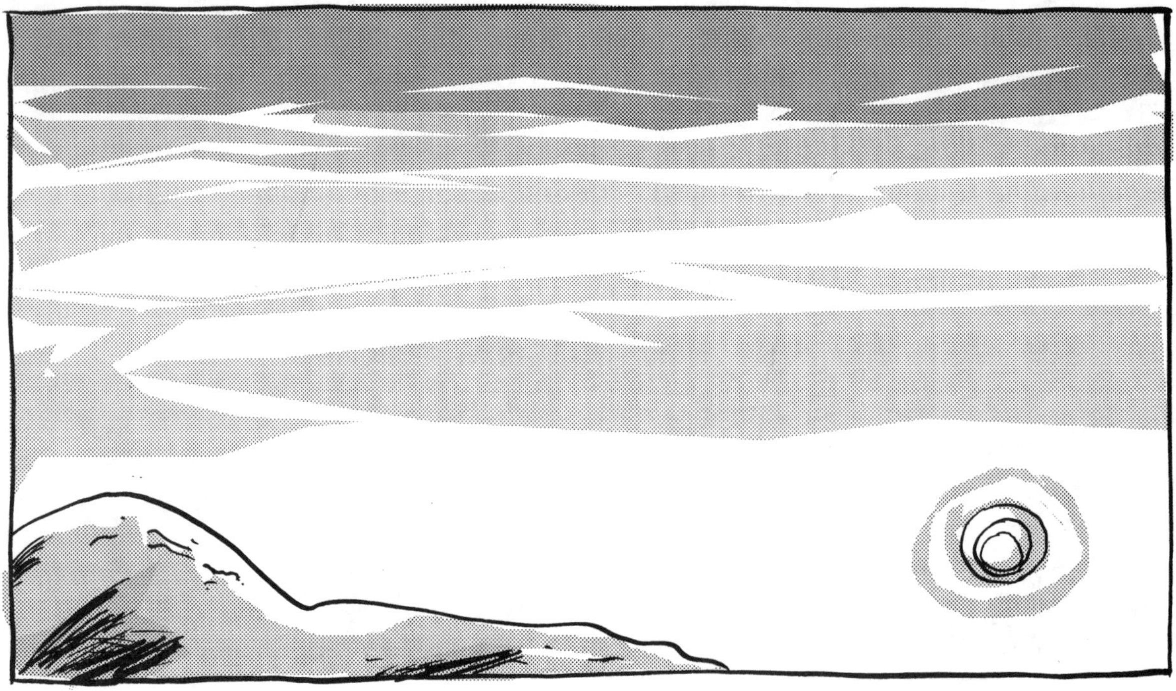

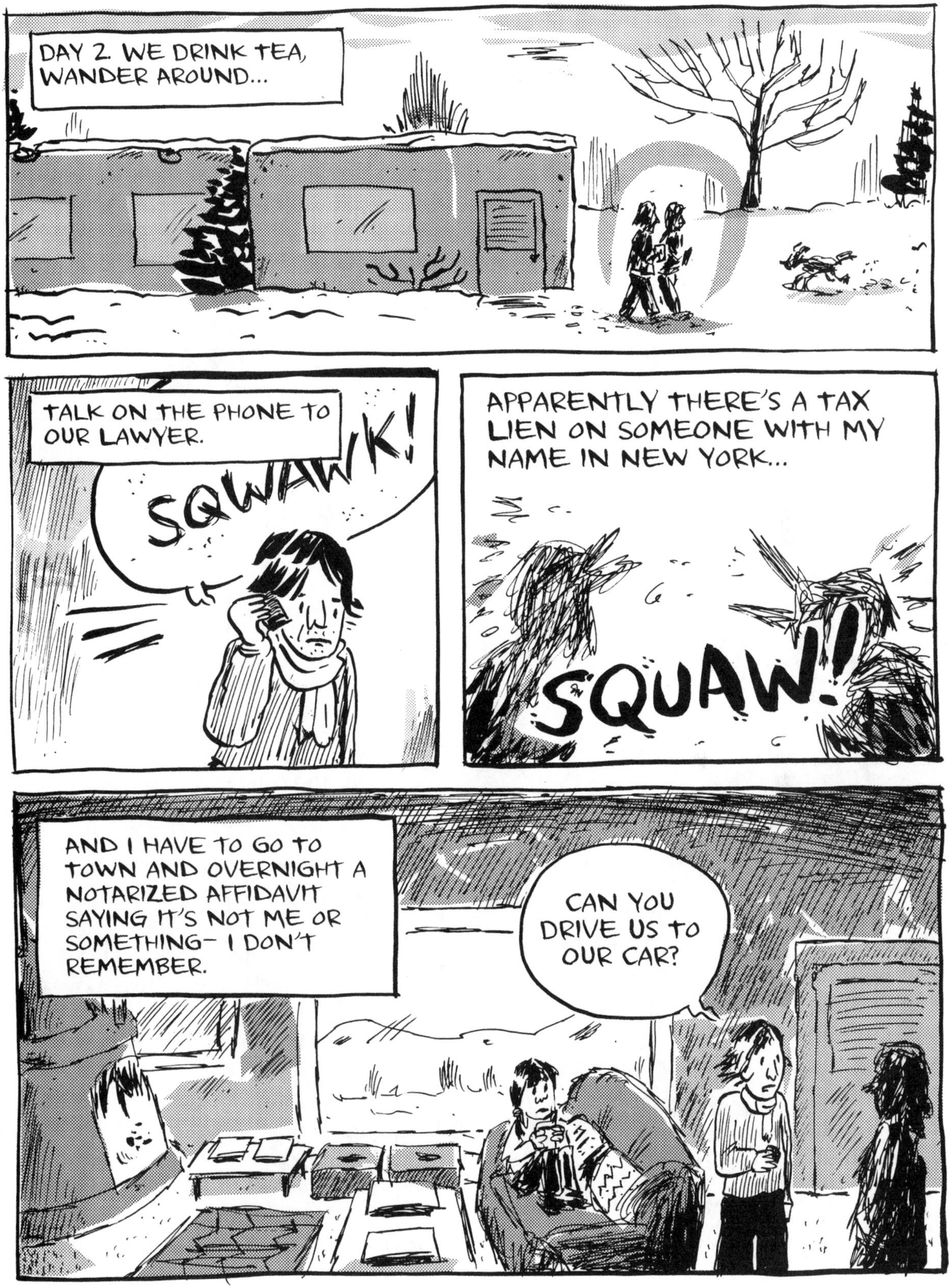
DAY 2. WE DRINK TEA, WANDER AROUND...
TALK ON THE PHONE TO OUR LAWYER.
SQWAWK!
APPARENTLY THERE'S A TAX LIEN ON SOMEONE WITH MY NAME IN NEW YORK...
SQUAW!
AND I HAVE TO GO TO TOWN AND OVERNIGHT A NOTARIZED AFFIDAVIT SAYING IT'S NOT ME OR SOMETHING— I DON'T REMEMBER.
CAN YOU DRIVE US TO OUR CAR?

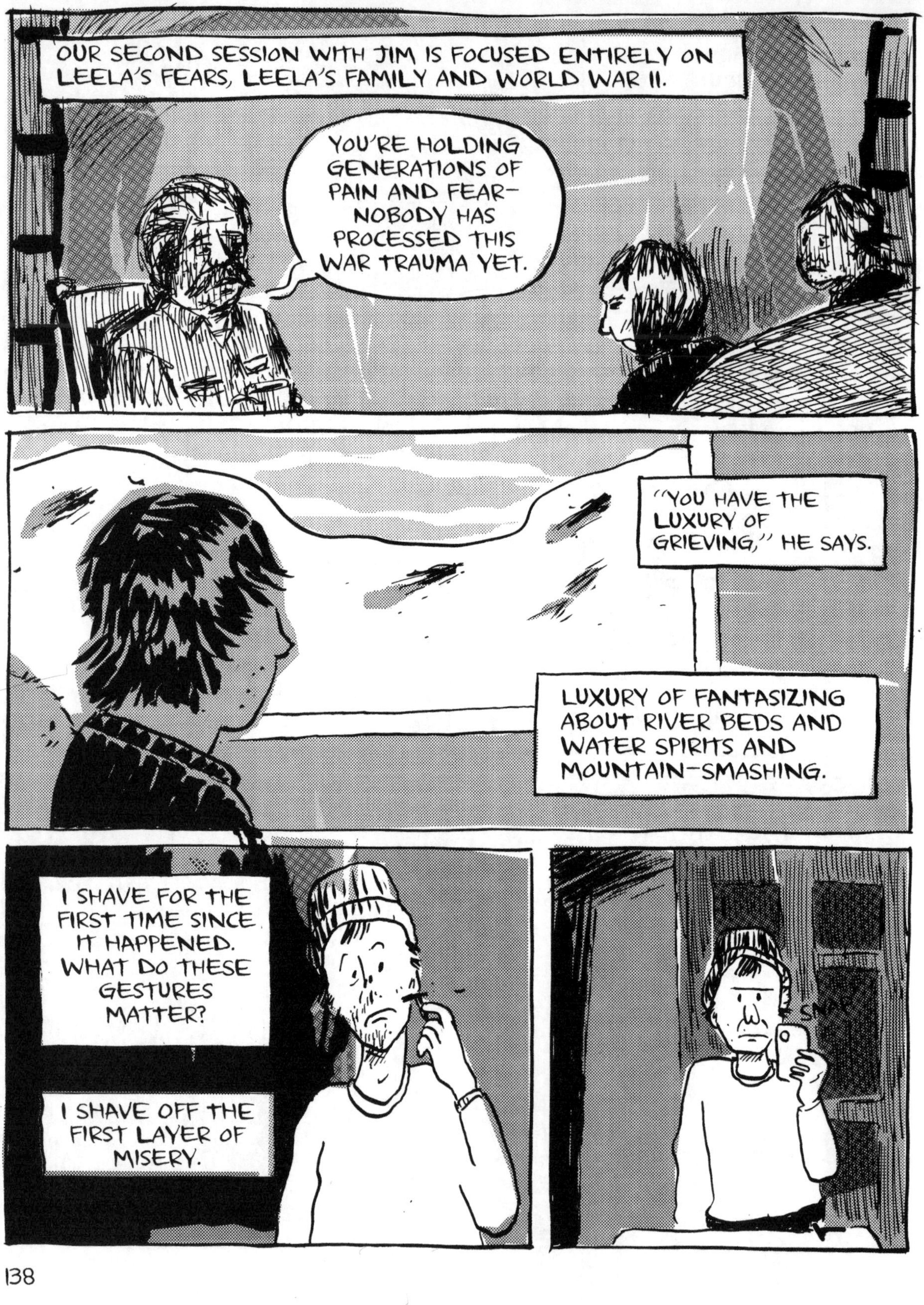
OUR SECOND SESSION WITH JIM IS FOCUSED ENTIRELY ON LEELA'S FEARS, LEELA'S FAMILY AND WORLD WAR II.
YOU'RE HOLDING GENERATIONS OF PAIN AND FEAR- NOBODY HAS PROCESSED THIS WAR TRAUMA YET.
"YOU HAVE THE LUXURY OF GRIEVING," HE SAYS.
LUXURY OF FANTASIZING ABOUT RIVER BEDS AND WATER SPIRITS AND MOUNTAIN-SMASHING.
I SHAVE FOR THE FIRST TIME SINCE IT HAPPENED. WHAT DO THESE GESTURES MATTER?
I SHAVE OFF THE FIRST LAYER OF MISERY.

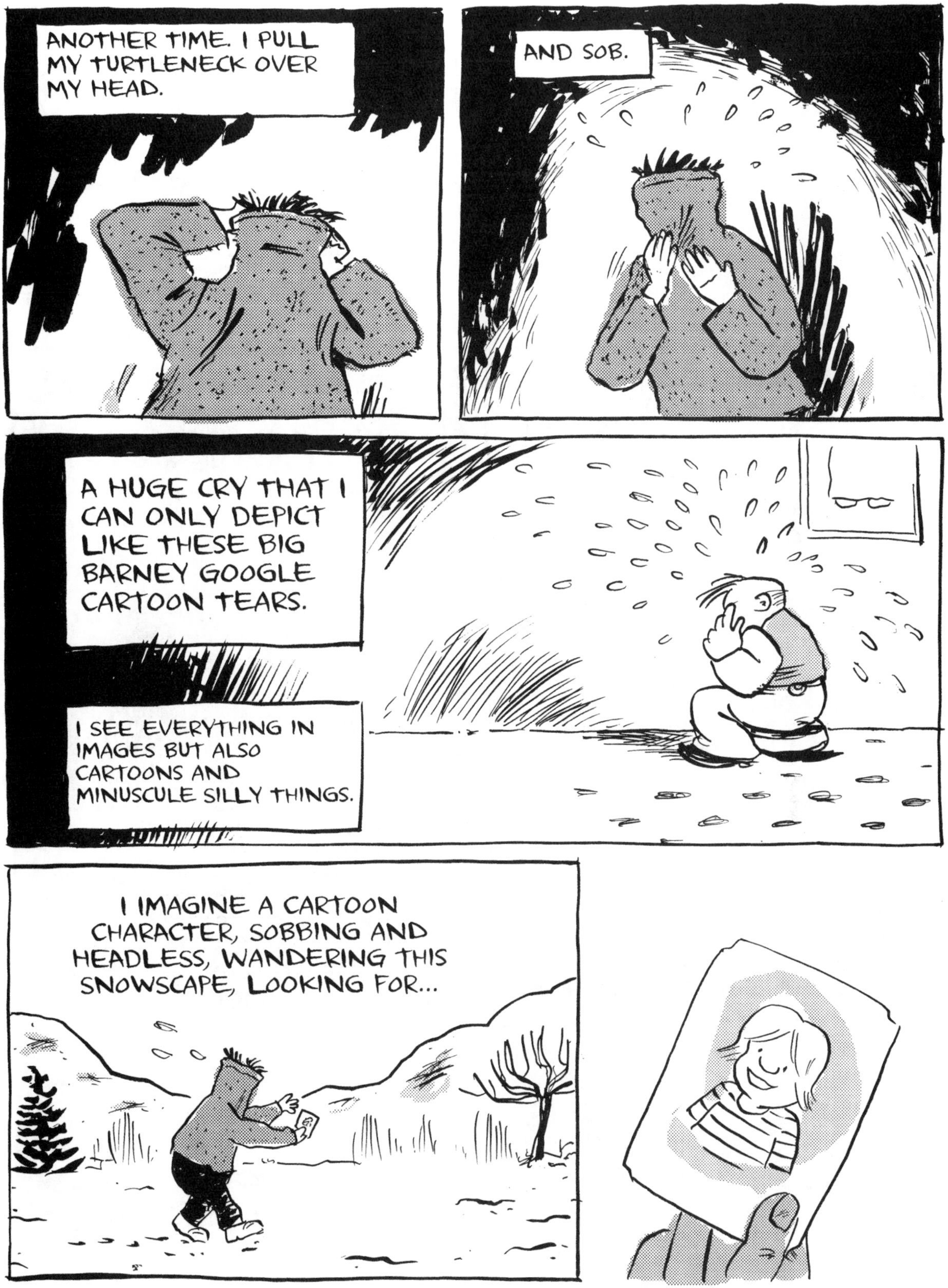
ANOTHER TIME. I PULL MY TURTLENECK OVER MY HEAD.
AND SOB.
A HUGE CRY THAT I CAN ONLY DEPICT LIKE THESE BIG BARNEY GOOGLE CARTOON TEARS.
I SEE EVERYTHING IN IMAGES BUT ALSO CARTOONS AND MINUSCULE SILLY THINGS.
I IMAGINE A CARTOON CHARACTER, SOBBING AND HEADLESS, WANDERING THIS SNOWSCAPE, LOOKING FOR...

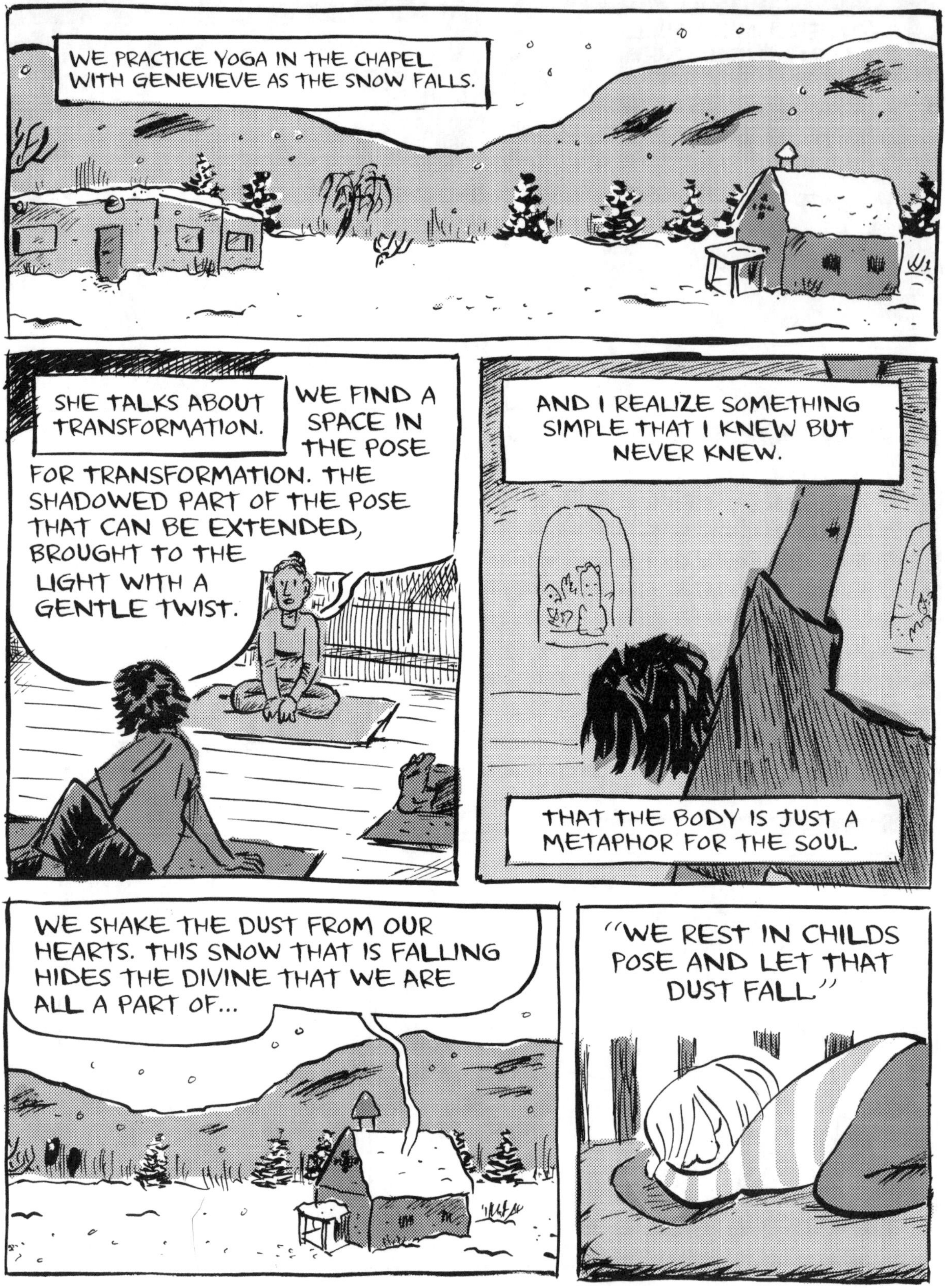
WE PRACTICE YOGA IN THE CHAPEL WITH GENEVIEVE AS THE SNOW FALLS.
SHE TALKS ABOUT TRANSFORMATION.
WE FIND A SPACE IN THE POSE FOR TRANSFORMATION. THE SHADOWED PART OF THE POSE THAT CAN BE EXTENDED, BROUGHT TO THE LIGHT WITH A GENTLE TWIST.
AND I REALIZE SOMETHING SIMPLE THAT I KNEW BUT NEVER KNEW.
THAT THE BODY IS JUST A METAPHOR FOR THE SOUL.
WE SHAKE THE DUST FROM OUR HEARTS. THIS SNOW THAT IS FALLING HIDES THE DIVINE THAT WE ARE ALL A PART OF...
"WE REST IN CHILDS POSE AND LET THAT DUST FALL."

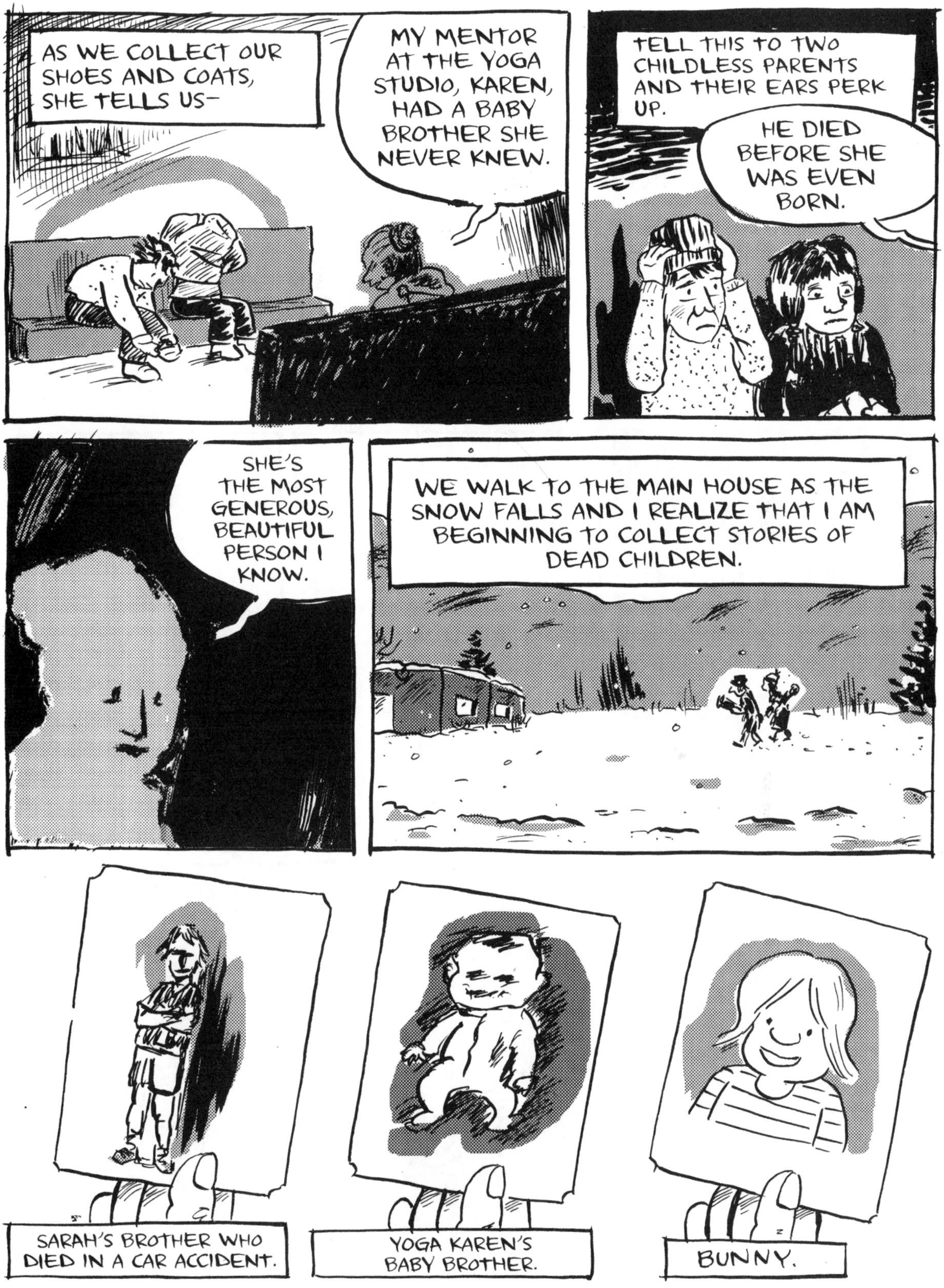

AS WE COLLECT OUR SHOES AND COATS, SHE TELLS US–
MY MENTOR AT THE YOGA STUDIO, KAREN, HAD A BABY BROTHER SHE NEVER KNEW.
TELL THIS TO TWO CHILDLESS PARENTS AND THEIR EARS PERK UP.
HE DIED BEFORE SHE WAS EVEN BORN.
SHE'S THE MOST GENEROUS, BEAUTIFUL PERSON I KNOW.
WE WALK TO THE MAIN HOUSE AS THE SNOW FALLS AND I REALIZE THAT I AM BEGINNING TO COLLECT STORIES OF DEAD CHILDREN.
SARAH'S BROTHER WHO DIED IN A CAR ACCIDENT.
YOGA KAREN'S BABY BROTHER.
BUNNY.

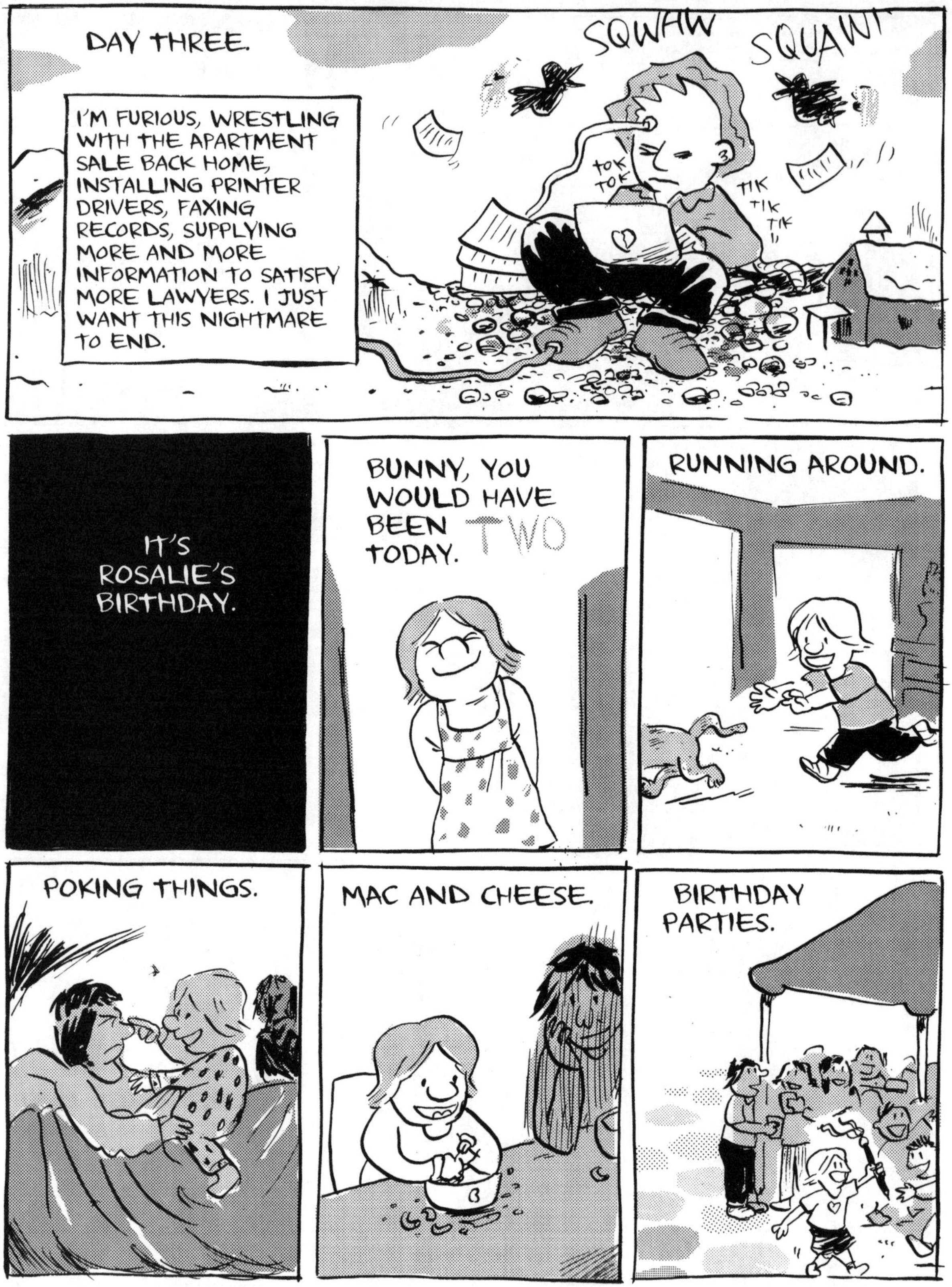
DAY THREE.
SQWAW
SQUAW
I'M FURIOUS, WRESTLING WITH THE APARTMENT SALE BACK HOME, INSTALLING PRINTER DRIVERS, FAXING RECORDS, SUPPLYING MORE AND MORE INFORMATION TO SATISFY MORE LAWYERS. I JUST WANT THIS NIGHTMARE TO END.
TOK TOK
TIK TIK TIK
IT'S ROSALIE'S BIRTHDAY.
BUNNY, YOU WOULD HAVE BEEN TODAY.
TWO
RUNNING AROUND.
POKING THINGS.
MAC AND CHEESE.
BIRTHDAY PARTIES.

THREE
WEEKS
AGO—

WASN'T I
A FATHER?

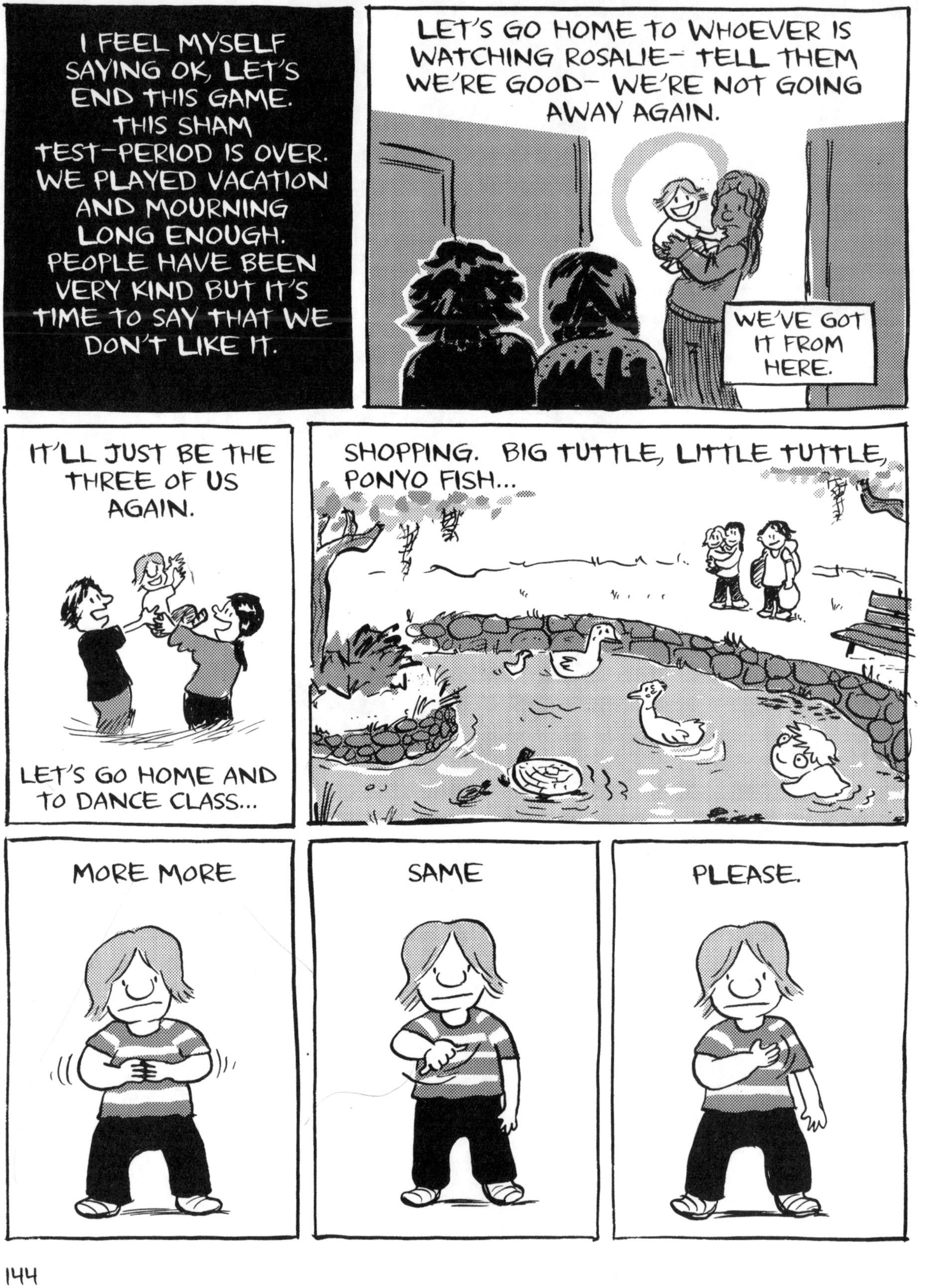
I FEEL MYSELF SAYING OK, LET'S END THIS GAME. THIS SHAM TEST-PERIOD IS OVER. WE PLAYED VACATION AND MOURNING LONG ENOUGH. PEOPLE HAVE BEEN VERY KIND BUT IT'S TIME TO SAY THAT WE DON'T LIKE IT.
LET'S GO HOME TO WHOEVER IS WATCHING ROSALIE- TELL THEM WE'RE GOOD- WE'RE NOT GOING AWAY AGAIN.
WE'VE GOT IT FROM HERE.
IT'LL JUST BE THE THREE OF US AGAIN.
LET'S GO HOME AND TO DANCE CLASS...
SHOPPING. BIG TUTTLE, LITTLE TUTTLE, PONYO FISH...
MORE MORE
SAME
PLEASE.

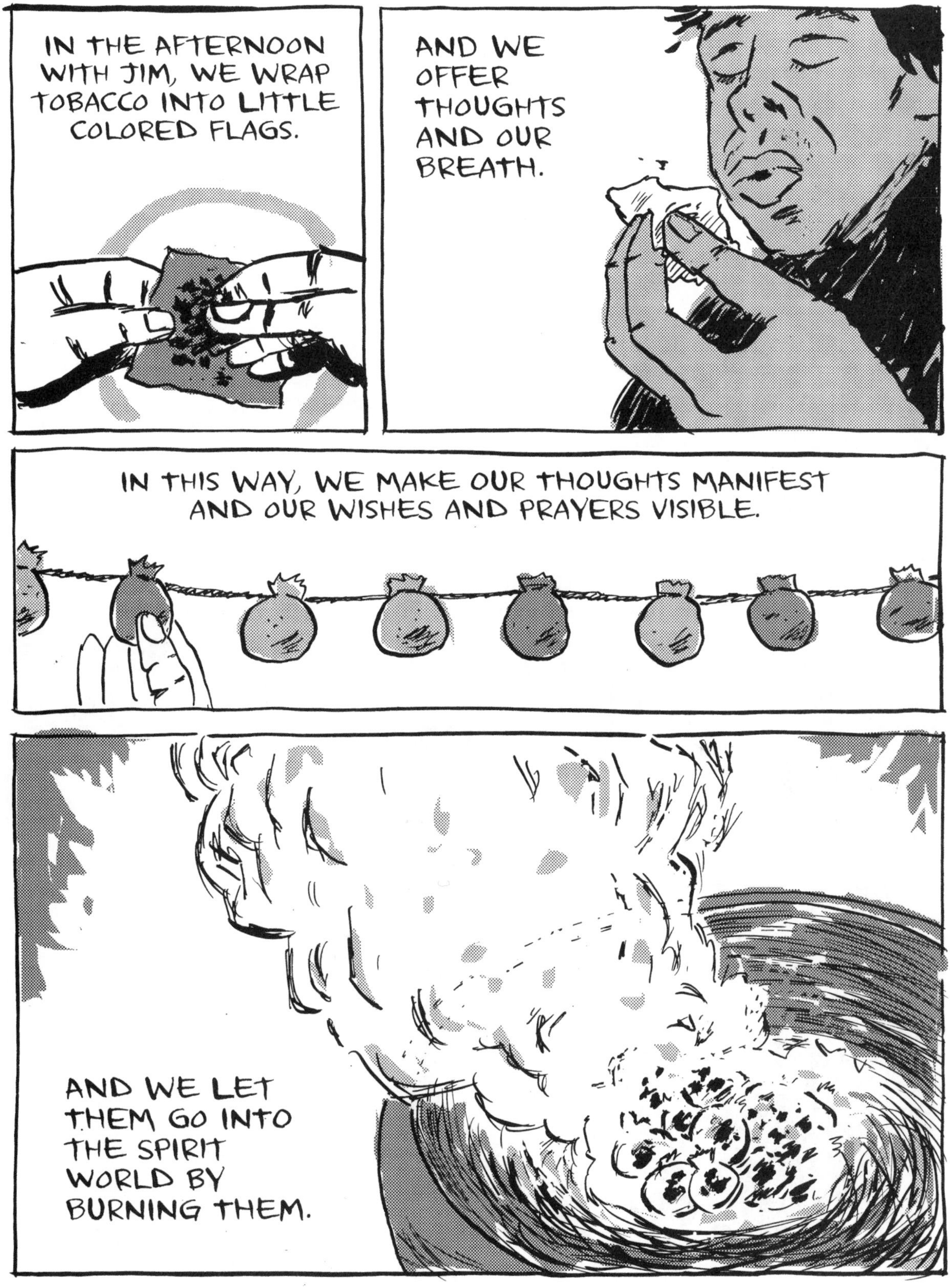
IN THE AFTERNOON WITH JIM, WE WRAP TOBACCO INTO LITTLE COLORED FLAGS.
AND WE OFFER THOUGHTS AND OUR BREATH.
IN THIS WAY, WE MAKE OUR THOUGHTS MANIFEST AND OUR WISHES AND PRAYERS VISIBLE.
AND WE LET THEM GO INTO THE SPIRIT WORLD BY BURNING THEM.

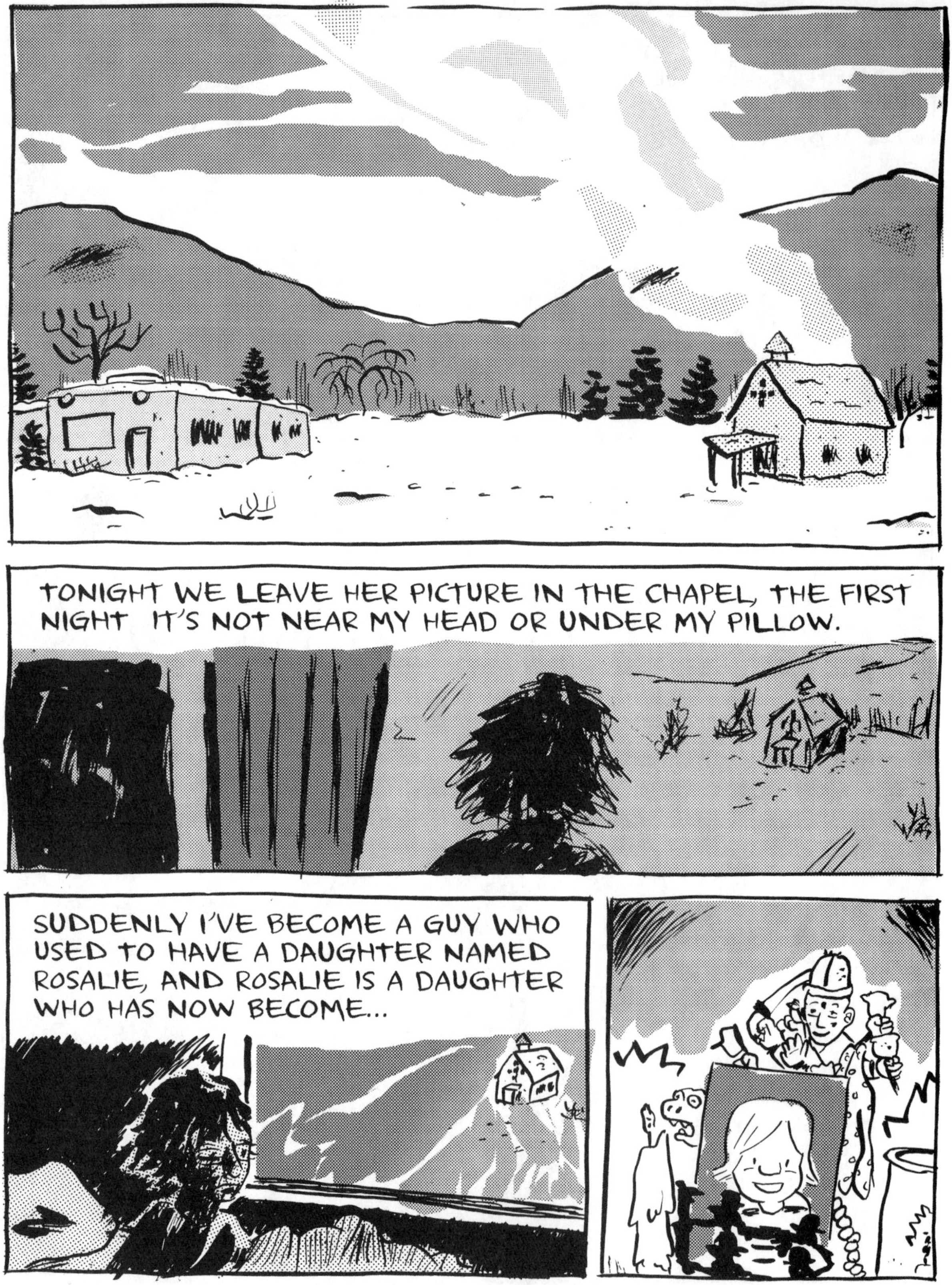
TONIGHT WE LEAVE HER PICTURE IN THE CHAPEL, THE FIRST NIGHT IT'S NOT NEAR MY HEAD OR UNDER MY PILLOW.
SUDDENLY I'VE BECOME A GUY WHO USED TO HAVE A DAUGHTER NAMED ROSALIE, AND ROSALIE IS A DAUGHTER WHO HAS NOW BECOME...

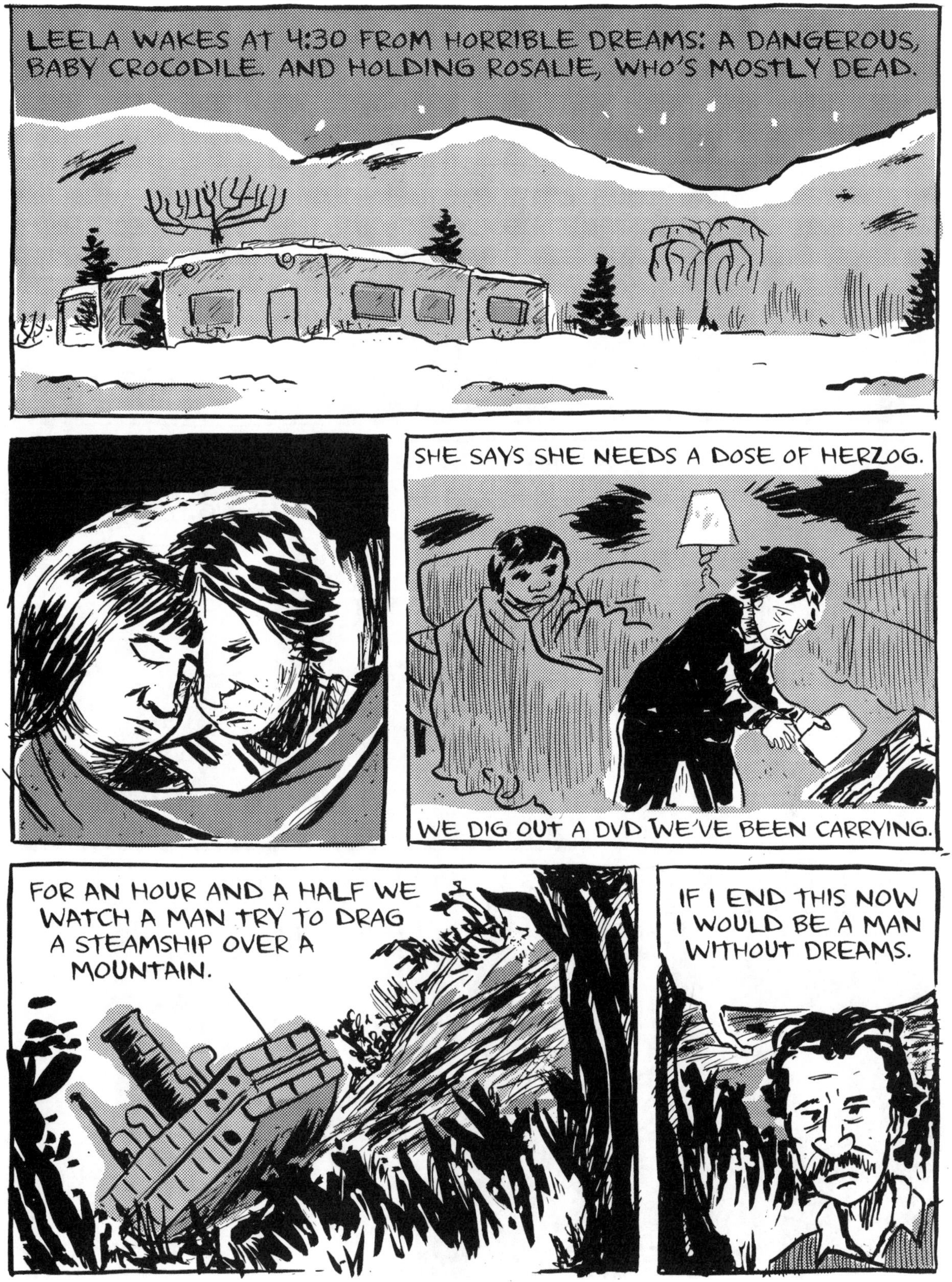
LEELA WAKES AT 4:30 FROM HORRIBLE DREAMS: A DANGEROUS, BABY CROCODILE. AND HOLDING ROSALIE, WHO'S MOSTLY DEAD.
SHE SAYS SHE NEEDS A DOSE OF HERZOG.
WE DIG OUT A DVD WE'VE BEEN CARRYING.
FOR AN HOUR AND A HALF WE WATCH A MAN TRY TO DRAG A STEAMSHIP OVER A MOUNTAIN.
IF I END THIS NOW I WOULD BE A MAN WITHOUT DREAMS.

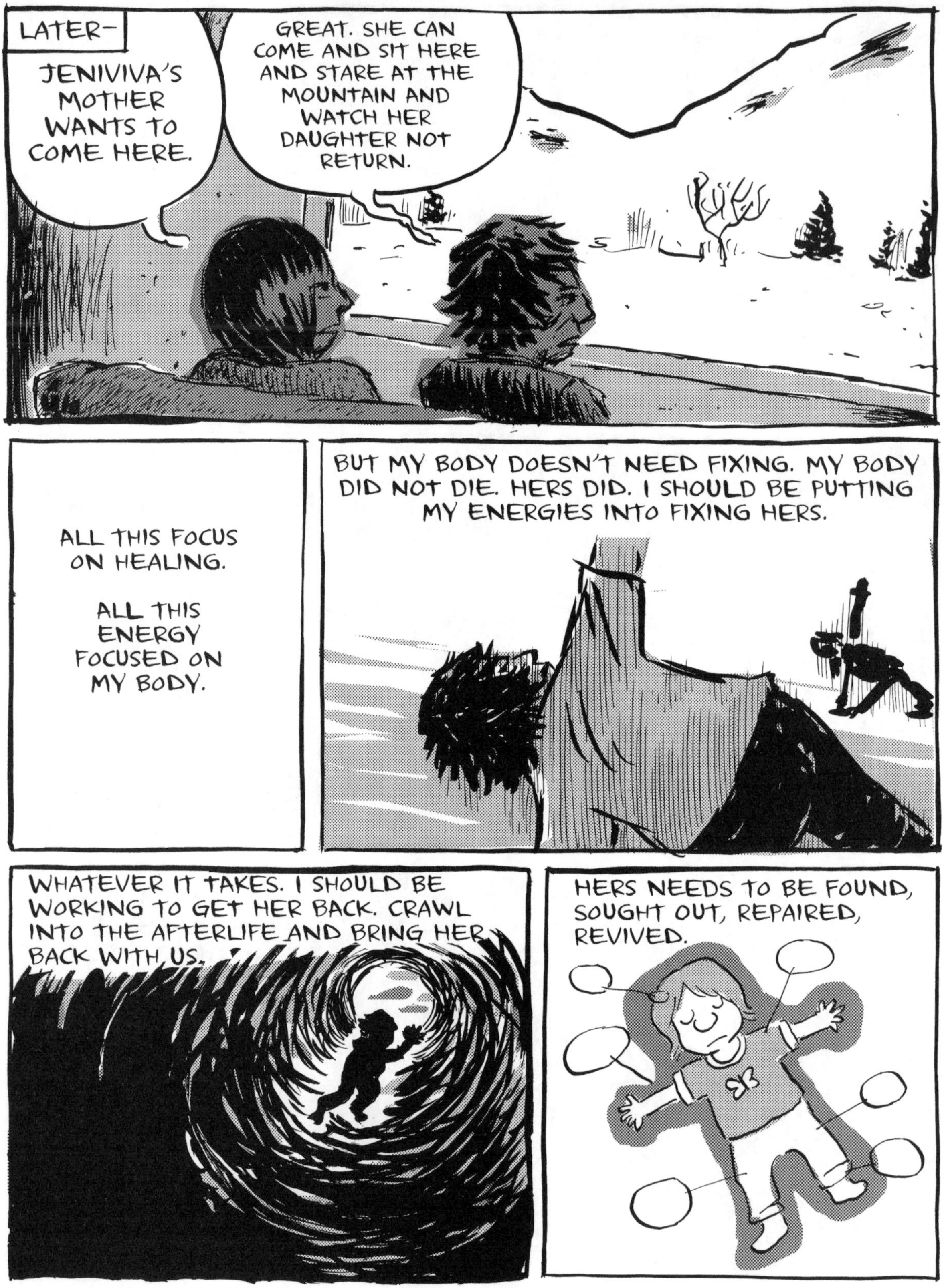
LATER–
JENIVIVA'S MOTHER WANTS TO COME HERE.
GREAT. SHE CAN COME AND SIT HERE AND STARE AT THE MOUNTAIN AND WATCH HER DAUGHTER NOT RETURN.
ALL THIS FOCUS ON HEALING.
ALL THIS ENERGY FOCUSED ON MY BODY.
BUT MY BODY DOESN'T NEED FIXING. MY BODY DID NOT DIE. HERS DID. I SHOULD BE PUTTING MY ENERGIES INTO FIXING HERS.
WHATEVER IT TAKES. I SHOULD BE WORKING TO GET HER BACK. CRAWL INTO THE AFTERLIFE AND BRING HER BACK WITH US.
HERS NEEDS TO BE FOUND, SOUGHT OUT, REPAIRED, REVIVED.

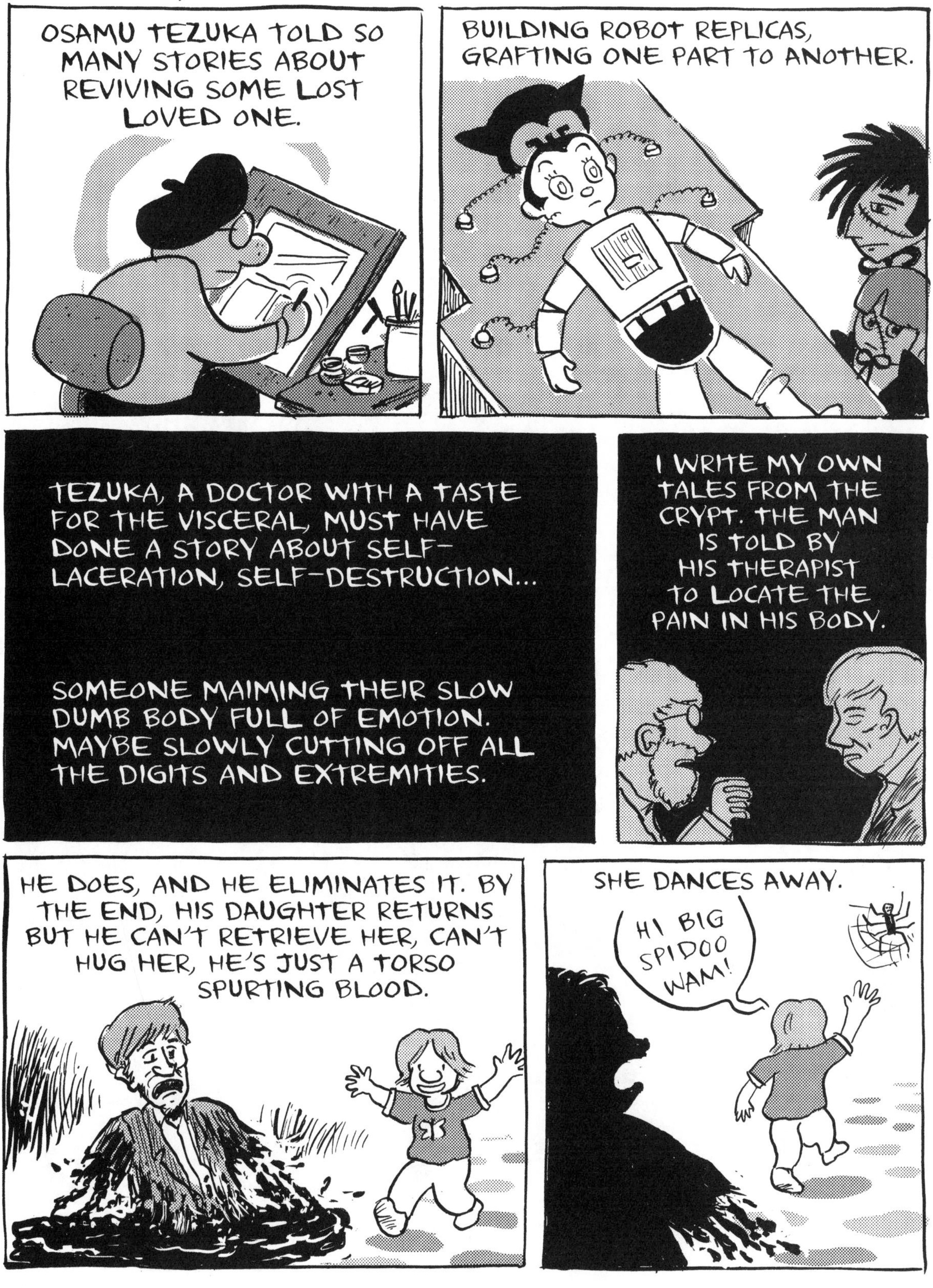
OSAMU TEZUKA TOLD SO MANY STORIES ABOUT REVIVING SOME LOST LOVED ONE.
BUILDING ROBOT REPLICAS, GRAFTING ONE PART TO ANOTHER.
TEZUKA, A DOCTOR WITH A TASTE FOR THE VISCERAL, MUST HAVE DONE A STORY ABOUT SELF-LACERATION, SELF-DESTRUCTION...
SOMEONE MAIMING THEIR SLOW DUMB BODY FULL OF EMOTION. MAYBE SLOWLY CUTTING OFF ALL THE DIGITS AND EXTREMITIES.
I WRITE MY OWN TALES FROM THE CRYPT. THE MAN IS TOLD BY HIS THERAPIST TO LOCATE THE PAIN IN HIS BODY.
HE DOES, AND HE ELIMINATES IT. BY THE END, HIS DAUGHTER RETURNS BUT HE CAN'T RETRIEVE HER, CAN'T HUG HER, HE'S JUST A TORSO SPURTING BLOOD.
SHE DANCES AWAY.
HI BIG SPIDOO WAM!

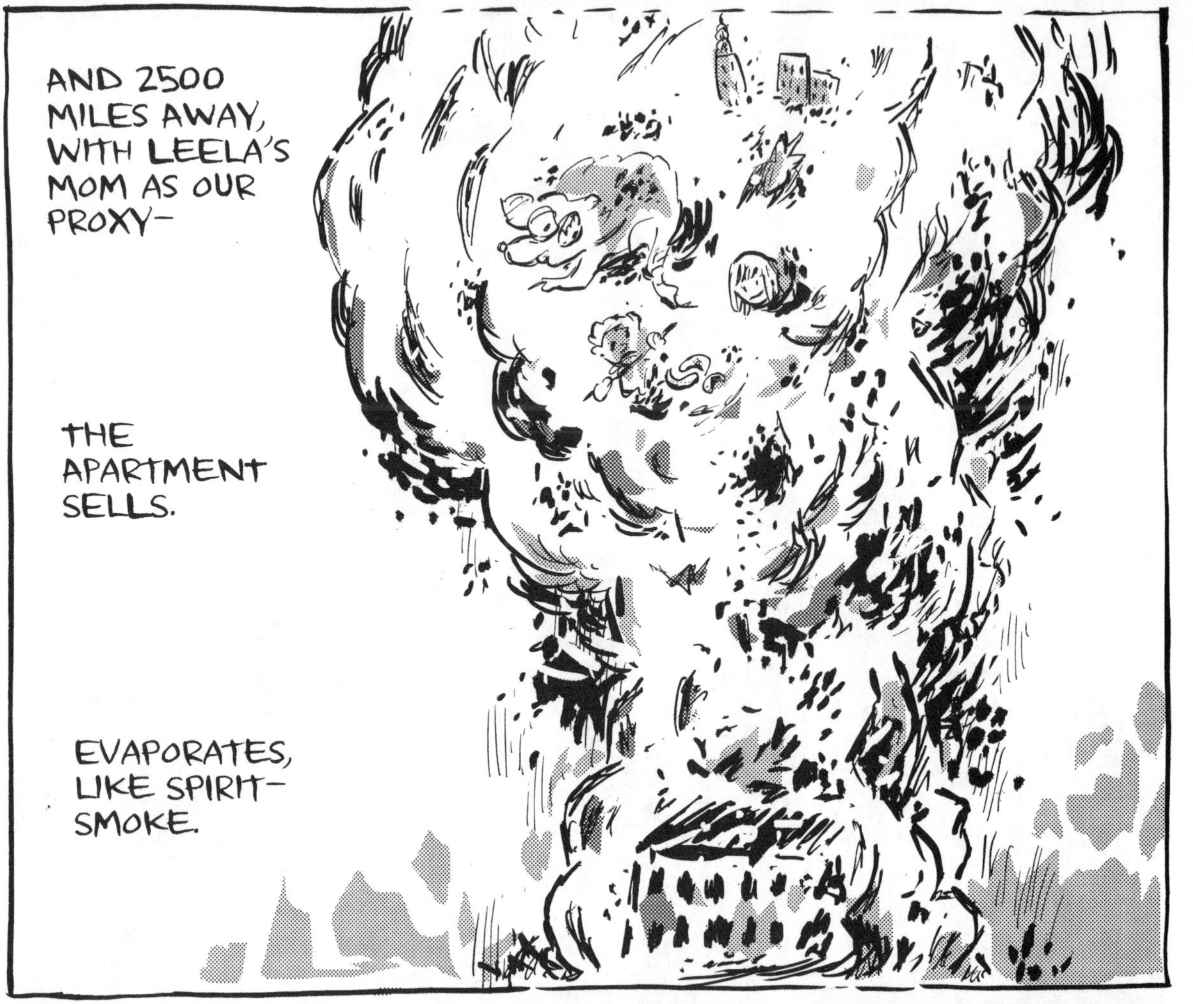
AND 2500 MILES AWAY, WITH LEELA'S MOM AS OUR PROXY–
THE APARTMENT SELLS.
EVAPORATES, LIKE SPIRIT-SMOKE.
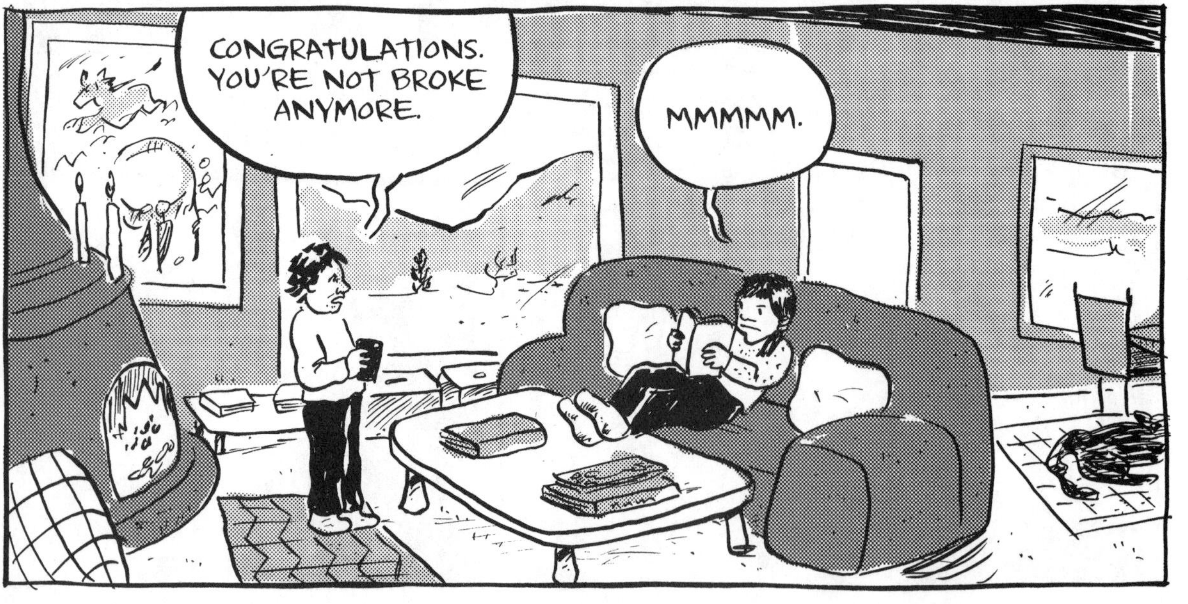
CONGRATULATIONS. YOU'RE NOT BROKE ANYMORE.
MMMMM.

VIII

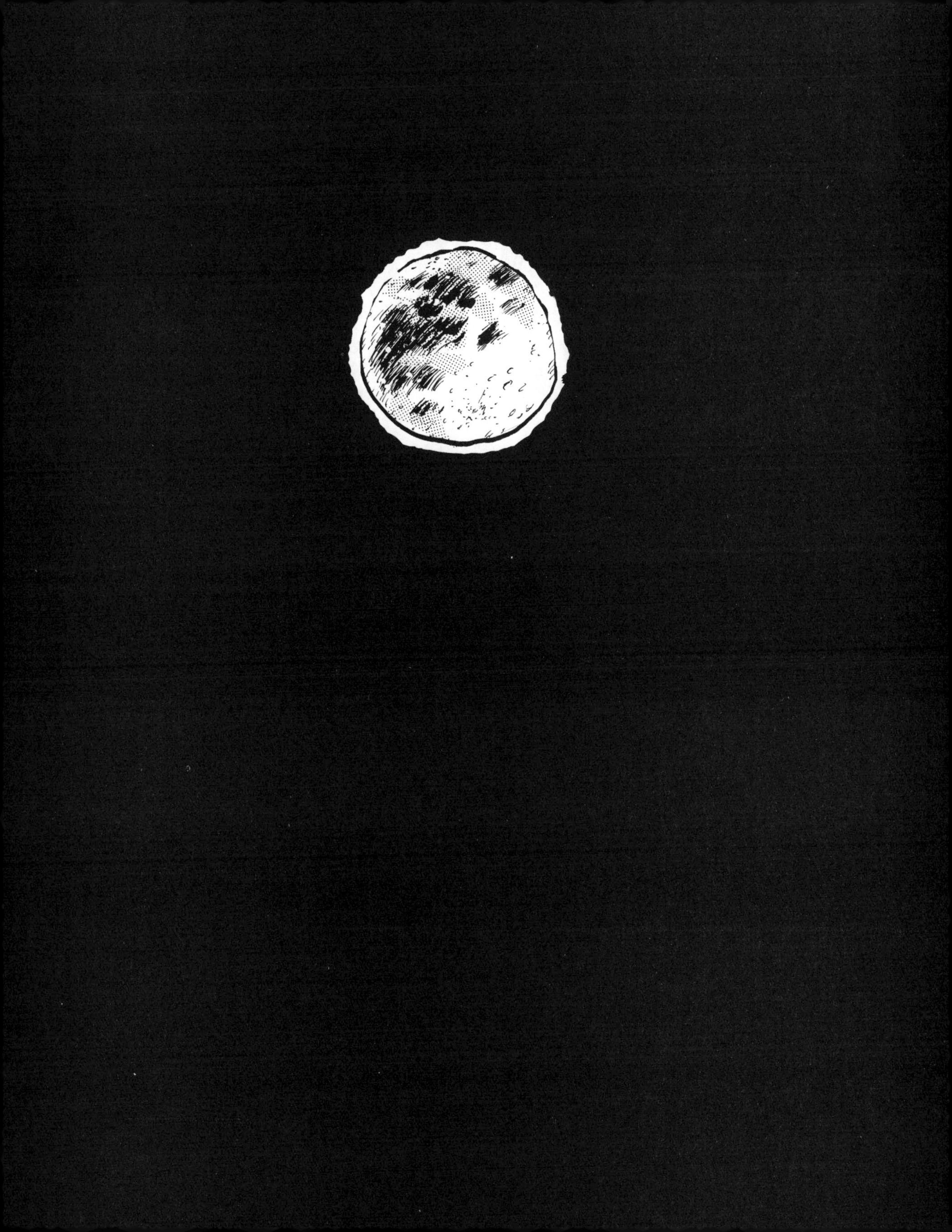

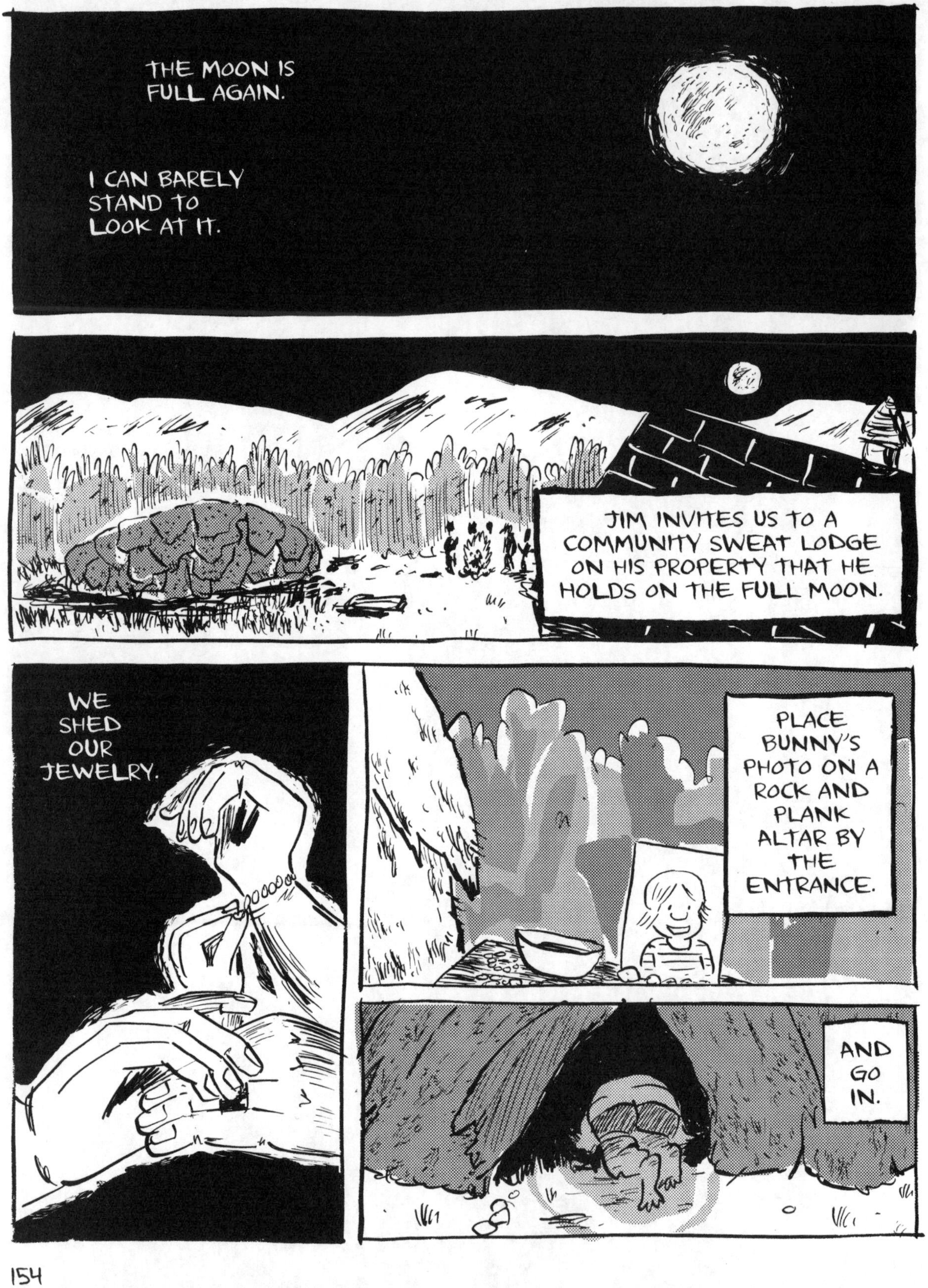
THE MOON IS FULL AGAIN.
I CAN BARELY STAND TO LOOK AT IT.
JIM INVITES US TO A COMMUNITY SWEAT LODGE ON HIS PROPERTY THAT HE HOLDS ON THE FULL MOON.
WE SHED OUR JEWELRY.
PLACE BUNNY'S PHOTO ON A ROCK AND PLANK ALTAR BY THE ENTRANCE.
AND GO IN.

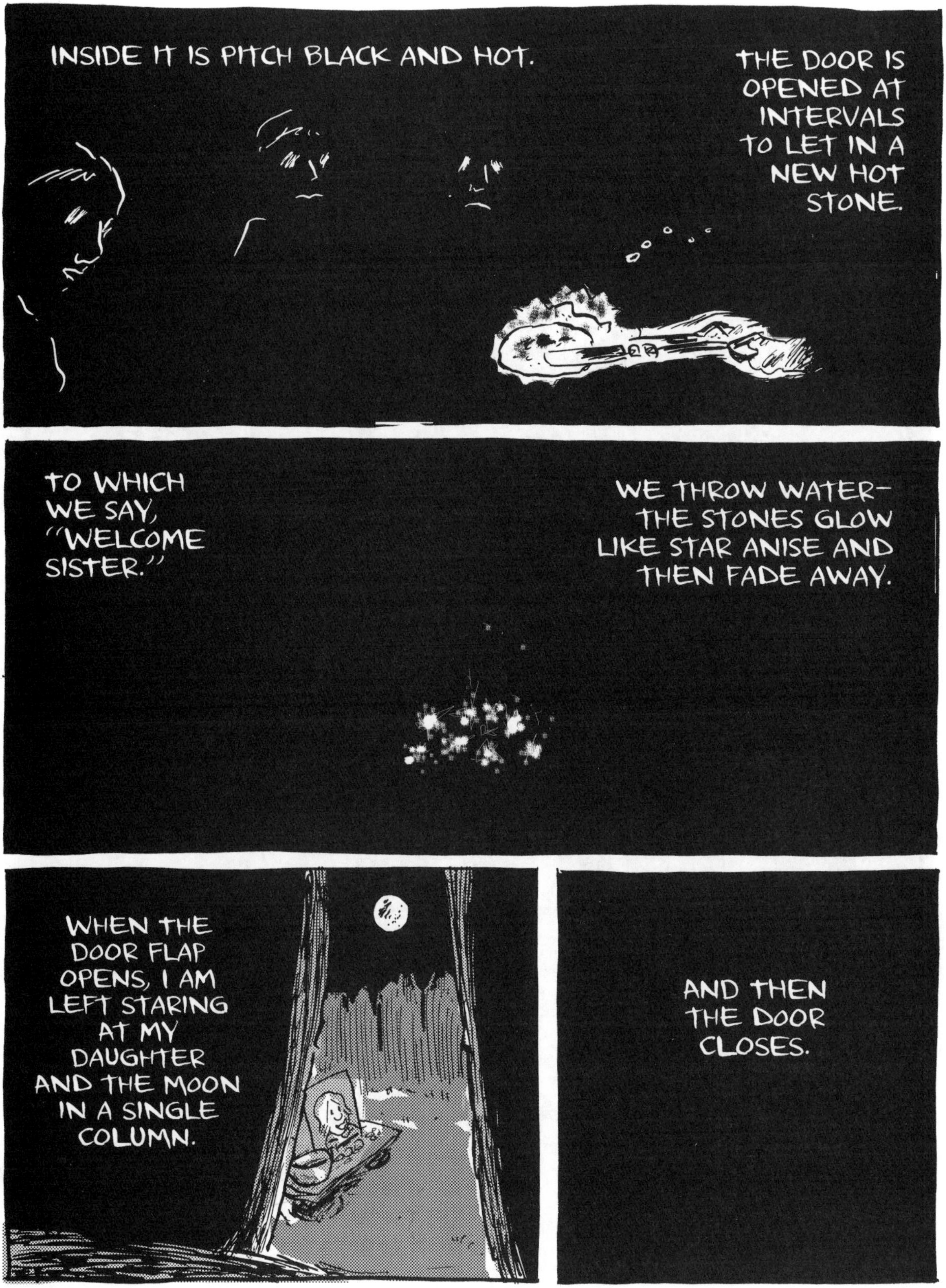
INSIDE IT IS PITCH BLACK AND HOT.
THE DOOR IS OPENED AT INTERVALS TO LET IN A NEW HOT STONE.
TO WHICH WE SAY, "WELCOME SISTER."
WE THROW WATER– THE STONES GLOW LIKE STAR ANISE AND THEN FADE AWAY.
WHEN THE DOOR FLAP OPENS, I AM LEFT STARING AT MY DAUGHTER AND THE MOON IN A SINGLE COLUMN.
AND THEN THE DOOR CLOSES.

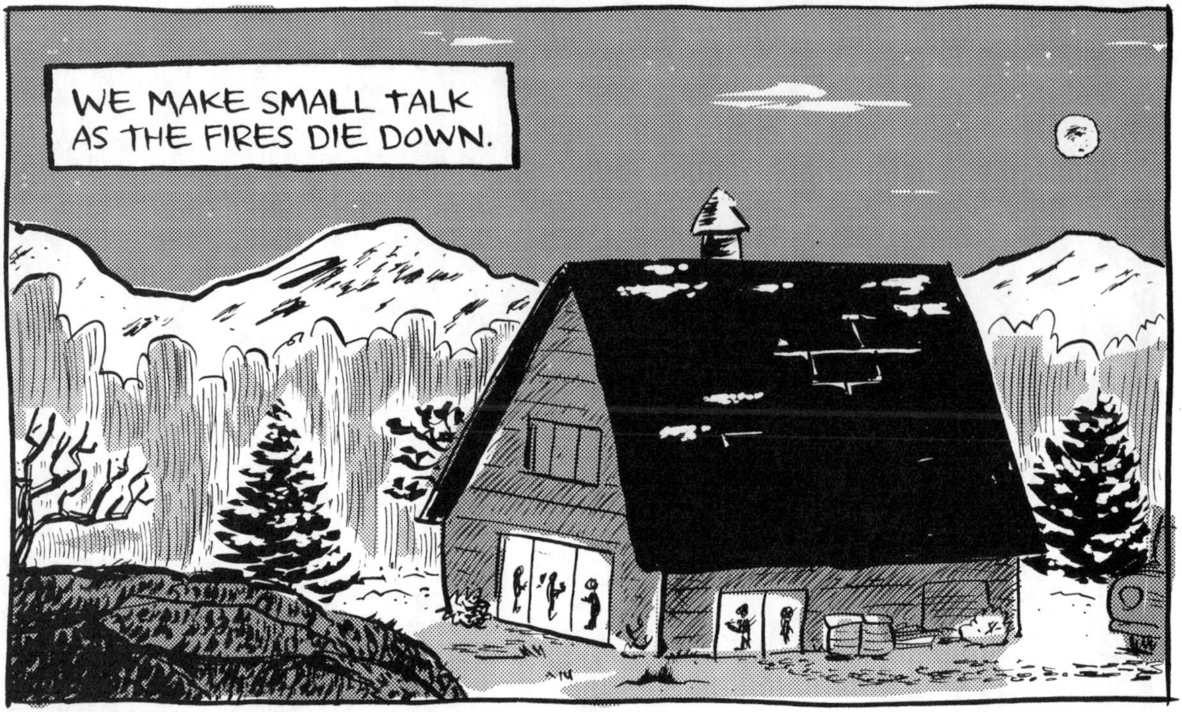
WE MAKE SMALL TALK AS THE FIRES DIE DOWN.

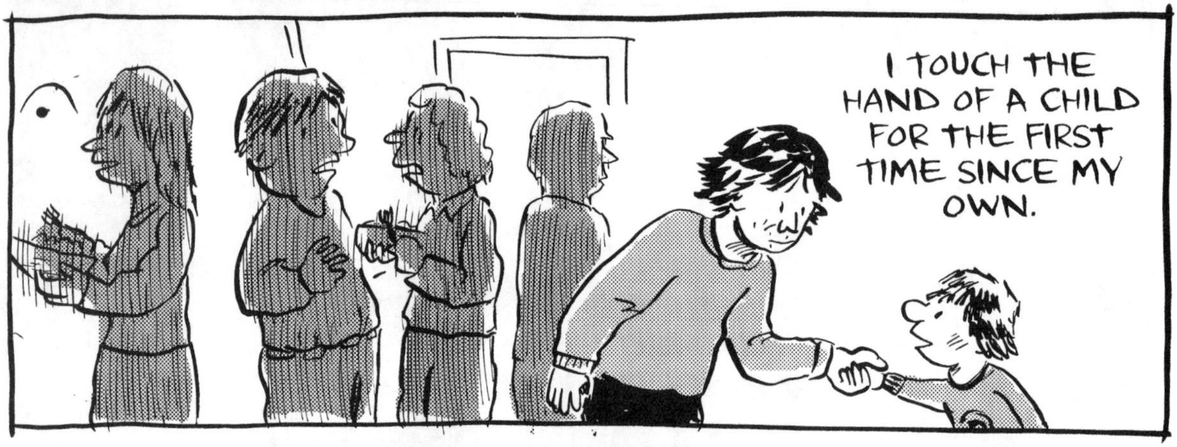
I TOUCH THE HAND OF A CHILD FOR THE FIRST TIME SINCE MY OWN.

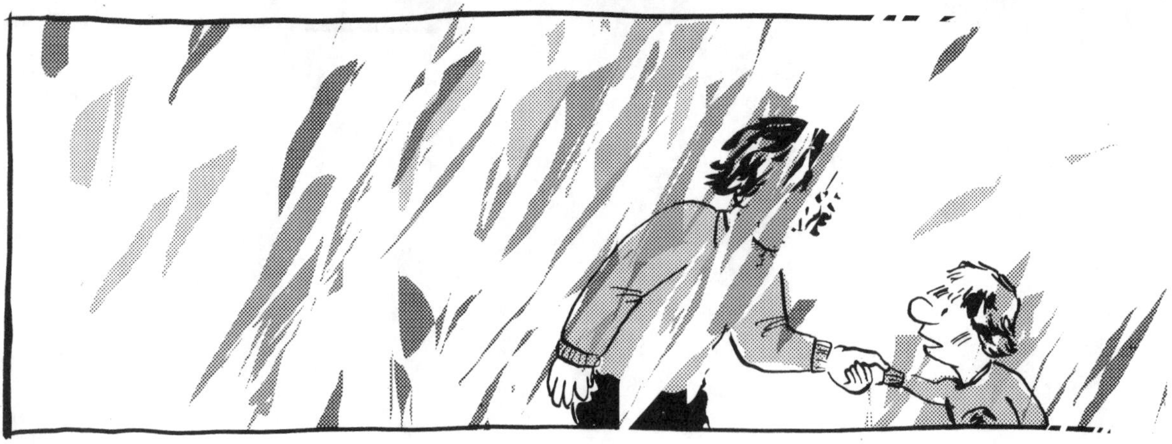

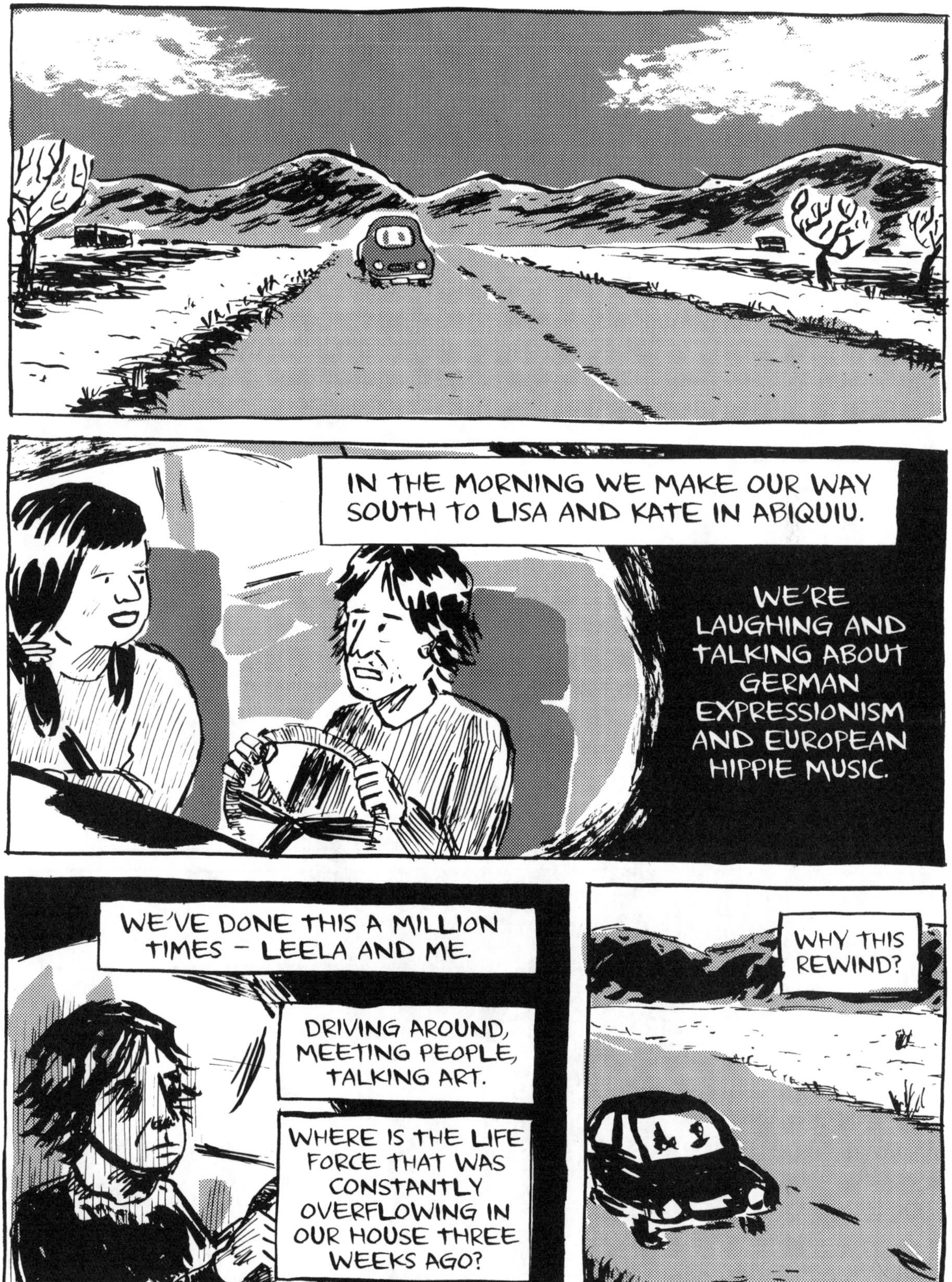
IN THE MORNING WE MAKE OUR WAY SOUTH TO LISA AND KATE IN ABIQUIU.
WE'RE LAUGHING AND TALKING ABOUT GERMAN EXPRESSIONISM AND EUROPEAN HIPPIE MUSIC.
WE'VE DONE THIS A MILLION TIMES – LEELA AND ME.
DRIVING AROUND, MEETING PEOPLE, TALKING ART.
WHERE IS THE LIFE FORCE THAT WAS CONSTANTLY OVERFLOWING IN OUR HOUSE THREE WEEKS AGO?
WHY THIS REWIND?

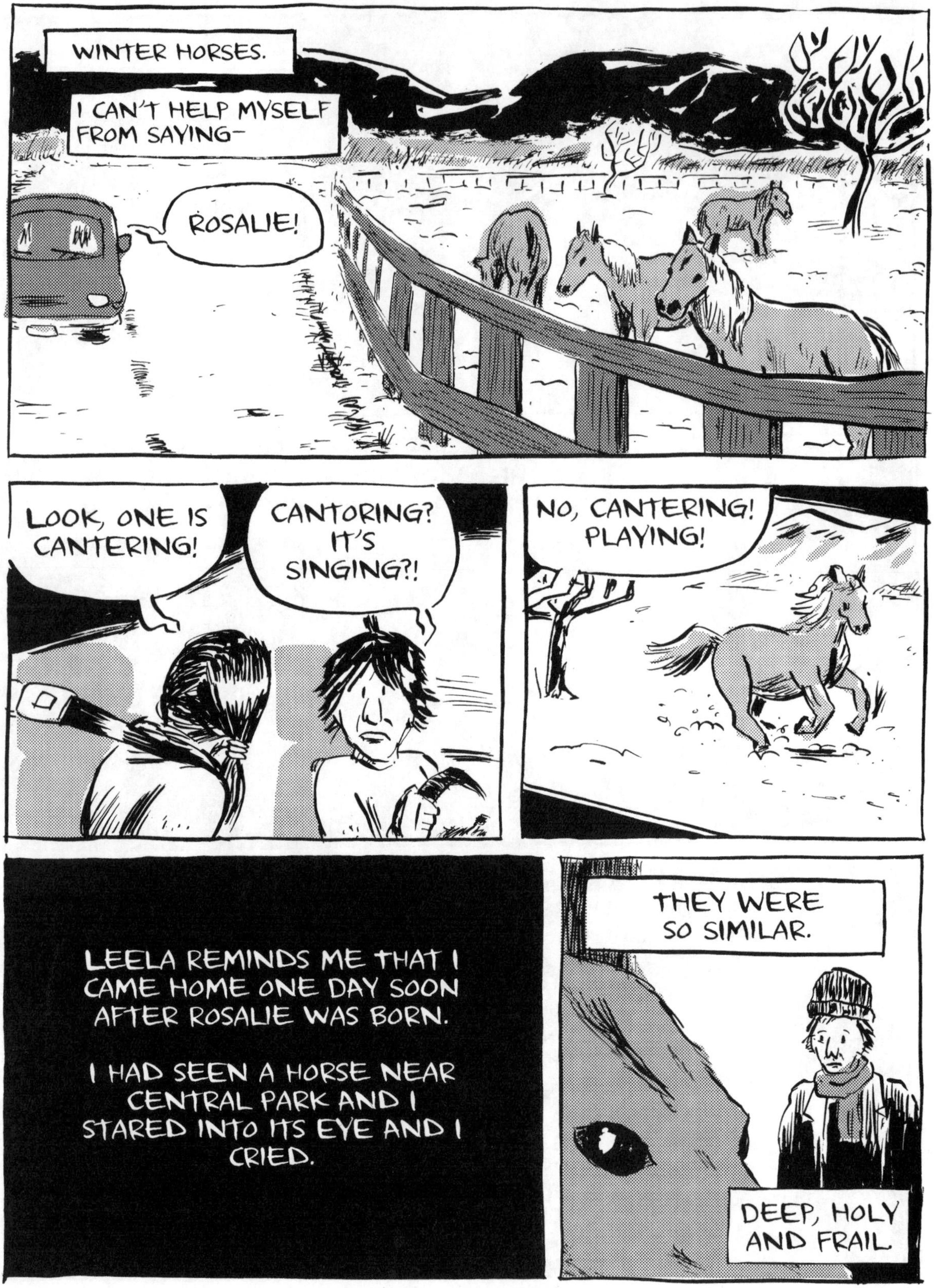
WINTER HORSES.
I CAN'T HELP MYSELF FROM SAYING-
ROSALIE!
LOOK, ONE IS CANTERING!
CANTORING? IT'S SINGING?!
NO, CANTERING! PLAYING!
LEELA REMINDS ME THAT I CAME HOME ONE DAY SOON AFTER ROSALIE WAS BORN.
I HAD SEEN A HORSE NEAR CENTRAL PARK AND I STARED INTO ITS EYE AND I CRIED.
THEY WERE SO SIMILAR.
DEEP, HOLY AND FRAIL.

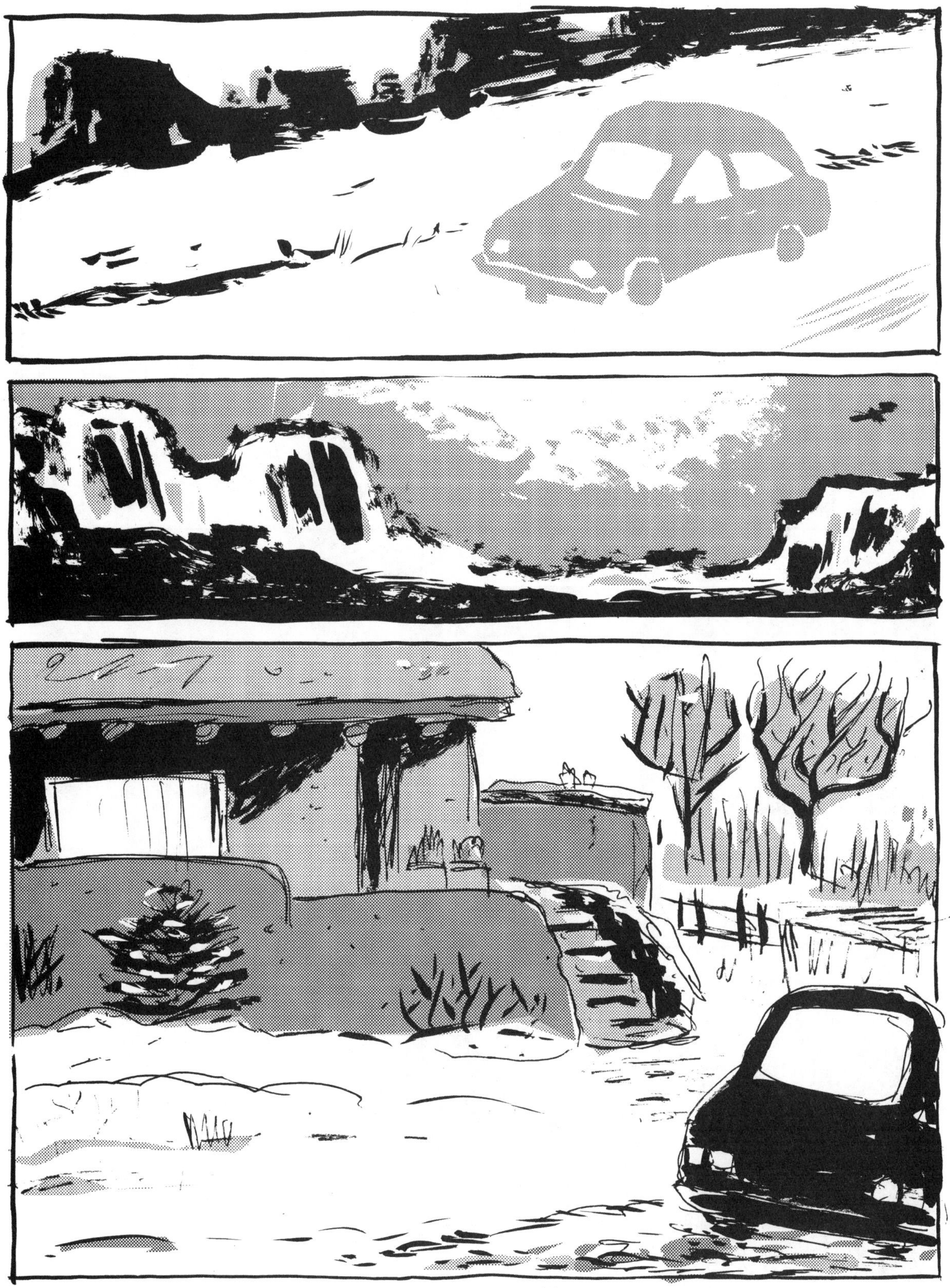

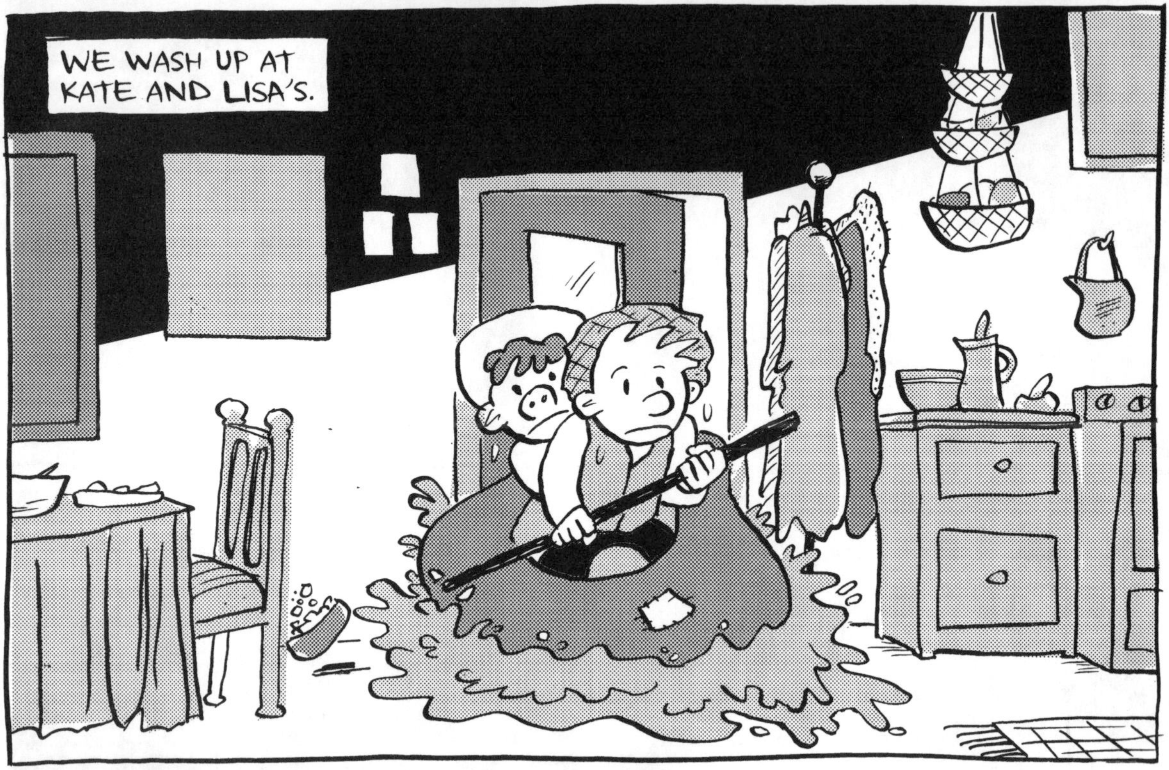
WE WASH UP AT KATE AND LISA'S.

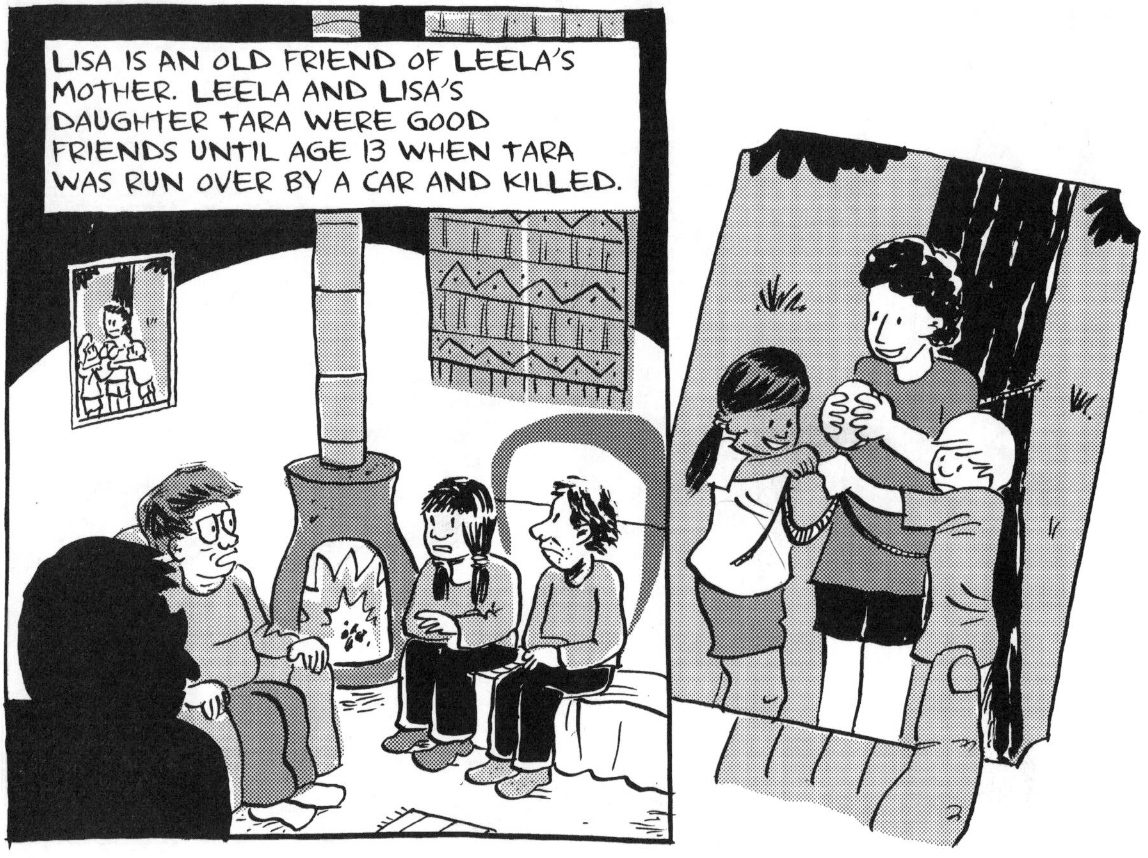
LISA IS AN OLD FRIEND OF LEELA'S MOTHER. LEELA AND LISA'S DAUGHTER TARA WERE GOOD FRIENDS UNTIL AGE 13 WHEN TARA WAS RUN OVER BY A CAR AND KILLED.

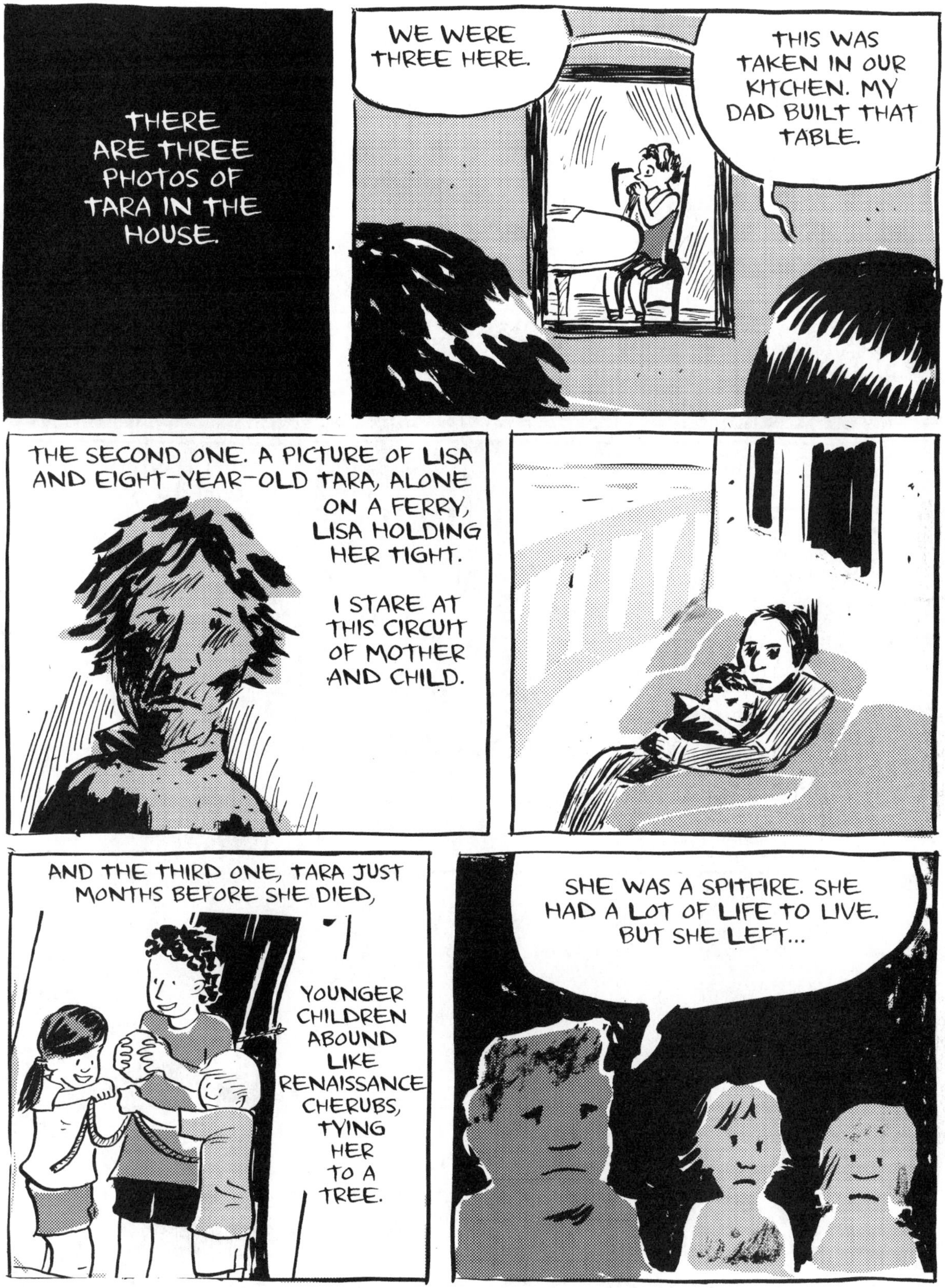
THERE ARE THREE PHOTOS OF TARA IN THE HOUSE.
WE WERE THREE HERE.
THIS WAS TAKEN IN OUR KITCHEN. MY DAD BUILT THAT TABLE.
THE SECOND ONE. A PICTURE OF LISA AND EIGHT-YEAR-OLD TARA, ALONE ON A FERRY, LISA HOLDING HER TIGHT.
I STARE AT THIS CIRCUIT OF MOTHER AND CHILD.
AND THE THIRD ONE, TARA JUST MONTHS BEFORE SHE DIED,
YOUNGER CHILDREN ABOUND LIKE RENAISSANCE CHERUBS, TYING HER TO A TREE.
SHE WAS A SPITFIRE. SHE HAD A LOT OF LIFE TO LIVE. BUT SHE LEFT...

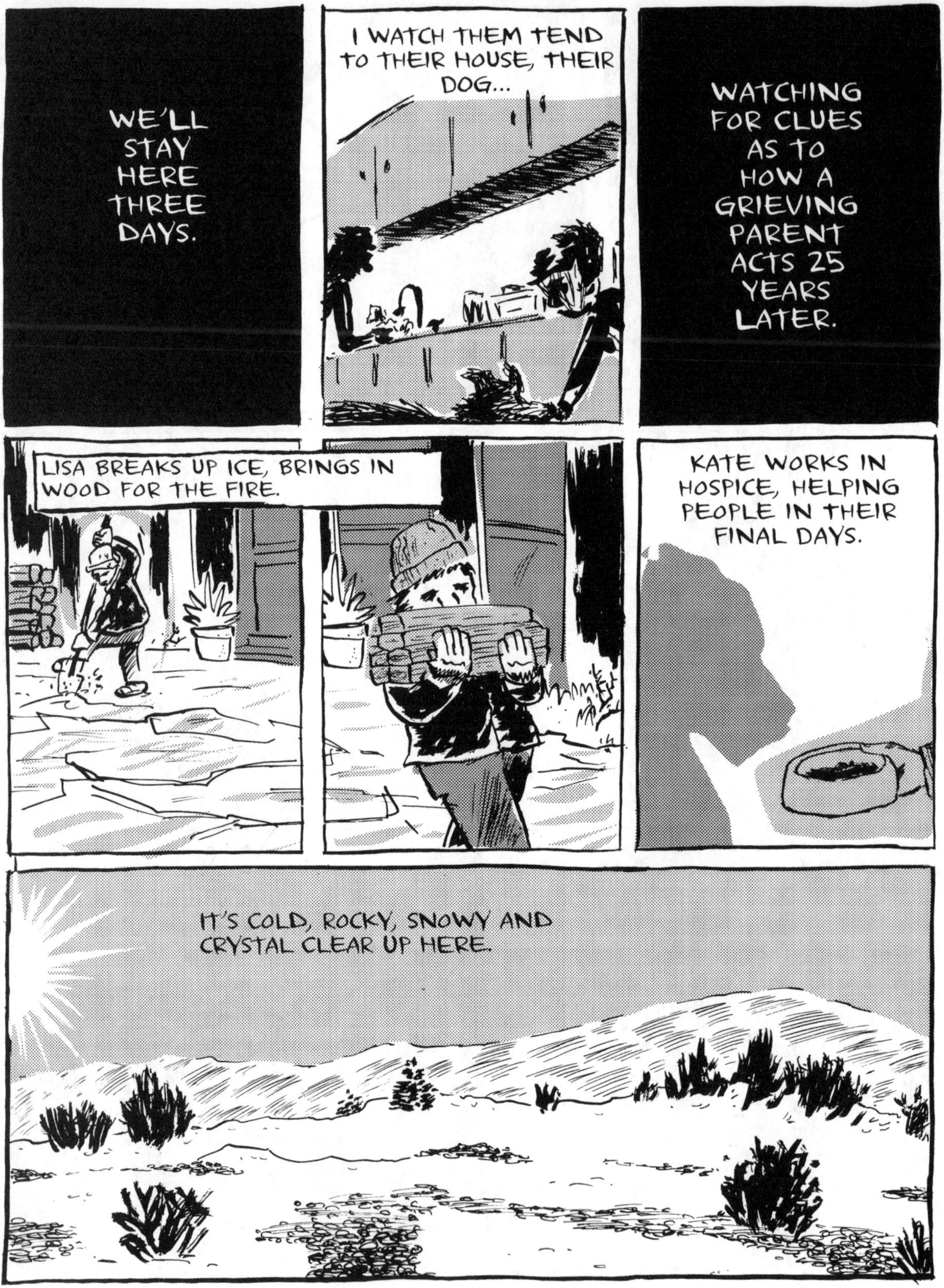
WE'LL STAY HERE THREE DAYS.
I WATCH THEM TEND TO THEIR HOUSE, THEIR DOG...
WATCHING FOR CLUES AS TO HOW A GRIEVING PARENT ACTS 25 YEARS LATER.
LISA BREAKS UP ICE, BRINGS IN WOOD FOR THE FIRE.
KATE WORKS IN HOSPICE, HELPING PEOPLE IN THEIR FINAL DAYS.
IT'S COLD, ROCKY, SNOWY AND CRYSTAL CLEAR UP HERE.

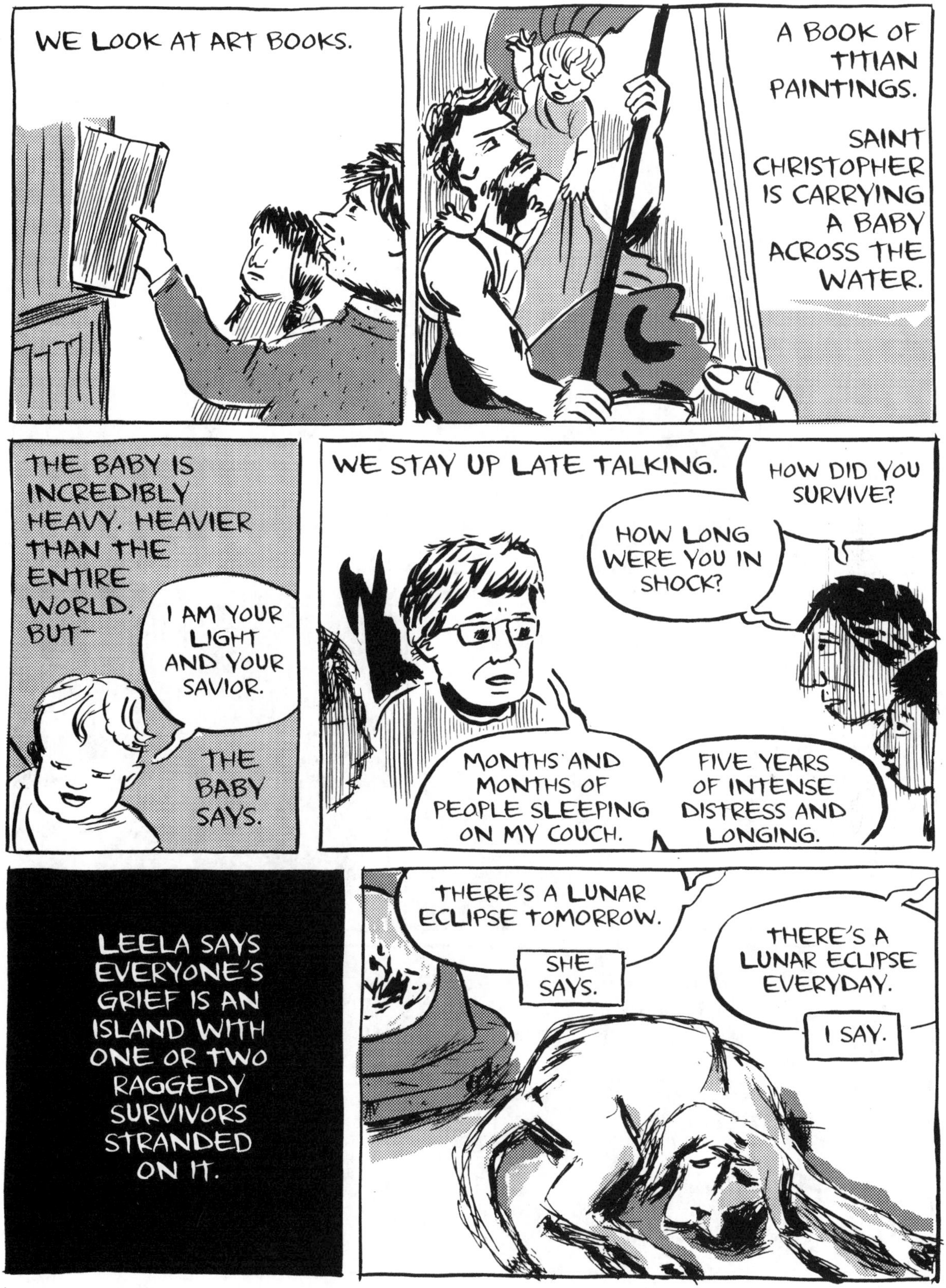
WE LOOK AT ART BOOKS.
A BOOK OF TITIAN PAINTINGS.
SAINT CHRISTOPHER IS CARRYING A BABY ACROSS THE WATER.
THE BABY IS INCREDIBLY HEAVY. HEAVIER THAN THE ENTIRE WORLD. BUT–
I AM YOUR LIGHT AND YOUR SAVIOR.
THE BABY SAYS.
WE STAY UP LATE TALKING.
HOW DID YOU SURVIVE?
HOW LONG WERE YOU IN SHOCK?
MONTHS AND MONTHS OF PEOPLE SLEEPING ON MY COUCH.
FIVE YEARS OF INTENSE DISTRESS AND LONGING.
LEELA SAYS EVERYONE'S GRIEF IS AN ISLAND WITH ONE OR TWO RAGGEDY SURVIVORS STRANDED ON IT.
THERE'S A LUNAR ECLIPSE TOMORROW.
SHE SAYS.
THERE'S A LUNAR ECLIPSE EVERYDAY.
I SAY.

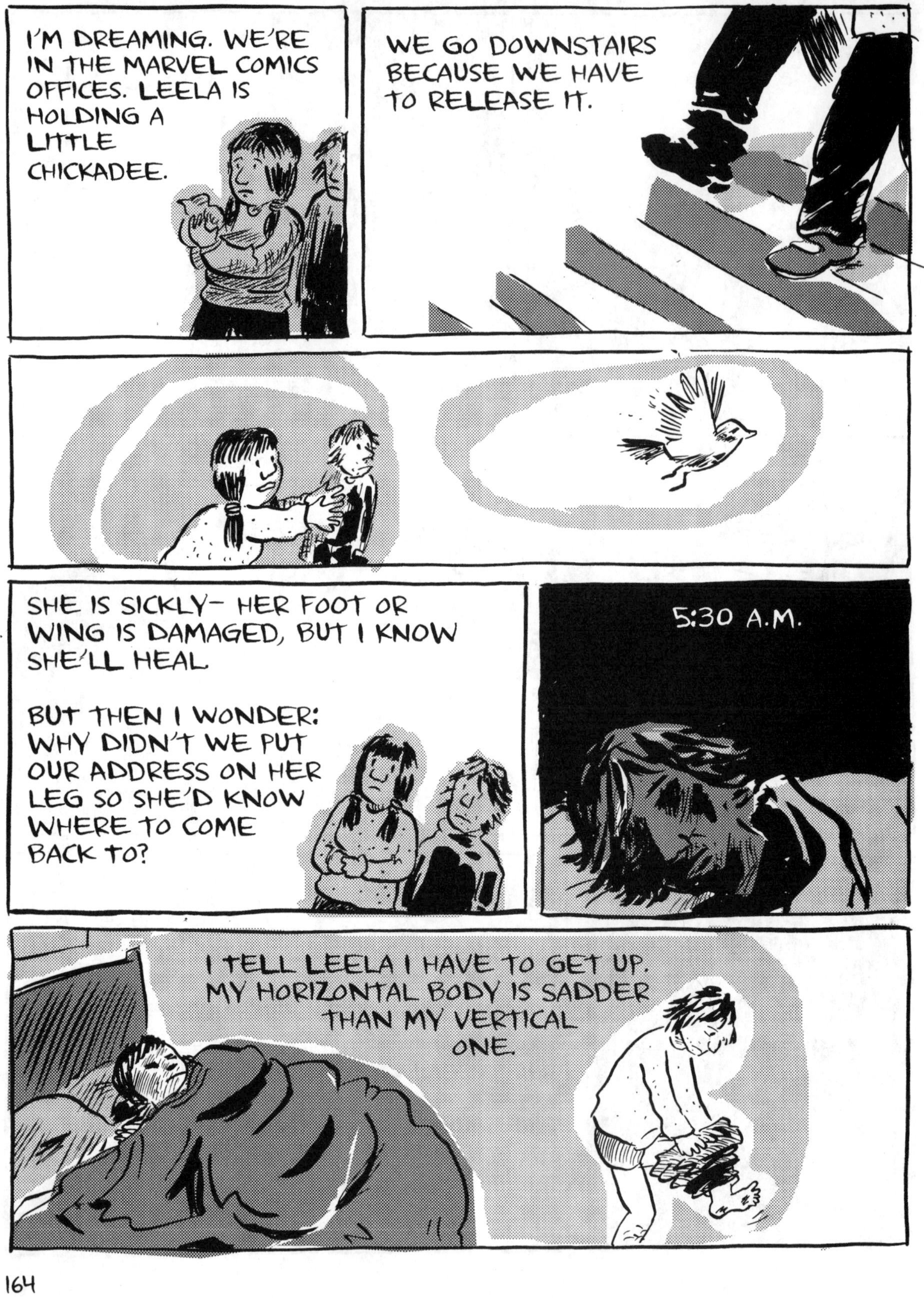
I'M DREAMING. WE'RE IN THE MARVEL COMICS OFFICES. LEELA IS HOLDING A LITTLE CHICKADEE.
WE GO DOWNSTAIRS BECAUSE WE HAVE TO RELEASE IT.
SHE IS SICKLY— HER FOOT OR WING IS DAMAGED, BUT I KNOW SHE'LL HEAL.
BUT THEN I WONDER: WHY DIDN'T WE PUT OUR ADDRESS ON HER LEG SO SHE'D KNOW WHERE TO COME BACK TO?
5:30 A.M.
I TELL LEELA I HAVE TO GET UP. MY HORIZONTAL BODY IS SADDER THAN MY VERTICAL ONE.

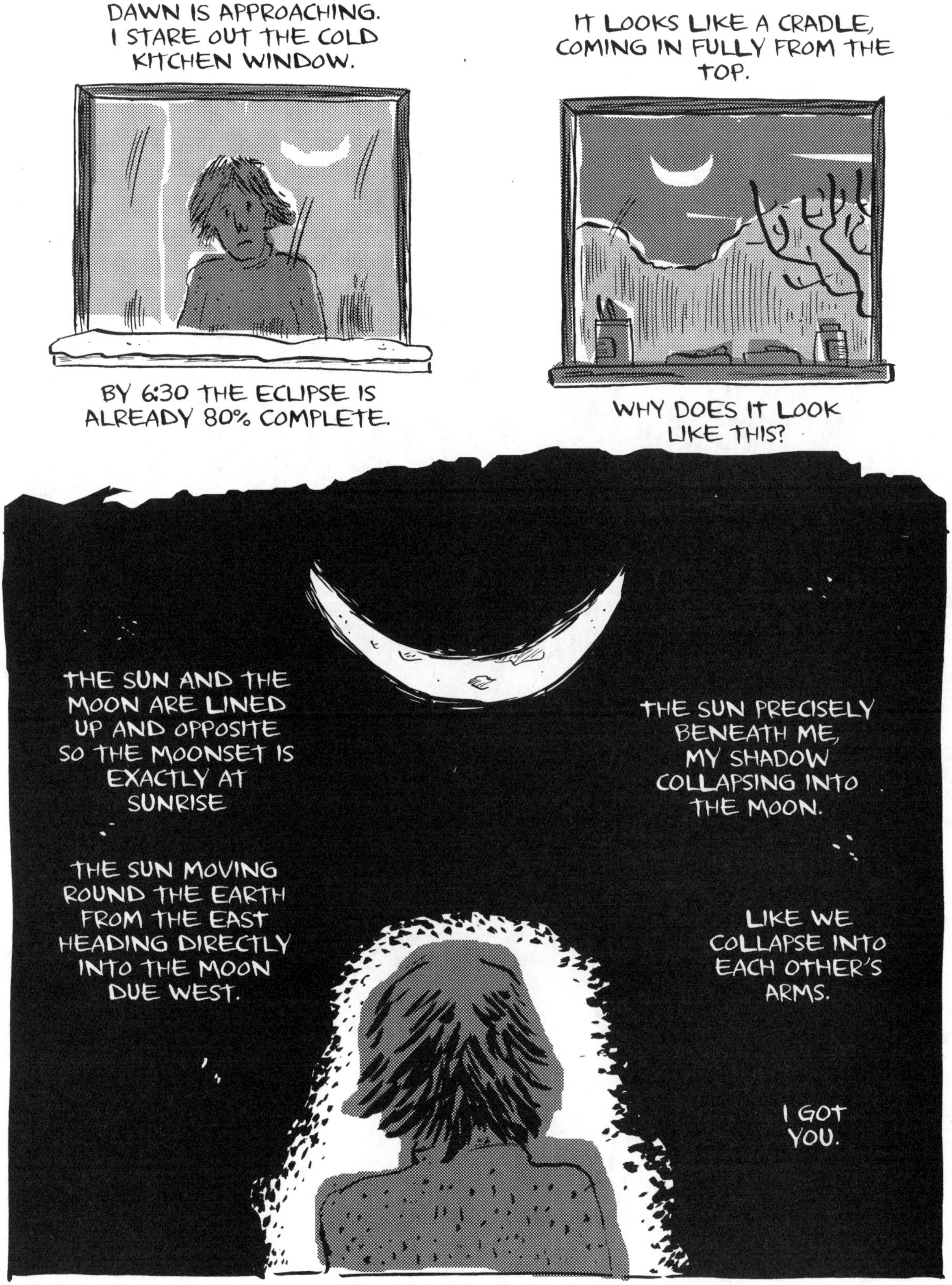
DAWN IS APPROACHING. I STARE OUT THE COLD KITCHEN WINDOW.
BY 6:30 THE ECLIPSE IS ALREADY 80% COMPLETE.
IT LOOKS LIKE A CRADLE, COMING IN FULLY FROM THE TOP.
WHY DOES IT LOOK LIKE THIS?
THE SUN AND THE MOON ARE LINED UP AND OPPOSITE SO THE MOONSET IS EXACTLY AT SUNRISE
THE SUN MOVING ROUND THE EARTH FROM THE EAST HEADING DIRECTLY INTO THE MOON DUE WEST.
THE SUN PRECISELY BENEATH ME, MY SHADOW COLLAPSING INTO THE MOON.
LIKE WE COLLAPSE INTO EACH OTHER'S ARMS.
I GOT YOU.

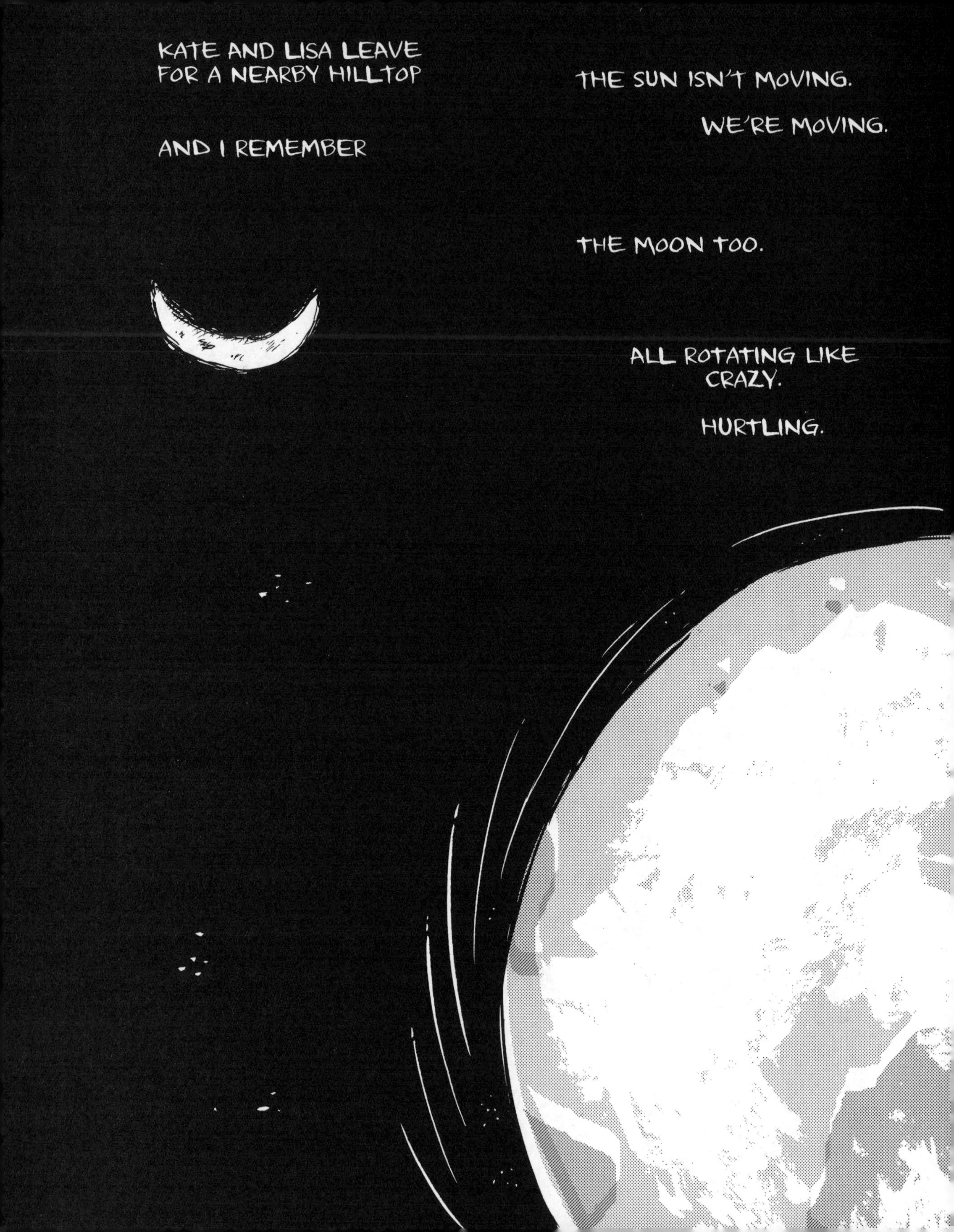
KATE AND LISA LEAVE FOR A NEARBY HILLTOP
AND I REMEMBER
THE SUN ISN'T MOVING.
WE'RE MOVING.
THE MOON TOO.
ALL ROTATING LIKE CRAZY.
HURTLING.

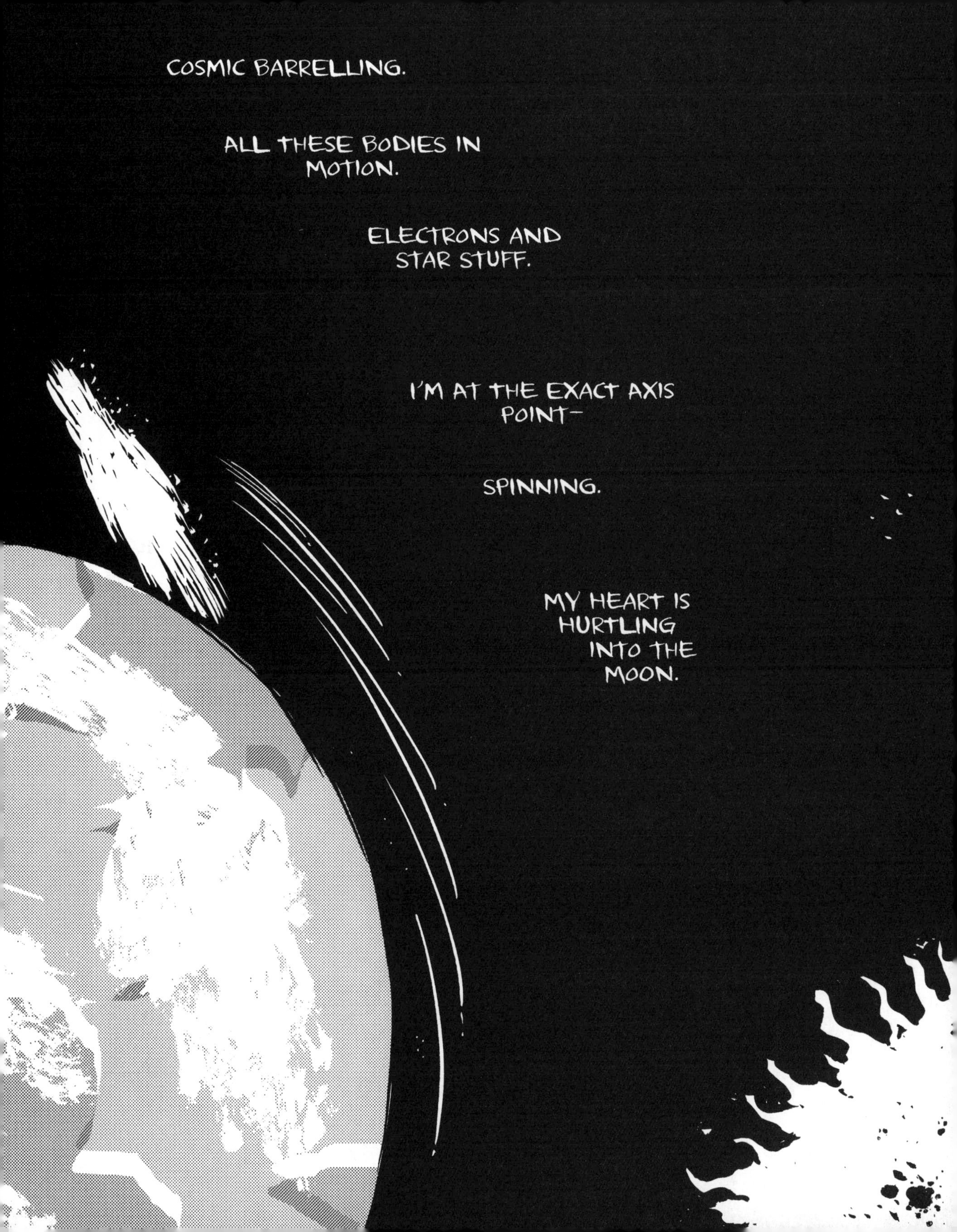
COSMIC BARRELLING.
ALL THESE BODIES IN MOTION.
ELECTRONS AND STAR STUFF.
I'M AT THE EXACT AXIS POINT–
SPINNING.
MY HEART IS HURTLING INTO THE MOON.

THE MOON IS A
SLIVER.

I STEP OUTSIDE
AND PUT ON MY
HURTLING SHOES
TO WATCH IT
DOUBLY
DISAPPEAR.

DISAPPEAR
BEHIND MY
SHADOW
AND
BENEATH
THE ROCKY
MESAS.

GONE.

WHERE DID THE
BIG MOON GO?

WHERE DID
RODZY GO?

WHERE DID
MY STAR
STUFF GO?

OUTSIDE, ROCKS ON A LEDGE, HAND PAINTED AS LADYBUGS.

LAST NIGHT, DREAMS OF CHICKADEES TAKING ME TO MY GIRL

THE SHADOW OF THE EARTH COLLAPSES INTO THE MOON.

I GOT YOU.

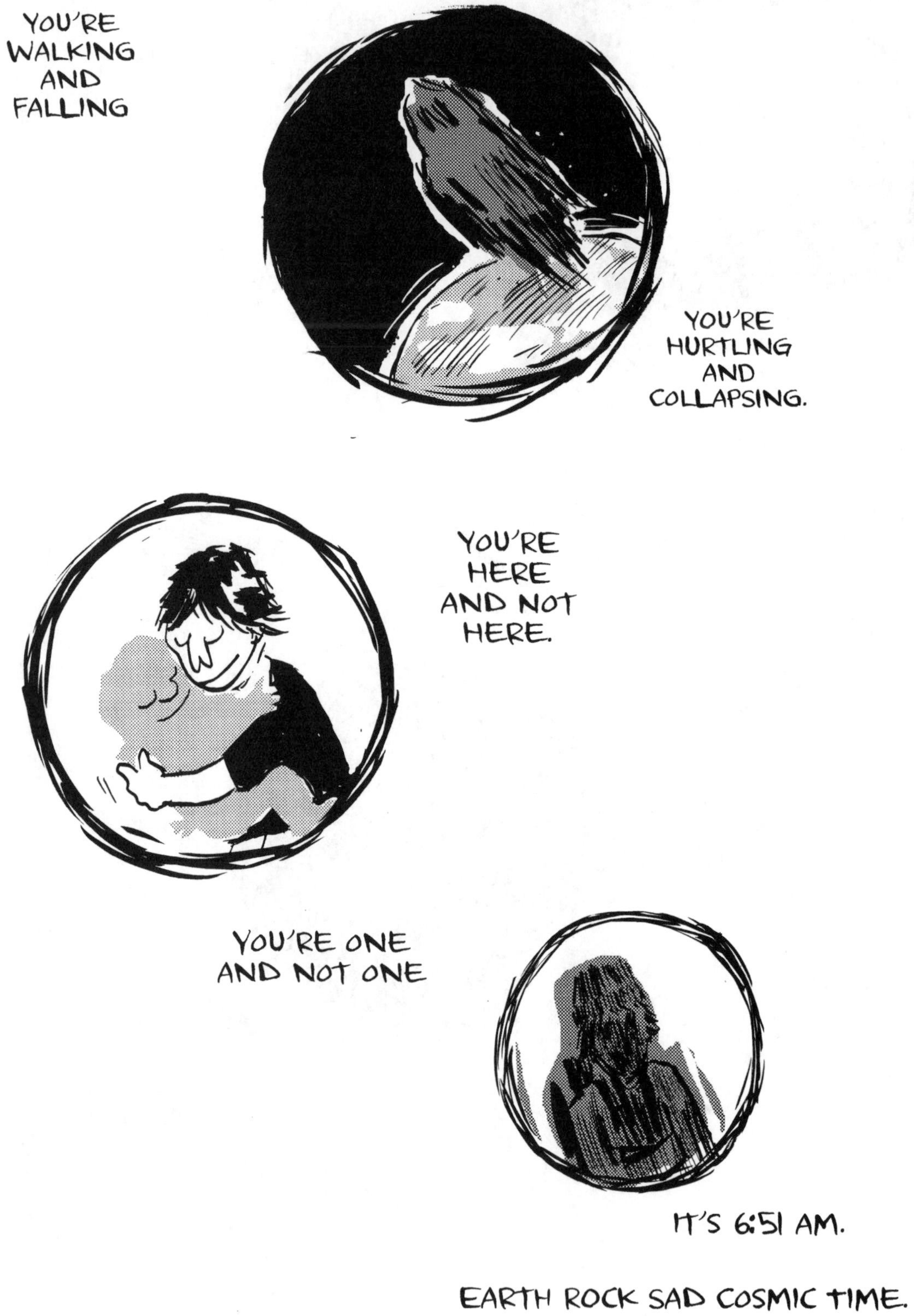
YOU'RE WALKING AND FALLING
YOU'RE HURTLING AND COLLAPSING.
YOU'RE HERE AND NOT HERE.
YOU'RE ONE AND NOT ONE
IT'S 6:51 AM.
EARTH ROCK SAD COSMIC TIME.

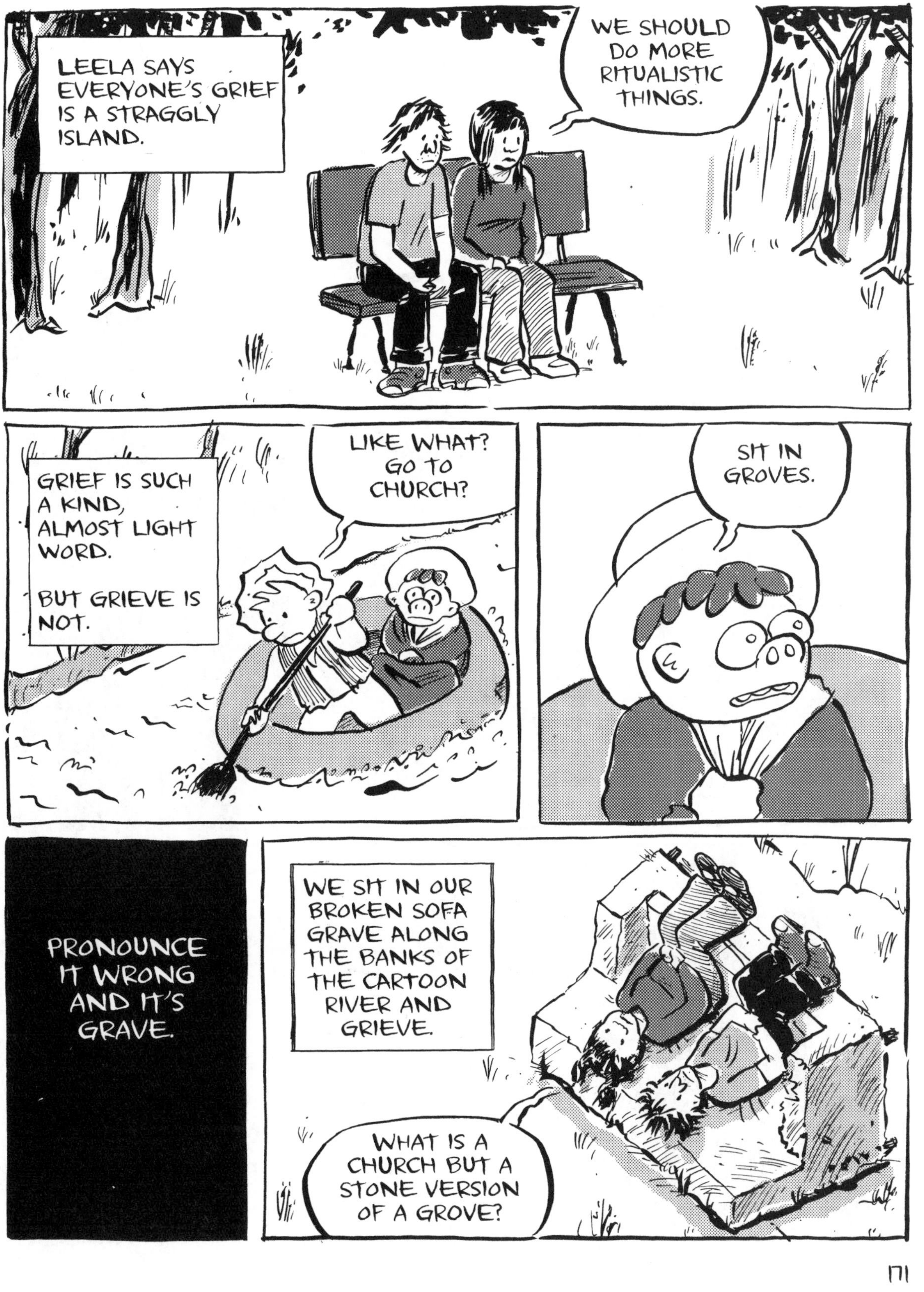

LEELA SAYS EVERYONE'S GRIEF IS A STRAGGLY ISLAND.
WE SHOULD DO MORE RITUALISTIC THINGS.
GRIEF IS SUCH A KIND, ALMOST LIGHT WORD.
BUT GRIEVE IS NOT.
LIKE WHAT? GO TO CHURCH?
SIT IN GROVES.
PRONOUNCE IT WRONG AND IT'S GRAVE.
WE SIT IN OUR BROKEN SOFA GRAVE ALONG THE BANKS OF THE CARTOON RIVER AND GRIEVE.
WHAT IS A CHURCH BUT A STONE VERSION OF A GROVE?

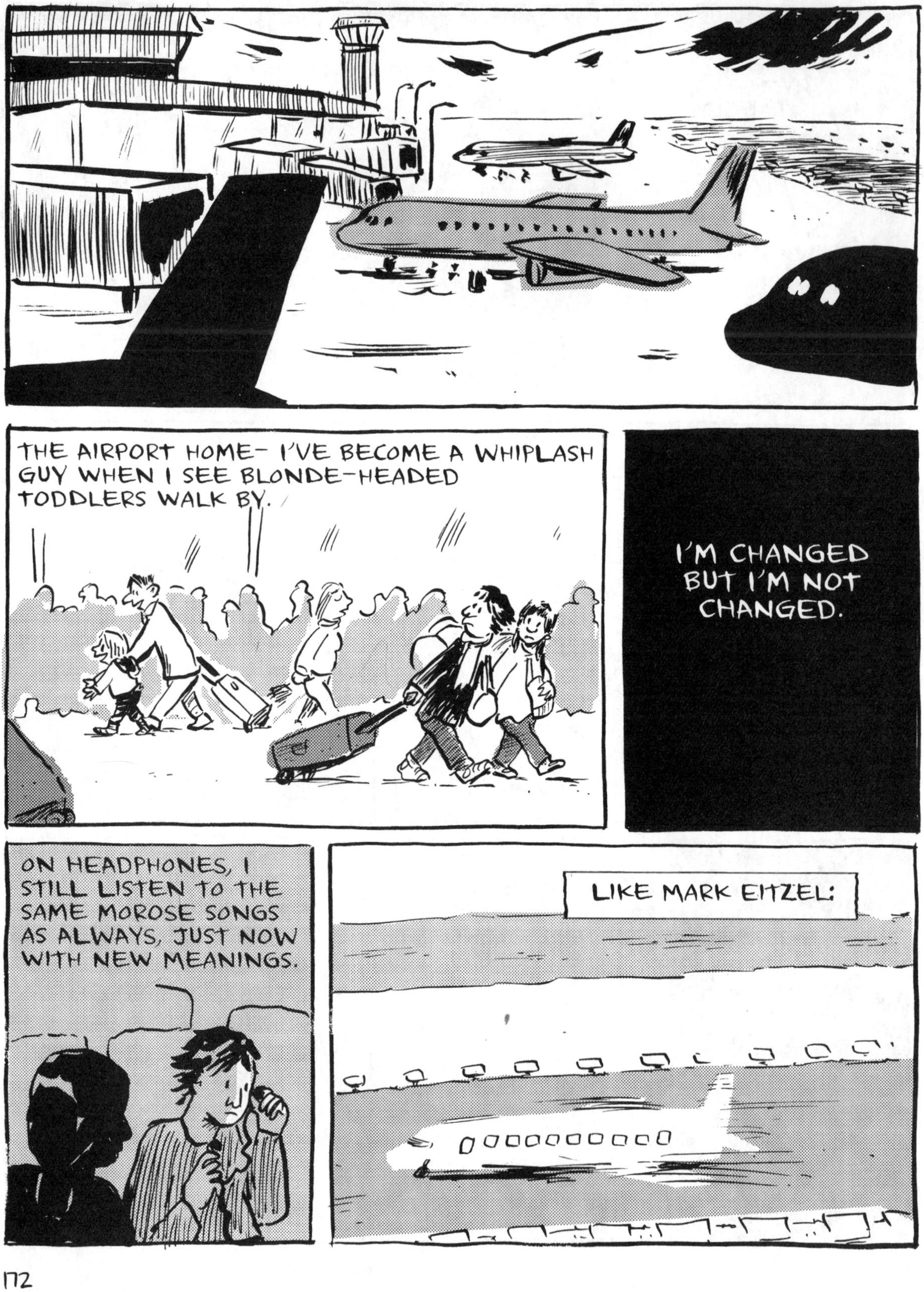
THE AIRPORT HOME– I'VE BECOME A WHIPLASH GUY WHEN I SEE BLONDE-HEADED TODDLERS WALK BY.
I'M CHANGED BUT I'M NOT CHANGED.
ON HEADPHONES, I STILL LISTEN TO THE SAME MOROSE SONGS AS ALWAYS, JUST NOW WITH NEW MEANINGS.
LIKE MARK EITZEL:

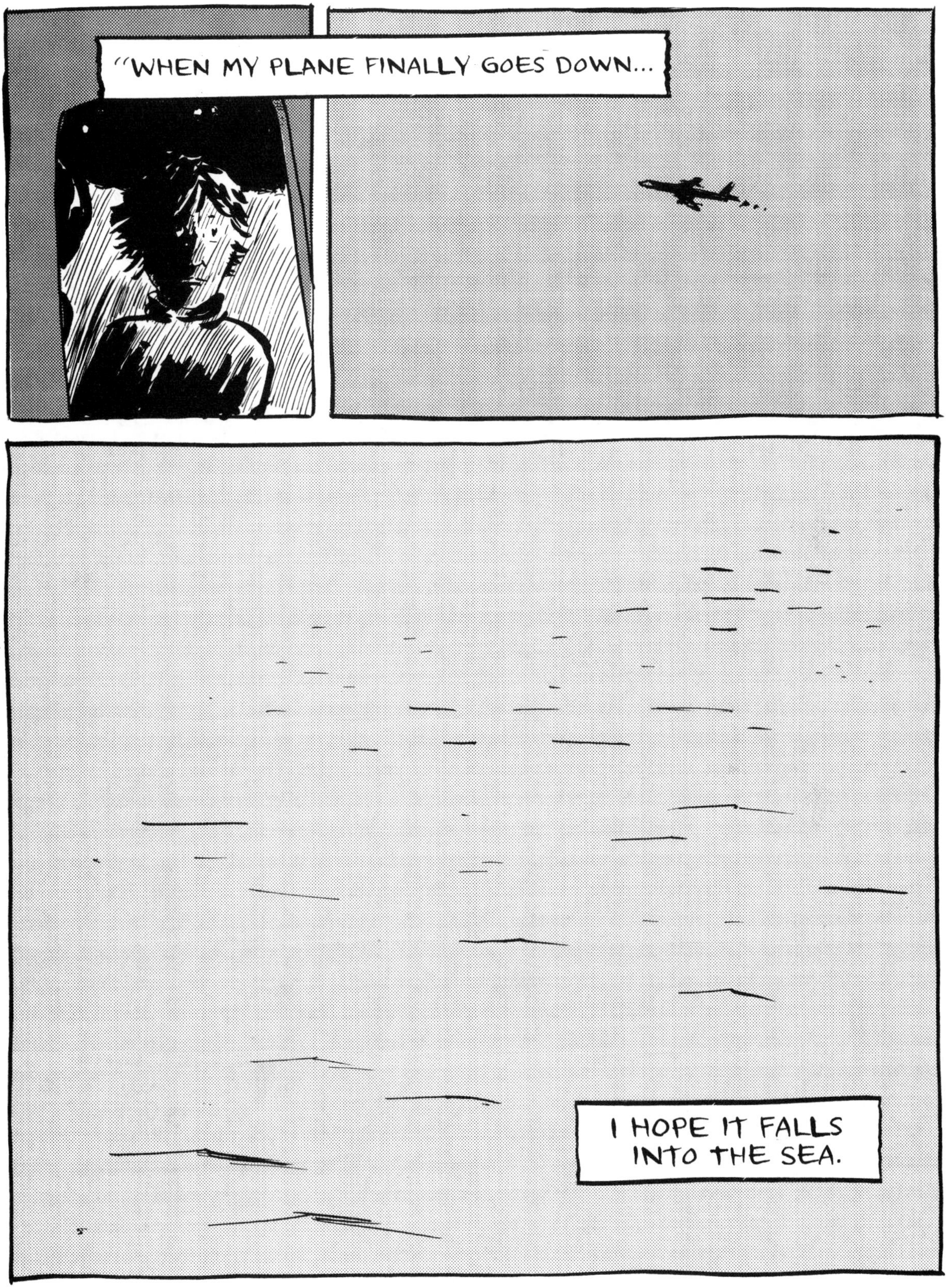
"WHEN MY PLANE FINALLY GOES DOWN...
I HOPE IT FALLS INTO THE SEA.

THEN THE FREEZING CLEAN WATER

WILL WASH AWAY WHATEVER'S LEFT OF ME."

IX

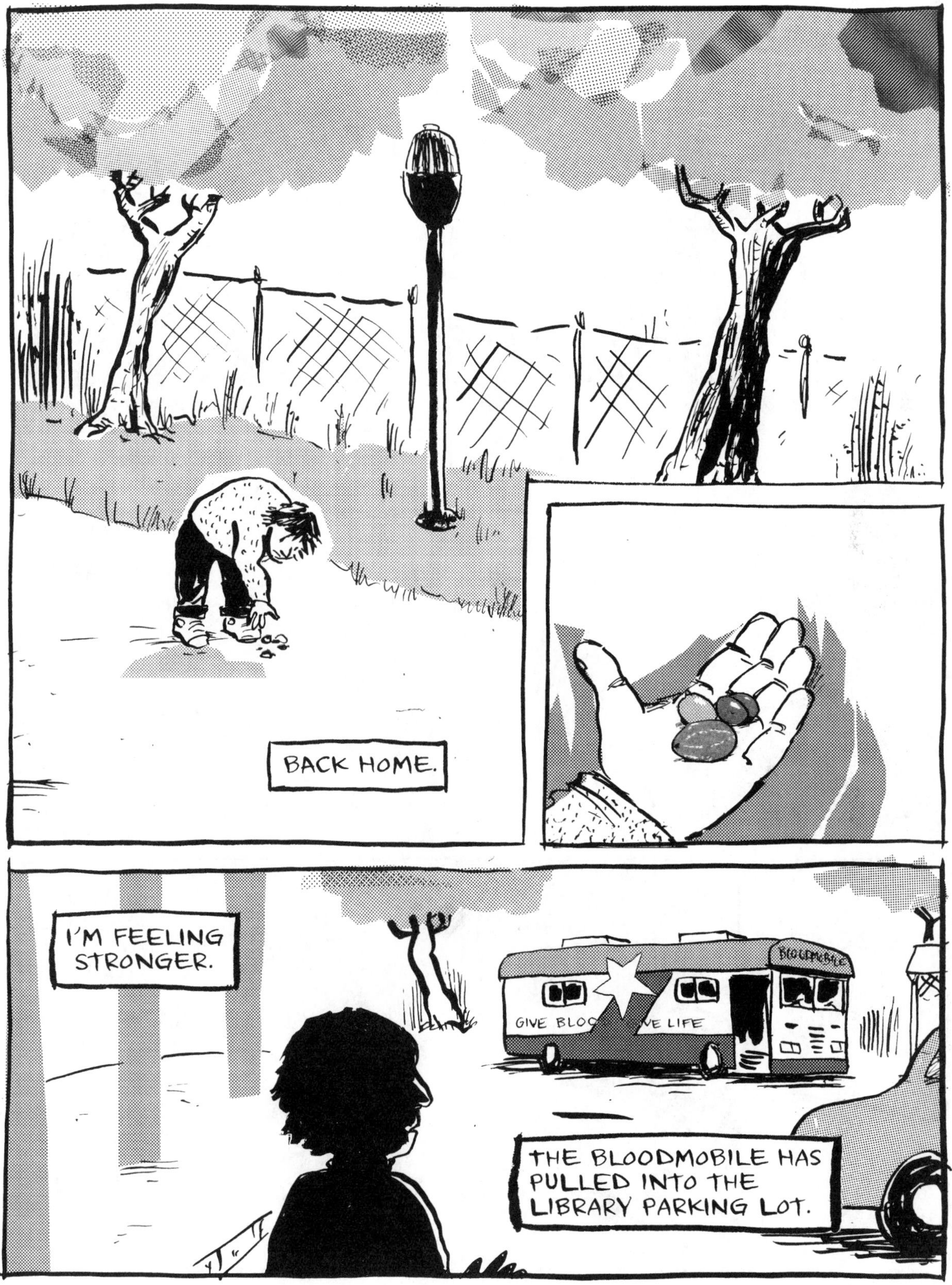
BACK HOME.
I'M FEELING STRONGER.
THE BLOODMOBILE HAS PULLED INTO THE LIBRARY PARKING LOT.

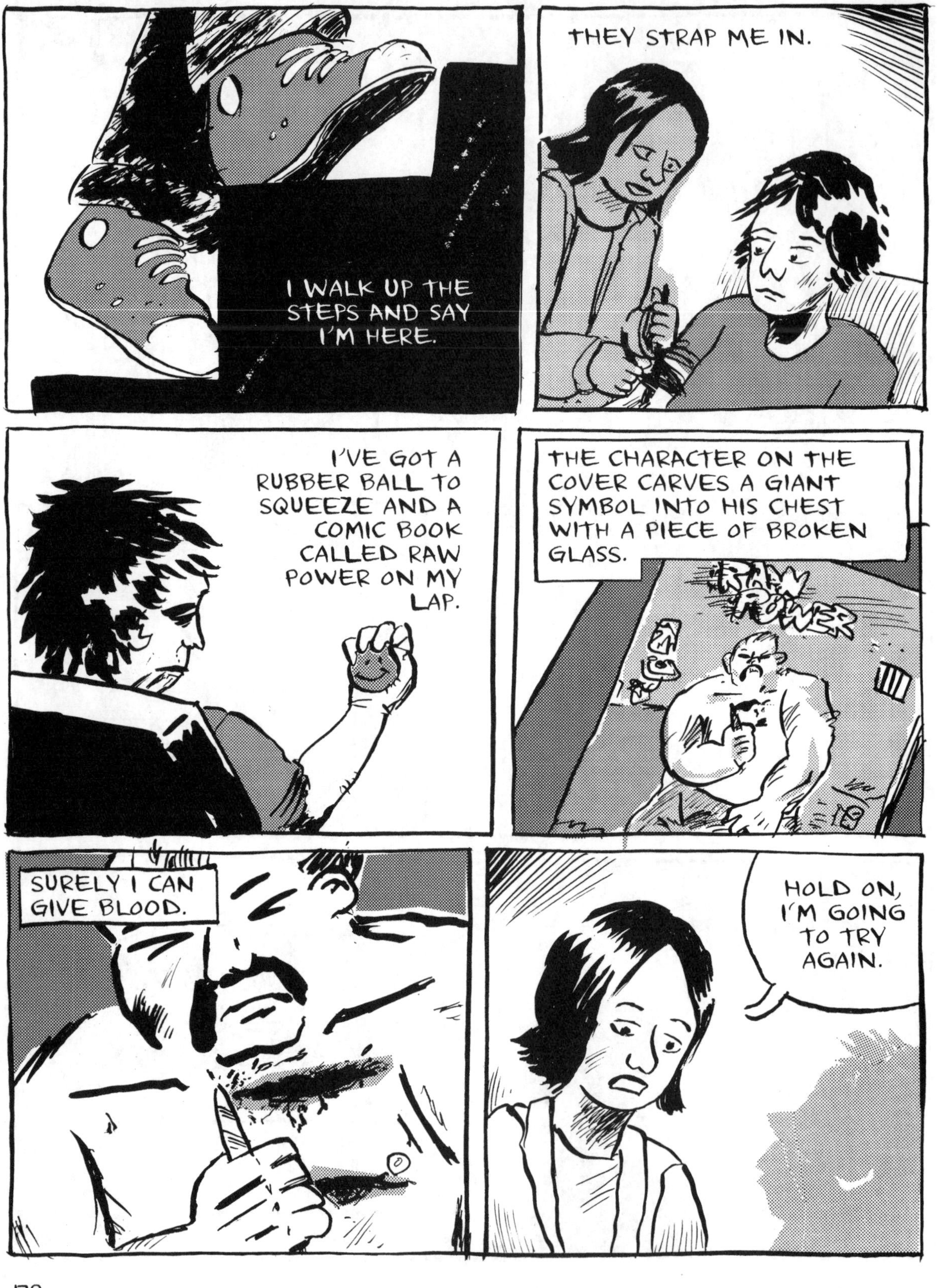
I WALK UP THE STEPS AND SAY I'M HERE.
THEY STRAP ME IN.
I'VE GOT A RUBBER BALL TO SQUEEZE AND A COMIC BOOK CALLED RAW POWER ON MY LAP.
THE CHARACTER ON THE COVER CARVES A GIANT SYMBOL INTO HIS CHEST WITH A PIECE OF BROKEN GLASS.
RAW POWER
SURELY I CAN GIVE BLOOD.
HOLD ON, I'M GOING TO TRY AGAIN.

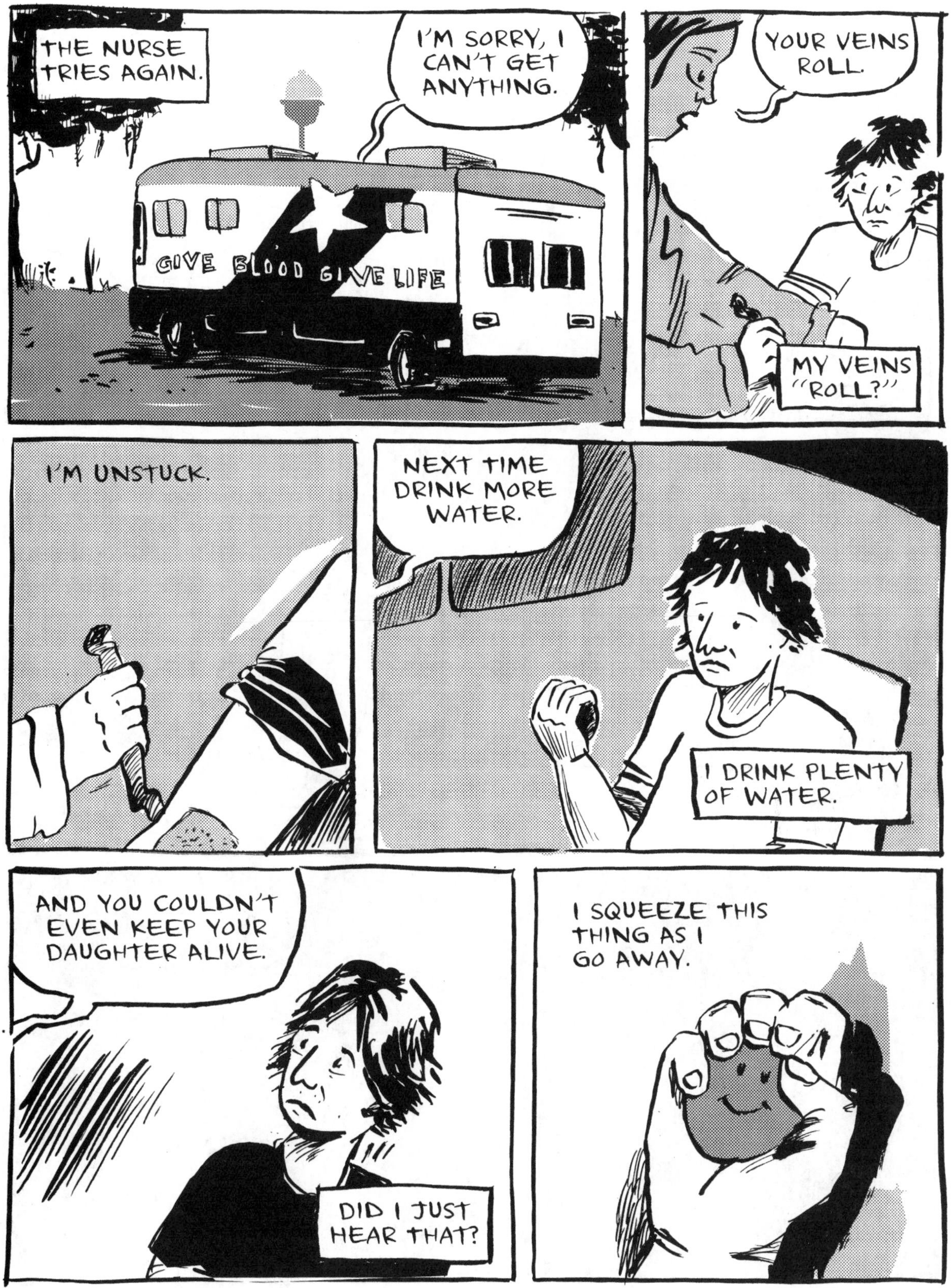
THE NURSE TRIES AGAIN.
I'M SORRY, I CAN'T GET ANYTHING.
GIVE BLOOD GIVE LIFE
YOUR VEINS ROLL.
MY VEINS "ROLL?"
I'M UNSTUCK.
NEXT TIME DRINK MORE WATER.
I DRINK PLENTY OF WATER.
AND YOU COULDN'T EVEN KEEP YOUR DAUGHTER ALIVE.
DID I JUST HEAR THAT?
I SQUEEZE THIS THING AS I GO AWAY.

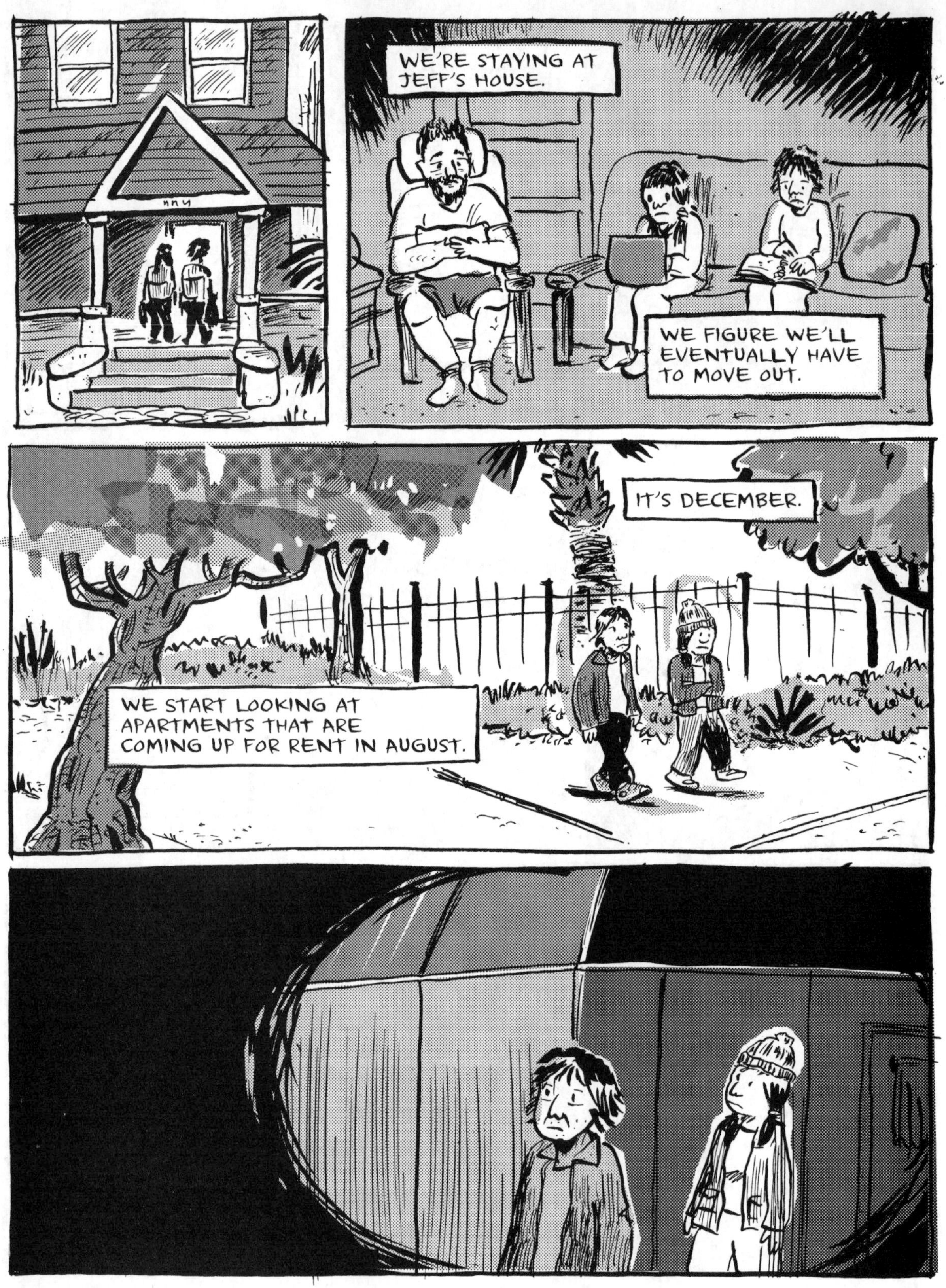

WE'RE STAYING AT JEFF'S HOUSE.
WE FIGURE WE'LL EVENTUALLY HAVE TO MOVE OUT.
IT'S DECEMBER.
WE START LOOKING AT APARTMENTS THAT ARE COMING UP FOR RENT IN AUGUST.

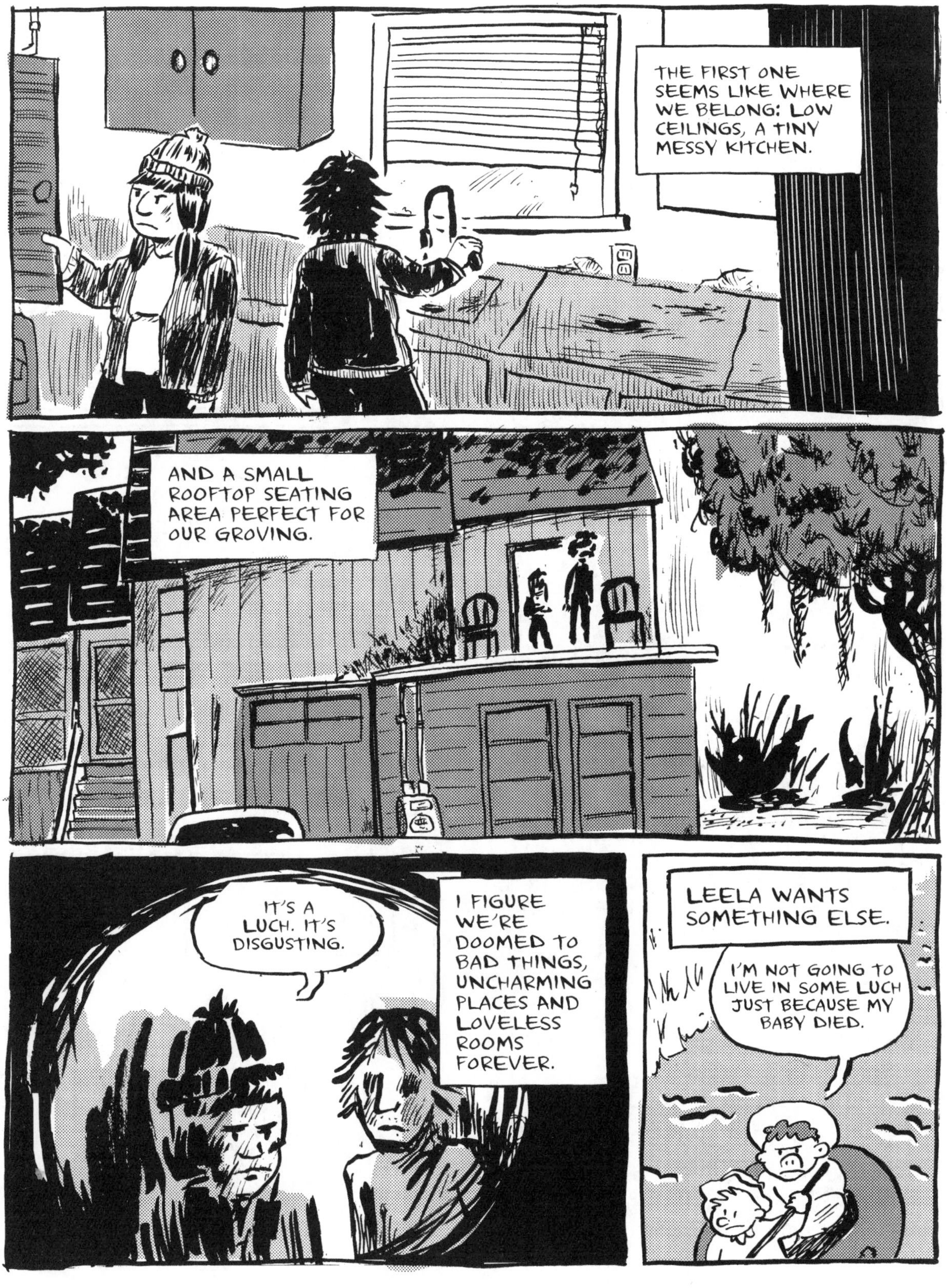

THE FIRST ONE SEEMS LIKE WHERE WE BELONG: LOW CEILINGS, A TINY MESSY KITCHEN.
AND A SMALL ROOFTOP SEATING AREA PERFECT FOR OUR GROVING.
IT'S A LUCH. IT'S DISGUSTING.
I FIGURE WE'RE DOOMED TO BAD THINGS, UNCHARMING PLACES AND LOVELESS ROOMS FOREVER.
LEELA WANTS SOMETHING ELSE.
I'M NOT GOING TO LIVE IN SOME LUCH JUST BECAUSE MY BABY DIED.

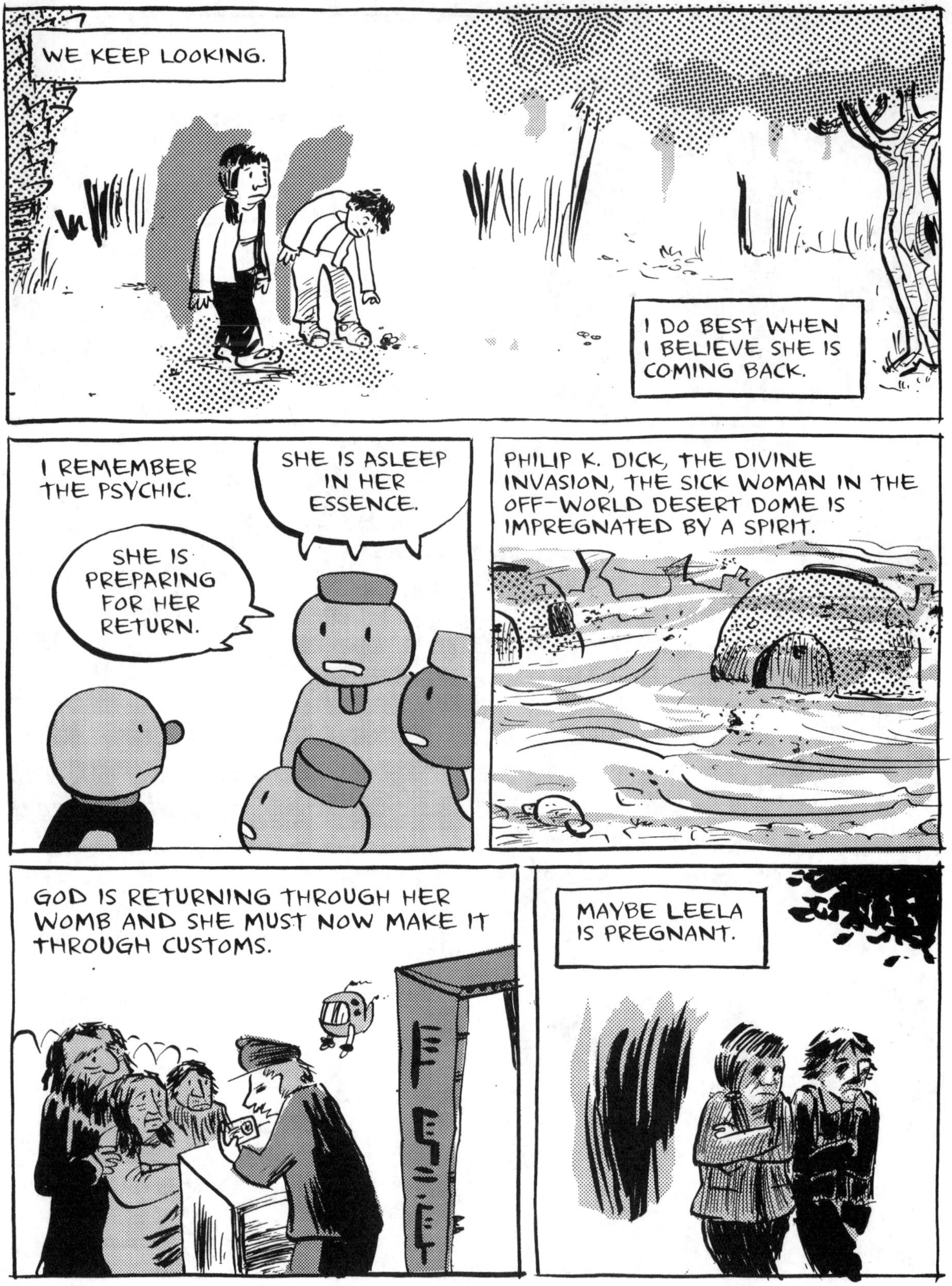
WE KEEP LOOKING.
I DO BEST WHEN I BELIEVE SHE IS COMING BACK.
I REMEMBER THE PSYCHIC.
SHE IS ASLEEP IN HER ESSENCE.
SHE IS PREPARING FOR HER RETURN.
PHILIP K. DICK, THE DIVINE INVASION, THE SICK WOMAN IN THE OFF-WORLD DESERT DOME IS IMPREGNATED BY A SPIRIT.
GOD IS RETURNING THROUGH HER WOMB AND SHE MUST NOW MAKE IT THROUGH CUSTOMS.
MAYBE LEELA IS PREGNANT.

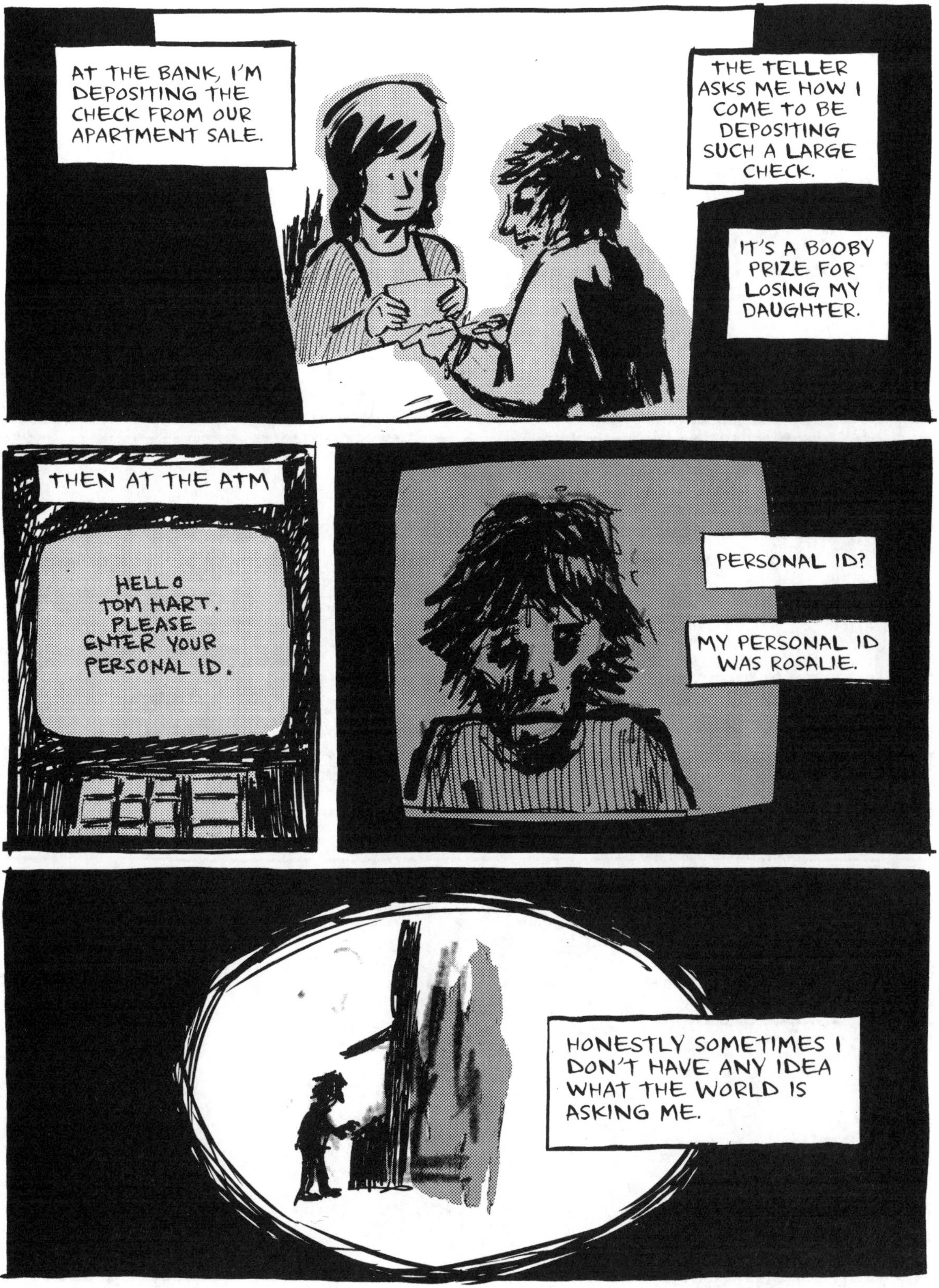
AT THE BANK, I'M DEPOSITING THE CHECK FROM OUR APARTMENT SALE.
THE TELLER ASKS ME HOW I COME TO BE DEPOSITING SUCH A LARGE CHECK.
IT'S A BOOBY PRIZE FOR LOSING MY DAUGHTER.
THEN AT THE ATM
HELLO TOM HART. PLEASE ENTER YOUR PERSONAL ID.
PERSONAL ID?
MY PERSONAL ID WAS ROSALIE.
HONESTLY SOMETIMES I DON'T HAVE ANY IDEA WHAT THE WORLD IS ASKING ME.

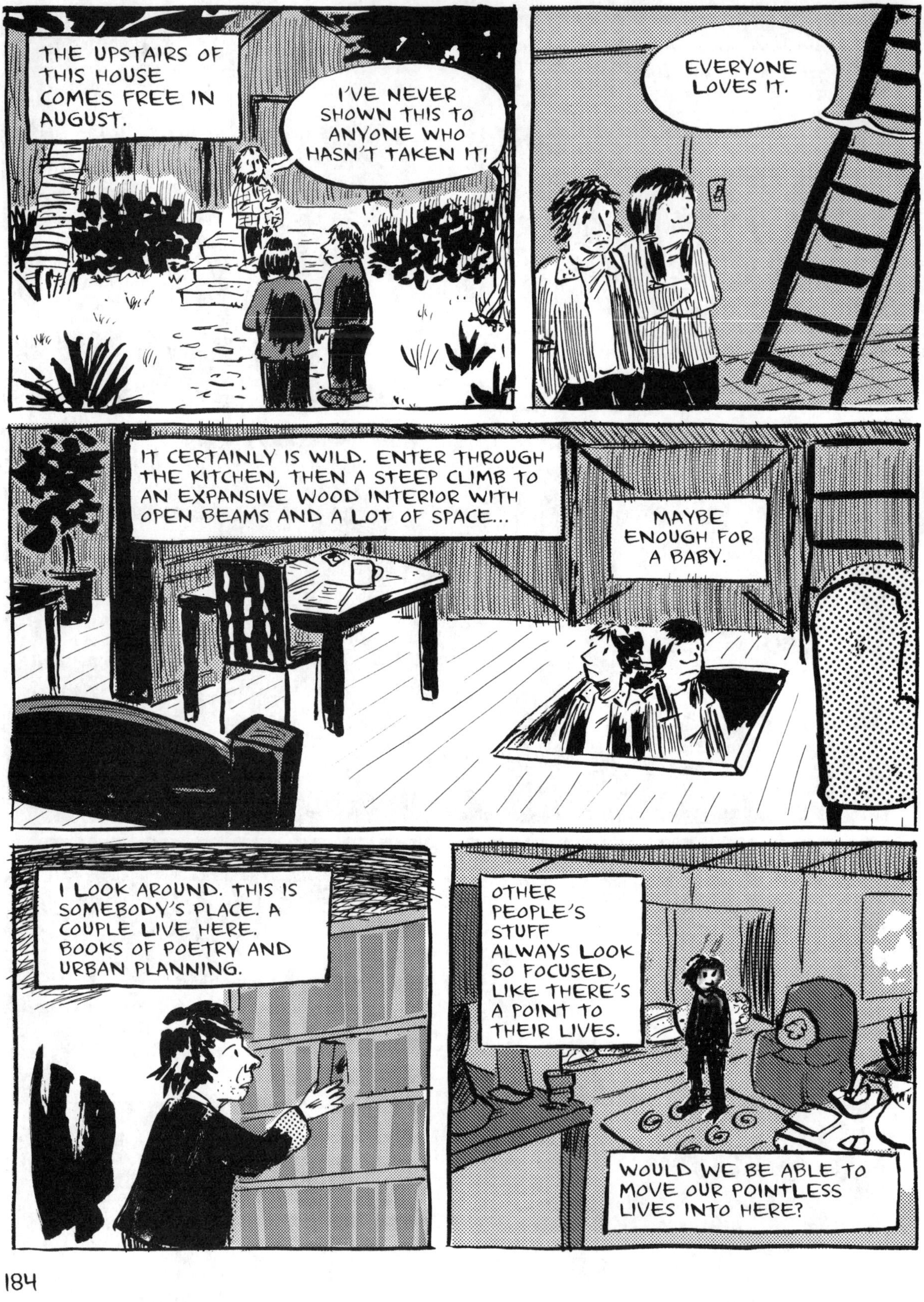
THE UPSTAIRS OF THIS HOUSE COMES FREE IN AUGUST.
I'VE NEVER SHOWN THIS TO ANYONE WHO HASN'T TAKEN IT!
EVERYONE LOVES IT.
IT CERTAINLY IS WILD. ENTER THROUGH THE KITCHEN, THEN A STEEP CLIMB TO AN EXPANSIVE WOOD INTERIOR WITH OPEN BEAMS AND A LOT OF SPACE...
MAYBE ENOUGH FOR A BABY.
I LOOK AROUND. THIS IS SOMEBODY'S PLACE. A COUPLE LIVE HERE. BOOKS OF POETRY AND URBAN PLANNING.
OTHER PEOPLE'S STUFF ALWAYS LOOK SO FOCUSED, LIKE THERE'S A POINT TO THEIR LIVES.
WOULD WE BE ABLE TO MOVE OUR POINTLESS LIVES INTO HERE?

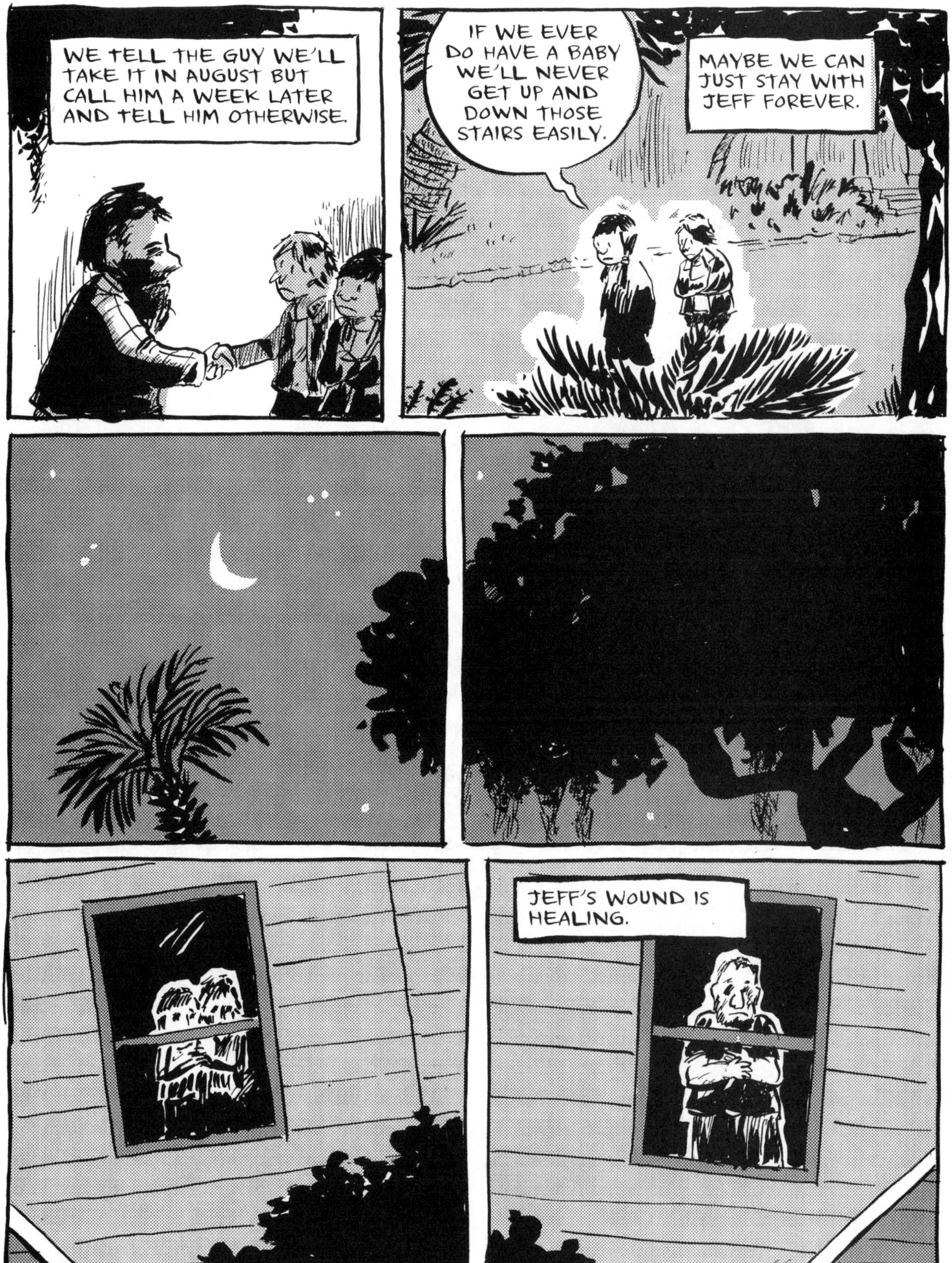
WE TELL THE GUY WE'LL TAKE IT IN AUGUST BUT CALL HIM A WEEK LATER AND TELL HIM OTHERWISE.
IF WE EVER DO HAVE A BABY WE'LL NEVER GET UP AND DOWN THOSE STAIRS EASILY.
MAYBE WE CAN JUST STAY WITH JEFF FOREVER.
JEFF'S WOUND IS HEALING.

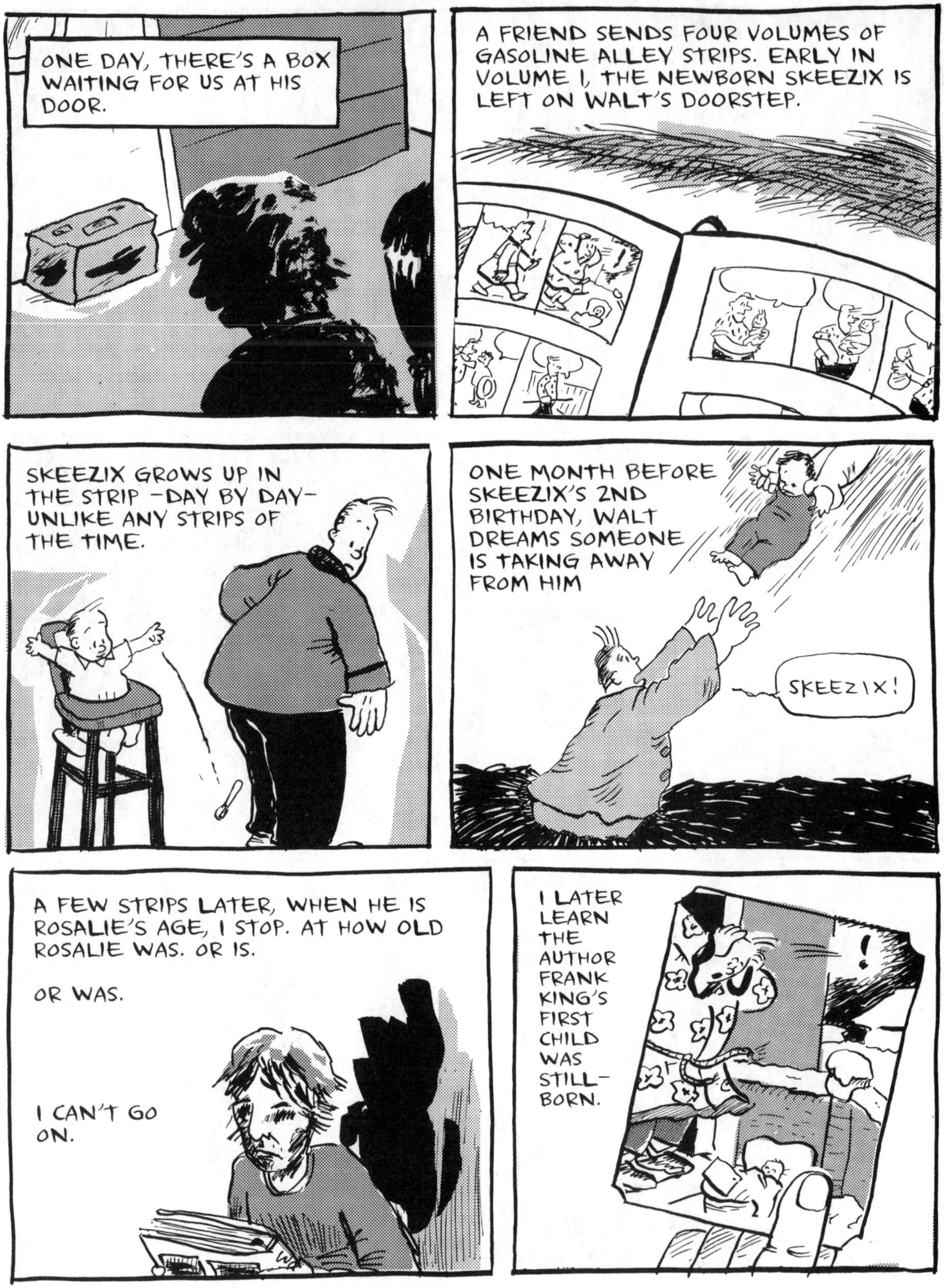

ONE DAY, THERE'S A BOX WAITING FOR US AT HIS DOOR.
A FRIEND SENDS FOUR VOLUMES OF GASOLINE ALLEY STRIPS. EARLY IN VOLUME I, THE NEWBORN SKEEZIX IS LEFT ON WALT'S DOORSTEP.
SKEEZIX GROWS UP IN THE STRIP —DAY BY DAY— UNLIKE ANY STRIPS OF THE TIME.
ONE MONTH BEFORE SKEEZIX'S 2ND BIRTHDAY, WALT DREAMS SOMEONE IS TAKING AWAY FROM HIM
SKEEZIX!
A FEW STRIPS LATER, WHEN HE IS ROSALIE'S AGE, I STOP. AT HOW OLD ROSALIE WAS. OR IS.
OR WAS.
I CAN'T GO ON.
I LATER LEARN THE AUTHOR FRANK KING'S FIRST CHILD WAS STILL-BORN.

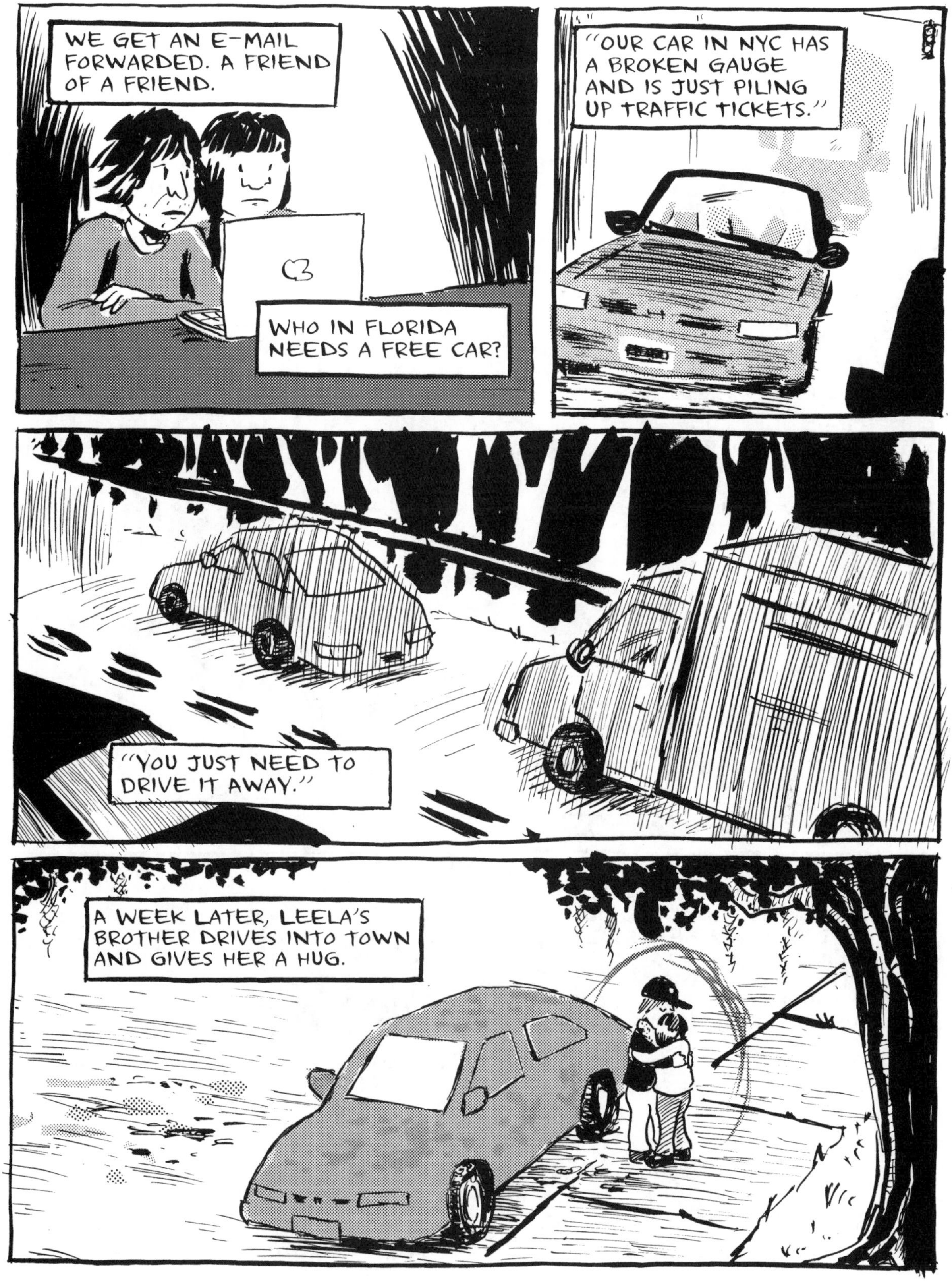
WE GET AN E-MAIL FORWARDED. A FRIEND OF A FRIEND.
WHO IN FLORIDA NEEDS A FREE CAR?
"OUR CAR IN NYC HAS A BROKEN GAUGE AND IS JUST PILING UP TRAFFIC TICKETS."
"YOU JUST NEED TO DRIVE IT AWAY."
A WEEK LATER, LEELA'S BROTHER DRIVES INTO TOWN AND GIVES HER A HUG.

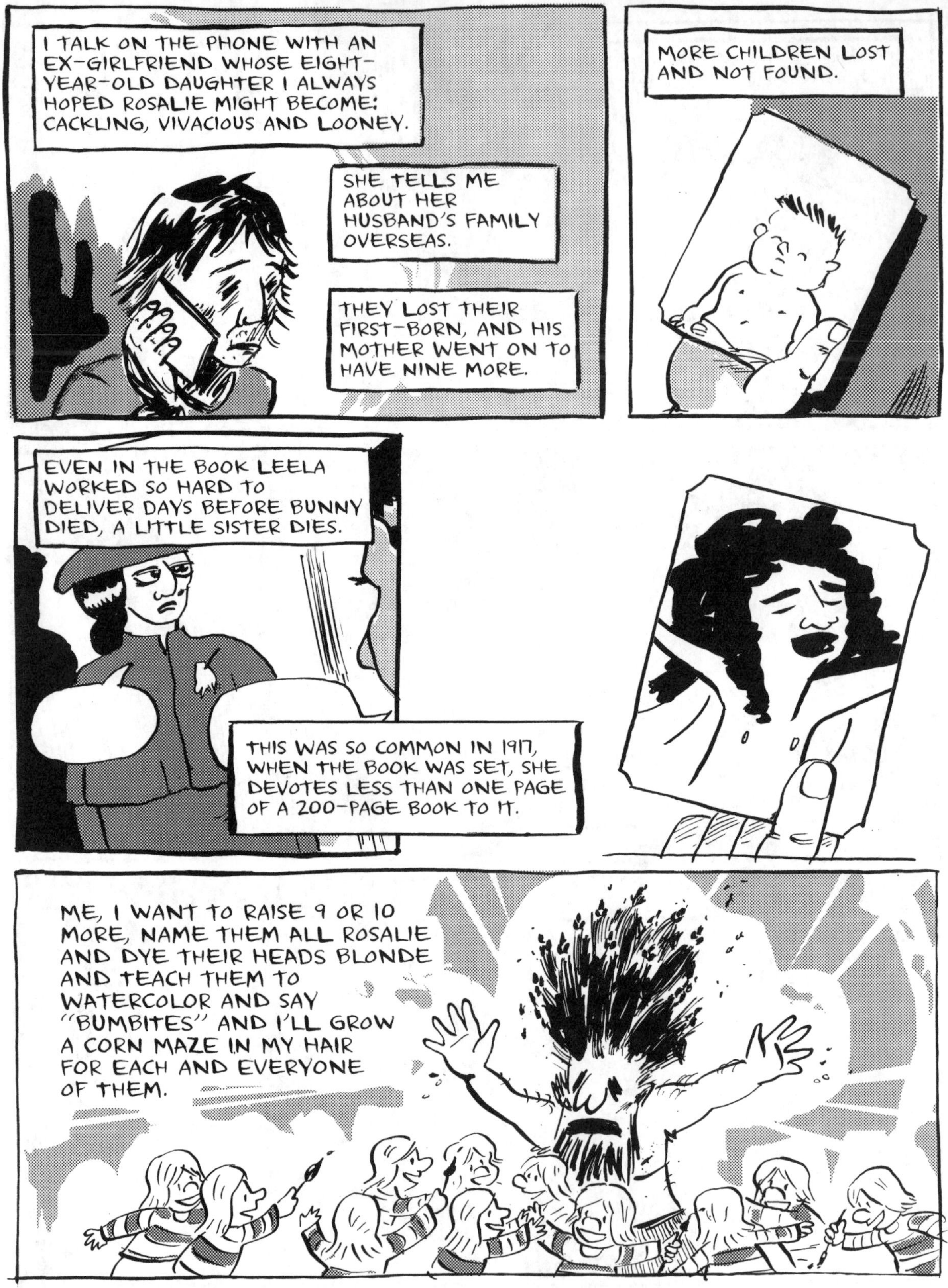
I TALK ON THE PHONE WITH AN EX-GIRLFRIEND WHOSE EIGHT-YEAR-OLD DAUGHTER I ALWAYS HOPED ROSALIE MIGHT BECOME: CACKLING, VIVACIOUS AND LOONEY.
SHE TELLS ME ABOUT HER HUSBAND'S FAMILY OVERSEAS.
THEY LOST THEIR FIRST-BORN, AND HIS MOTHER WENT ON TO HAVE NINE MORE.
MORE CHILDREN LOST AND NOT FOUND.
EVEN IN THE BOOK LEELA WORKED SO HARD TO DELIVER DAYS BEFORE BUNNY DIED, A LITTLE SISTER DIES.
THIS WAS SO COMMON IN 1917, WHEN THE BOOK WAS SET, SHE DEVOTES LESS THAN ONE PAGE OF A 200-PAGE BOOK TO IT.
ME, I WANT TO RAISE 9 OR 10 MORE, NAME THEM ALL ROSALIE AND DYE THEIR HEADS BLONDE AND TEACH THEM TO WATERCOLOR AND SAY "BUMBITES" AND I'LL GROW A CORN MAZE IN MY HAIR FOR EACH AND EVERYONE OF THEM.

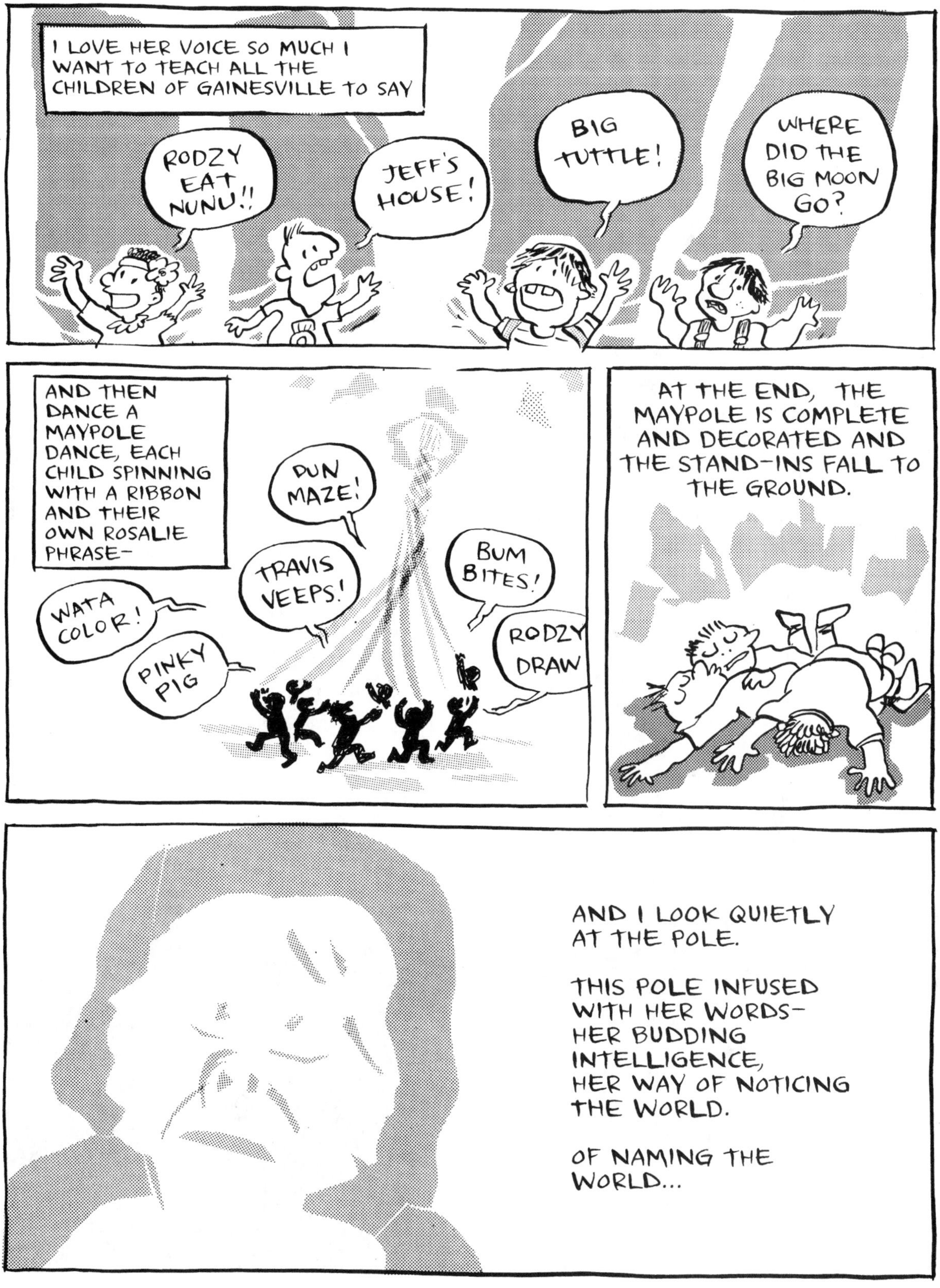
I LOVE HER VOICE SO MUCH I WANT TO TEACH ALL THE CHILDREN OF GAINESVILLE TO SAY
RODZY EAT NUNU!!
JEFF'S HOUSE!
BIG TUTTLE!
WHERE DID THE BIG MOON GO?
AND THEN DANCE A MAYPOLE DANCE, EACH CHILD SPINNING WITH A RIBBON AND THEIR OWN ROSALIE PHRASE—
DUN MAZE!
TRAVIS VEEPS!
BUM BITES!
WATA COLOR!
PINKY PIG
RODZY DRAW
AT THE END, THE MAYPOLE IS COMPLETE AND DECORATED AND THE STAND-INS FALL TO THE GROUND.
AND I LOOK QUIETLY AT THE POLE.
THIS POLE INFUSED WITH HER WORDS— HER BUDDING INTELLIGENCE, HER WAY OF NOTICING THE WORLD.
OF NAMING THE WORLD...

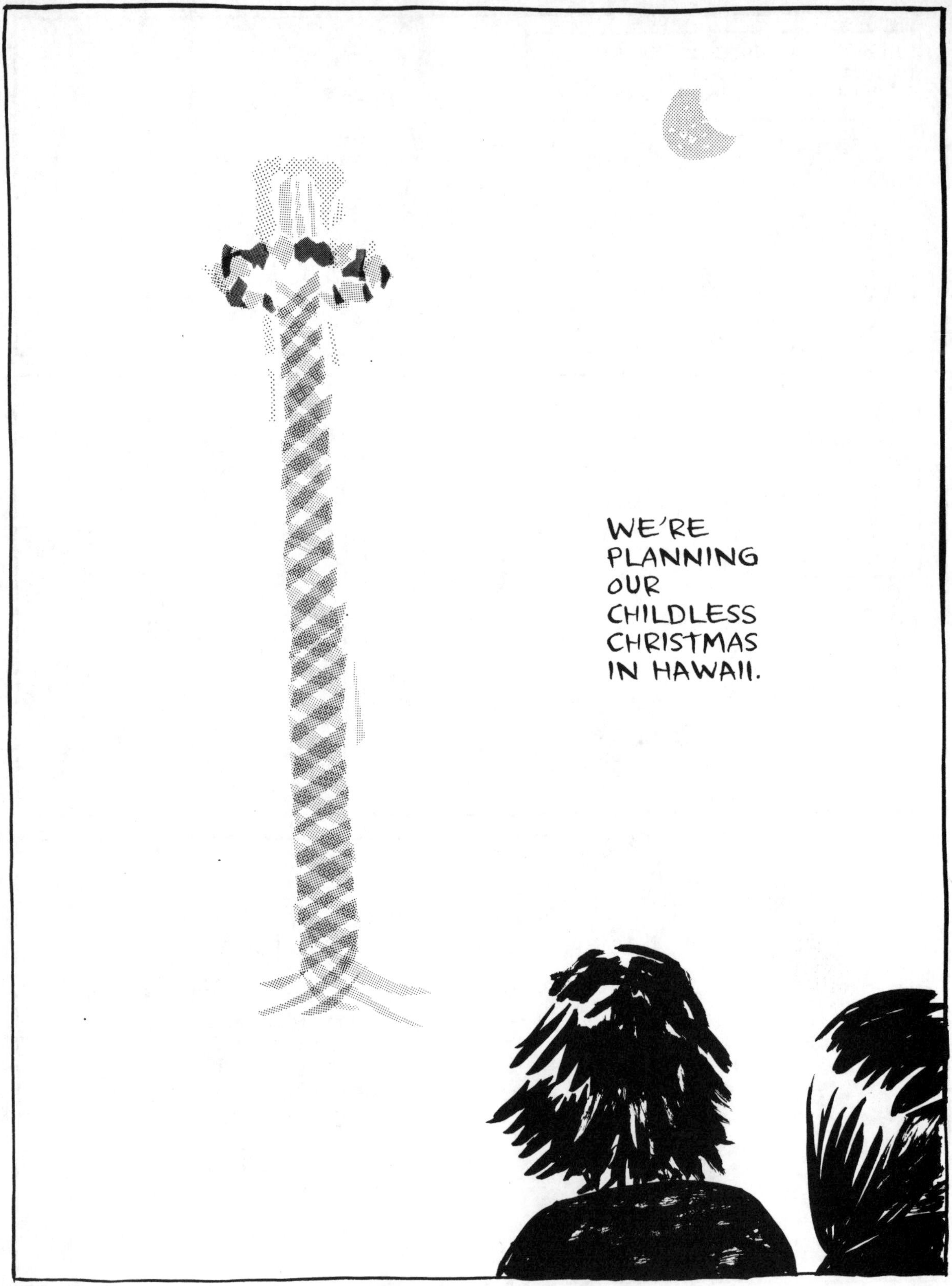
WE'RE PLANNING OUR CHILDLESS CHRISTMAS IN HAWAII.

X

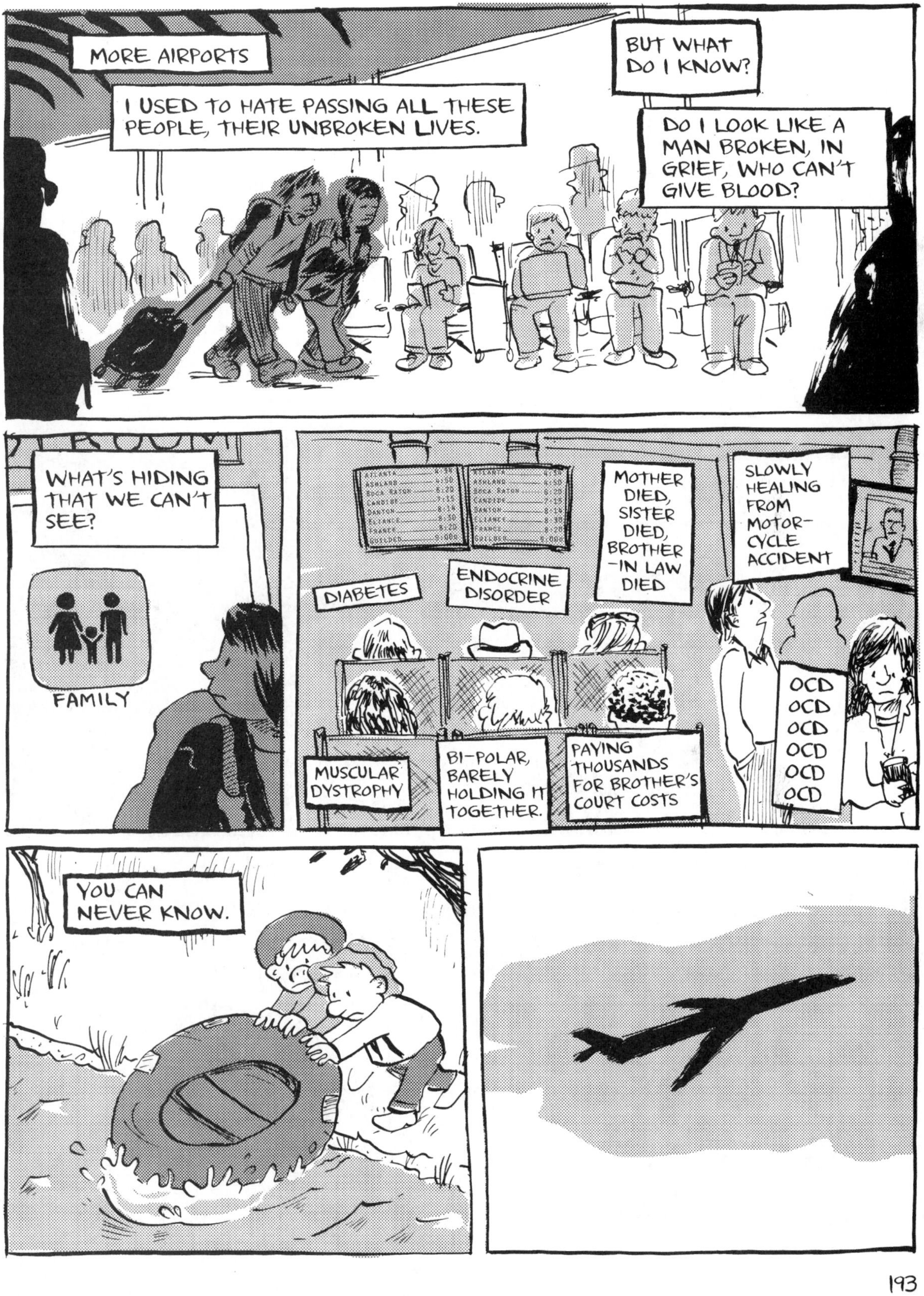
MORE AIRPORTS
I USED TO HATE PASSING ALL THESE PEOPLE, THEIR UNBROKEN LIVES.
BUT WHAT DO I KNOW?
DO I LOOK LIKE A MAN BROKEN, IN GRIEF, WHO CAN'T GIVE BLOOD?
WHAT'S HIDING THAT WE CAN'T SEE?
FAMILY
DIABETES
ENDOCRINE DISORDER
MOTHER DIED, SISTER DIED, BROTHER-IN LAW DIED
SLOWLY HEALING FROM MOTOR-CYCLE ACCIDENT
MUSCULAR DYSTROPHY
BI-POLAR, BARELY HOLDING IT TOGETHER.
PAYING THOUSANDS FOR BROTHER'S COURT COSTS
OCD
OCD
OCD
OCD
OCD
OCD
YOU CAN NEVER KNOW.

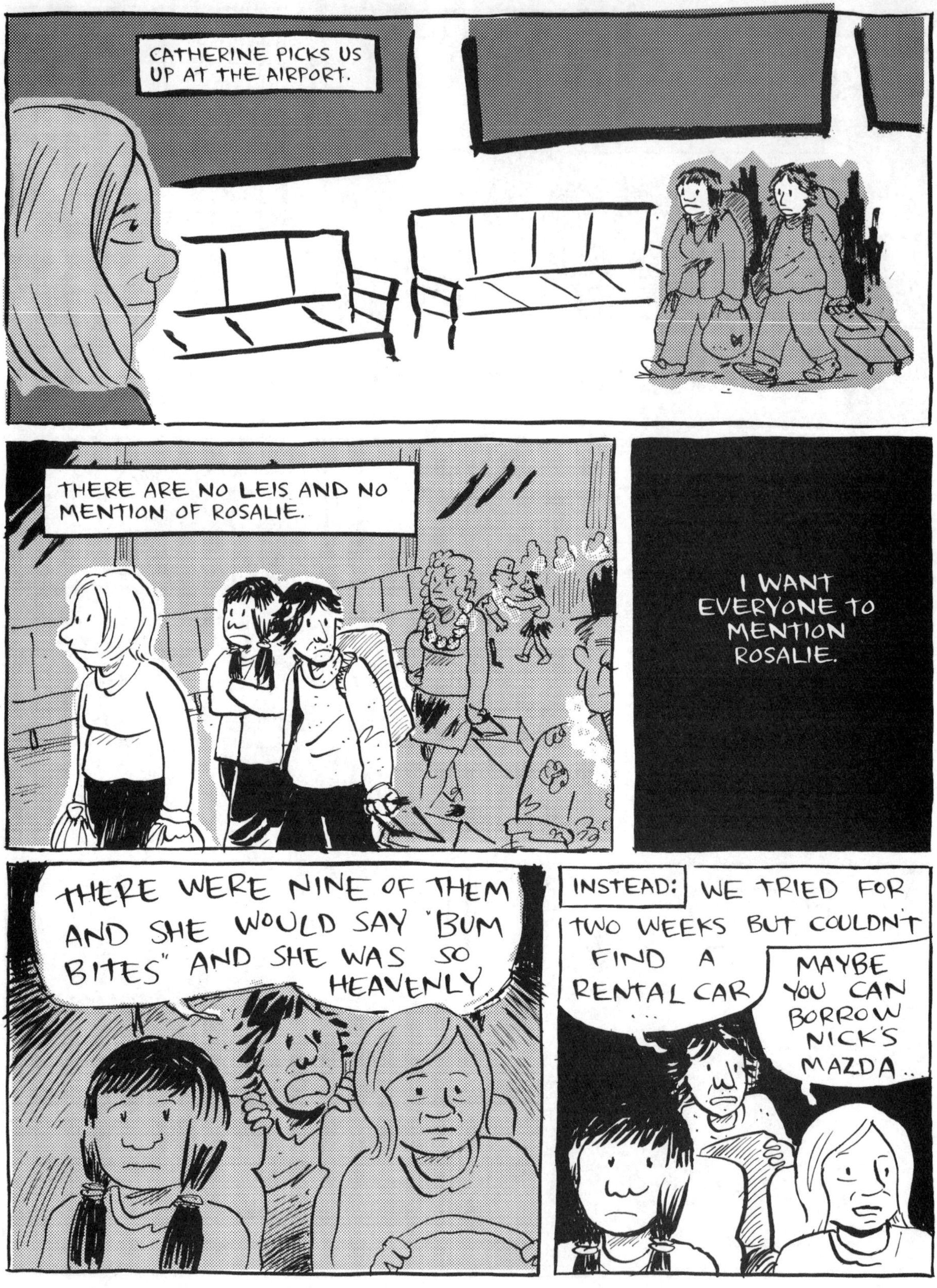
CATHERINE PICKS US UP AT THE AIRPORT.
THERE ARE NO LEIS AND NO MENTION OF ROSALIE.
I WANT EVERYONE TO MENTION ROSALIE.
THERE WERE NINE OF THEM AND SHE WOULD SAY "BUM BITES" AND SHE WAS SO HEAVENLY
INSTEAD:
WE TRIED FOR TWO WEEKS BUT COULDN'T FIND A RENTAL CAR ...
MAYBE YOU CAN BORROW NICK'S MAZDA ...

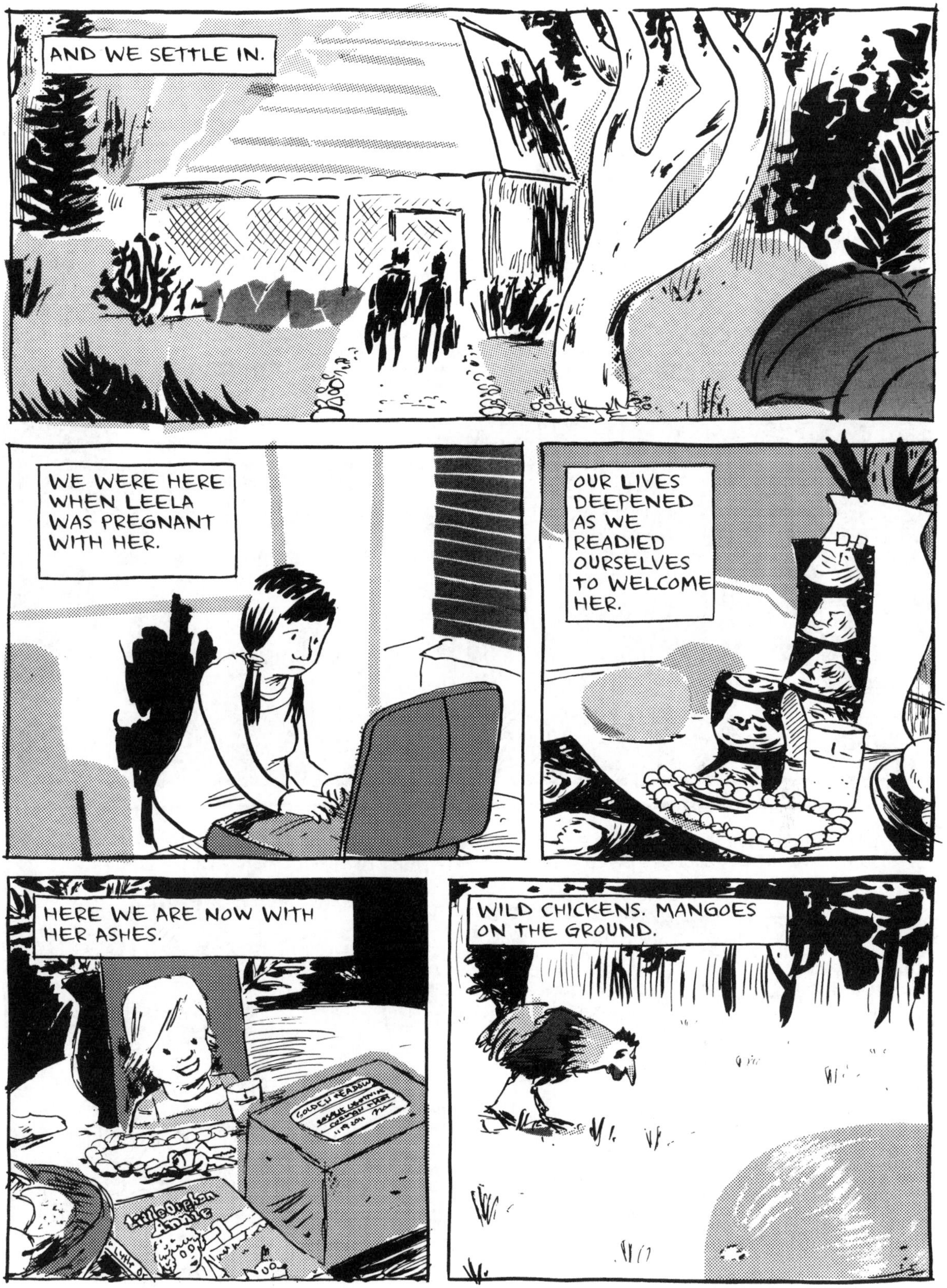
AND WE SETTLE IN.
WE WERE HERE WHEN LEELA WAS PREGNANT WITH HER.
OUR LIVES DEEPENED AS WE READIED OURSELVES TO WELCOME HER.
HERE WE ARE NOW WITH HER ASHES.
Little Orphan Annie
WILD CHICKENS. MANGOES ON THE GROUND.

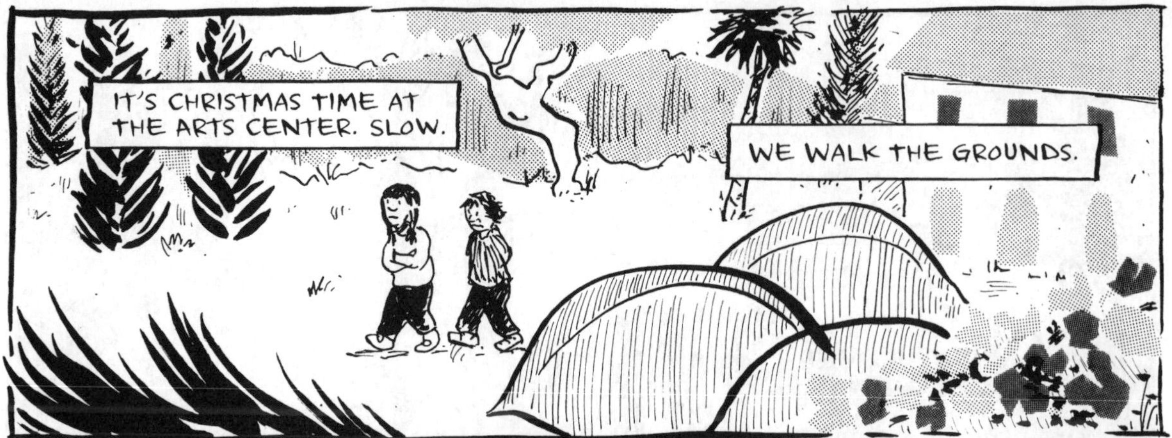
IT'S CHRISTMAS TIME AT THE ARTS CENTER. SLOW.
WE WALK THE GROUNDS.

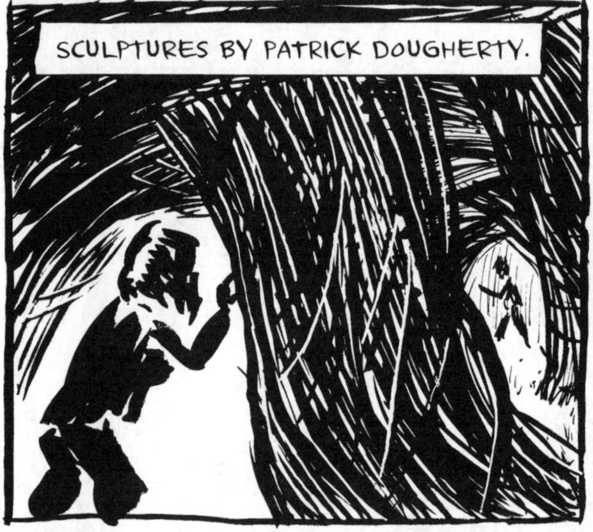
SCULPTURES BY PATRICK DOUGHERTY.

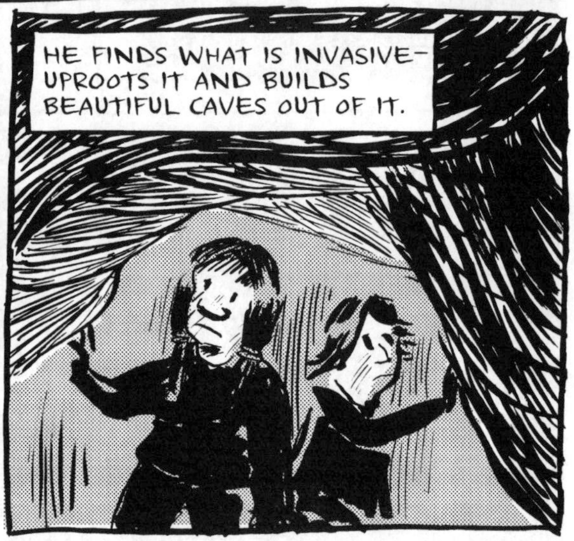
HE FINDS WHAT IS INVASIVE- UPROOTS IT AND BUILDS BEAUTIFUL CAVES OUT OF IT.

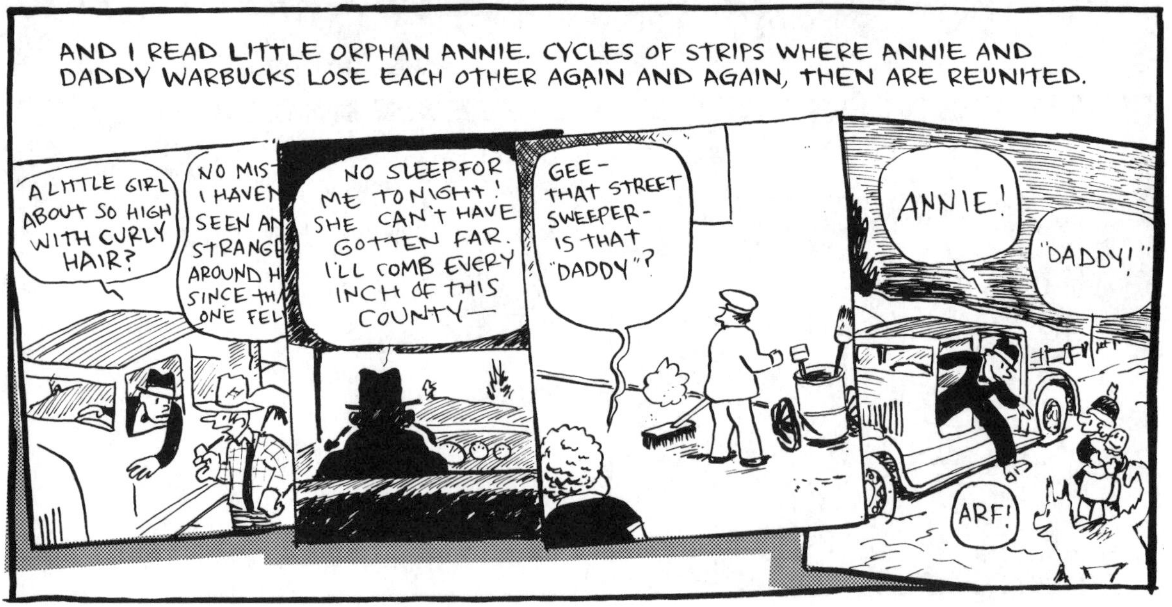
AND I READ LITTLE ORPHAN ANNIE. CYCLES OF STRIPS WHERE ANNIE AND DADDY WARBUCKS LOSE EACH OTHER AGAIN AND AGAIN, THEN ARE REUNITED.
A LITTLE GIRL ABOUT SO HIGH WITH CURLY HAIR?
NO MIS I HAVEN SEEN AN STRANGE AROUND H SINCE TH ONE FEL
NO SLEEP FOR ME TONIGHT! SHE CAN'T HAVE GOTTEN FAR. I'LL COMB EVERY INCH OF THIS COUNTY—
GEE— THAT STREET SWEEPER- IS THAT "DADDY"?
ANNIE!
"DADDY!"
ARF!

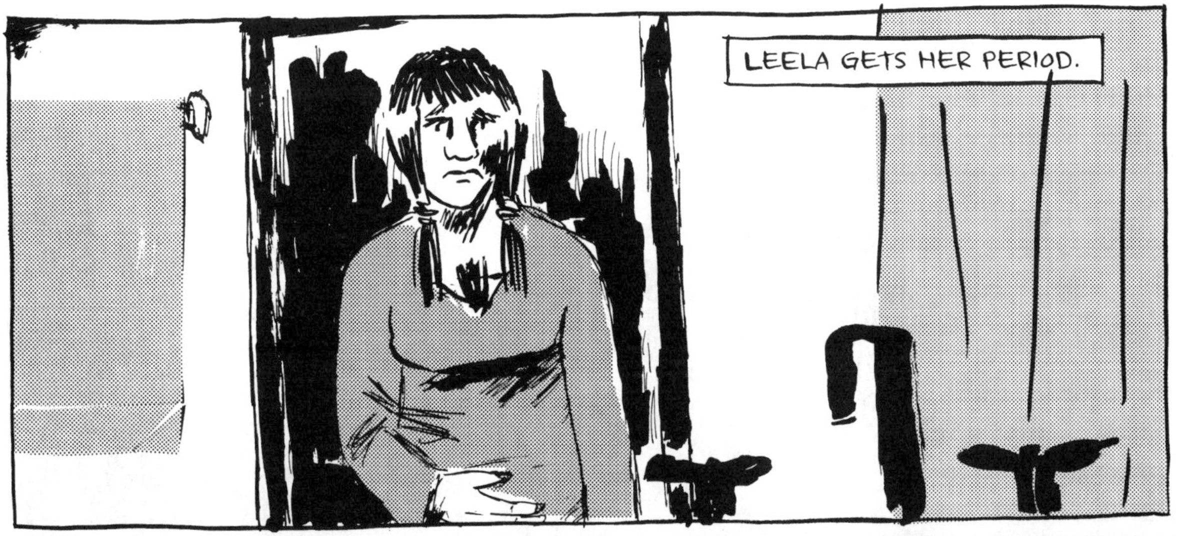
LEELA GETS HER PERIOD.

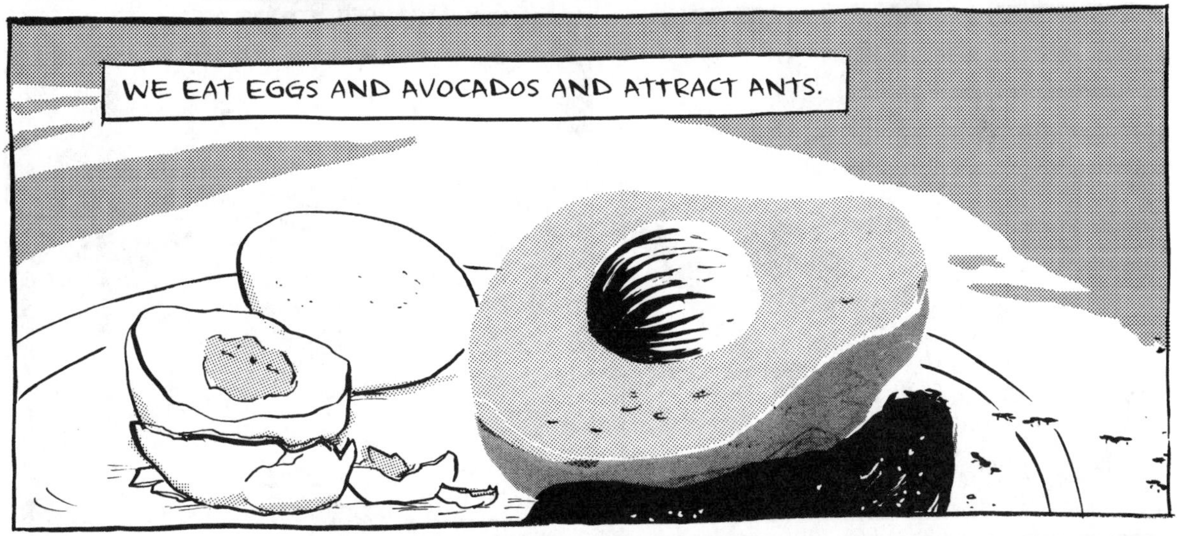
WE EAT EGGS AND AVOCADOS AND ATTRACT ANTS.

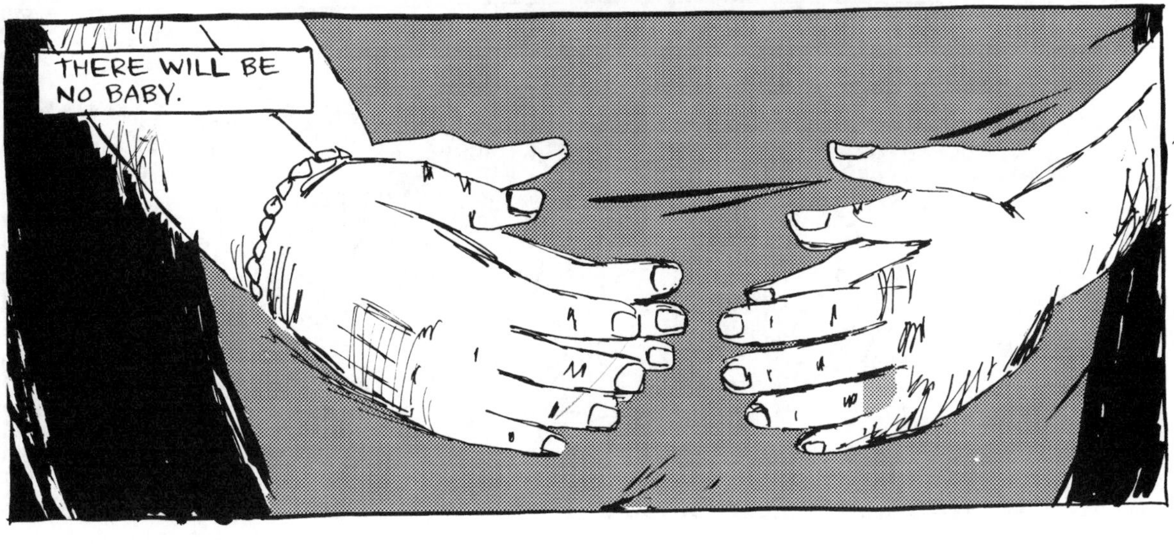
THERE WILL BE NO BABY.

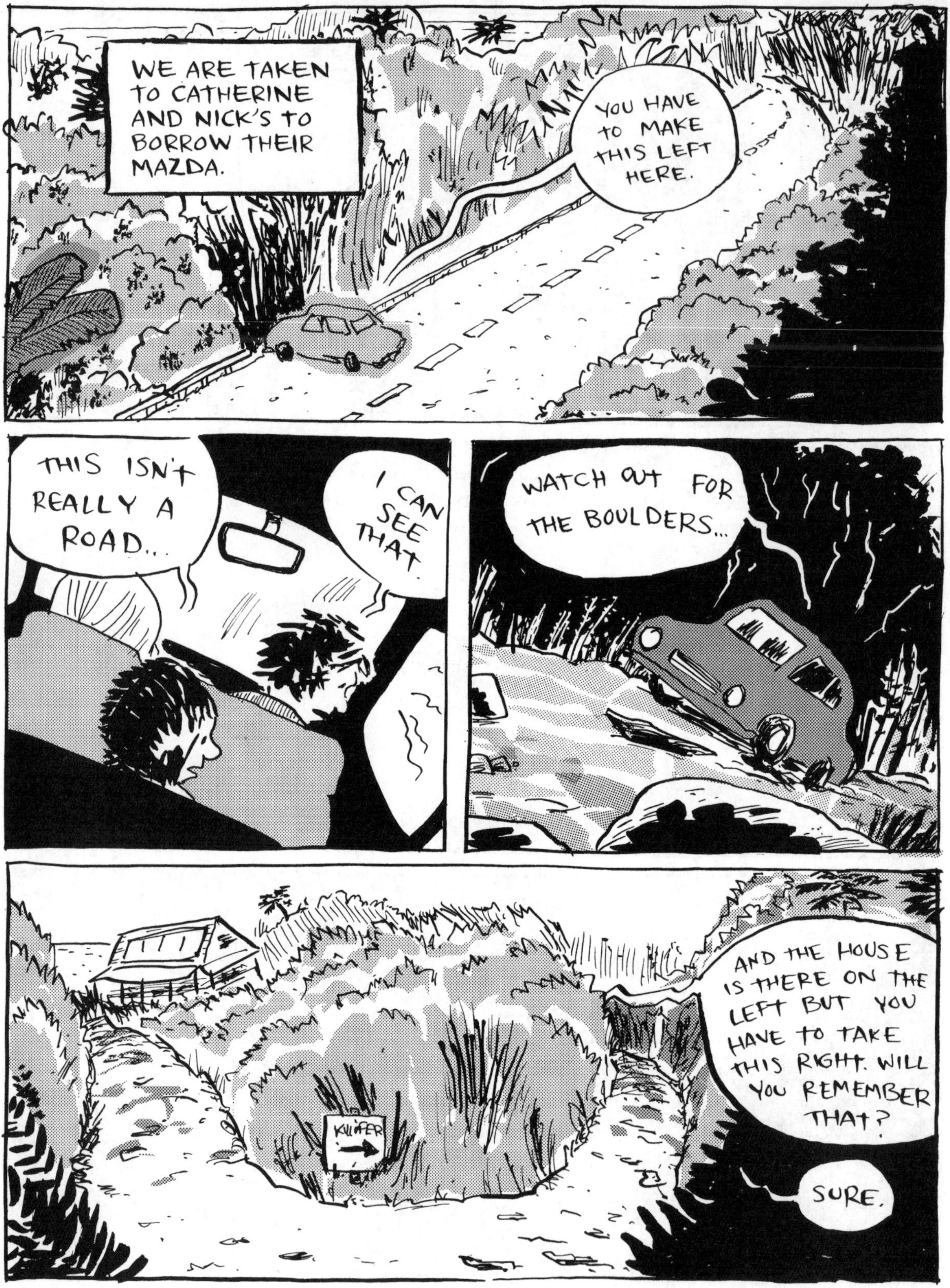
WE ARE TAKEN TO CATHERINE AND NICK'S TO BORROW THEIR MAZDA.
YOU HAVE TO MAKE THIS LEFT HERE.
THIS ISN'T REALLY A ROAD...
I CAN SEE THAT.
WATCH OUT FOR THE BOULDERS...
AND THE HOUSE IS THERE ON THE LEFT BUT YOU HAVE TO TAKE THIS RIGHT. WILL YOU REMEMBER THAT?
SURE.

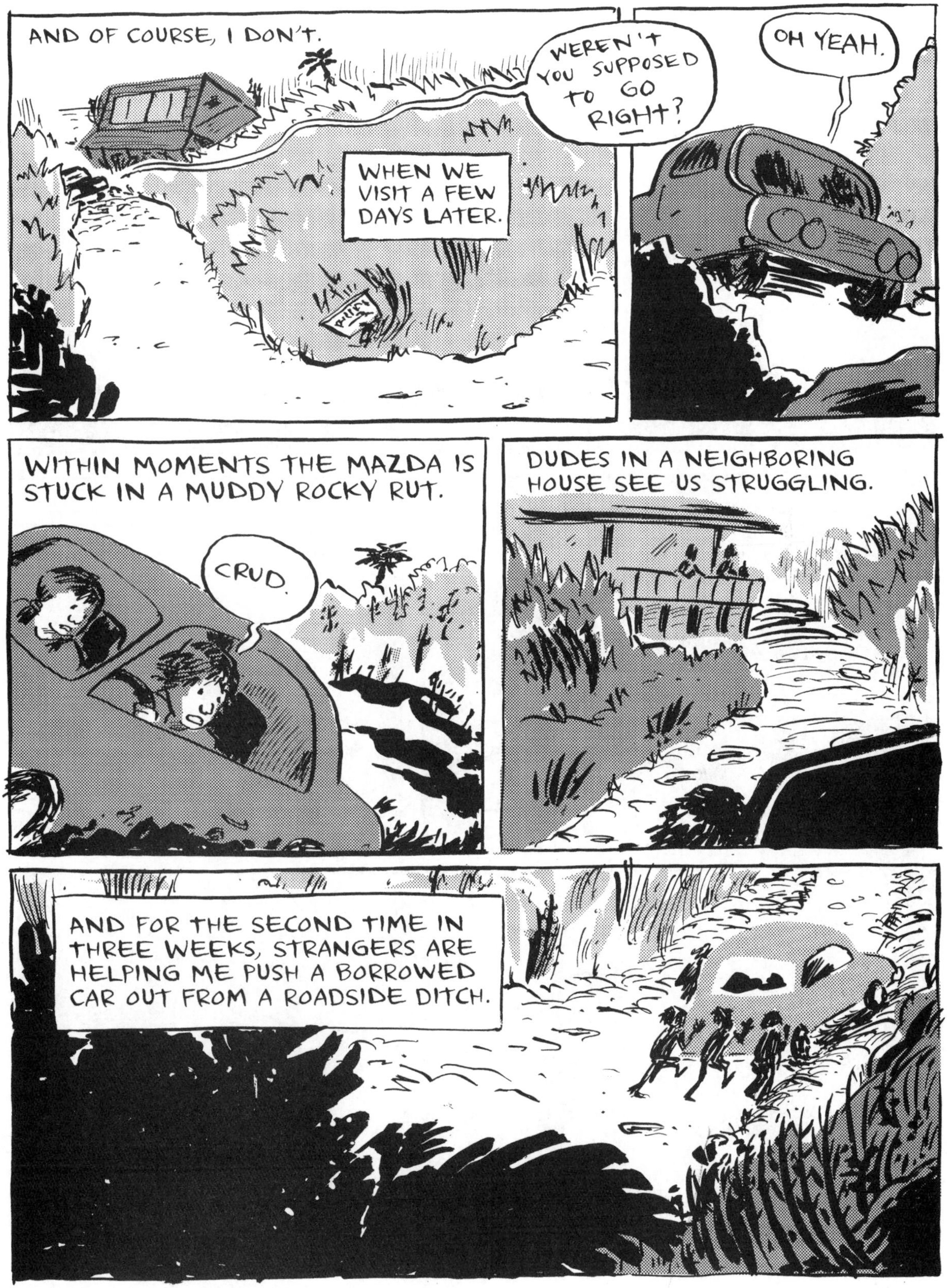
AND OF COURSE, I DON'T.
WHEN WE VISIT A FEW DAYS LATER.
WEREN'T YOU SUPPOSED TO GO RIGHT?
OH YEAH.
WITHIN MOMENTS THE MAZDA IS STUCK IN A MUDDY ROCKY RUT.
CRUD.
DUDES IN A NEIGHBORING HOUSE SEE US STRUGGLING.
AND FOR THE SECOND TIME IN THREE WEEKS, STRANGERS ARE HELPING ME PUSH A BORROWED CAR OUT FROM A ROADSIDE DITCH.

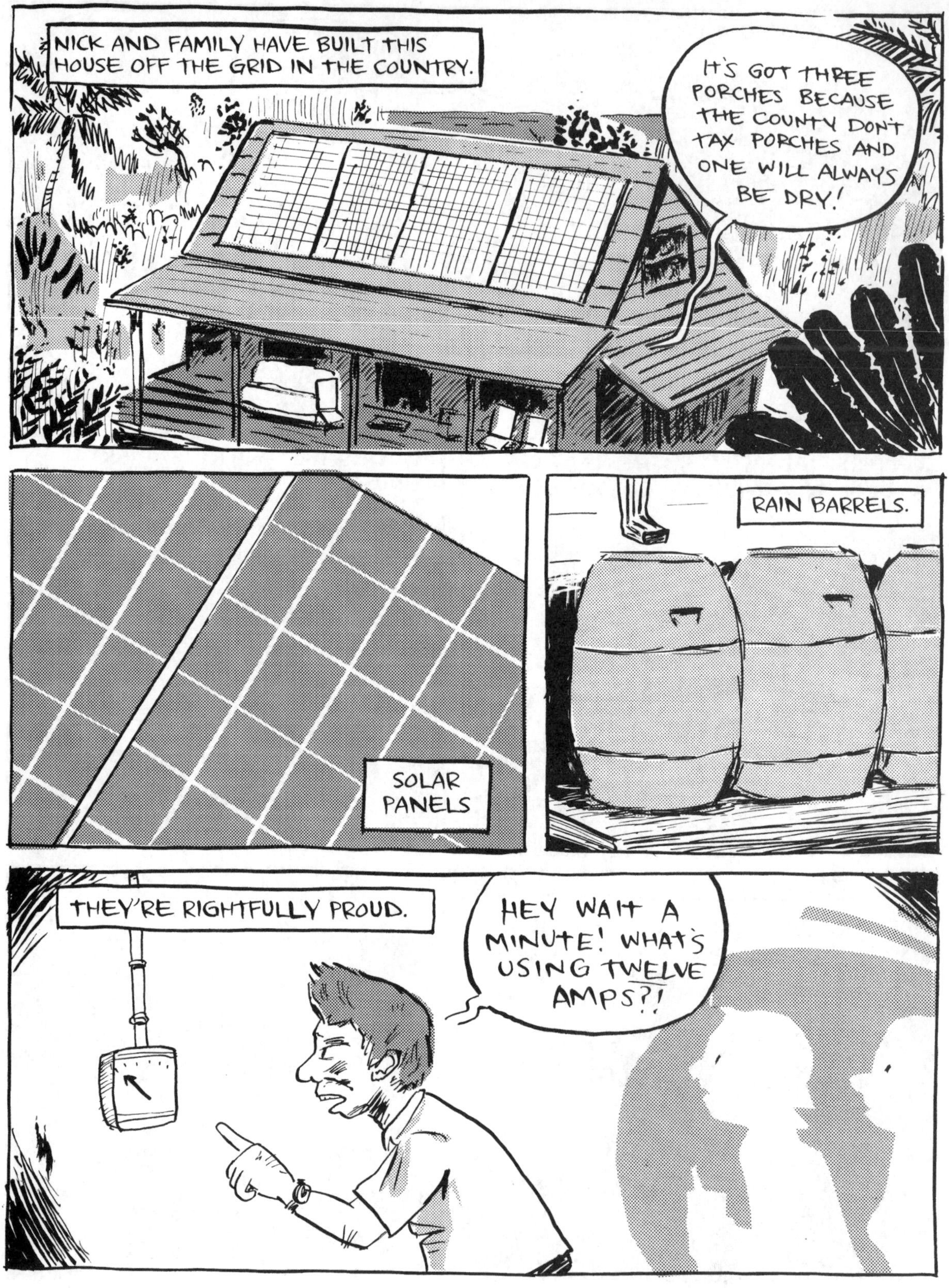
NICK AND FAMILY HAVE BUILT THIS HOUSE OFF THE GRID IN THE COUNTRY.
IT'S GOT THREE PORCHES BECAUSE THE COUNTY DON'T TAX PORCHES AND ONE WILL ALWAYS BE DRY!
SOLAR PANELS
RAIN BARRELS.
THEY'RE RIGHTFULLY PROUD.
HEY WAIT A MINUTE! WHAT'S USING TWELVE AMPS?!

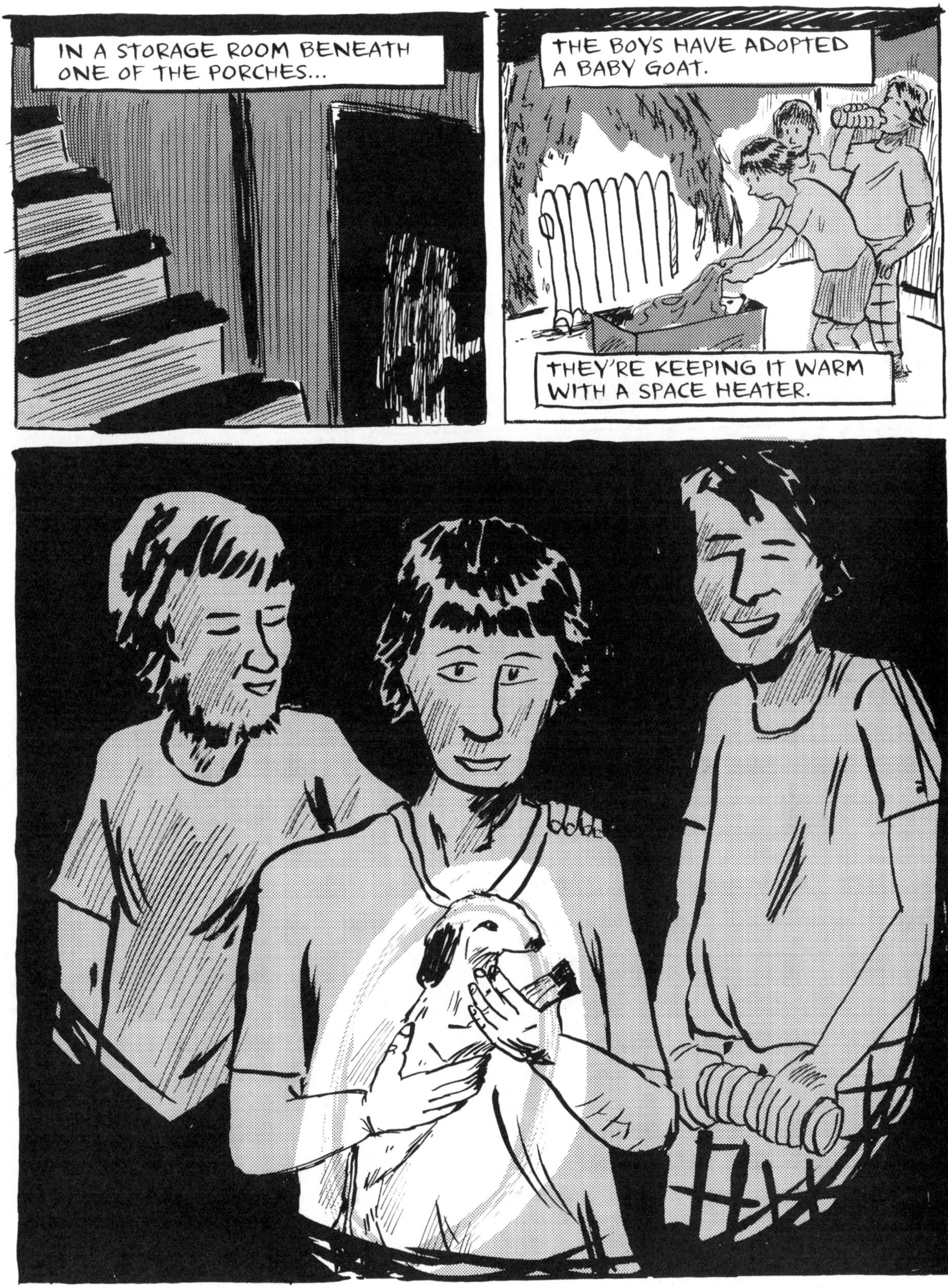
IN A STORAGE ROOM BENEATH ONE OF THE PORCHES...
THE BOYS HAVE ADOPTED A BABY GOAT.
THEY'RE KEEPING IT WARM WITH A SPACE HEATER.

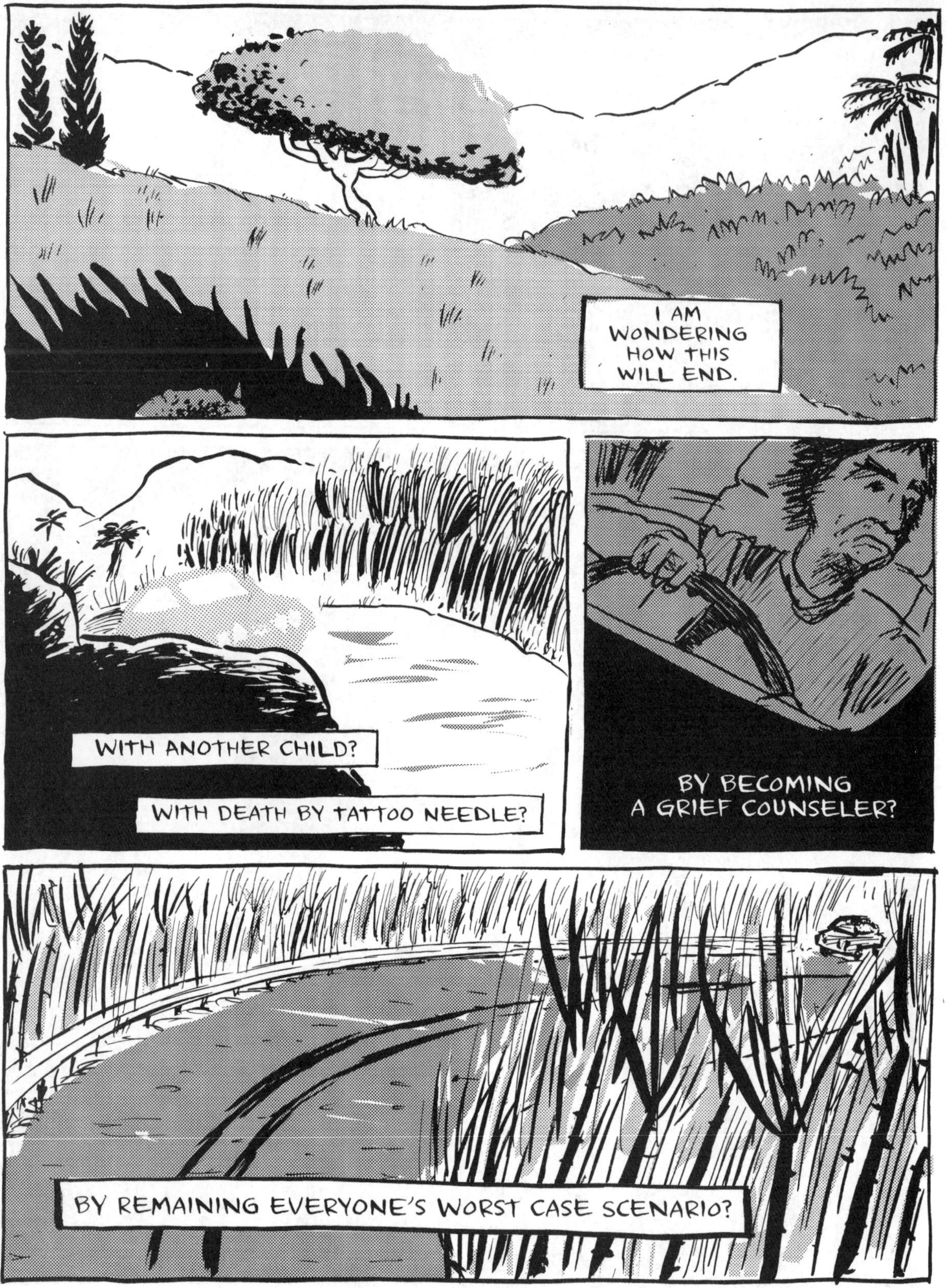
I AM WONDERING HOW THIS WILL END.
WITH ANOTHER CHILD?
WITH DEATH BY TATTOO NEEDLE?
BY BECOMING A GRIEF COUNSELER?
BY REMAINING EVERYONE'S WORST CASE SCENARIO?

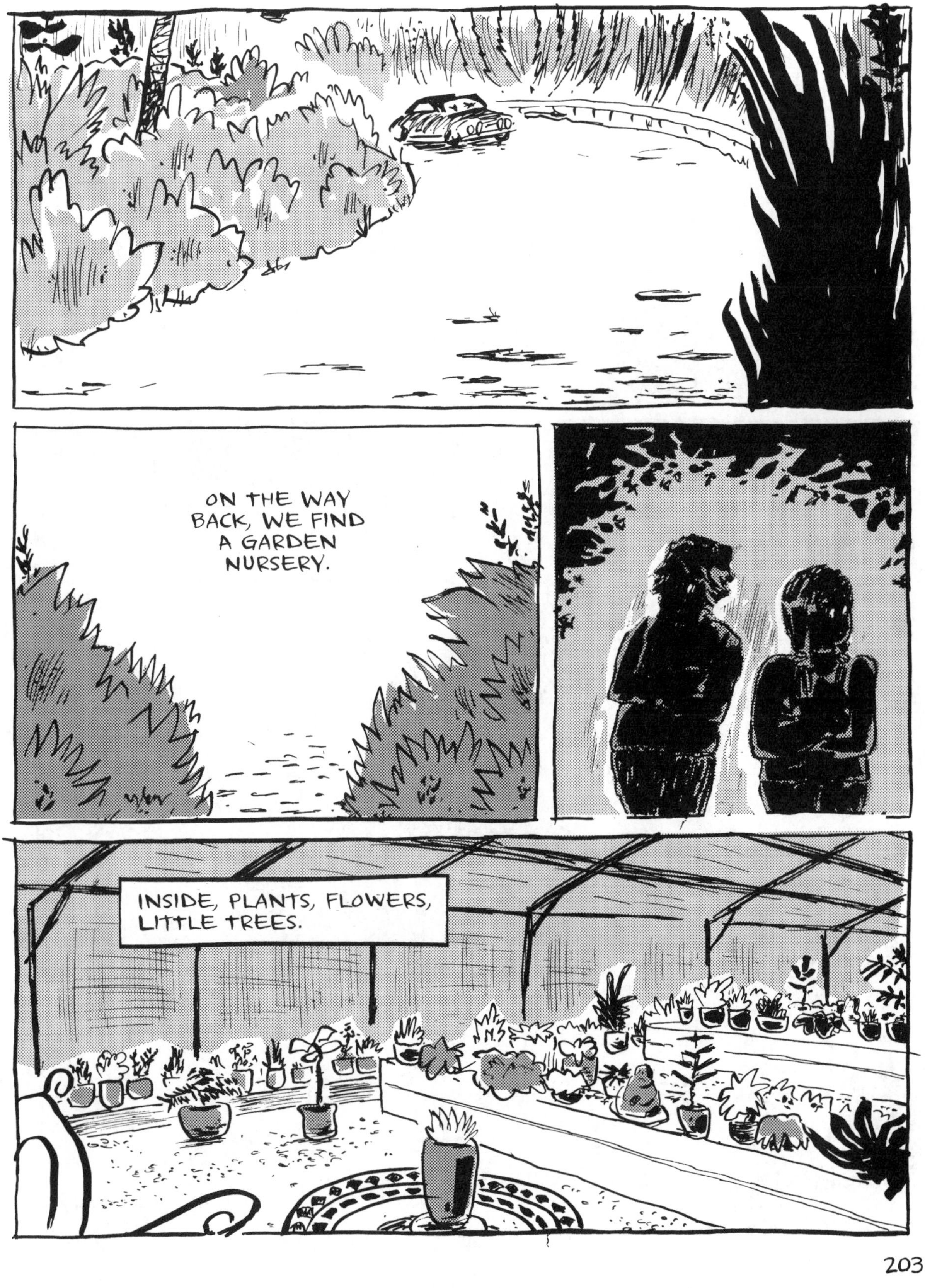
ON THE WAY BACK, WE FIND A GARDEN NURSERY.
INSIDE, PLANTS, FLOWERS, LITTLE TREES.

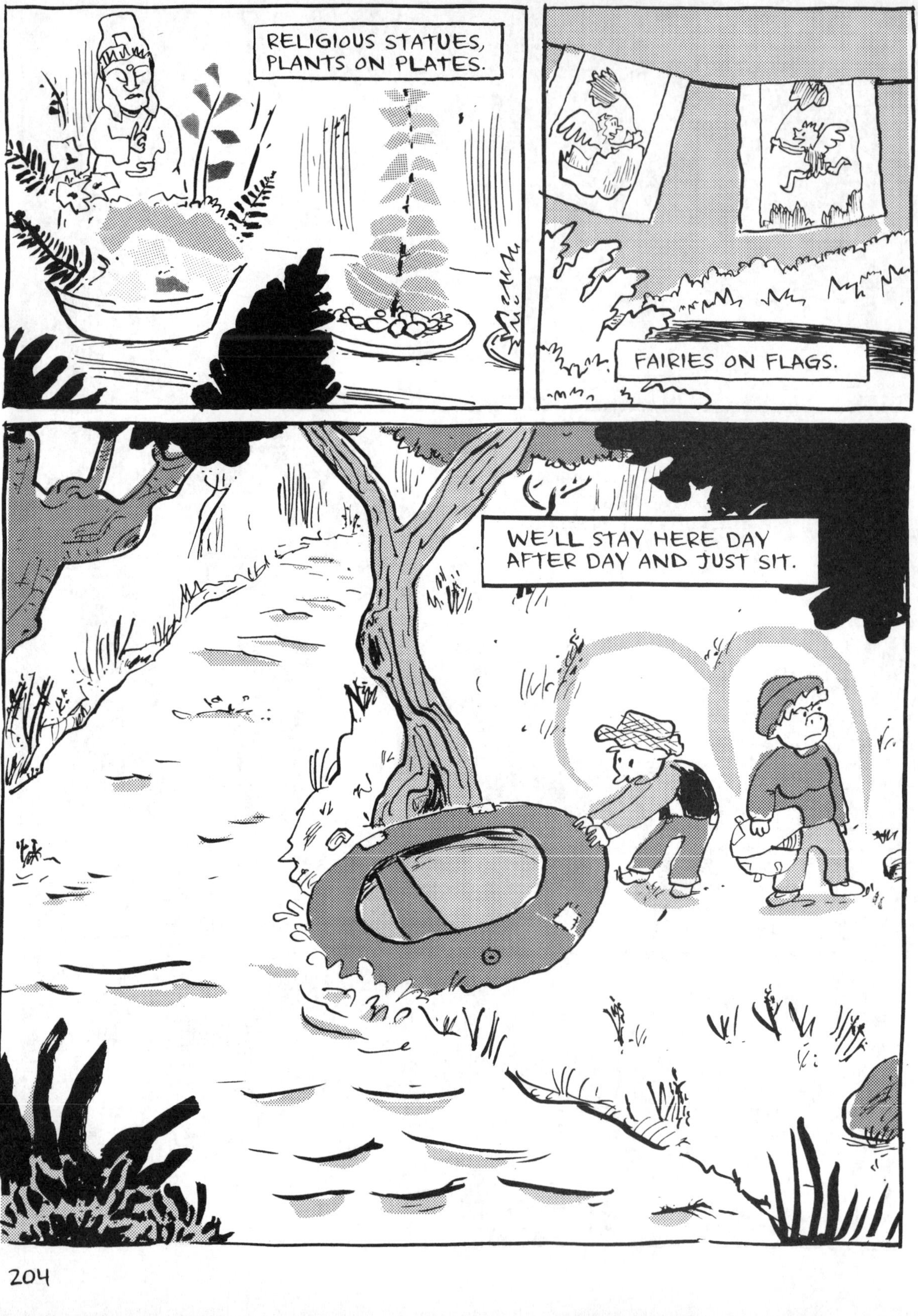
RELIGIOUS STATUES, PLANTS ON PLATES.
FAIRIES ON FLAGS.
WE'LL STAY HERE DAY AFTER DAY AND JUST SIT.

XI

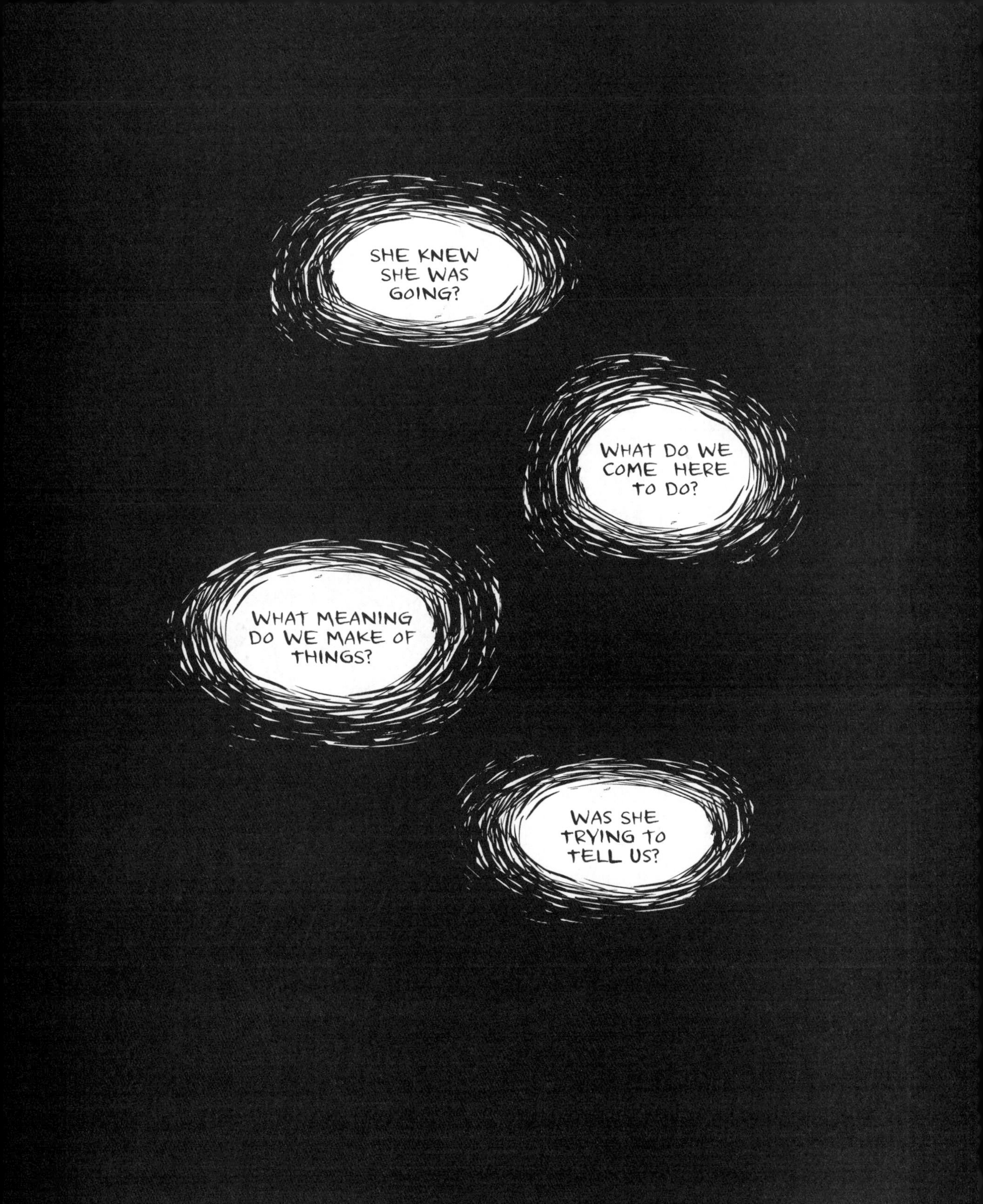
SHE KNEW SHE WAS GOING?
WHAT DO WE COME HERE TO DO?
WHAT MEANING DO WE MAKE OF THINGS?
WAS SHE TRYING TO TELL US?

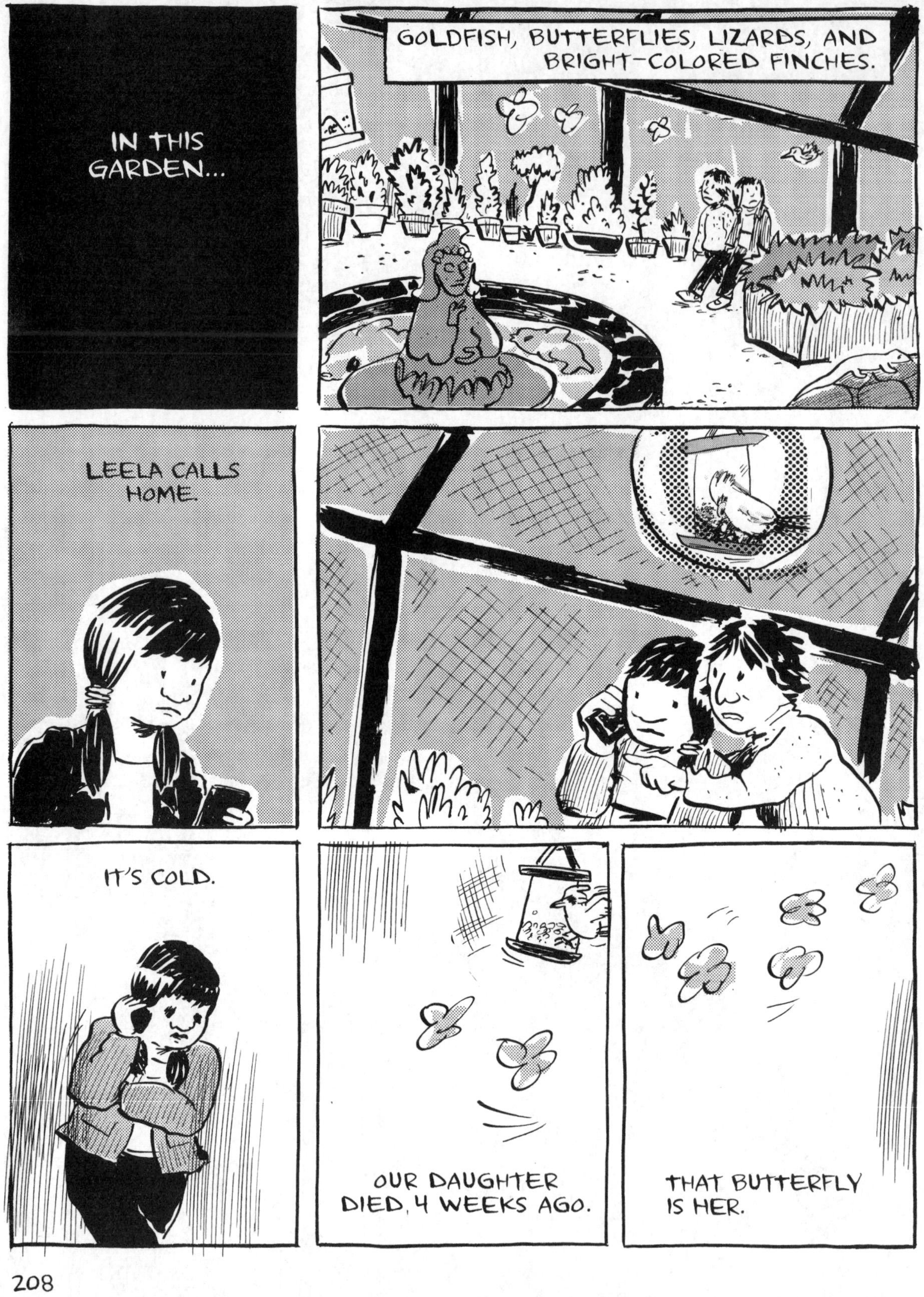
IN THIS GARDEN...
GOLDFISH, BUTTERFLIES, LIZARDS, AND BRIGHT-COLORED FINCHES.
LEELA CALLS HOME.
IT'S COLD.
OUR DAUGHTER DIED, 4 WEEKS AGO.
THAT BUTTERFLY IS HER.

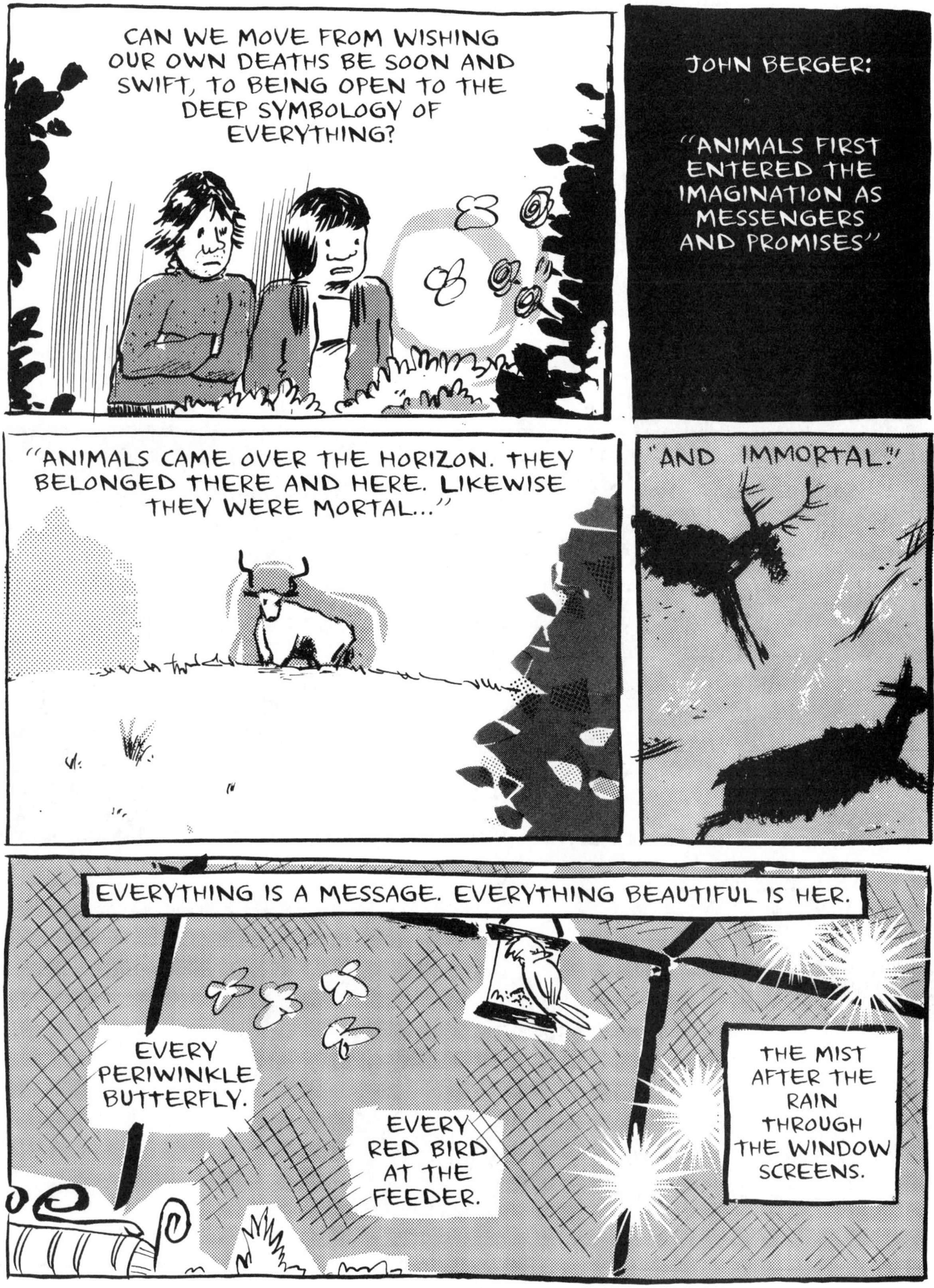
CAN WE MOVE FROM WISHING OUR OWN DEATHS BE SOON AND SWIFT, TO BEING OPEN TO THE DEEP SYMBOLOGY OF EVERYTHING?
JOHN BERGER:
"ANIMALS FIRST ENTERED THE IMAGINATION AS MESSENGERS AND PROMISES"
"ANIMALS CAME OVER THE HORIZON. THEY BELONGED THERE AND HERE. LIKEWISE THEY WERE MORTAL..."
"AND IMMORTAL."
EVERYTHING IS A MESSAGE. EVERYTHING BEAUTIFUL IS HER.
EVERY PERIWINKLE BUTTERFLY.
EVERY RED BIRD AT THE FEEDER.
THE MIST AFTER THE RAIN THROUGH THE WINDOW SCREENS.

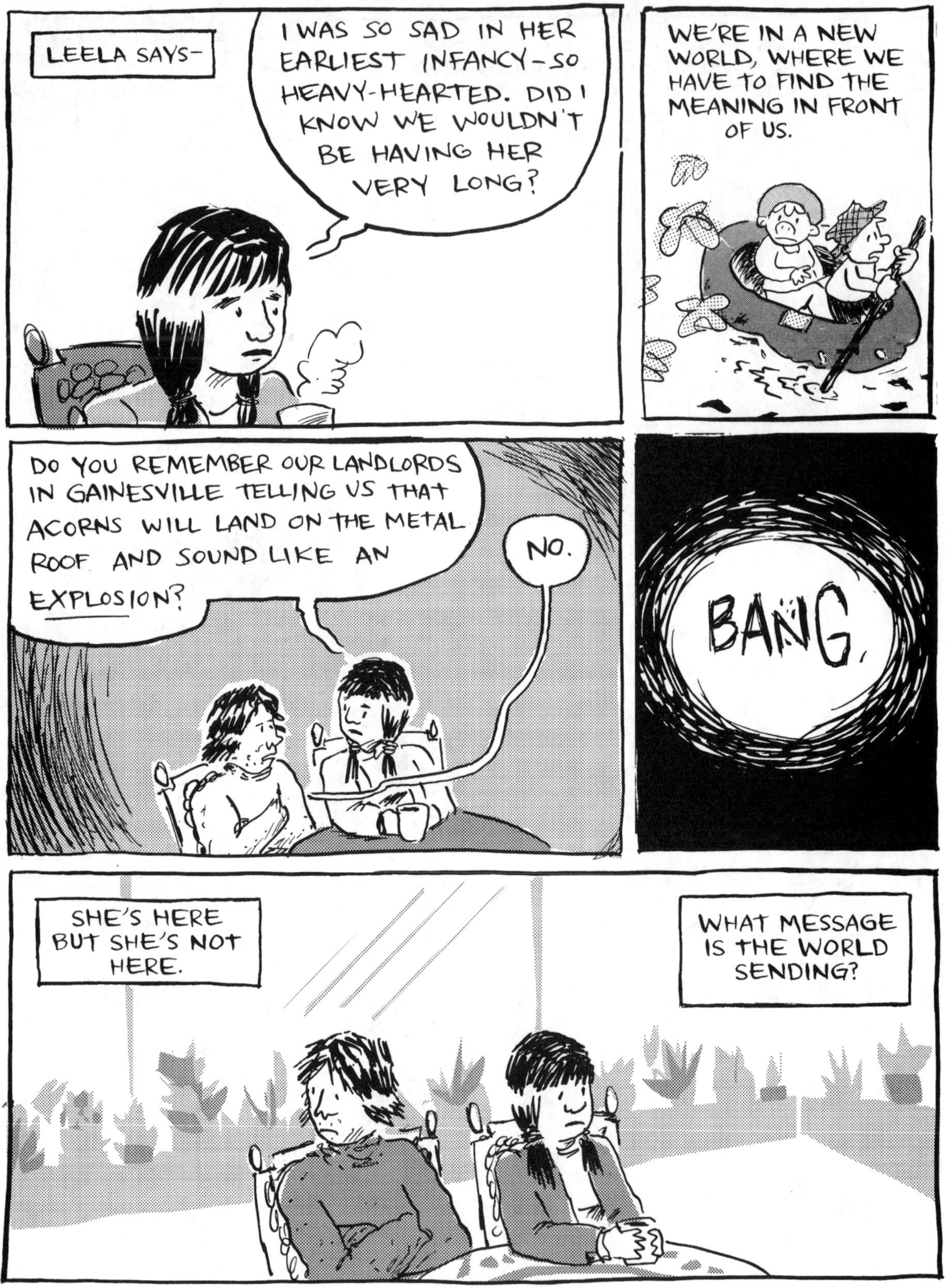
LEELA SAYS-
I WAS SO SAD IN HER EARLIEST INFANCY-SO HEAVY-HEARTED. DID I KNOW WE WOULDN'T BE HAVING HER VERY LONG?
WE'RE IN A NEW WORLD, WHERE WE HAVE TO FIND THE MEANING IN FRONT OF US.
DO YOU REMEMBER OUR LANDLORDS IN GAINESVILLE TELLING US THAT ACORNS WILL LAND ON THE METAL ROOF AND SOUND LIKE AN EXPLOSION?
NO.
BANG.
SHE'S HERE BUT SHE'S NOT HERE.
WHAT MESSAGE IS THE WORLD SENDING?

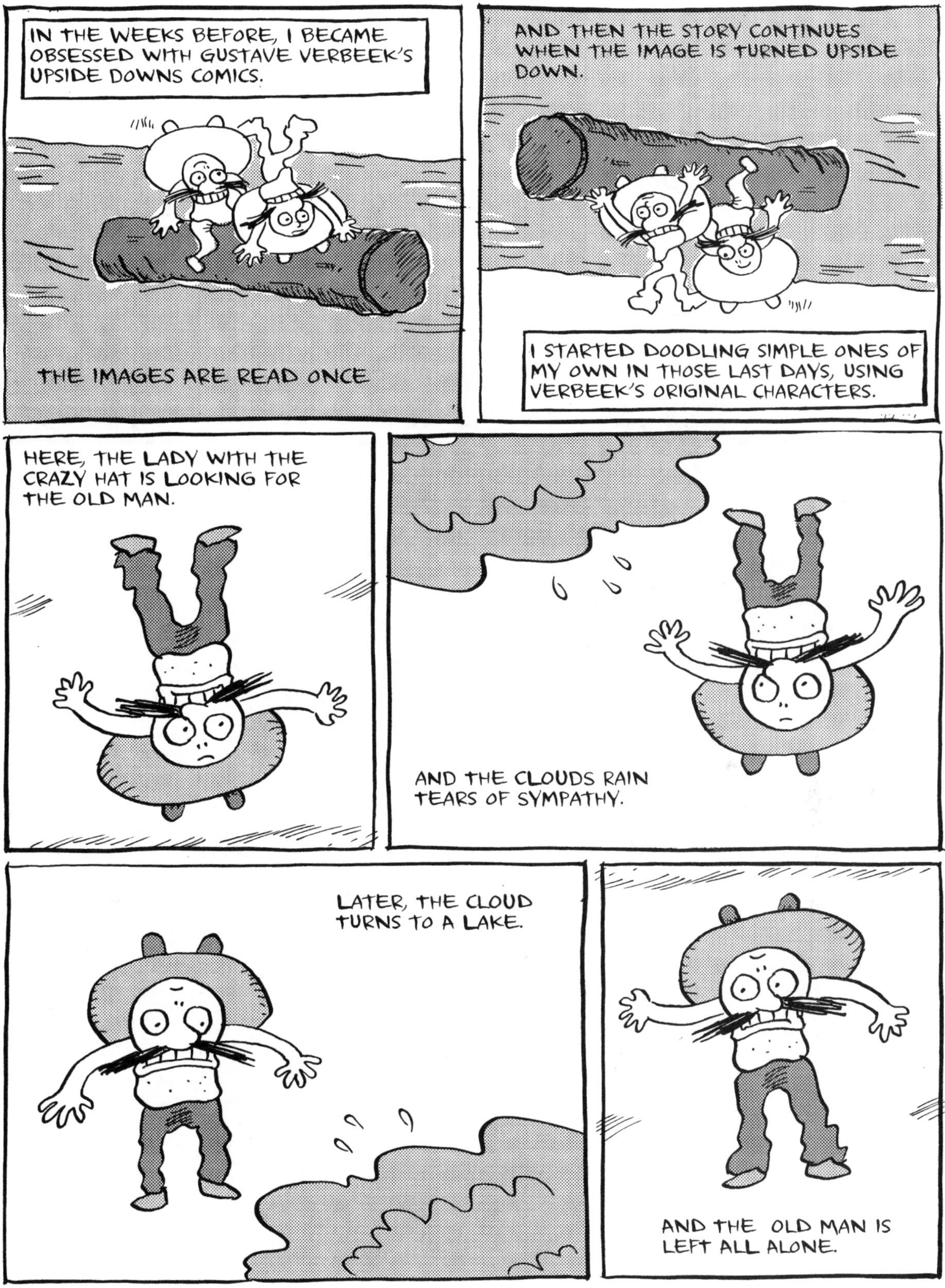
IN THE WEEKS BEFORE, I BECAME OBSESSED WITH GUSTAVE VERBEEK'S UPSIDE DOWNS COMICS.
THE IMAGES ARE READ ONCE
AND THEN THE STORY CONTINUES WHEN THE IMAGE IS TURNED UPSIDE DOWN.
I STARTED DOODLING SIMPLE ONES OF MY OWN IN THOSE LAST DAYS, USING VERBEEK'S ORIGINAL CHARACTERS.
HERE, THE LADY WITH THE CRAZY HAT IS LOOKING FOR THE OLD MAN.
AND THE CLOUDS RAIN TEARS OF SYMPATHY.
LATER, THE CLOUD TURNS TO A LAKE.
AND THE OLD MAN IS LEFT ALL ALONE.

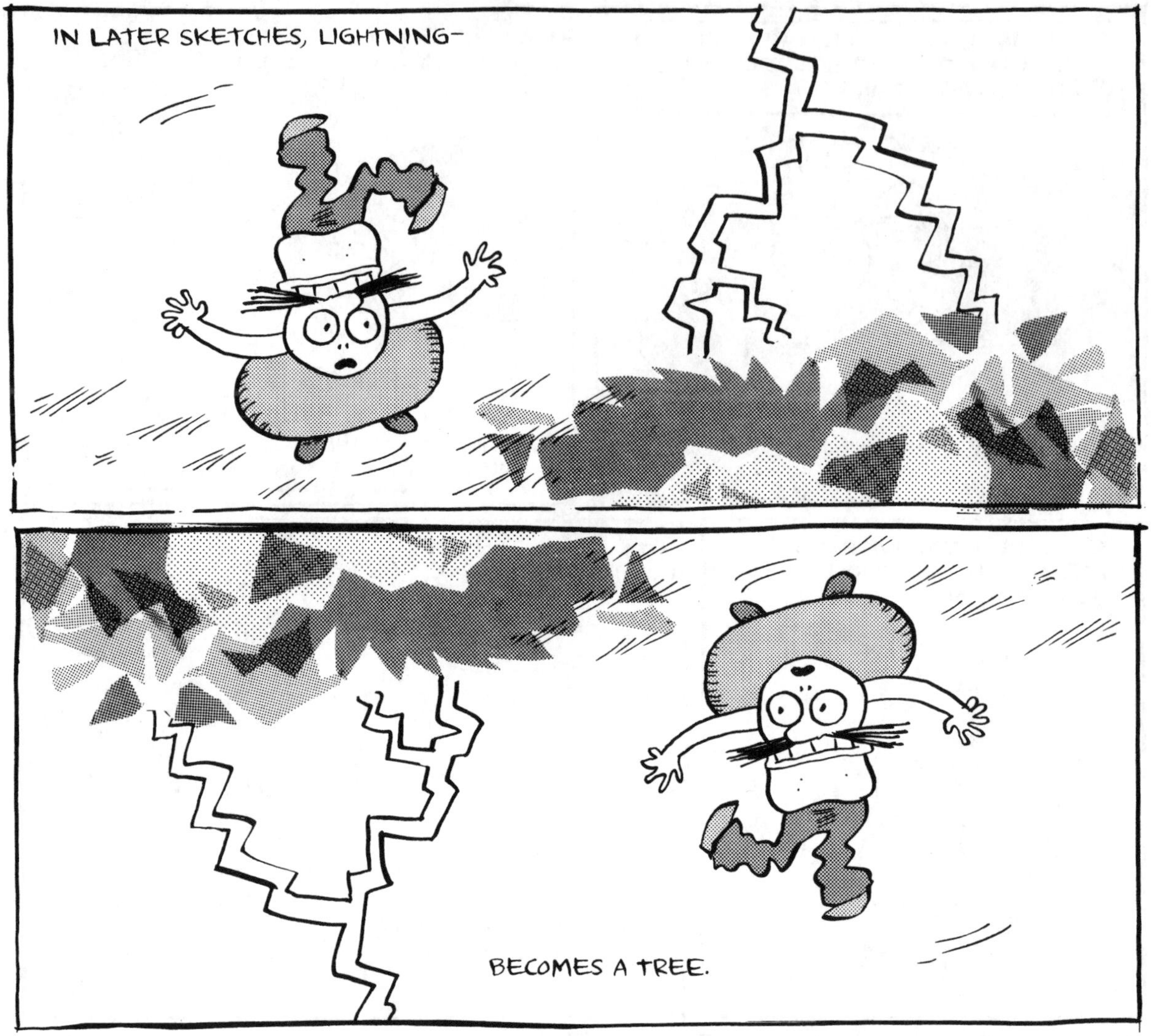
IN LATER SKETCHES, LIGHTNING–
BECOMES A TREE.

MY SKETCHBOOK AFTER THESE ENTRIES IS EMPTY EXCEPT FOR HER DRAWINGS.

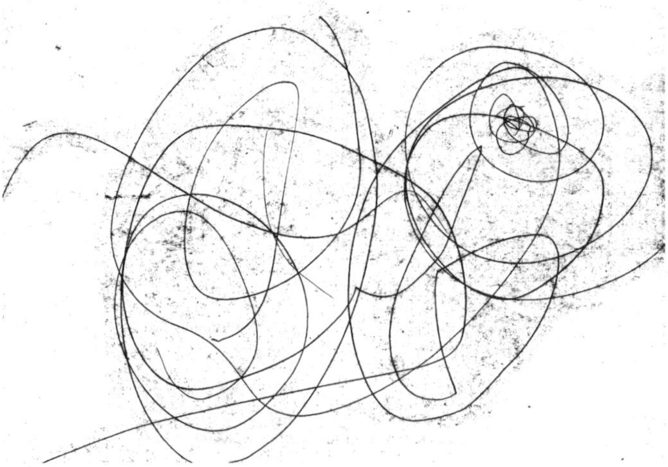

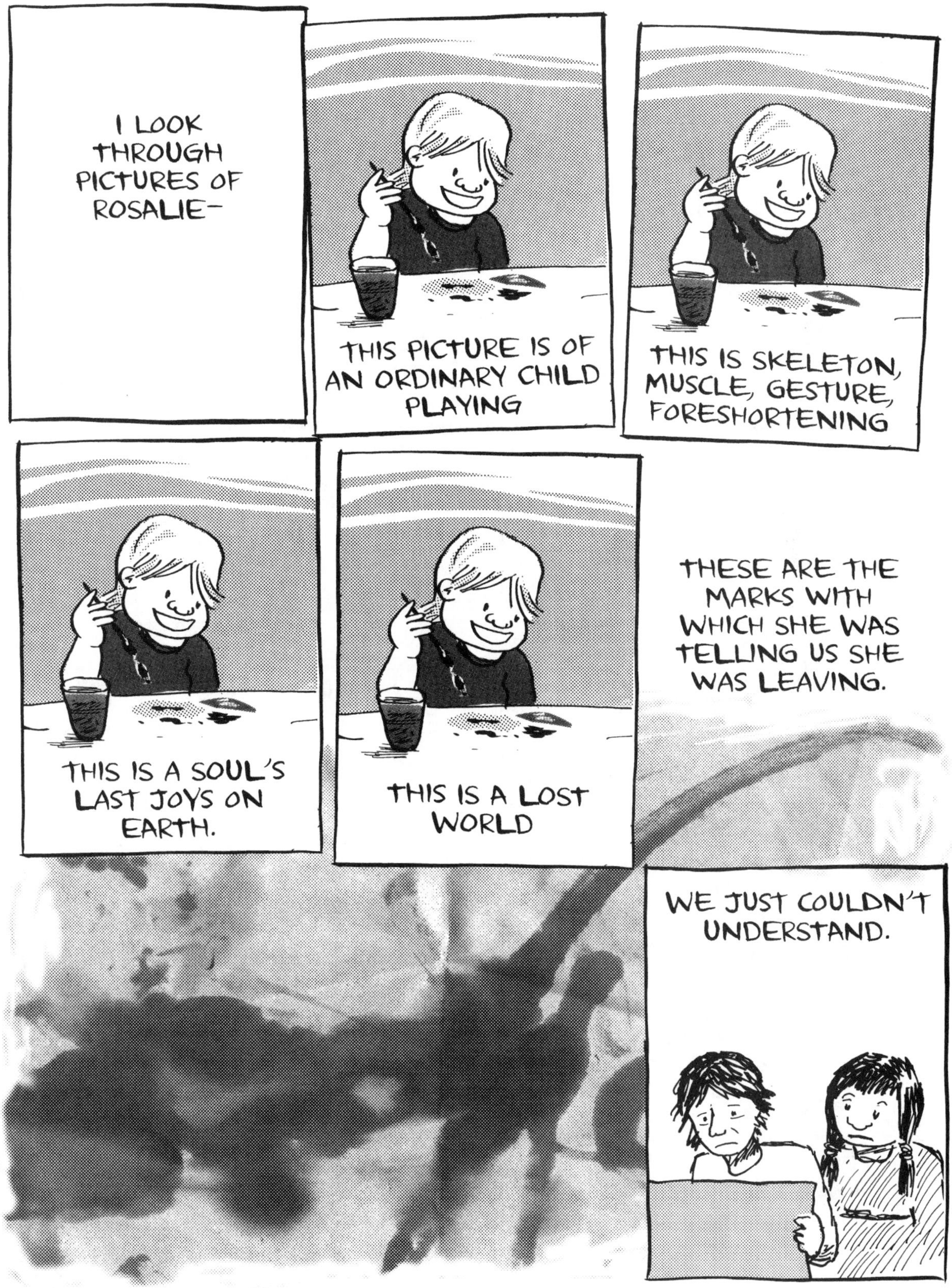
I LOOK THROUGH PICTURES OF ROSALIE–
THIS PICTURE IS OF AN ORDINARY CHILD PLAYING
THIS IS SKELETON, MUSCLE, GESTURE, FORESHORTENING
THIS IS A SOUL'S LAST JOYS ON EARTH.
THIS IS A LOST WORLD
THESE ARE THE MARKS WITH WHICH SHE WAS TELLING US SHE WAS LEAVING.
WE JUST COULDN'T UNDERSTAND.

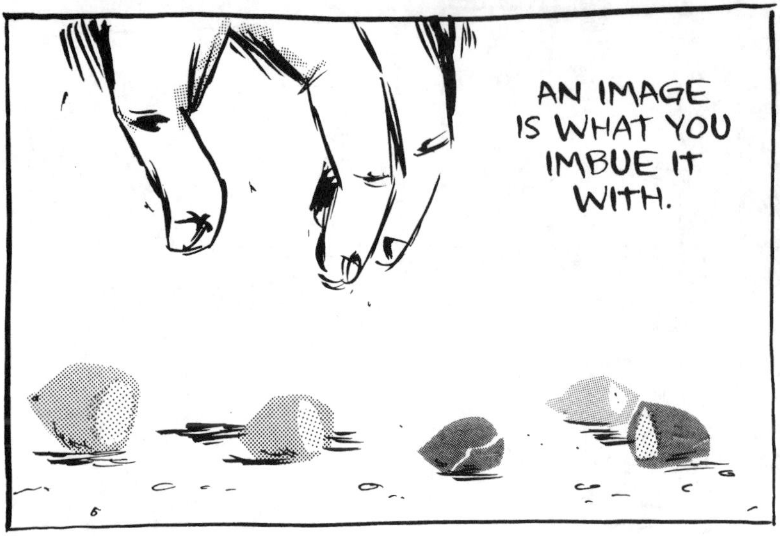
AN IMAGE IS WHAT YOU IMBUE IT WITH.

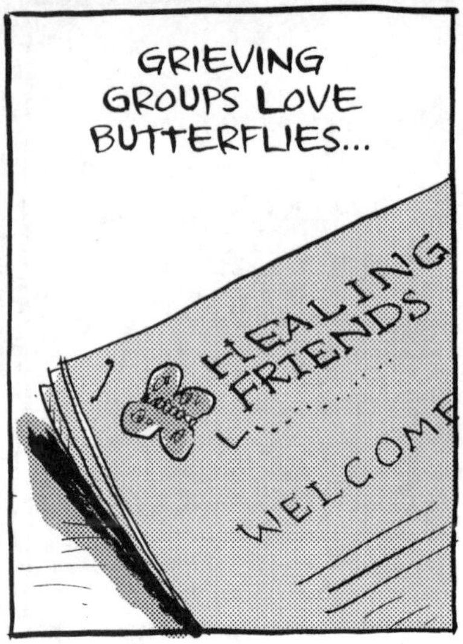
GRIEVING GROUPS LOVE BUTTERFLIES...
HEALING FRIENDS
WELCOME

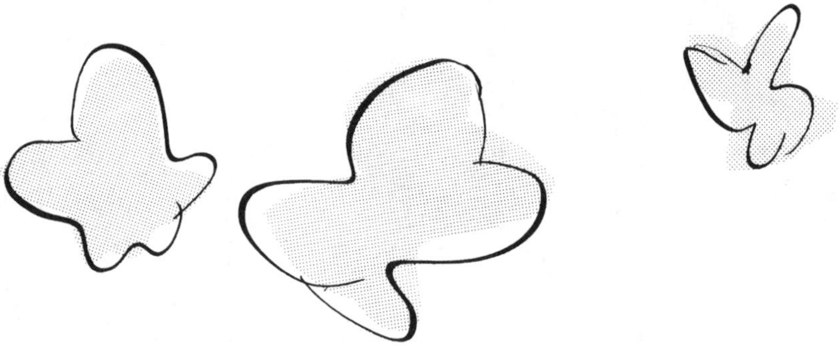

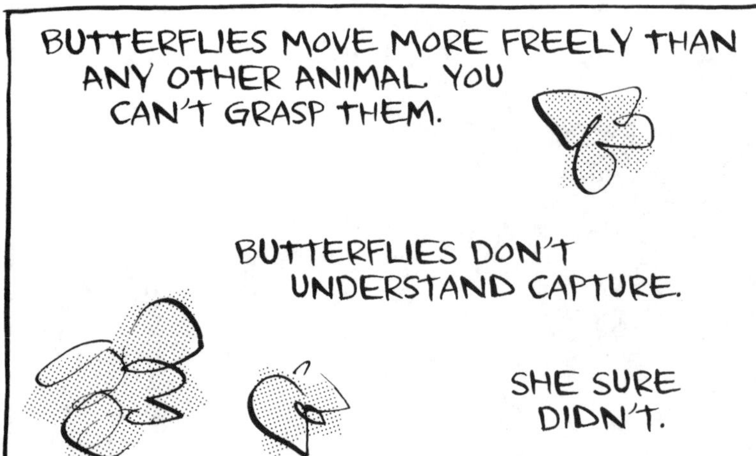
BUTTERFLIES MOVE MORE FREELY THAN ANY OTHER ANIMAL. YOU CAN'T GRASP THEM.
BUTTERFLIES DON'T UNDERSTAND CAPTURE.
SHE SURE DIDN'T.

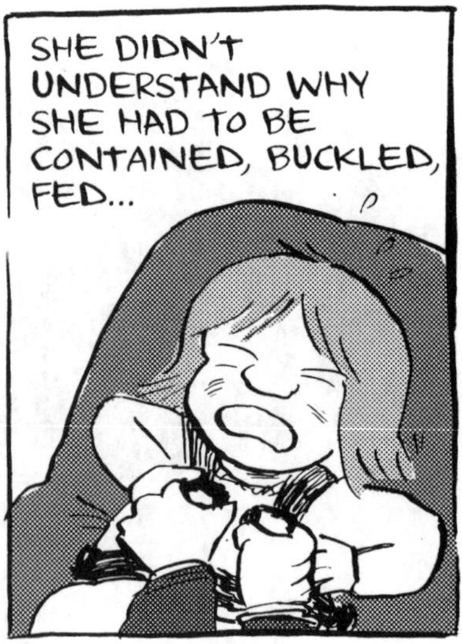
SHE DIDN'T UNDERSTAND WHY SHE HAD TO BE CONTAINED, BUCKLED, FED...

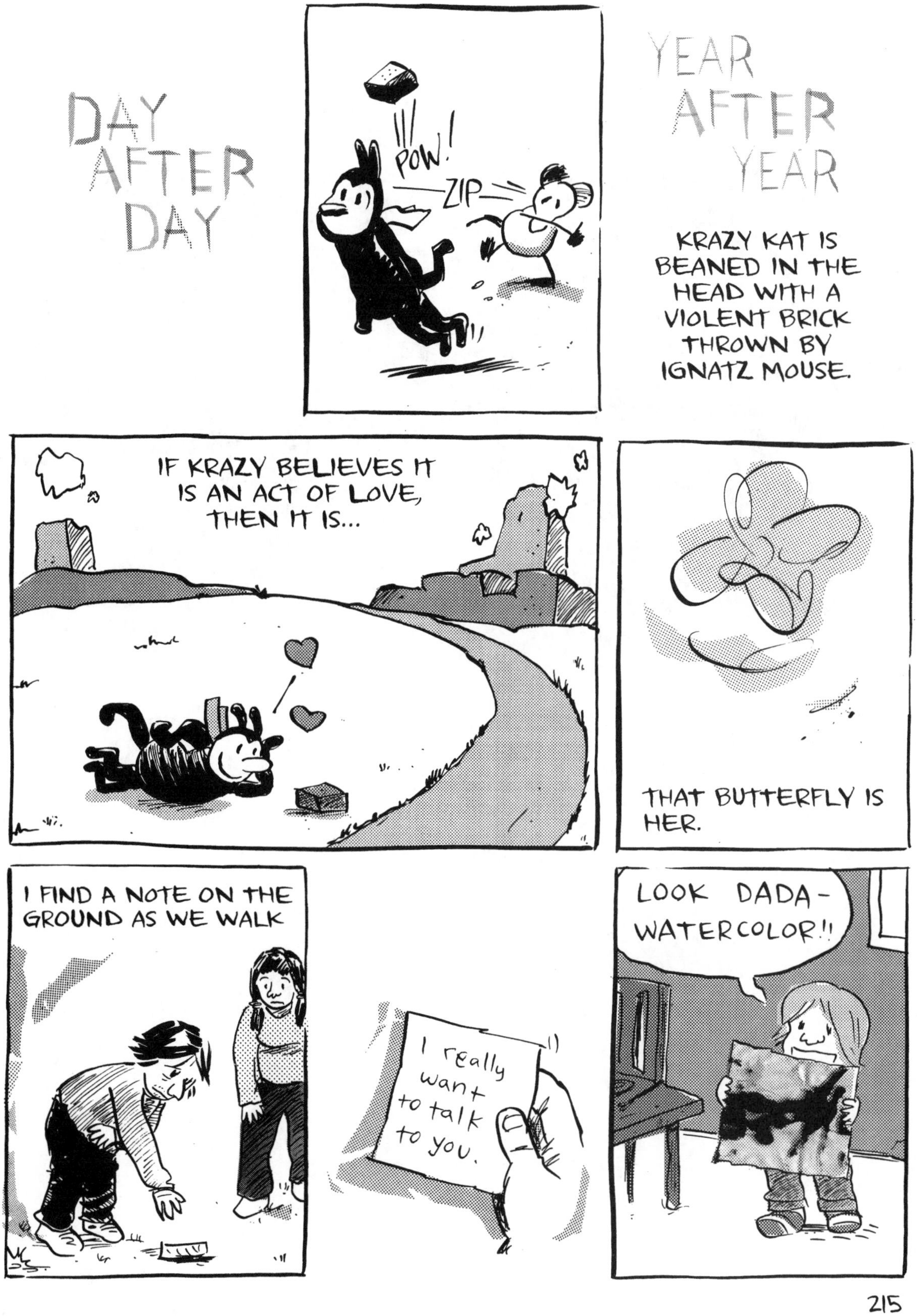
DAY AFTER DAY
POW!
ZIP
YEAR AFTER YEAR
KRAZY KAT IS BEANED IN THE HEAD WITH A VIOLENT BRICK THROWN BY IGNATZ MOUSE.
IF KRAZY BELIEVES IT IS AN ACT OF LOVE, THEN IT IS...
THAT BUTTERFLY IS HER.
I FIND A NOTE ON THE GROUND AS WE WALK
I really want to talk to you.
LOOK DADA - WATERCOLOR!!

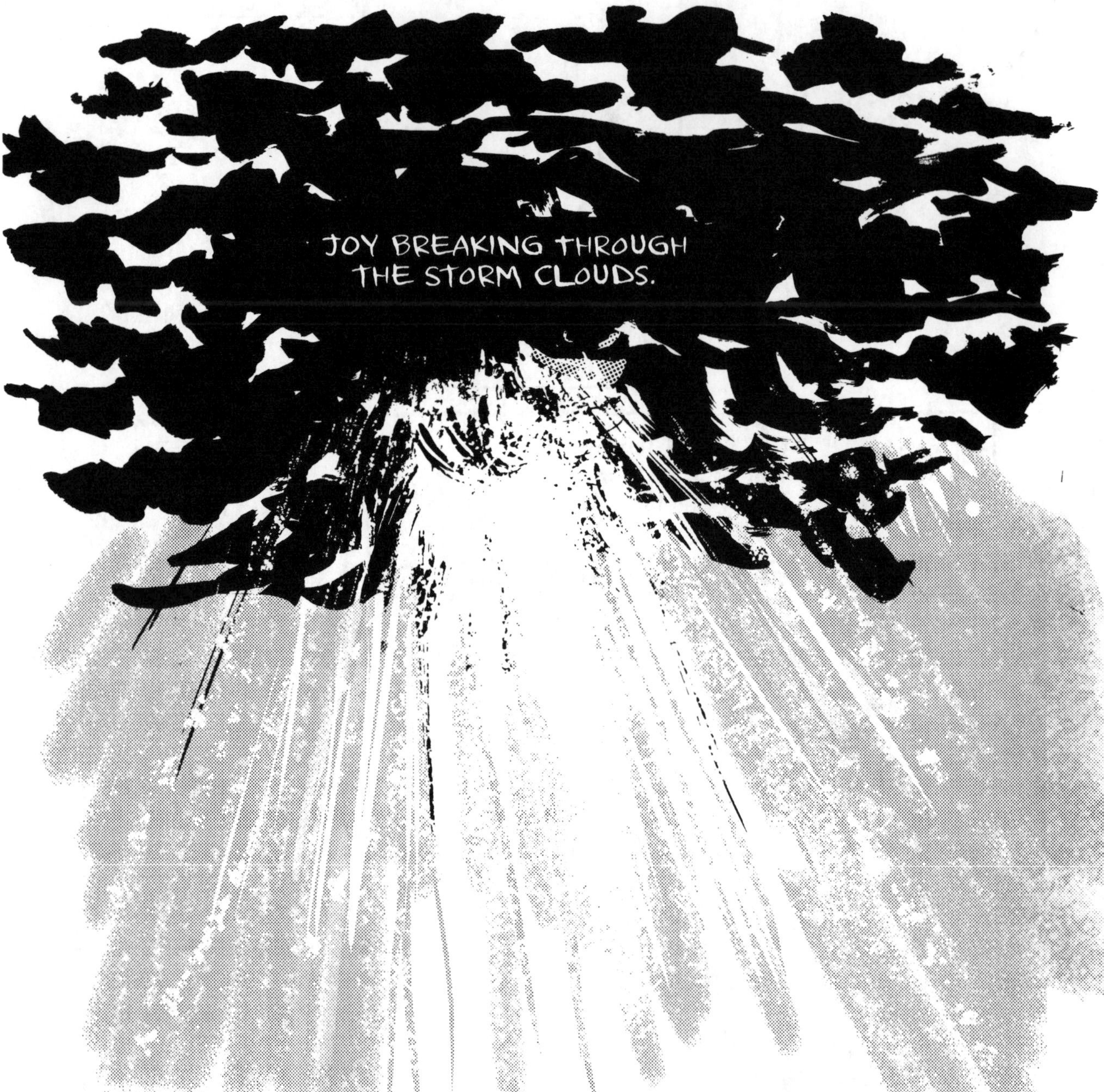
JOY BREAKING THROUGH THE STORM CLOUDS.

WE DECIDE TO GO
TO THE BEACH.

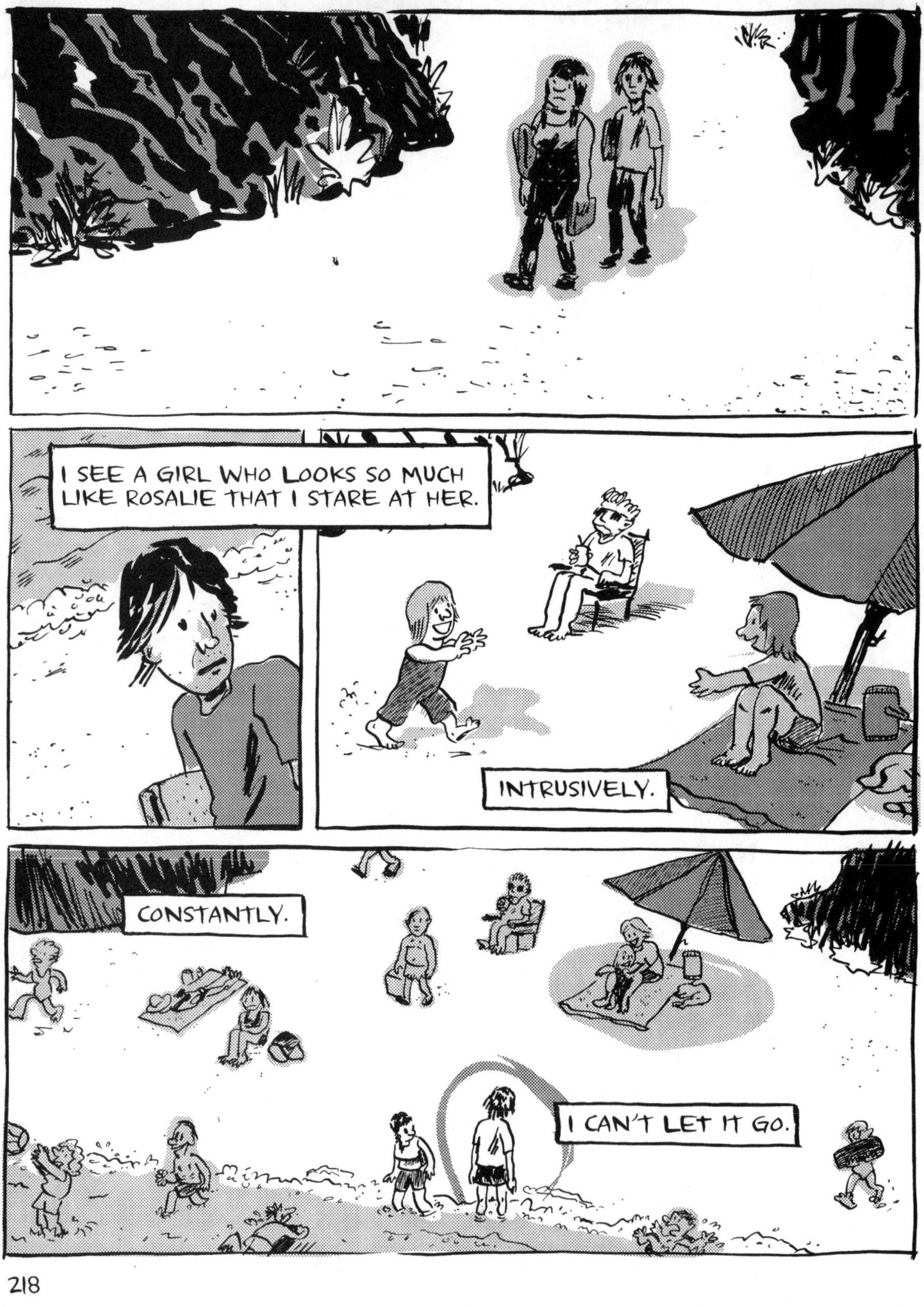
I SEE A GIRL WHO LOOKS SO MUCH LIKE ROSALIE THAT I STARE AT HER.
INTRUSIVELY.
CONSTANTLY.
I CAN'T LET IT GO.

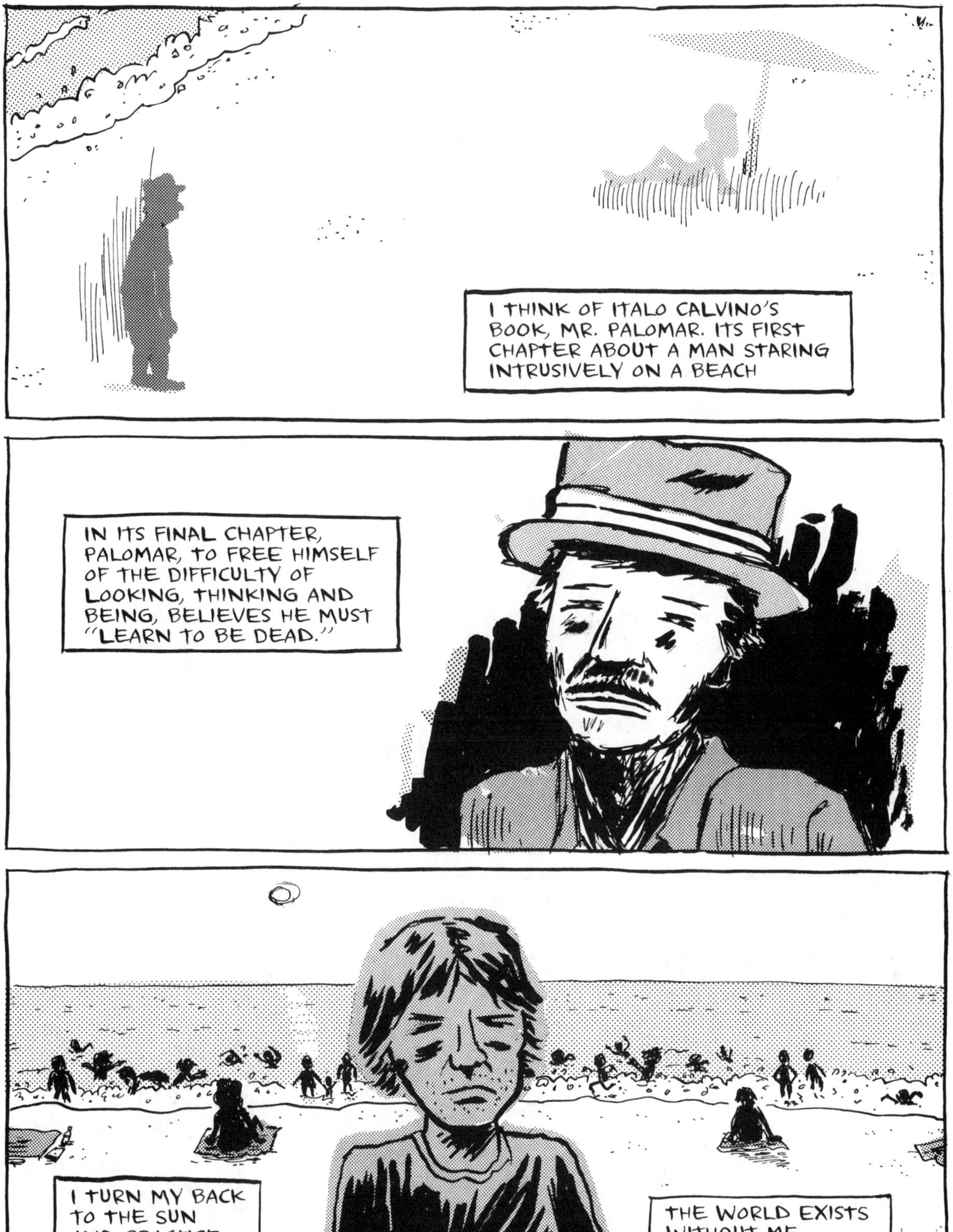
I THINK OF ITALO CALVINO'S BOOK, MR. PALOMAR. ITS FIRST CHAPTER ABOUT A MAN STARING INTRUSIVELY ON A BEACH
IN ITS FINAL CHAPTER, PALOMAR, TO FREE HIMSELF OF THE DIFFICULTY OF LOOKING, THINKING AND BEING, BELIEVES HE MUST "LEARN TO BE DEAD."
I TURN MY BACK TO THE SUN AND PRACTICE.
THE WORLD EXISTS WITHOUT ME.

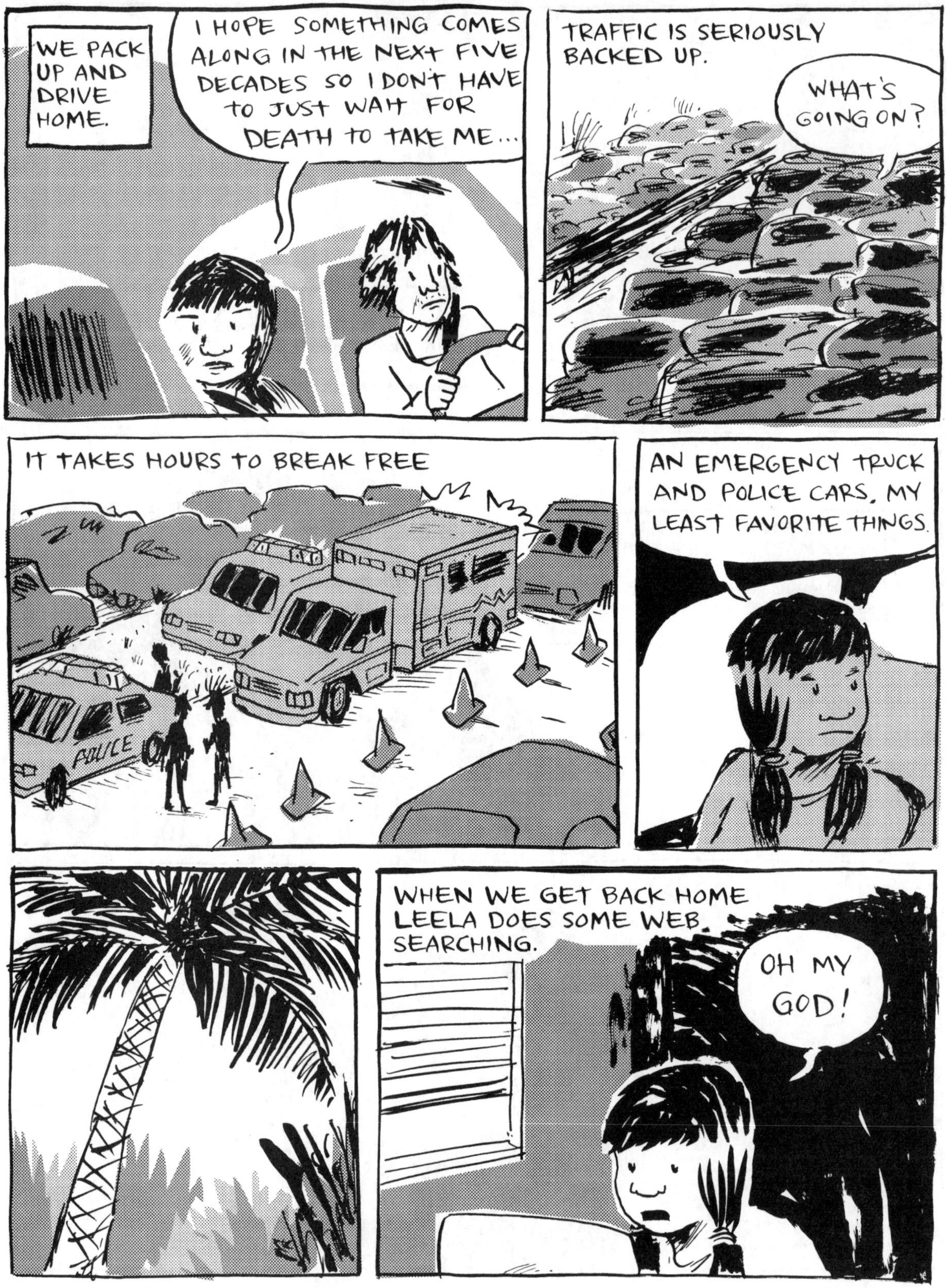
WE PACK UP AND DRIVE HOME.
I HOPE SOMETHING COMES ALONG IN THE NEXT FIVE DECADES SO I DON'T HAVE TO JUST WAIT FOR DEATH TO TAKE ME...
TRAFFIC IS SERIOUSLY BACKED UP.
WHAT'S GOING ON?
IT TAKES HOURS TO BREAK FREE
POLICE
AN EMERGENCY TRUCK AND POLICE CARS. MY LEAST FAVORITE THINGS.
WHEN WE GET BACK HOME LEELA DOES SOME WEB SEARCHING.
OH MY GOD!

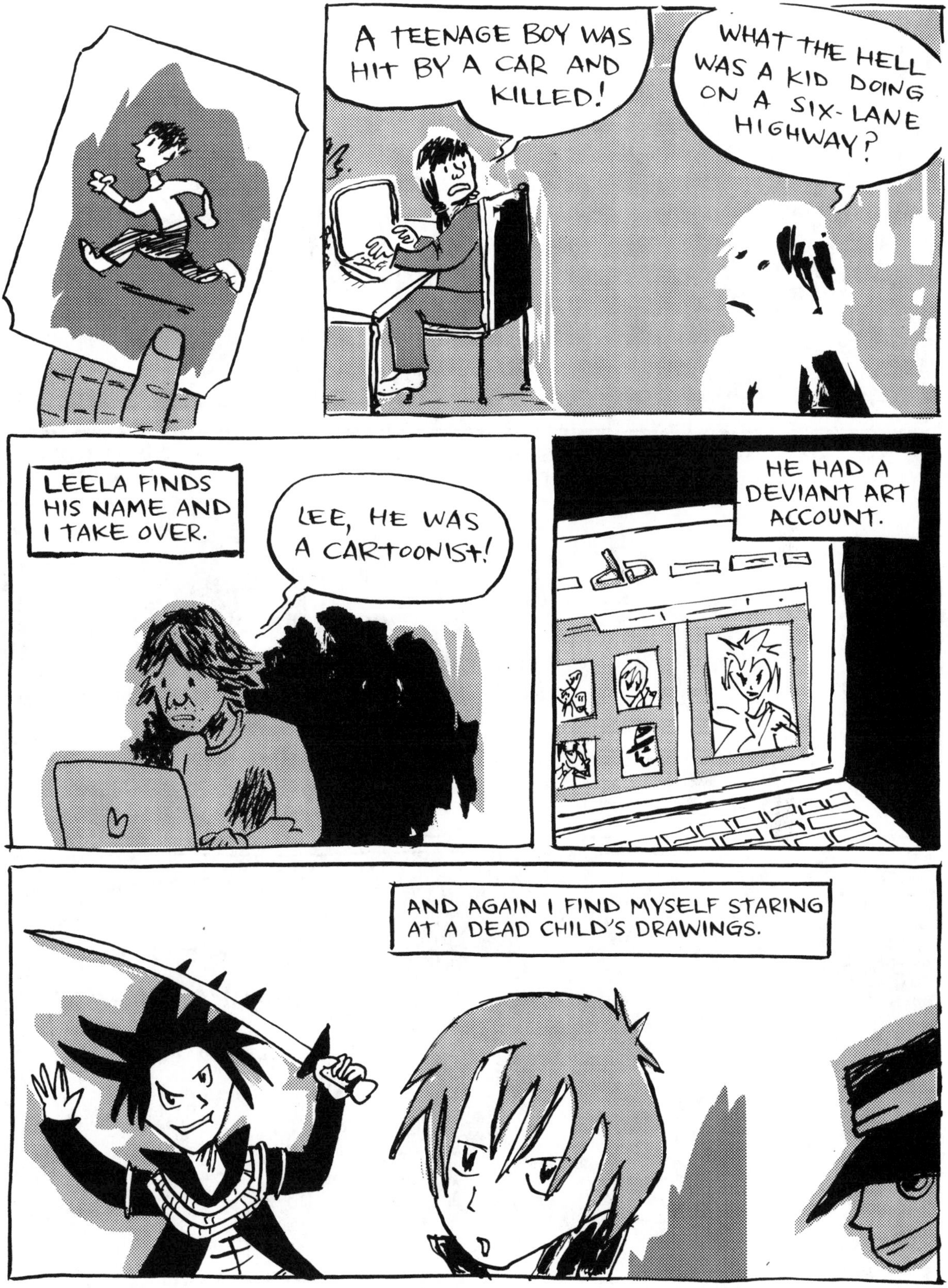
A TEENAGE BOY WAS HIT BY A CAR AND KILLED!
WHAT THE HELL WAS A KID DOING ON A SIX-LANE HIGHWAY?
LEELA FINDS HIS NAME AND I TAKE OVER.
LEE, HE WAS A CARTOONIST!
HE HAD A DEVIANT ART ACCOUNT.
AND AGAIN I FIND MYSELF STARING AT A DEAD CHILD'S DRAWINGS.

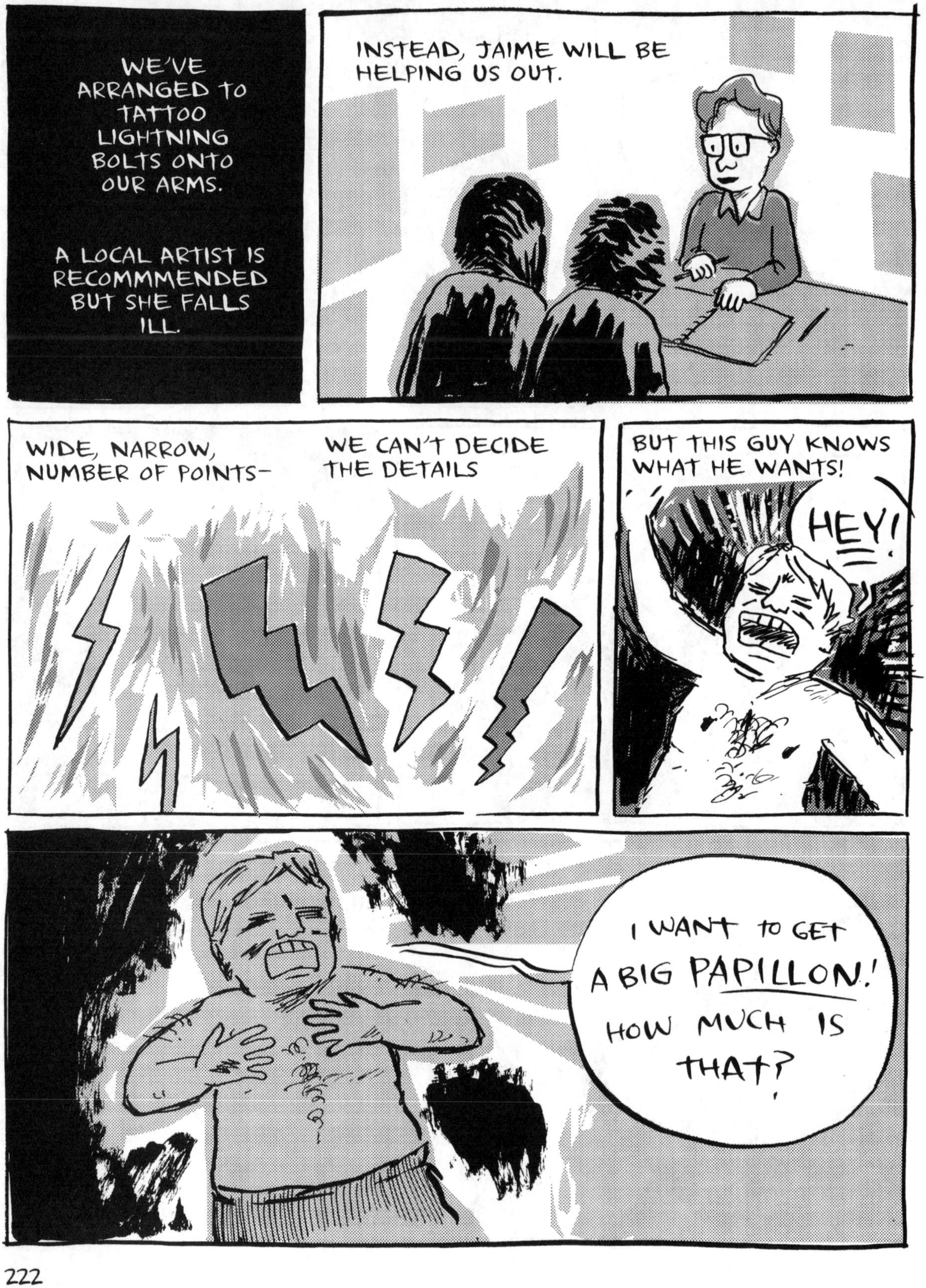
WE'VE ARRANGED TO TATTOO LIGHTNING BOLTS ONTO OUR ARMS.
A LOCAL ARTIST IS RECOMMMENDED BUT SHE FALLS ILL.
INSTEAD, JAIME WILL BE HELPING US OUT.
WIDE, NARROW, NUMBER OF POINTS-
WE CAN'T DECIDE THE DETAILS
BUT THIS GUY KNOWS WHAT HE WANTS!
HEY!
I WANT TO GET A BIG PAPILLON! HOW MUCH IS THAT?

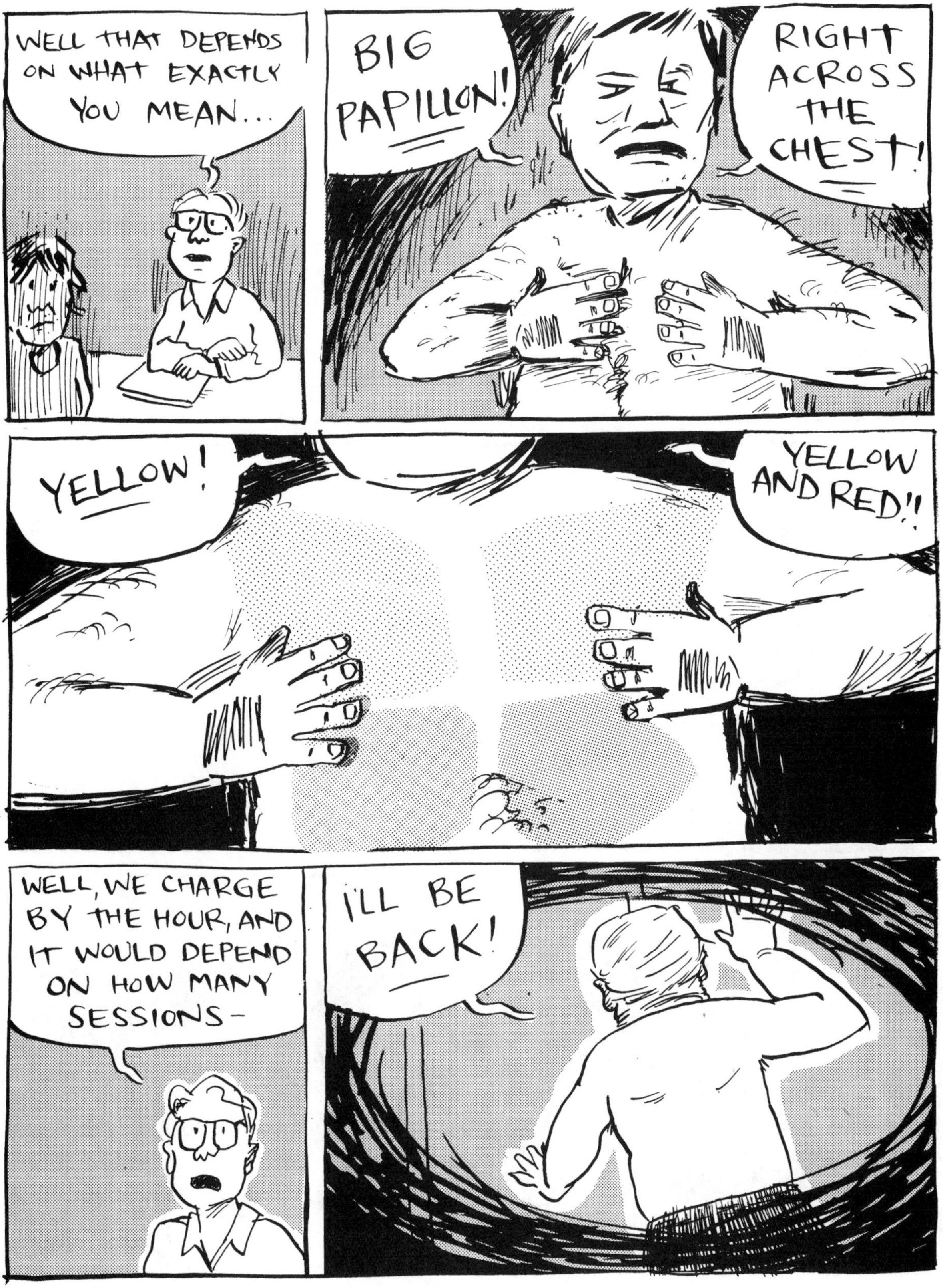
WELL THAT DEPENDS ON WHAT EXACTLY YOU MEAN...
BIG PAPILLON!
RIGHT ACROSS THE CHEST!
YELLOW!
YELLOW AND RED!!
WELL, WE CHARGE BY THE HOUR, AND IT WOULD DEPEND ON HOW MANY SESSIONS-
I'LL BE BACK!

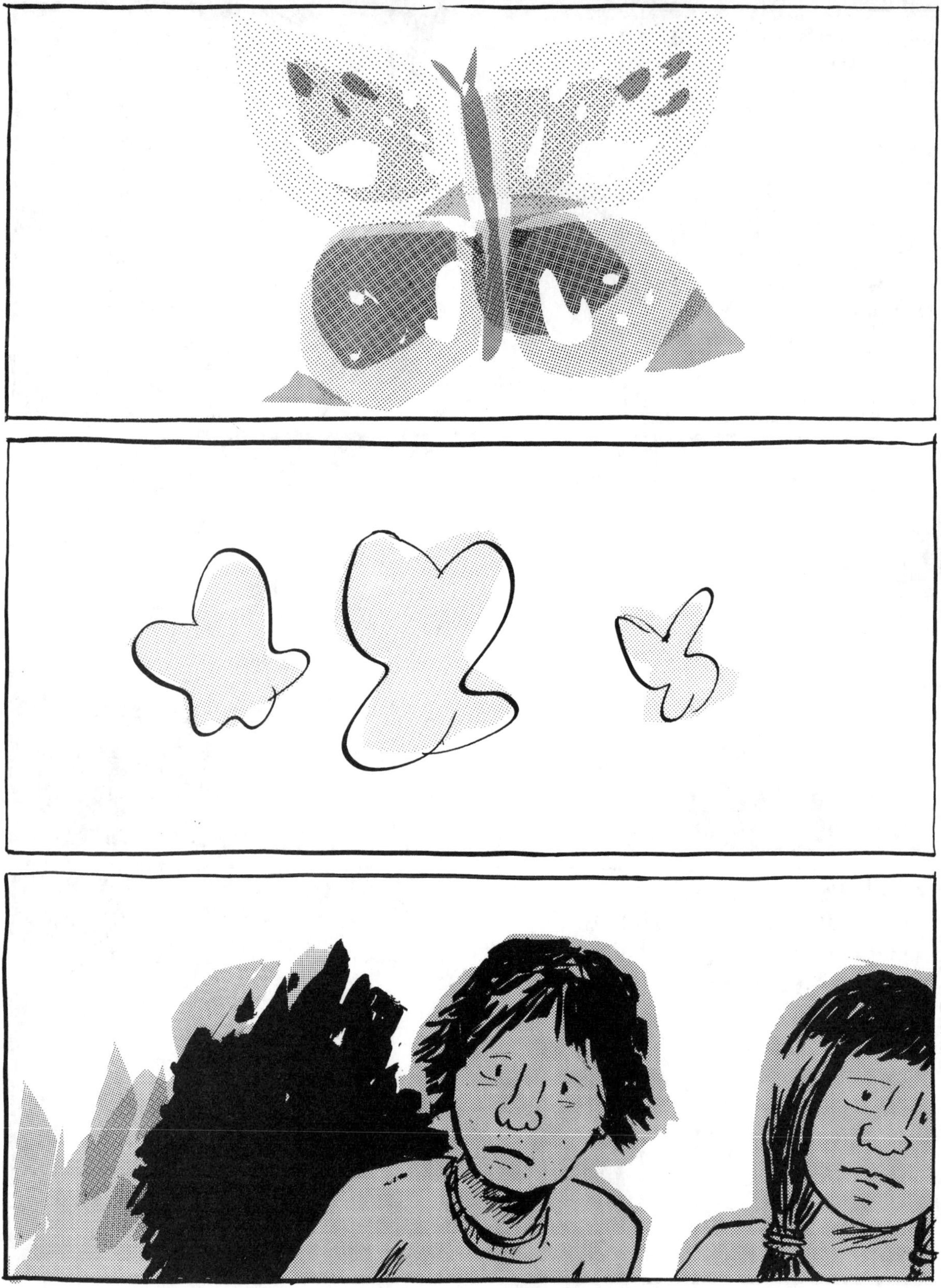

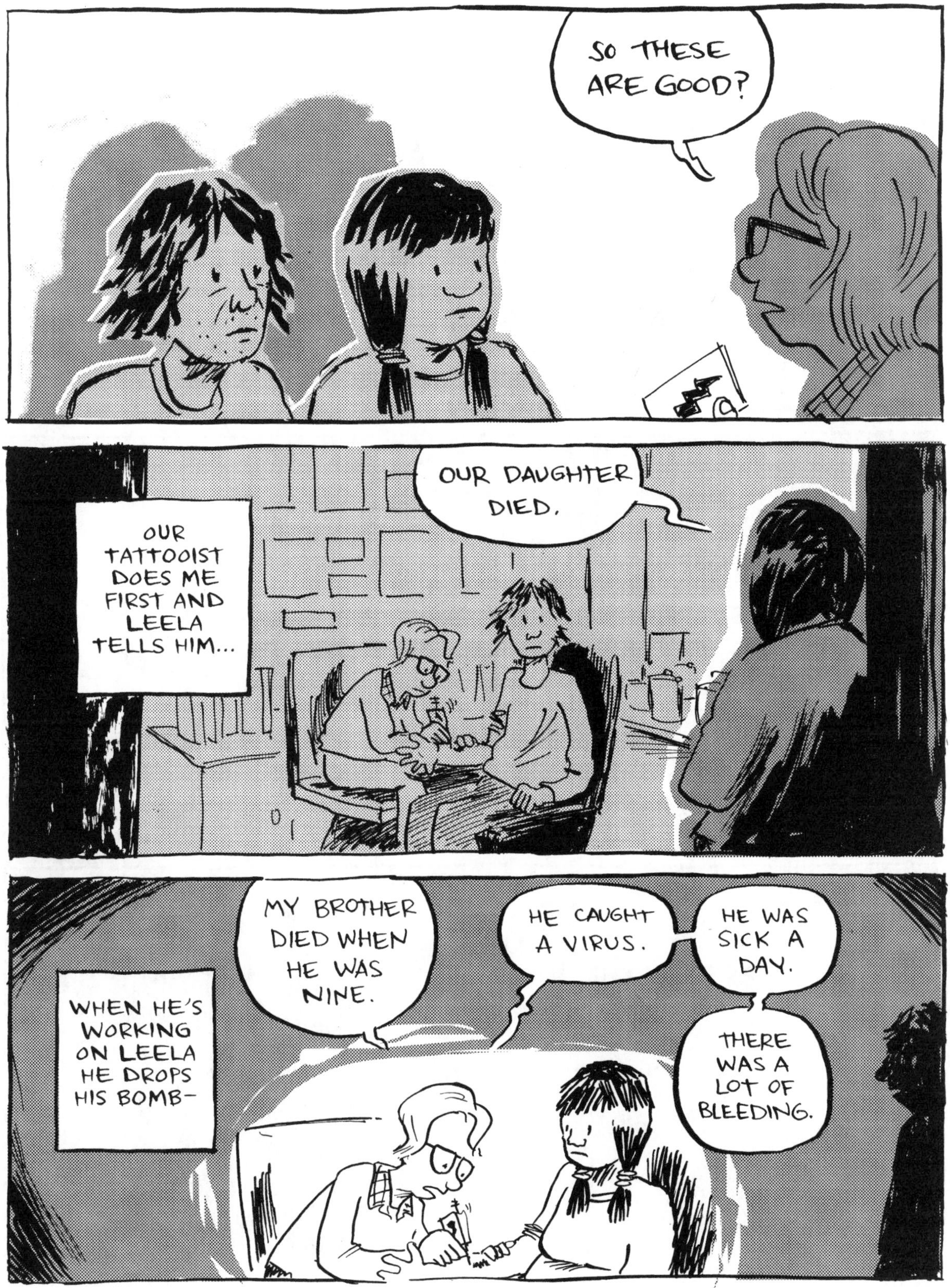
SO THESE ARE GOOD?
OUR TATTOOIST DOES ME FIRST AND LEELA TELLS HIM...
OUR DAUGHTER DIED.
WHEN HE'S WORKING ON LEELA HE DROPS HIS BOMB-
MY BROTHER DIED WHEN HE WAS NINE.
HE CAUGHT A VIRUS.
HE WAS SICK A DAY.
THERE WAS A LOT OF BLEEDING.

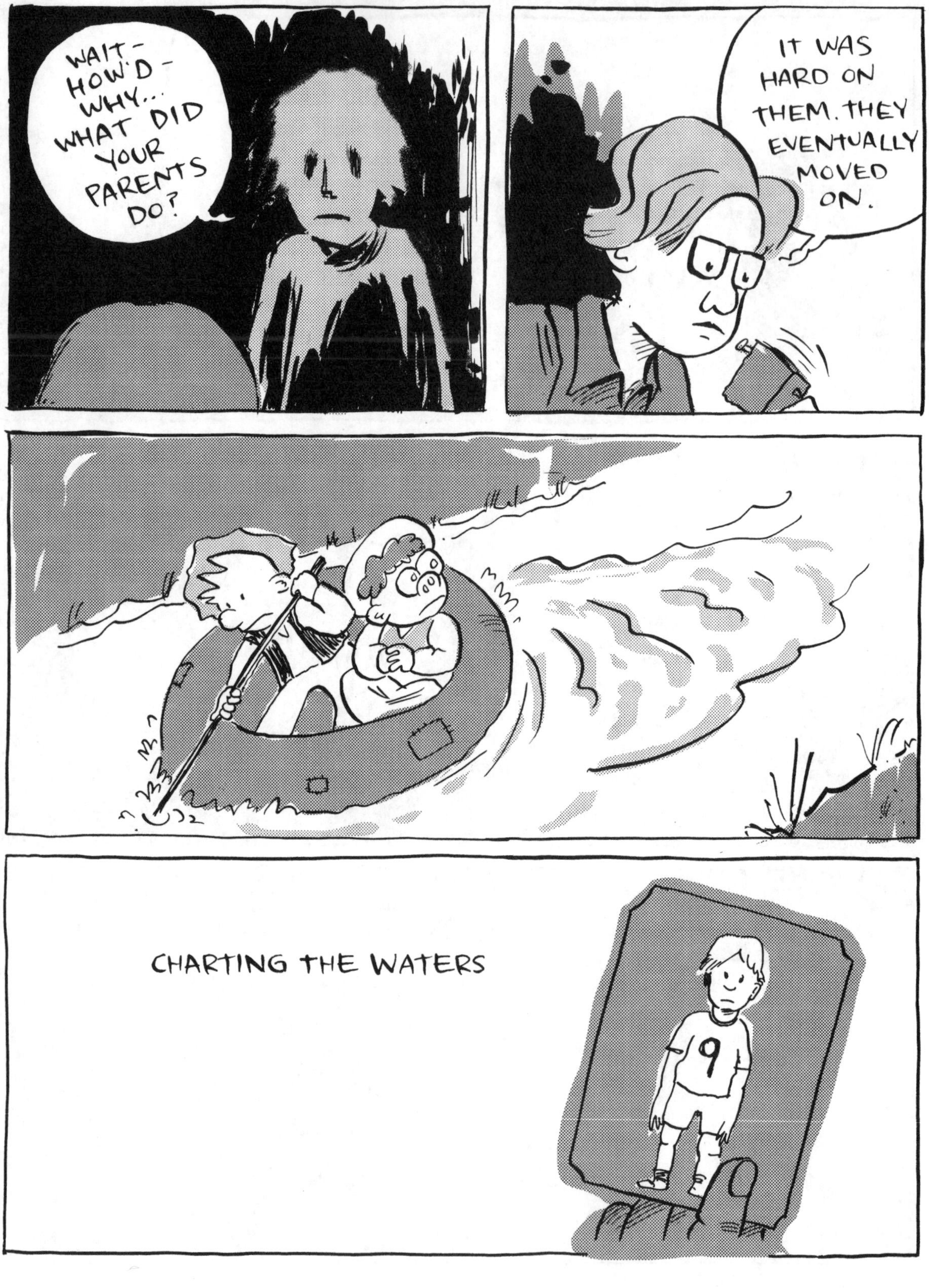
WAIT- HOW'D- WHY... WHAT DID YOUR PARENTS DO?
IT WAS HARD ON THEM. THEY EVENTUALLY MOVED ON.
CHARTING THE WATERS
9

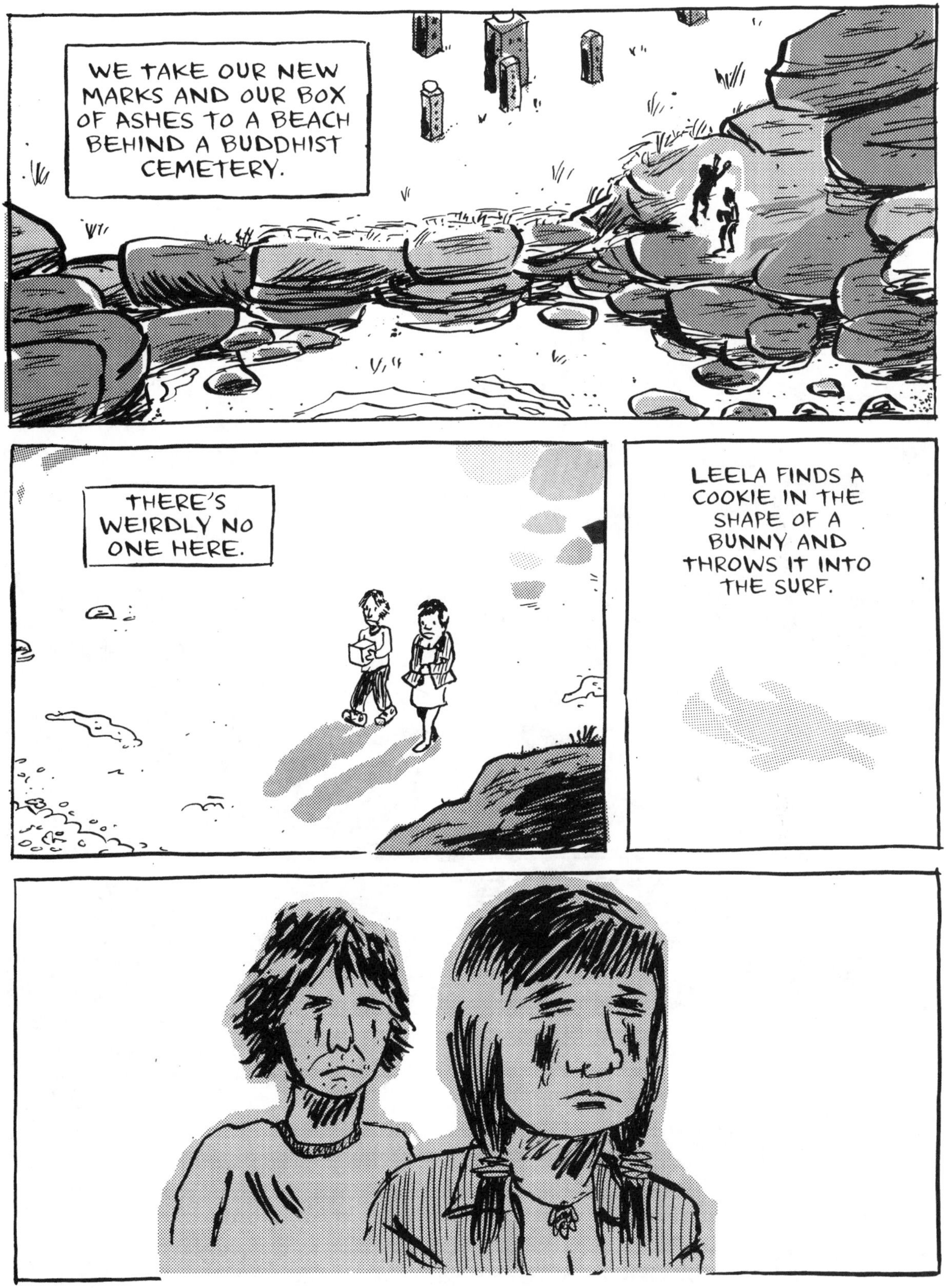
WE TAKE OUR NEW MARKS AND OUR BOX OF ASHES TO A BEACH BEHIND A BUDDHIST CEMETERY.
THERE'S WEIRDLY NO ONE HERE.
LEELA FINDS A COOKIE IN THE SHAPE OF A BUNNY AND THROWS IT INTO THE SURF.

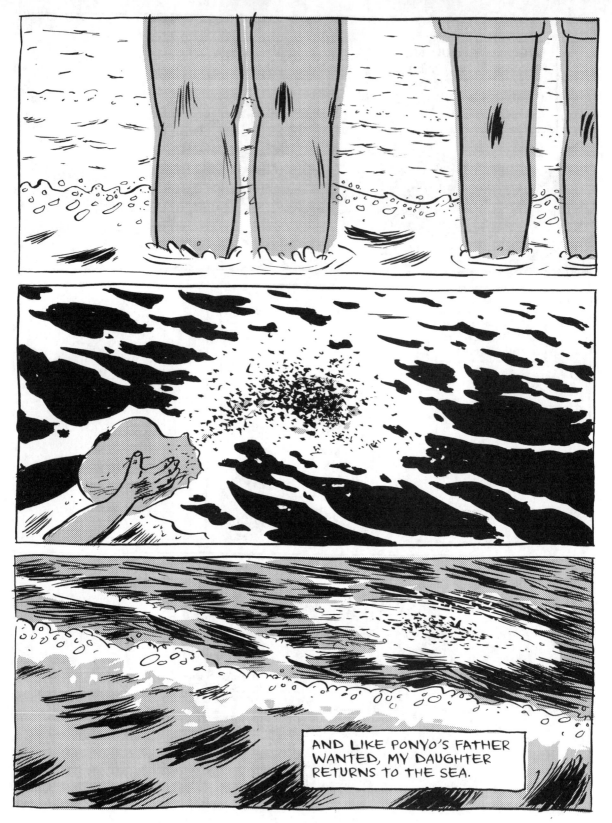

AND LIKE PONYO'S FATHER WANTED, MY DAUGHTER RETURNS TO THE SEA.

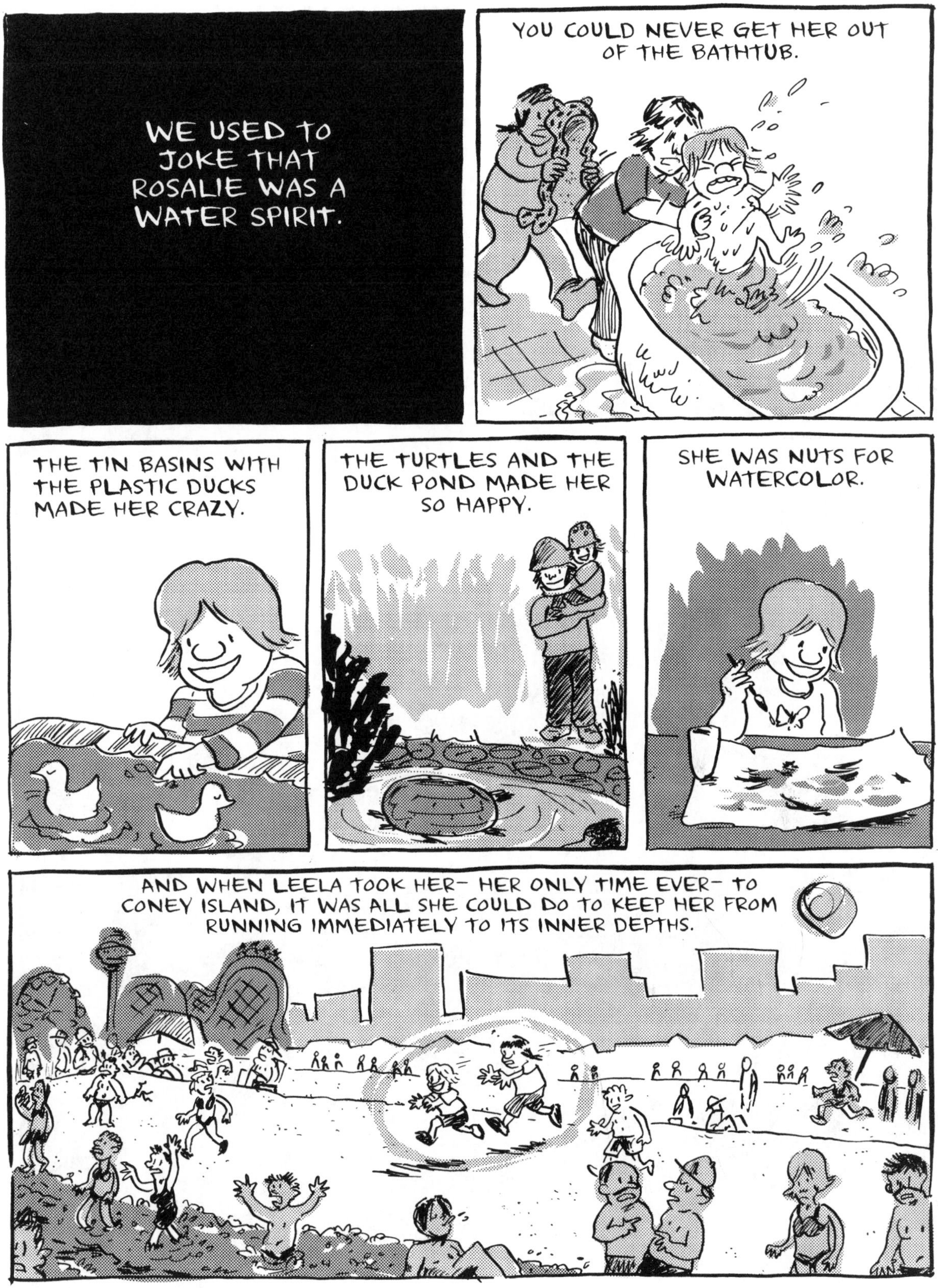
WE USED TO JOKE THAT ROSALIE WAS A WATER SPIRIT.
YOU COULD NEVER GET HER OUT OF THE BATHTUB.
THE TIN BASINS WITH THE PLASTIC DUCKS MADE HER CRAZY.
THE TURTLES AND THE DUCK POND MADE HER SO HAPPY.
SHE WAS NUTS FOR WATERCOLOR.
AND WHEN LEELA TOOK HER— HER ONLY TIME EVER— TO CONEY ISLAND, IT WAS ALL SHE COULD DO TO KEEP HER FROM RUNNING IMMEDIATELY TO ITS INNER DEPTHS.

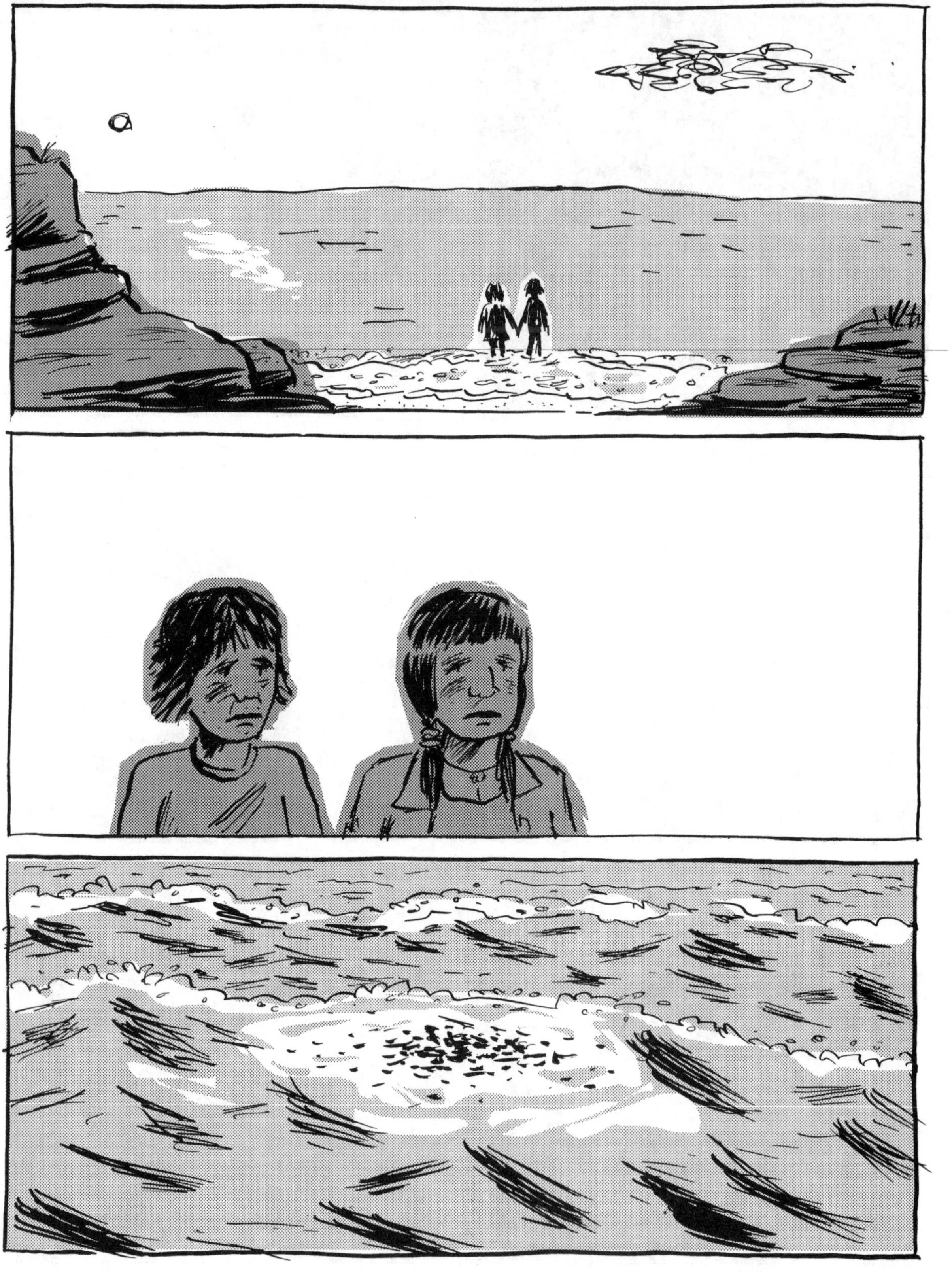

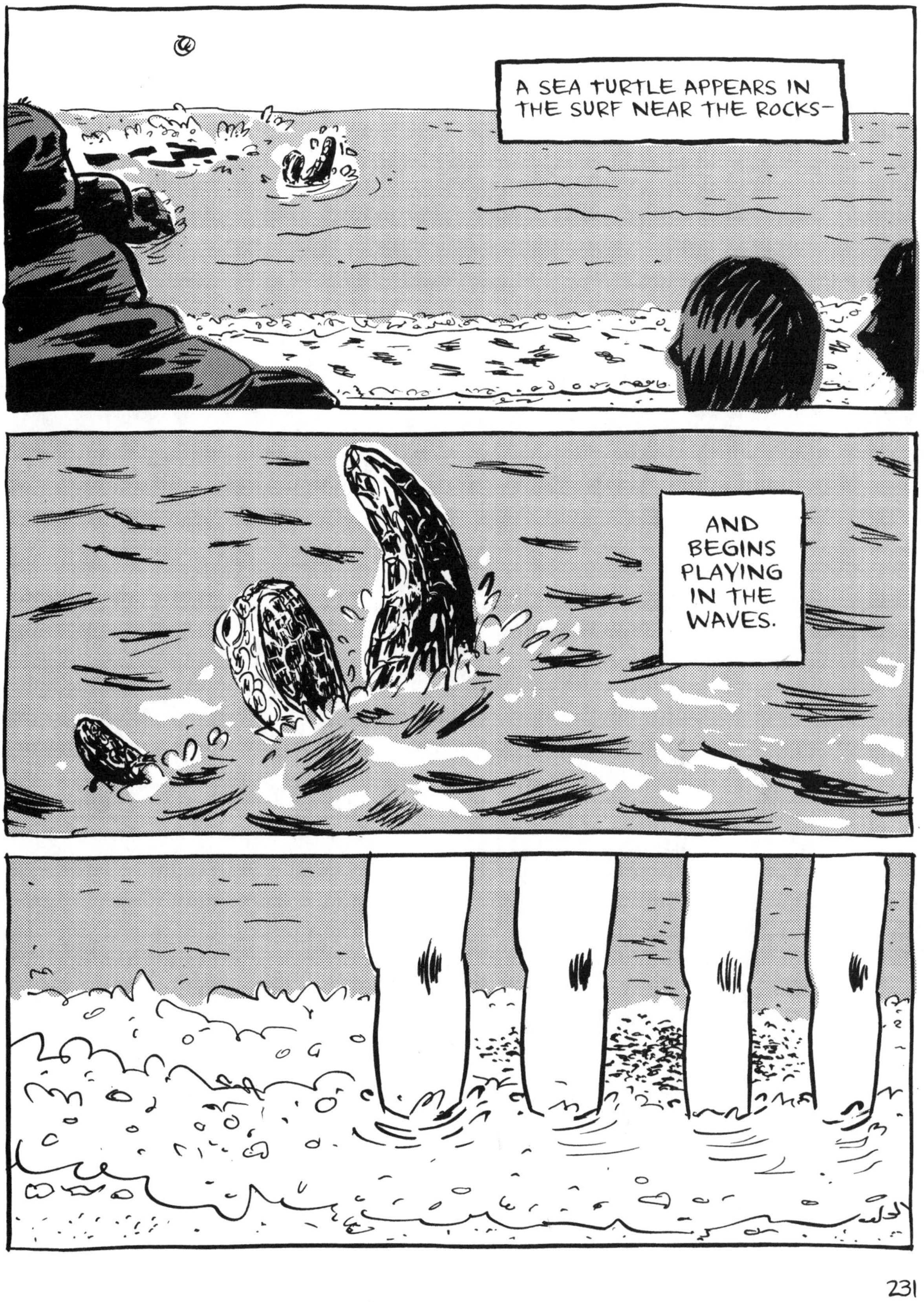
A SEA TURTLE APPEARS IN THE SURF NEAR THE ROCKS-
AND BEGINS PLAYING IN THE WAVES.

EVERYTHING MERGES

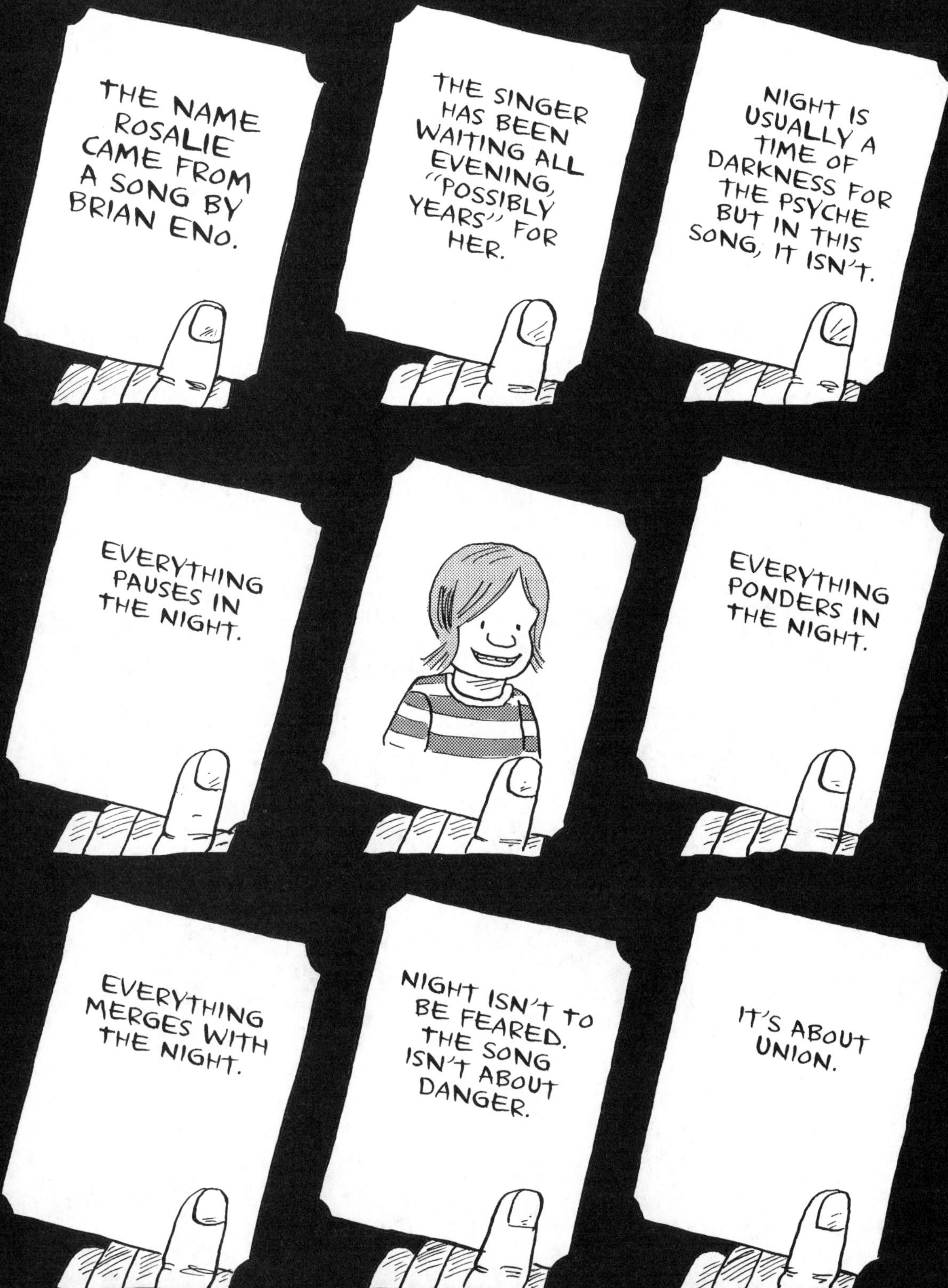

THE NAME ROSALIE CAME FROM A SONG BY BRIAN ENO.
THE SINGER HAS BEEN WAITING ALL EVENING, "POSSIBLY YEARS" FOR HER.
NIGHT IS USUALLY A TIME OF DARKNESS FOR THE PSYCHE BUT IN THIS SONG, IT ISN'T.
EVERYTHING PAUSES IN THE NIGHT.
EVERYTHING PONDERS IN THE NIGHT.
EVERYTHING MERGES WITH THE NIGHT.
NIGHT ISN'T TO BE FEARED. THE SONG ISN'T ABOUT DANGER.
IT'S ABOUT UNION.

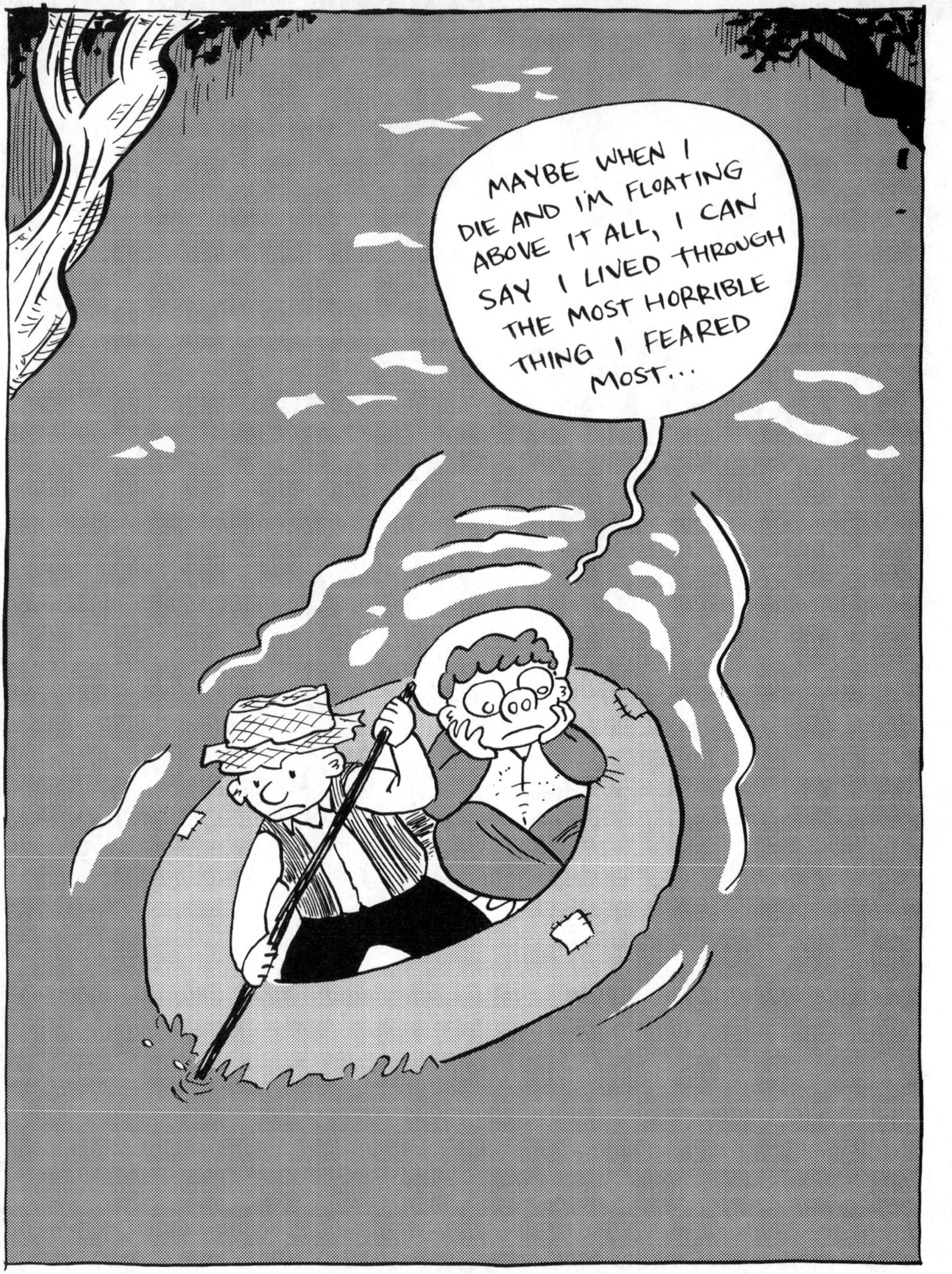
MAYBE WHEN I DIE AND I'M FLOATING ABOVE IT ALL, I CAN SAY I LIVED THROUGH THE MOST HORRIBLE THING I FEARED MOST...

XII

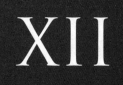

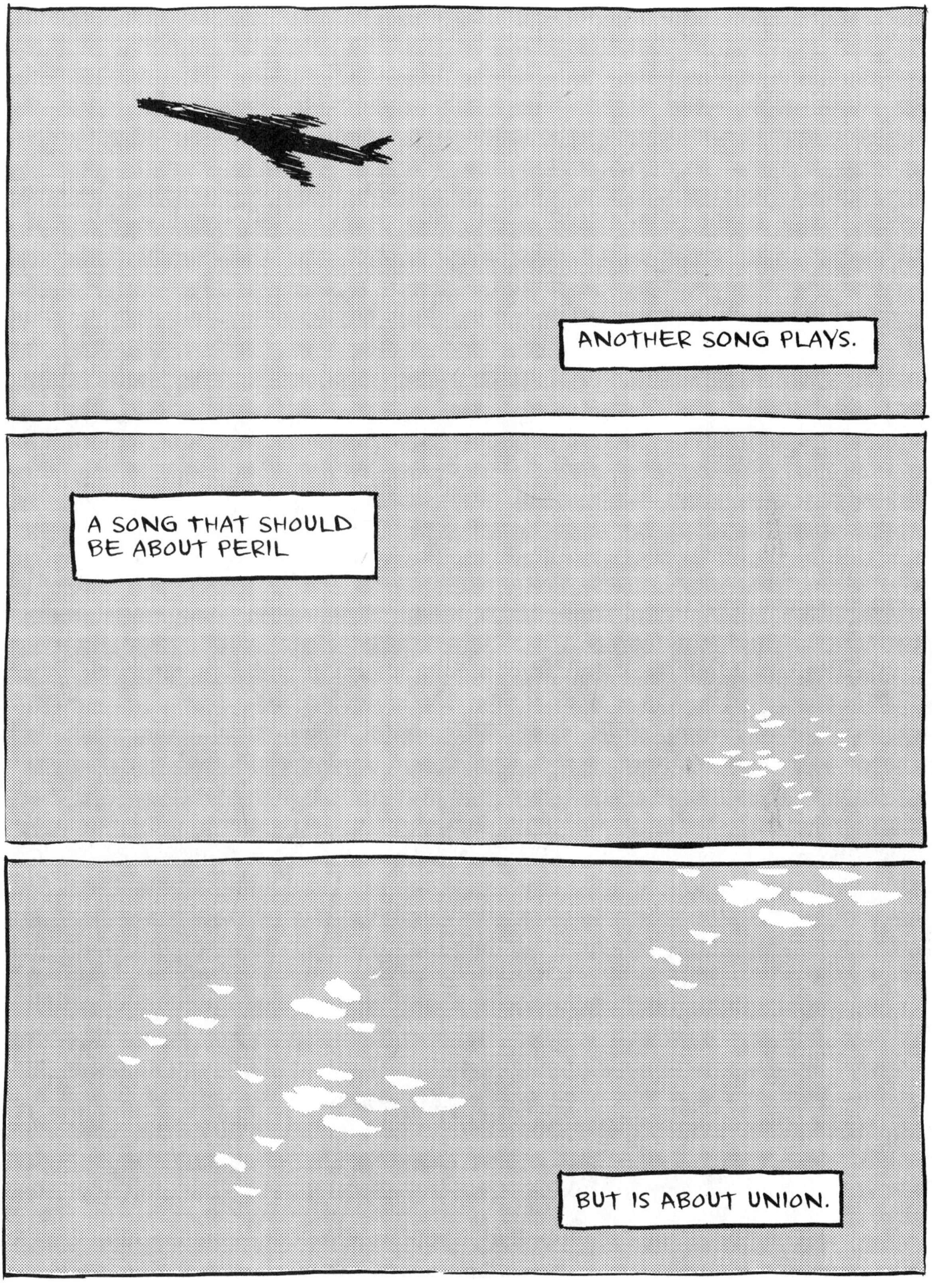
ANOTHER SONG PLAYS.
A SONG THAT SHOULD BE ABOUT PERIL
BUT IS ABOUT UNION.

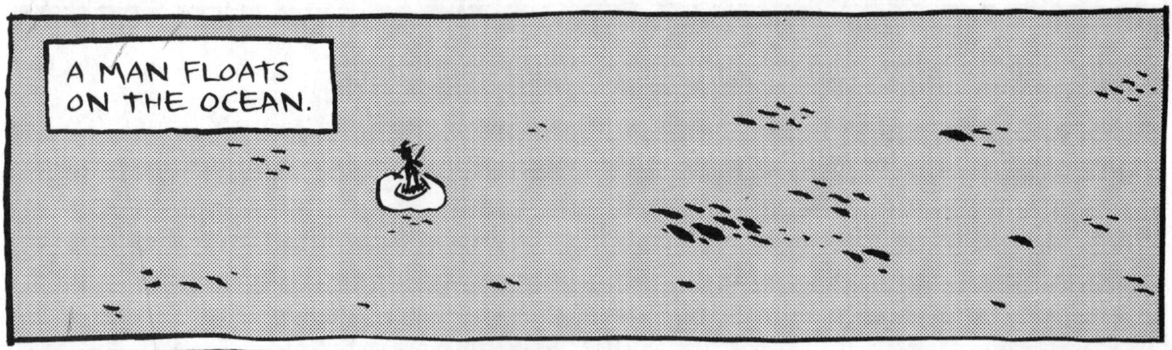
A MAN FLOATS ON THE OCEAN.
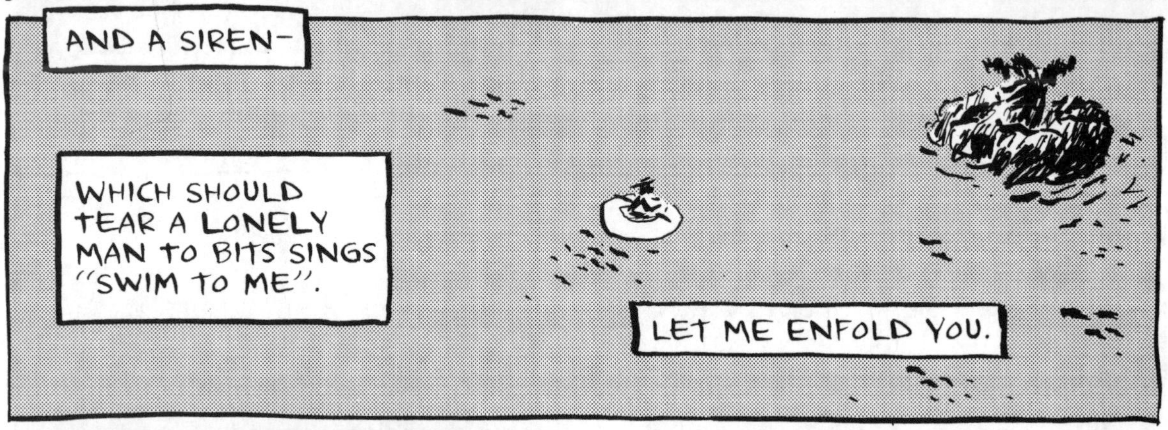
AND A SIREN-
WHICH SHOULD TEAR A LONELY MAN TO BITS SINGS "SWIM TO ME".
LET ME ENFOLD YOU.
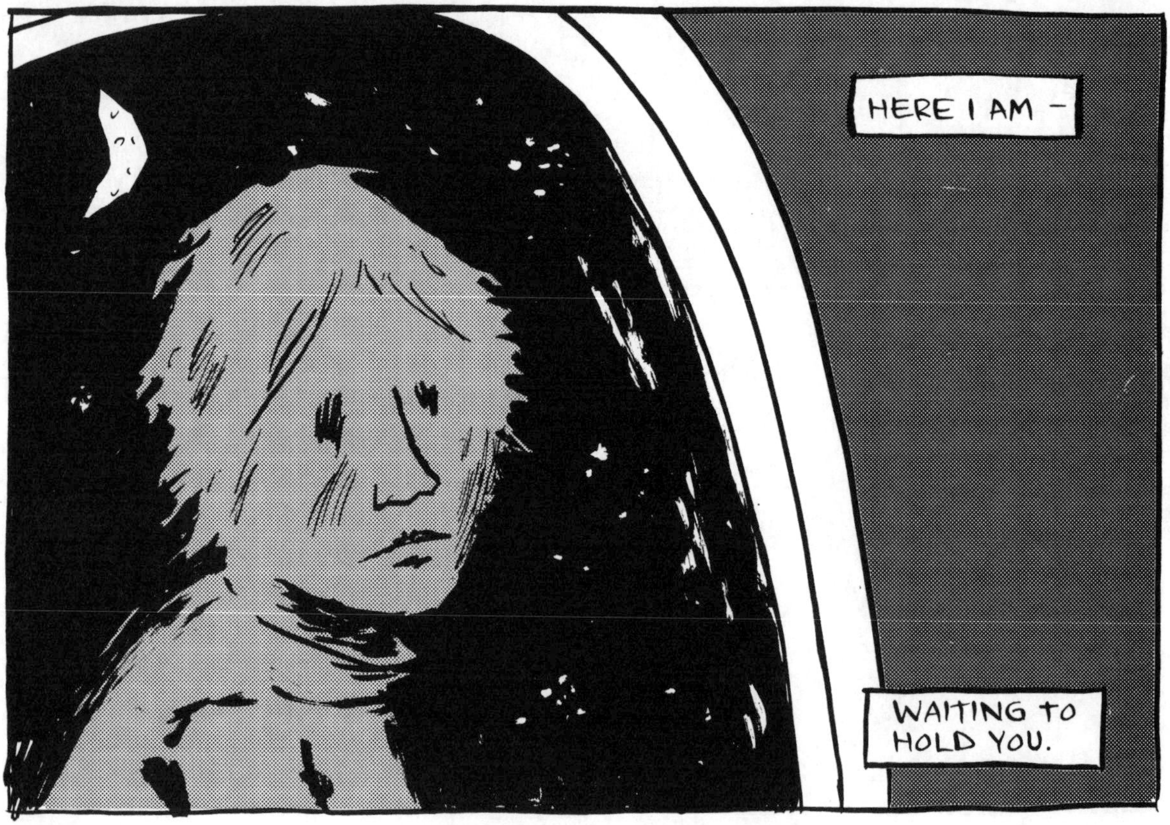
HERE I AM -
WAITING TO HOLD YOU.

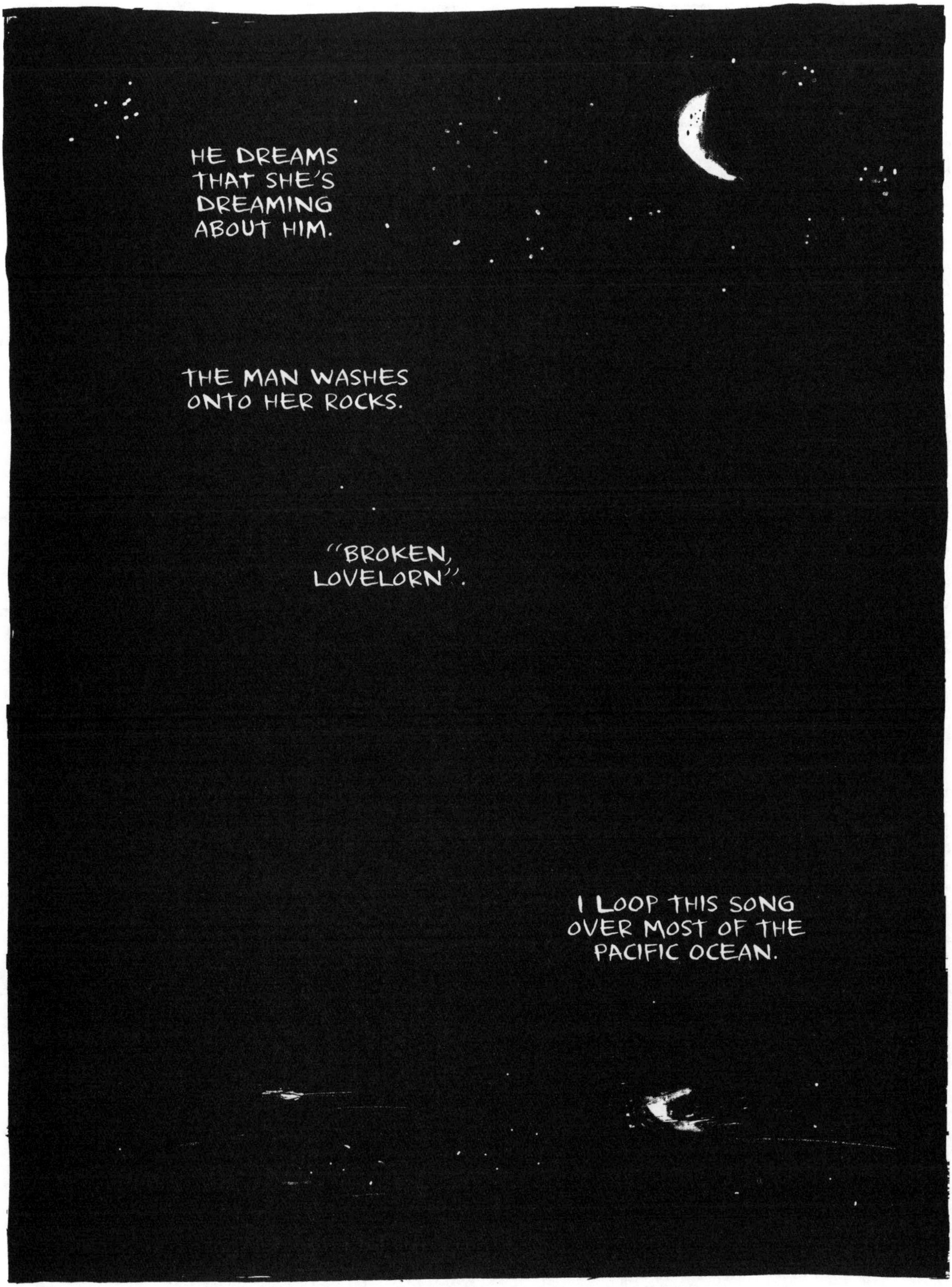
HE DREAMS THAT SHE'S DREAMING ABOUT HIM.
THE MAN WASHES ONTO HER ROCKS.
"BROKEN, LOVELORN".
I LOOP THIS SONG OVER MOST OF THE PACIFIC OCEAN.

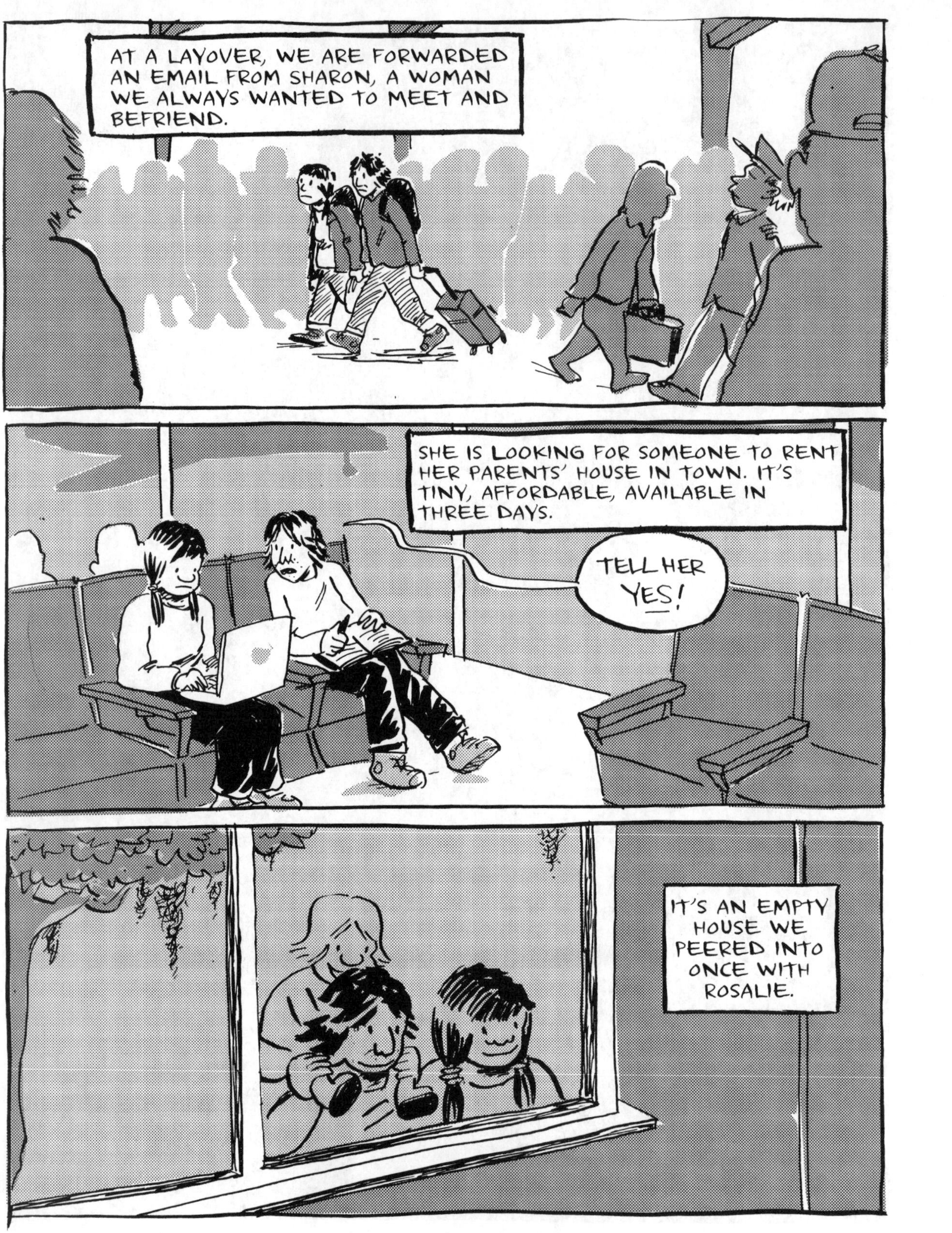
AT A LAYOVER, WE ARE FORWARDED AN EMAIL FROM SHARON, A WOMAN WE ALWAYS WANTED TO MEET AND BEFRIEND.
SHE IS LOOKING FOR SOMEONE TO RENT HER PARENTS' HOUSE IN TOWN. IT'S TINY, AFFORDABLE, AVAILABLE IN THREE DAYS.
TELL HER YES!
IT'S AN EMPTY HOUSE WE PEERED INTO ONCE WITH ROSALIE.

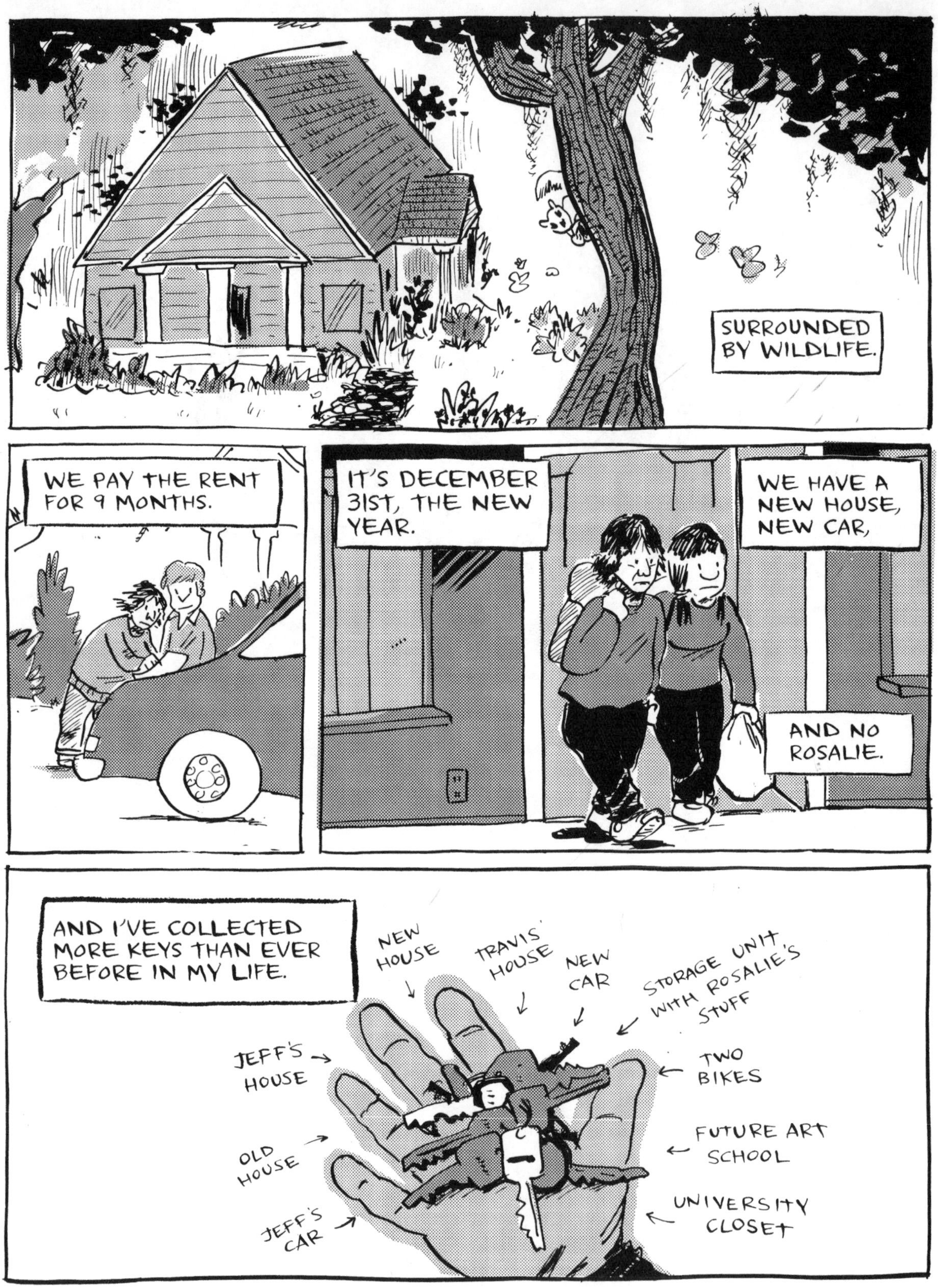
SURROUNDED BY WILDLIFE.
WE PAY THE RENT FOR 9 MONTHS.
IT'S DECEMBER 31ST, THE NEW YEAR.
WE HAVE A NEW HOUSE, NEW CAR,
AND NO ROSALIE.
AND I'VE COLLECTED MORE KEYS THAN EVER BEFORE IN MY LIFE.
NEW HOUSE
TRAVIS' HOUSE
NEW CAR
STORAGE UNIT WITH ROSALIE'S STUFF
JEFF'S HOUSE
TWO BIKES
OLD HOUSE
FUTURE ART SCHOOL
JEFF'S CAR
UNIVERSITY CLOSET

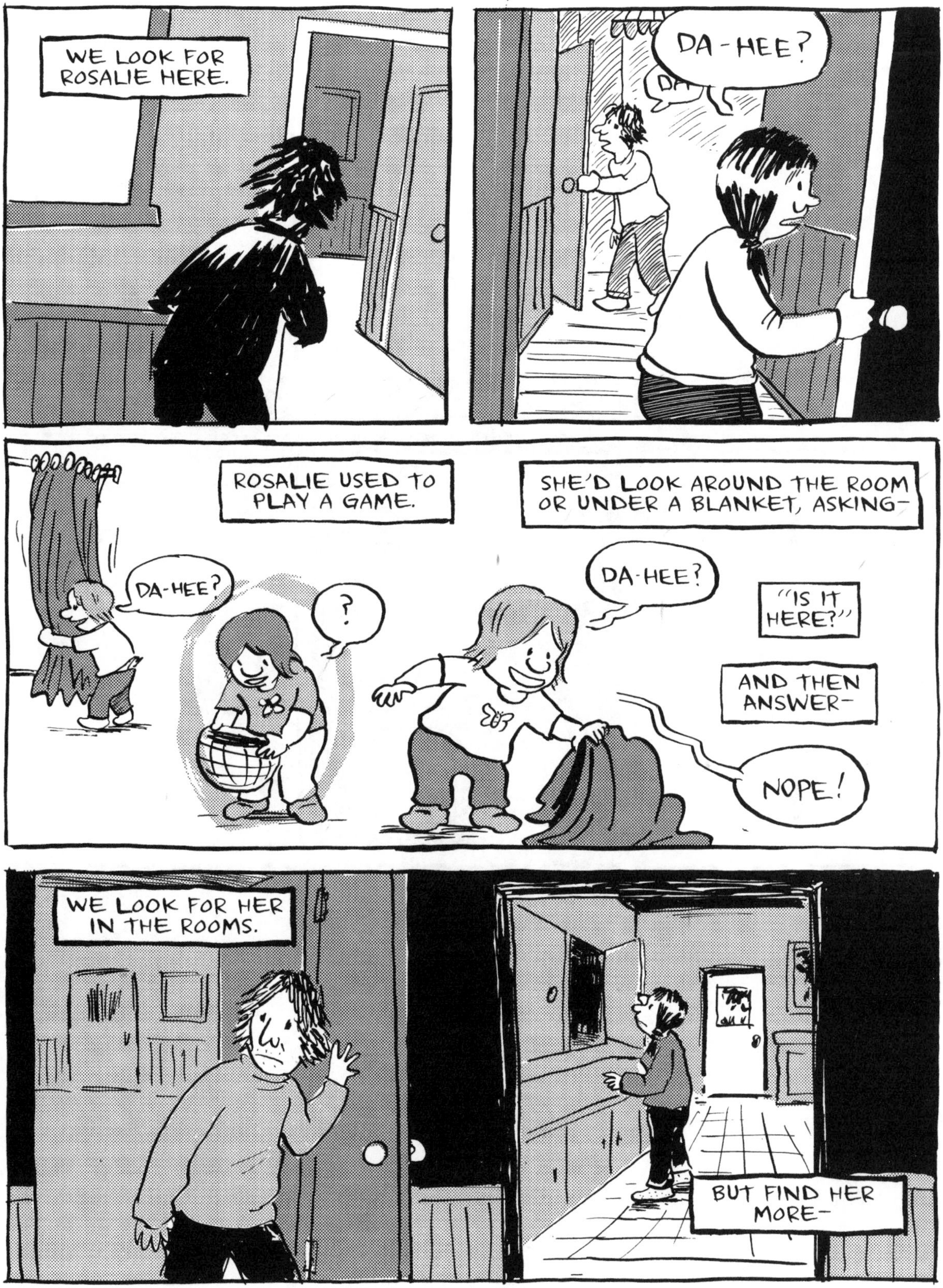
WE LOOK FOR ROSALIE HERE.
DA-HEE?
ROSALIE USED TO PLAY A GAME.
SHE'D LOOK AROUND THE ROOM OR UNDER A BLANKET, ASKING–
DA-HEE?
?
DA-HEE?
"IS IT HERE?"
AND THEN ANSWER–
NOPE!
WE LOOK FOR HER IN THE ROOMS.
BUT FIND HER MORE–

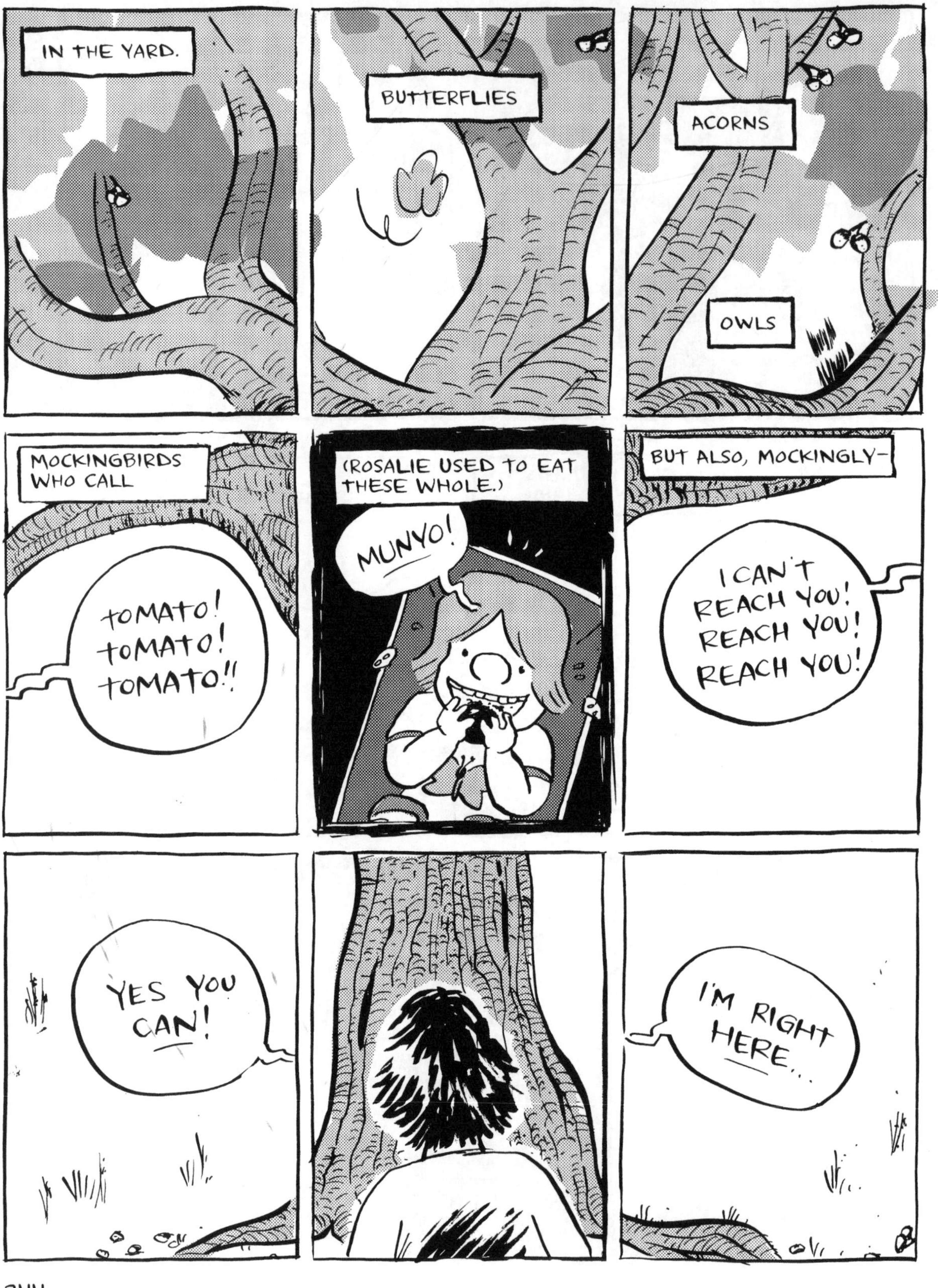
IN THE YARD.
BUTTERFLIES
ACORNS
OWLS
MOCKINGBIRDS WHO CALL
TOMATO! TOMATO! TOMATO!!
(ROSALIE USED TO EAT THESE WHOLE.)
MUNYO!
BUT ALSO, MOCKINGLY-
I CAN'T REACH YOU! REACH YOU! REACH YOU!
YES YOU CAN!
I'M RIGHT HERE...

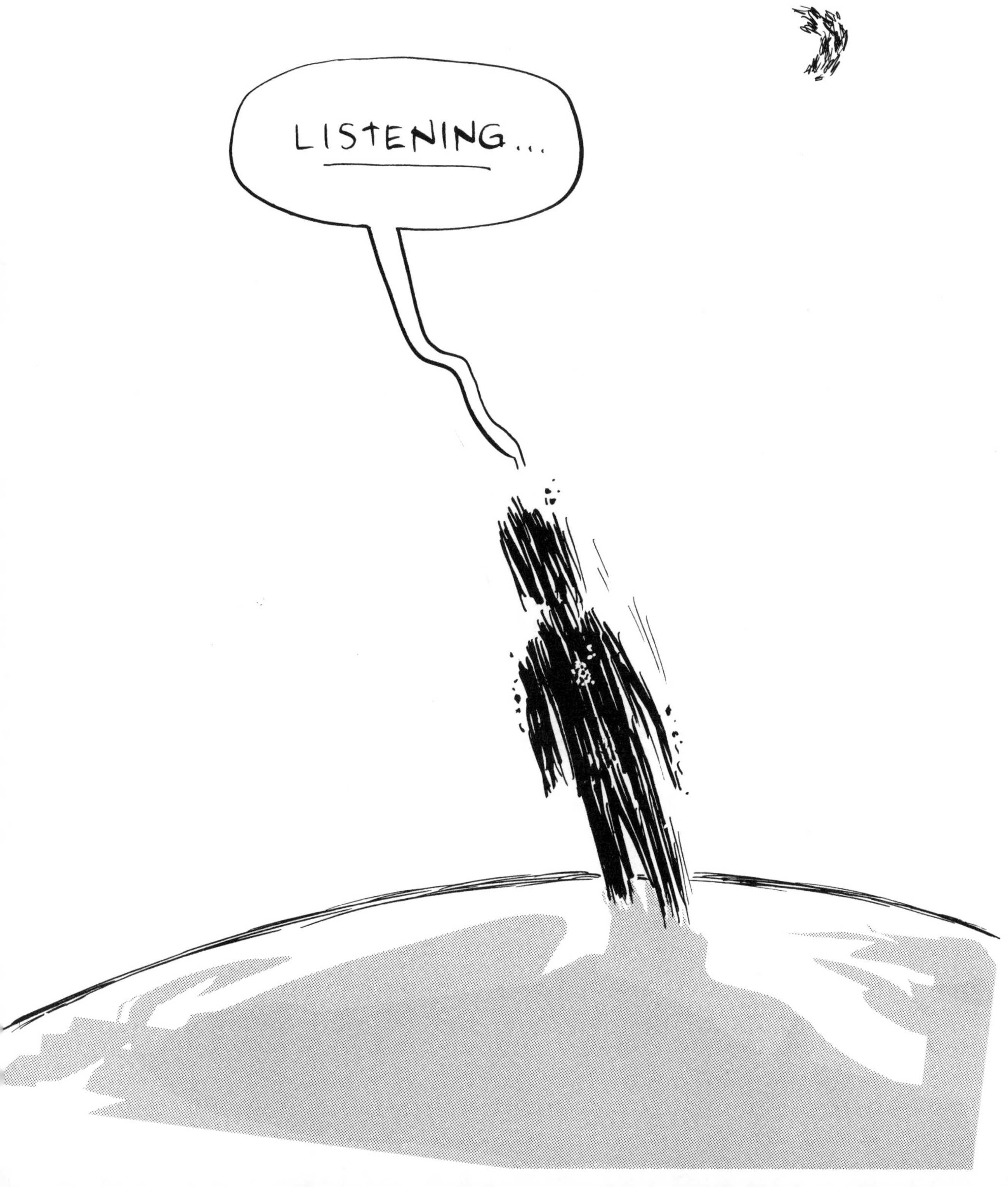
LISTENING...

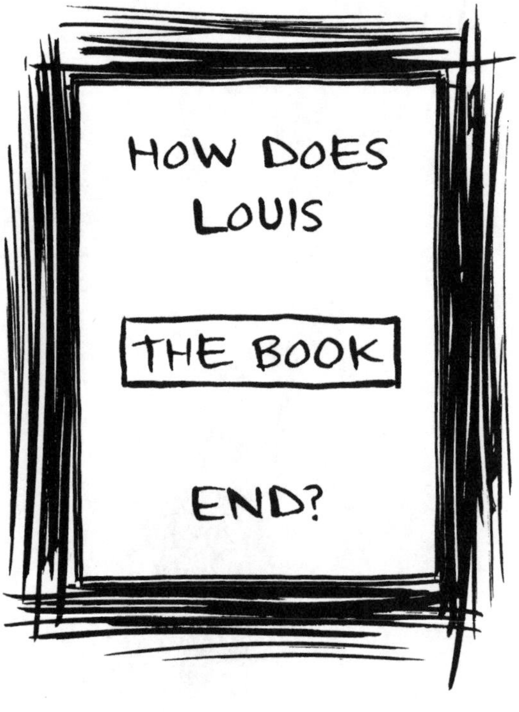
HOW DOES
LOUIS
THE BOOK
END?

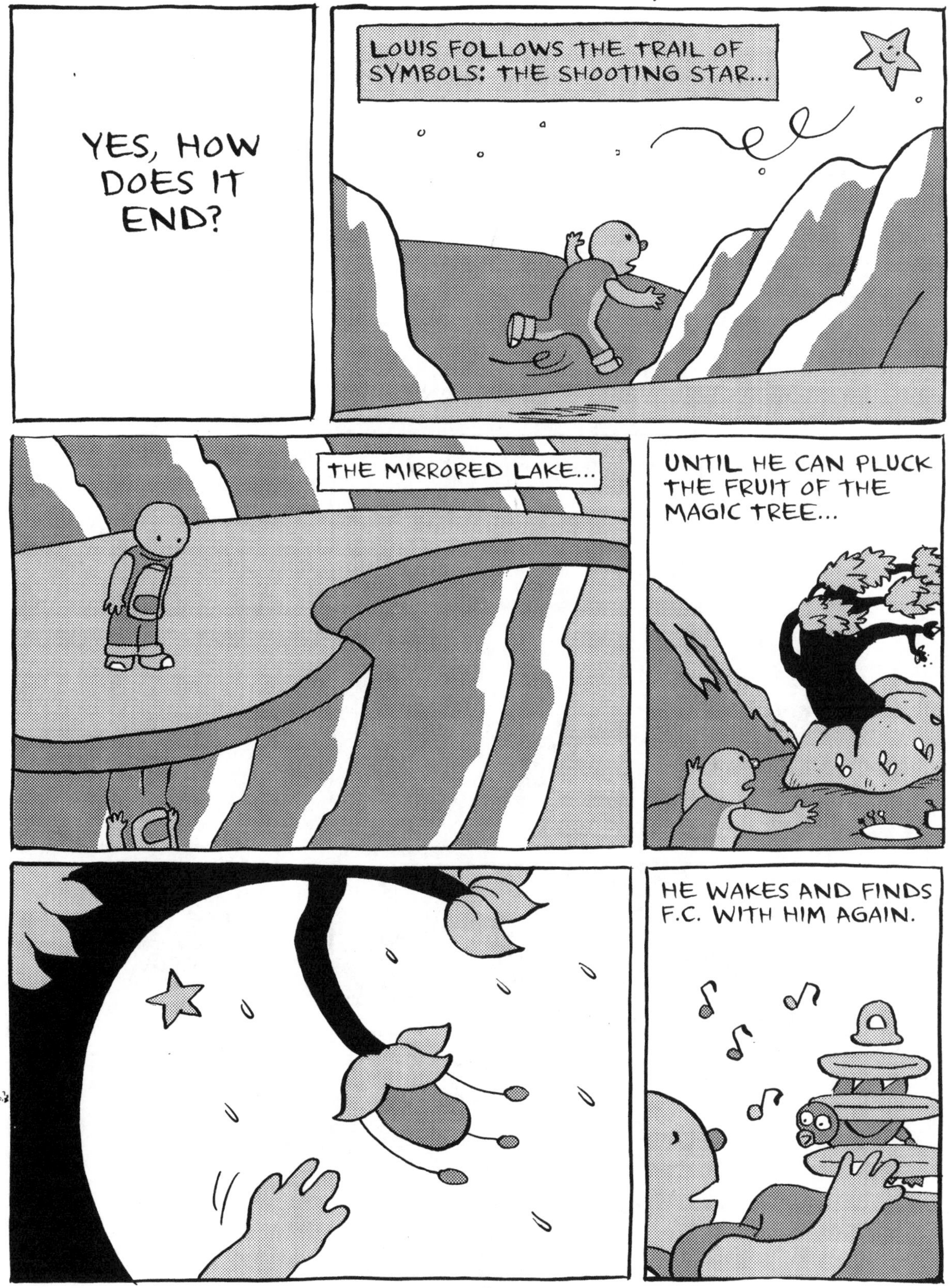
YES, HOW DOES IT END?
LOUIS FOLLOWS THE TRAIL OF SYMBOLS: THE SHOOTING STAR...
THE MIRRORED LAKE...
UNTIL HE CAN PLUCK THE FRUIT OF THE MAGIC TREE...
HE WAKES AND FINDS F.C. WITH HIM AGAIN.

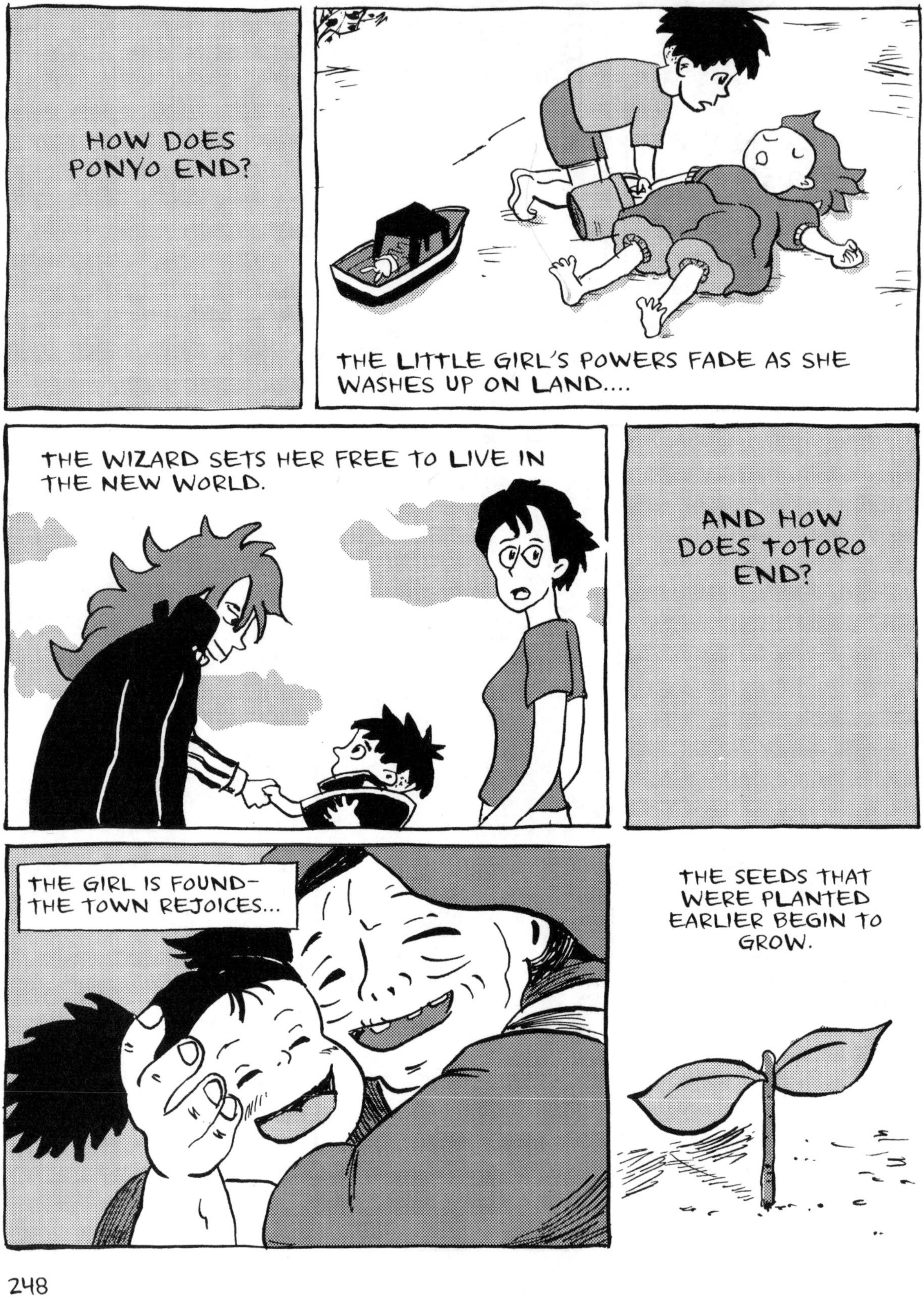
HOW DOES PONYO END?
THE LITTLE GIRL'S POWERS FADE AS SHE WASHES UP ON LAND....
THE WIZARD SETS HER FREE TO LIVE IN THE NEW WORLD.
AND HOW DOES TOTORO END?
THE GIRL IS FOUND– THE TOWN REJOICES...
THE SEEDS THAT WERE PLANTED EARLIER BEGIN TO GROW.

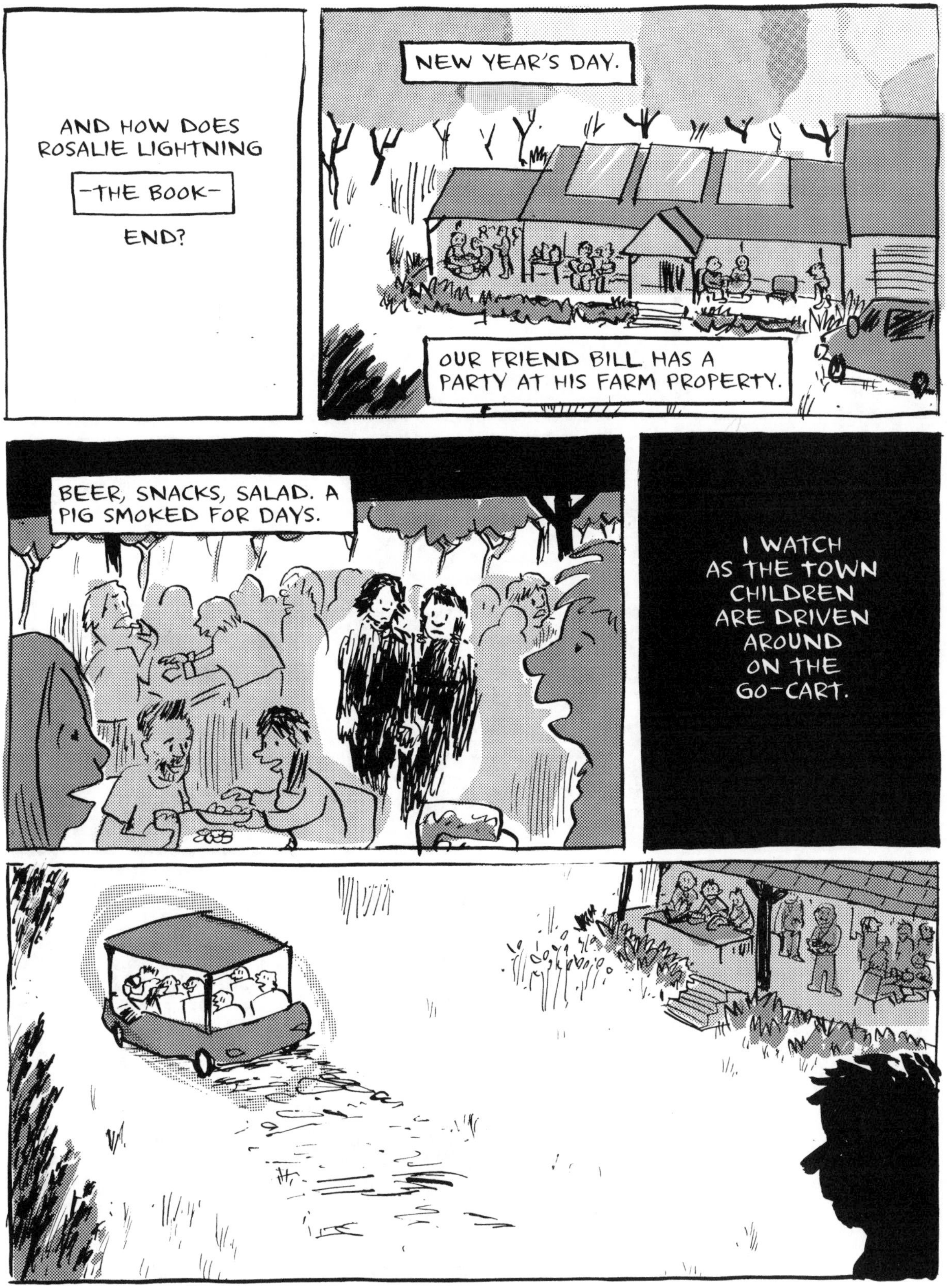
AND HOW DOES ROSALIE LIGHTNING
-THE BOOK-
END?
NEW YEAR'S DAY.
OUR FRIEND BILL HAS A PARTY AT HIS FARM PROPERTY.
BEER, SNACKS, SALAD. A PIG SMOKED FOR DAYS.
I WATCH AS THE TOWN CHILDREN ARE DRIVEN AROUND ON THE GO-CART.

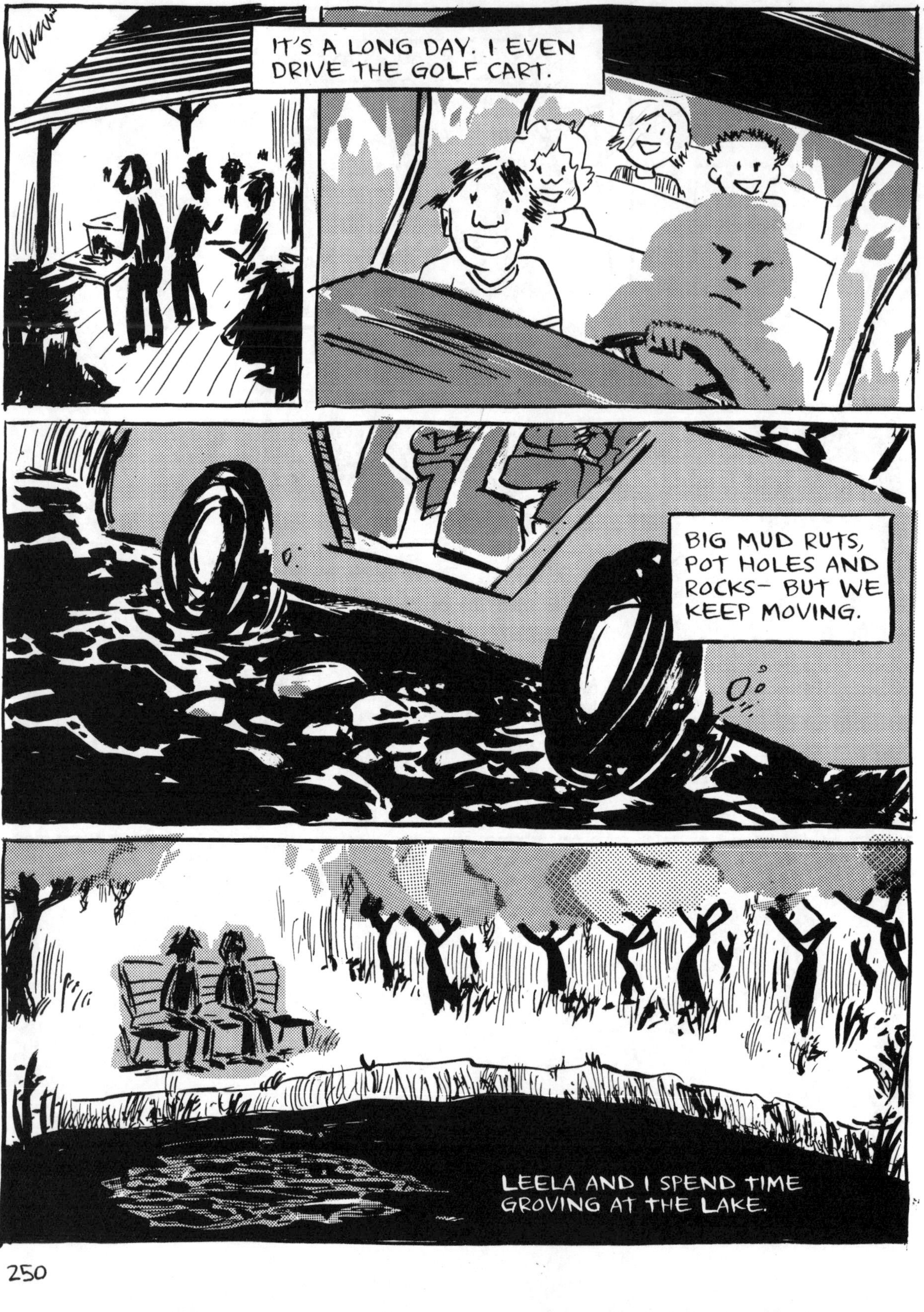
IT'S A LONG DAY. I EVEN DRIVE THE GOLF CART.
BIG MUD RUTS, POT HOLES AND ROCKS– BUT WE KEEP MOVING.
LEELA AND I SPEND TIME GROVING AT THE LAKE.

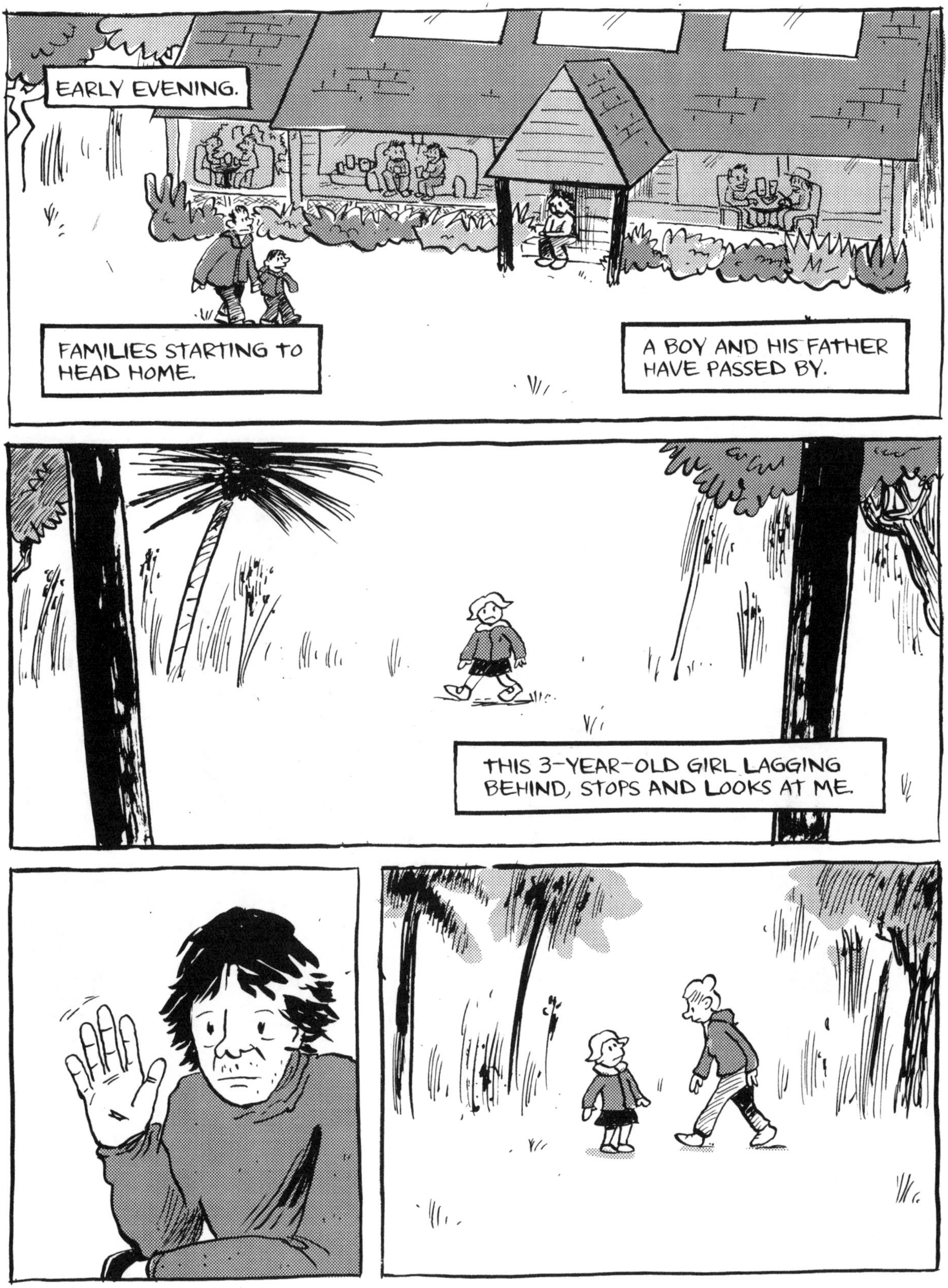
EARLY EVENING.
FAMILIES STARTING TO HEAD HOME.
A BOY AND HIS FATHER HAVE PASSED BY.
THIS 3-YEAR-OLD GIRL LAGGING BEHIND, STOPS AND LOOKS AT ME.

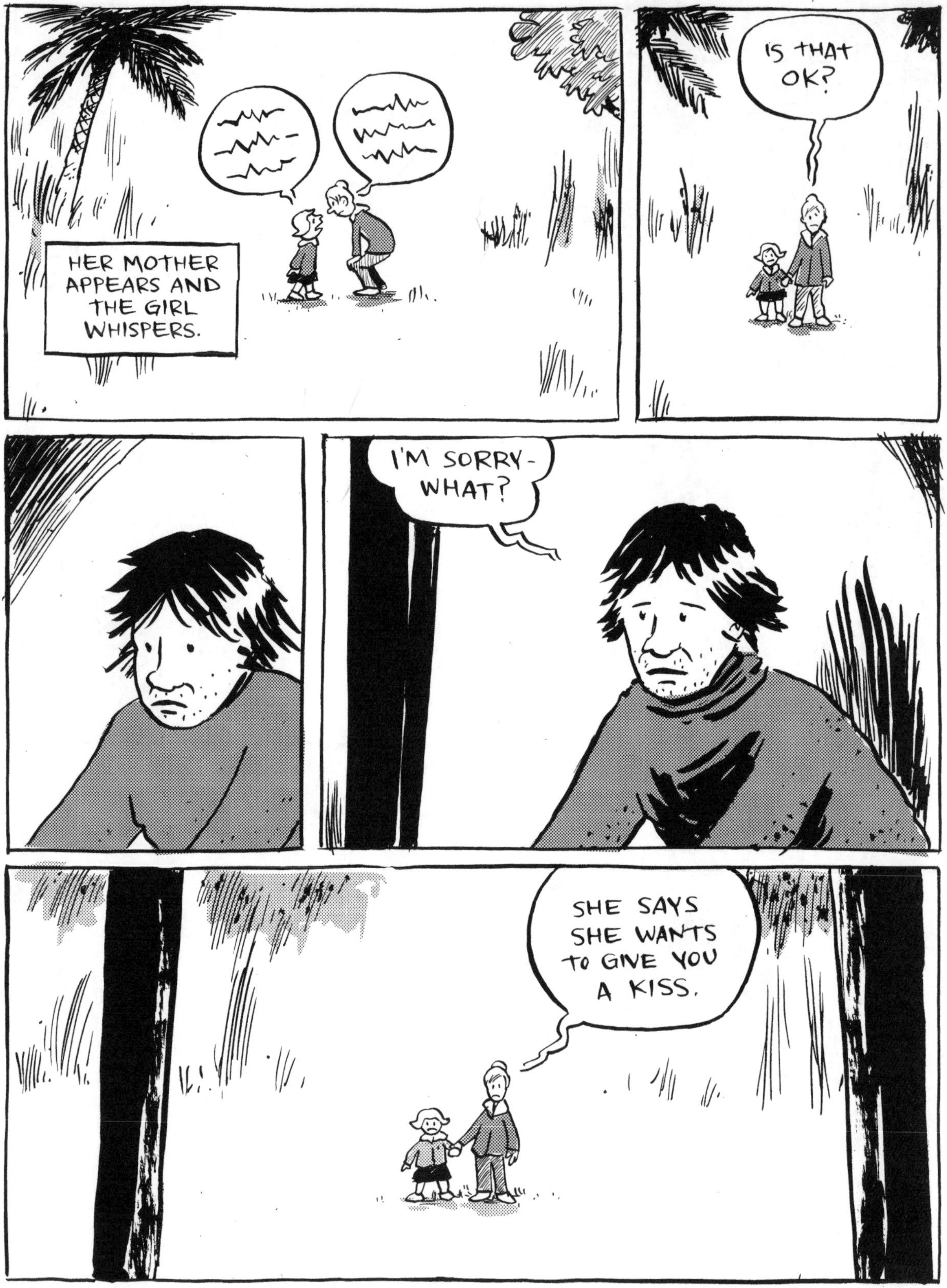
HER MOTHER APPEARS AND THE GIRL WHISPERS.
IS THAT OK?
I'M SORRY- WHAT?
SHE SAYS SHE WANTS TO GIVE YOU A KISS.

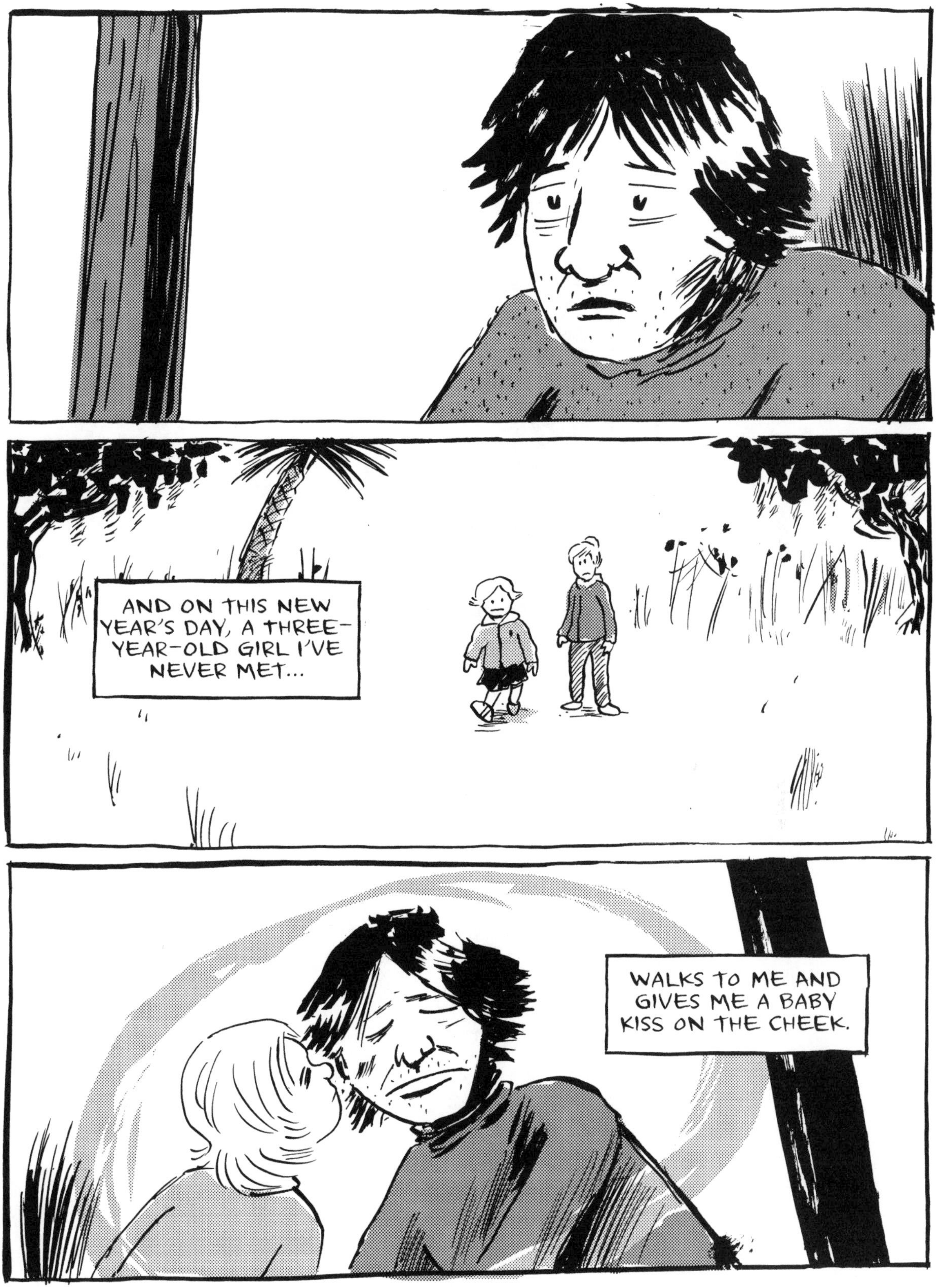
AND ON THIS NEW YEAR'S DAY, A THREE-YEAR-OLD GIRL I'VE NEVER MET...
WALKS TO ME AND GIVES ME A BABY KISS ON THE CHEEK.

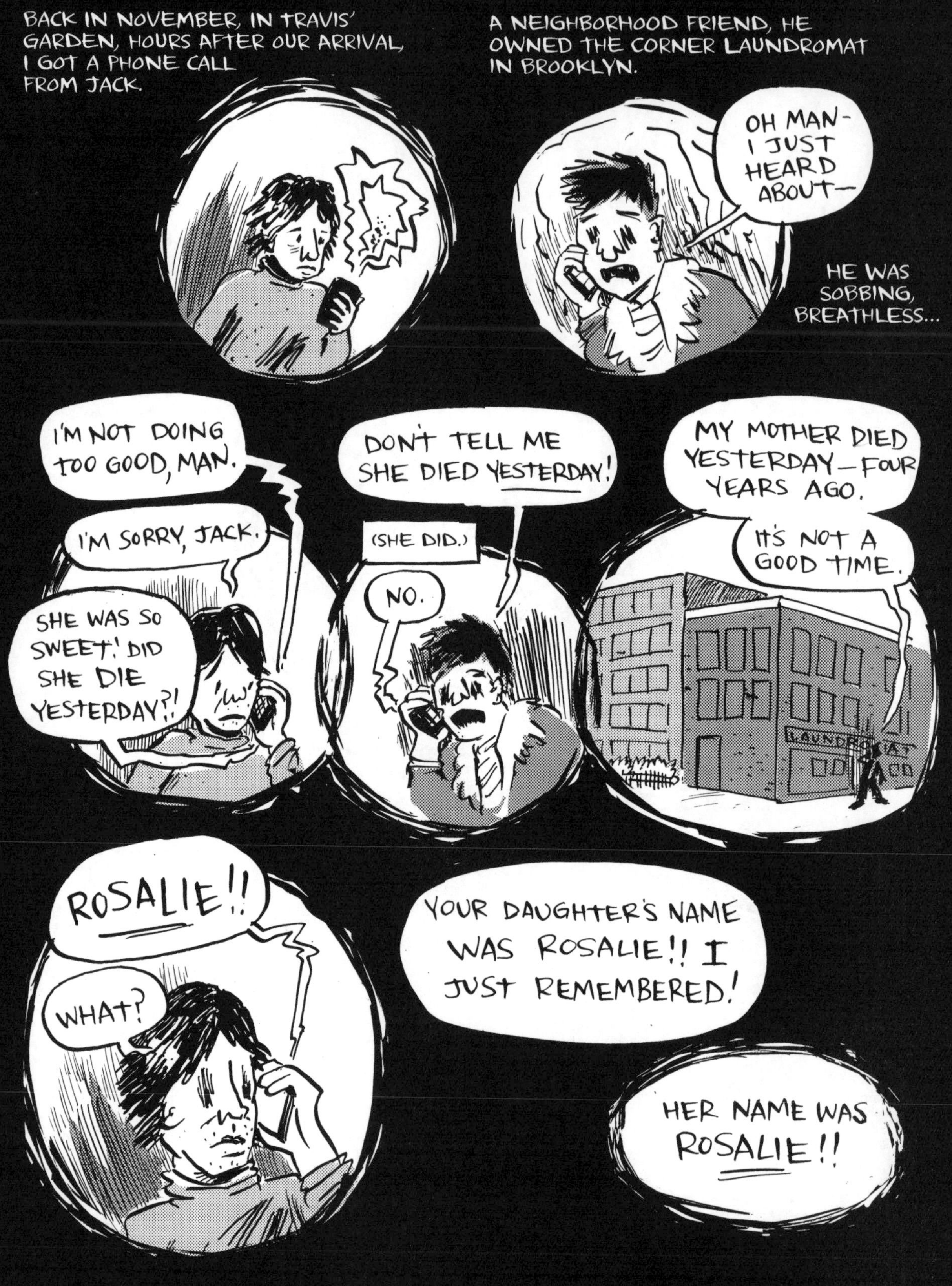
BACK IN NOVEMBER, IN TRAVIS' GARDEN, HOURS AFTER OUR ARRIVAL, I GOT A PHONE CALL FROM JACK.
A NEIGHBORHOOD FRIEND, HE OWNED THE CORNER LAUNDROMAT IN BROOKLYN.
OH MAN- I JUST HEARD ABOUT—
HE WAS SOBBING, BREATHLESS...
I'M NOT DOING TOO GOOD, MAN.
I'M SORRY, JACK.
SHE WAS SO SWEET! DID SHE DIE YESTERDAY?!
DON'T TELL ME SHE DIED YESTERDAY!
(SHE DID.)
NO.
MY MOTHER DIED YESTERDAY—FOUR YEARS AGO.
IT'S NOT A GOOD TIME.
ROSALIE!!
WHAT?
YOUR DAUGHTER'S NAME WAS ROSALIE!! I JUST REMEMBERED!
HER NAME WAS ROSALIE!!

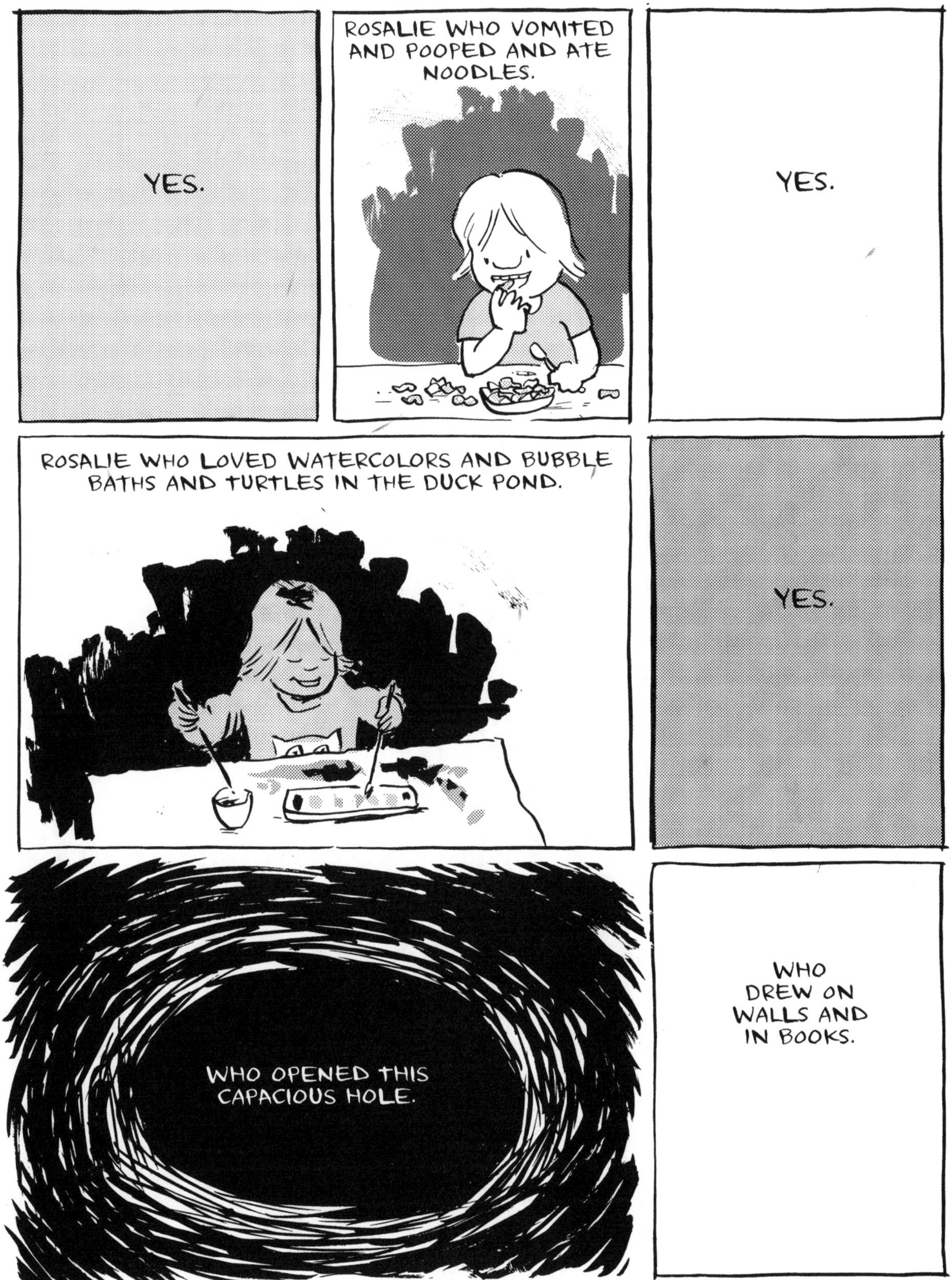
YES.
ROSALIE WHO VOMITED AND POOPED AND ATE NOODLES.
YES.
ROSALIE WHO LOVED WATERCOLORS AND BUBBLE BATHS AND TURTLES IN THE DUCK POND.
YES.
WHO OPENED THIS CAPACIOUS HOLE.
WHO DREW ON WALLS AND IN BOOKS.

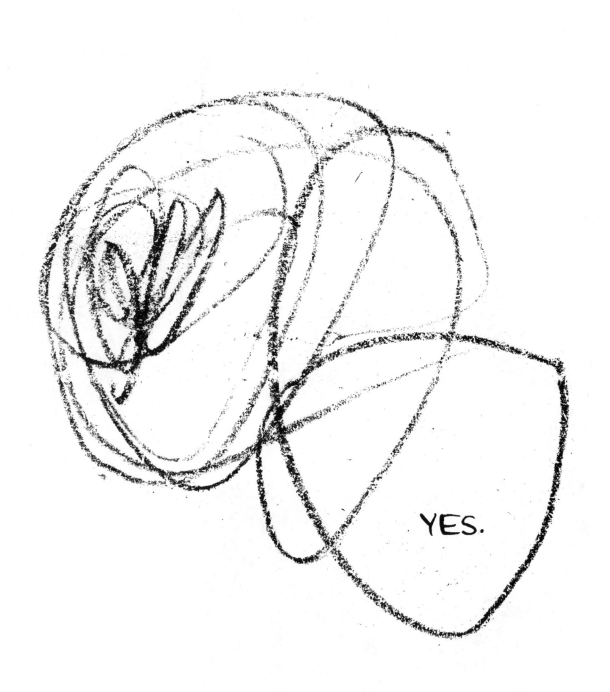

YES.

YES.

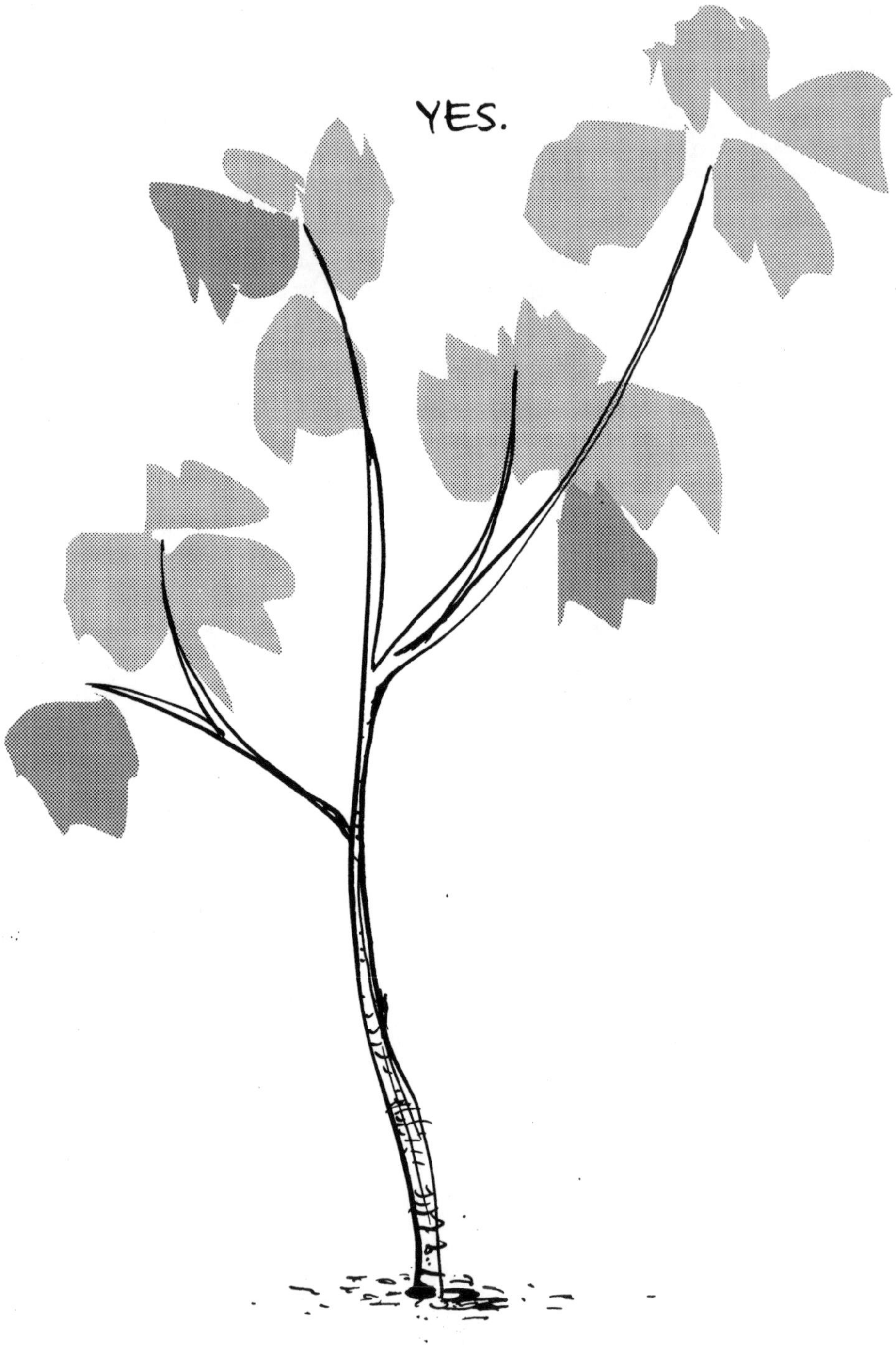
YES.

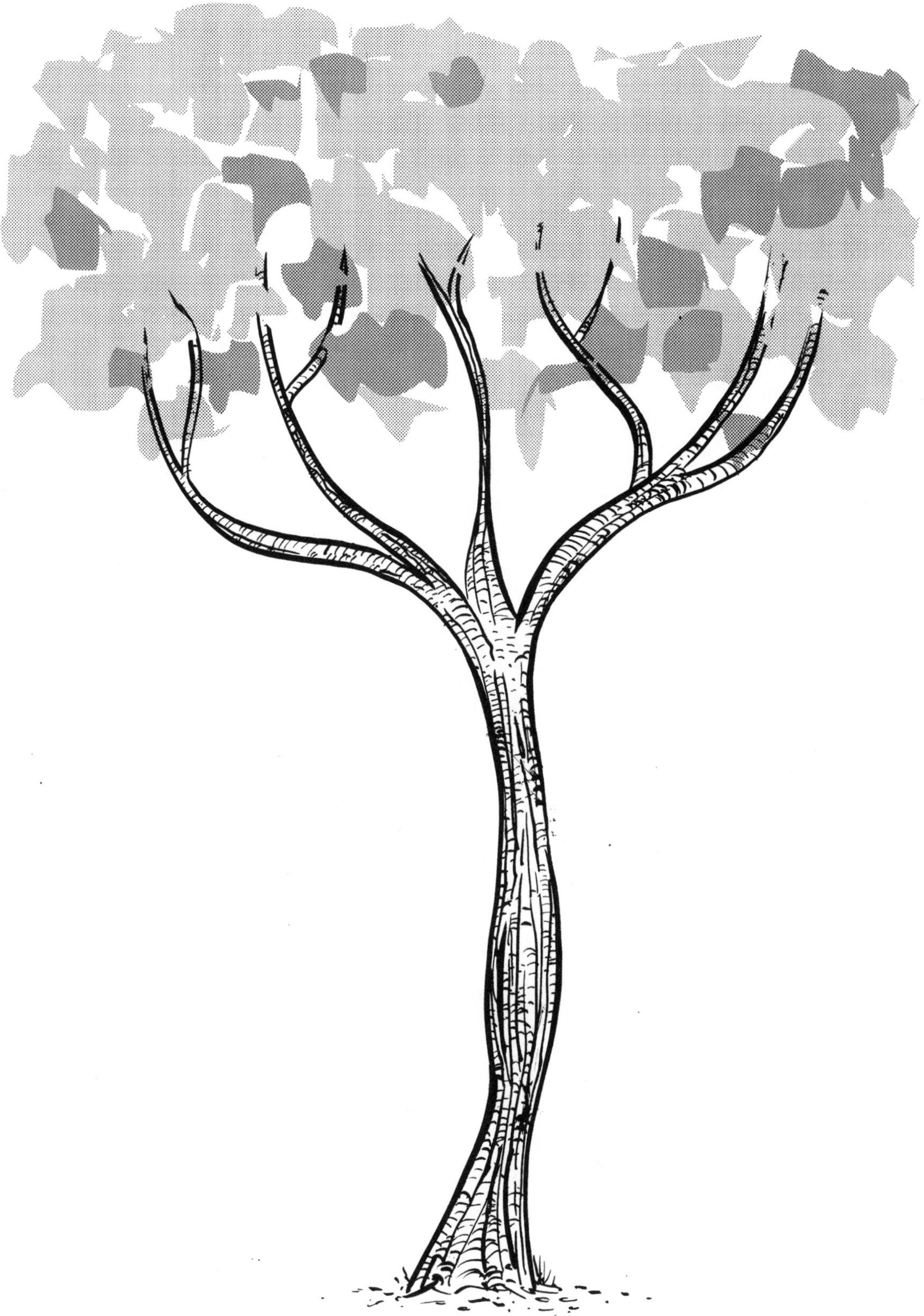

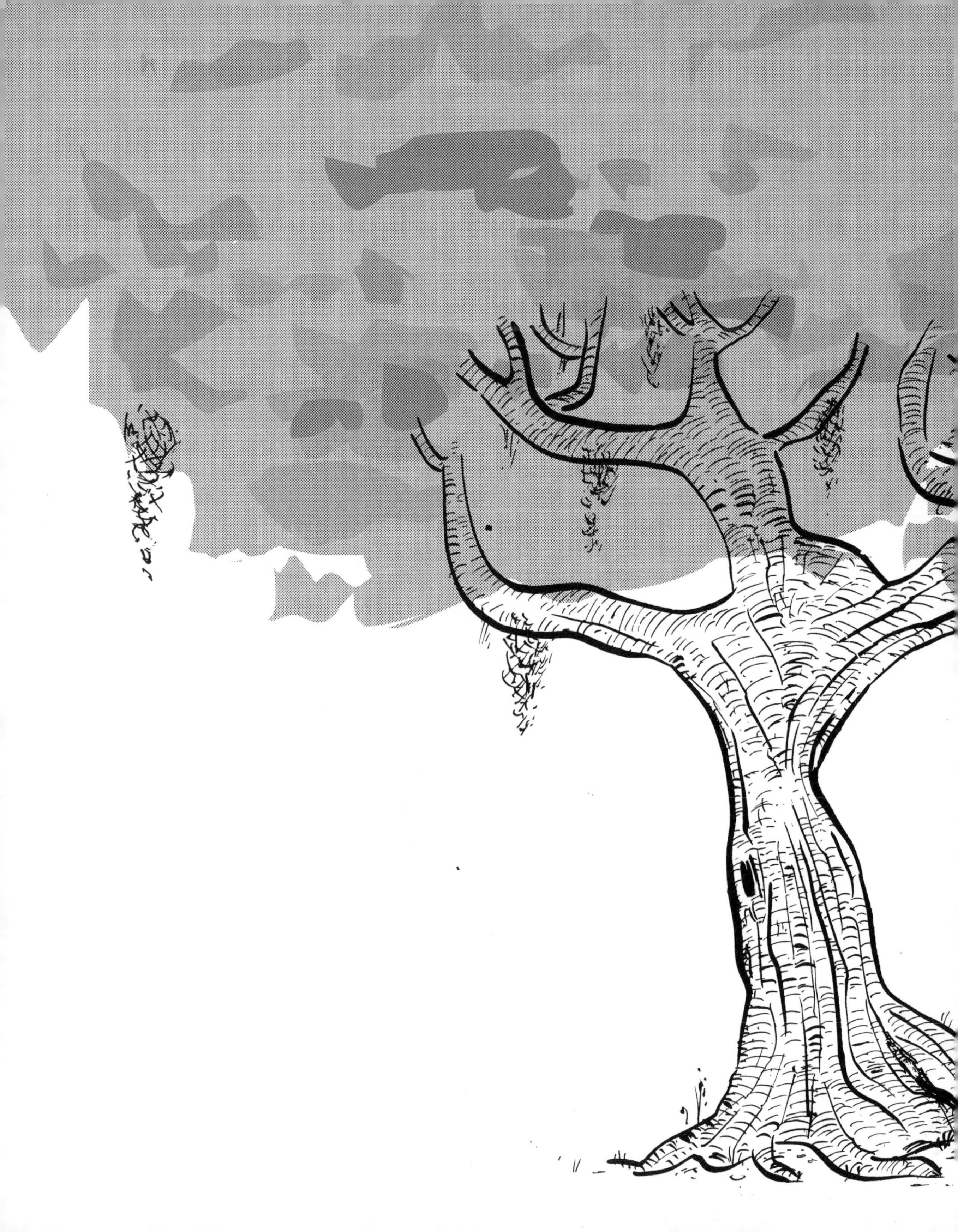

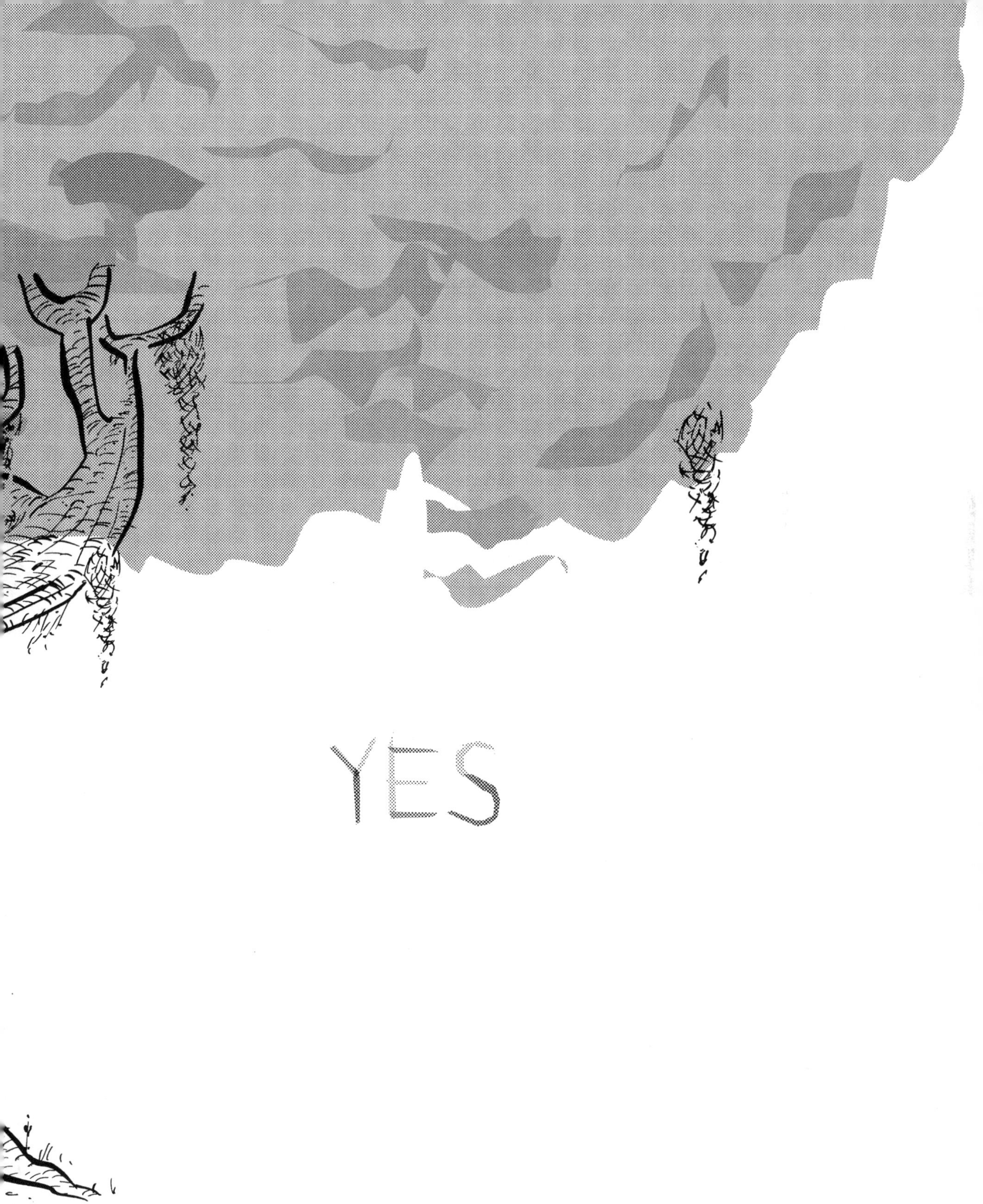YES

ROSALIE

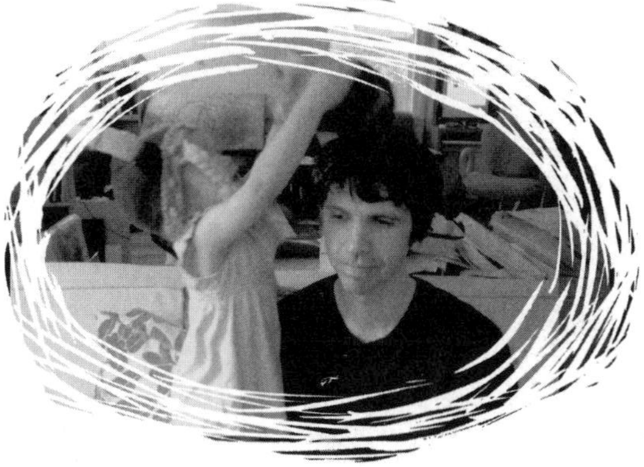

Tom Hart runs The Sequential Artists Workshop, a not-for-profit school for comics and graphic novels in Gainesville, Florida. He lives there with his wife Leela, and their daughter, Molly Rose.

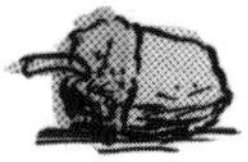

ACKNOWLEDGEMENTS

The breadth of people I should properly thank, who helped us in our neediest times, is incredibly large and I'm almost certain to make enormous omissions due to errors of judgement or just forgetfulness. So instead, this short list of people who helped specifically, privately in many ways, or in ways they didn't even know, to the making of this document. I hope that in mentioning our friends in Gainesville, New York and around the world, everyone else will recognize themselves there. I thank you all.

Enormous thanks to Travis Fristoe and Meredith Kite, whose friendship at our darkest hour never wavered. Big souls, you. Travis, safe travels. To Jeff Mason, generous soul.

To Don Fitzpatrick and Valrie Davis, who should have appeared in here, but didn't. My enormous thanks to Bill Bryson, Dale Gunnoe, Rick Stepp and Rayne Hurzeler, Elif Ackali, Margaret Tolbert, Tia Ma, Sam Jones, John Orth, Nina Hofer (the list could be 10 times this) for inspiration and sustenance in so many ways.

To Myla Goldberg and Lauren Weinstein. To Sarah Glidden and Tim Kreider. To Jenny Offill, David Hirmes and Theodora Hirmes, my dears. To Whitney Mutch and family. To John Darnielle and family. To Lauren Groff and family. To Austin Kleon and family. To Scott McCloud and family.

To Rosalie's and our friends in New York: Maddie Fix and Ellie, Jo Greep and Penny, Emma Assin and Egon and all your families, thank you.

To the people of Gainesville, especially circa 2012, including Chelsea Carnes, Julie and Shaenah Metheney and family, Sheila Bishop, Chris Fillie and family, Erin, Colin Curry, Tommy Akin and family, Tom Aycock, Joe Courter, Jasmine, Kyla, Elaine and Emma, Mandy, Gil Murray and about a million others of you, please know what your vibrant sprits did for mine. To Vine Bakery.

To the people of Gainesville, pre- and post-2011: Phil, Josh, Tanya, Andrew, Candi, Andrew, Laura, Sarah, Joe, Allison, Denise, Apestrong.

To the people of SAW, thanks as large as I can muster. Larger. Special thanks to Sally, Eric, Adrian and Anna. To Kurt Wolfgang, "Durt."

To the people in this story, you are forces in our field. Thank you. Thanks to Kirby Ruffner.

Thanks to Meg Thompson. Thanks to Michael Homler and Lauren Jablonski. To Karlyn Hixson and Dori Weintraub. To Peter Kuper and Bill Kartalopoulos.

Thanks to Dan Stepp. Thanks to Joey Manley, I miss you. To Bryan Doerries for your profound work and Tom Baxter for your collaboration. Thanks to colleagues, friends and inspirations at SVA. Thanks to Mark Newgarden and Meagan Montigue Cash. To Sascha Krader, Alabaster, Monica Hunken, Mandy Keifetz, Zoe Abrahams. Thanks forever to Matt Madden.

Thanks to Skip Major, Zannah Marsh, and Jason Little for early readings.

To Eddie Campbell, David B., Carol Tyler, Alison Bechdel, Art Spiegelman, and hundreds more; inspirational thanks.

To Mark Cousins, for The Story of Film.

To Leela, my love, I offer no consolation about anything, I am only glad you have been my partner on so many journeys.

And my enormous gratitude to Justine Mara Andersen.

The Sudden Unexplained Death of a Child Foundation (SUDC) is an organization dedicated to increasing awareness of sudden unexpected deaths in childhood, funding crucial research into the causes and prevention of SUDC, and advocating for the needs of families affected by these tragedies. They are the only organization worldwide devoted solely to the needs of families and professionals touched by unexplained death in childhood.

Please visit: sudc.org

My prayers go to any parents who have lost children, and especially through war, poverty, disease, violence, chaos, and to children who have lived with deprivation.

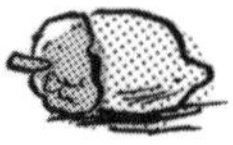